econoguide '96

Las Vegas, Reno, Laughlin, Lake Tahoe

Corey Sandler

CB

CONTEMPORARY
BOOKS

A TRIBUNE NEW MEDIA COMPANY

Library of Congress Cataloging-in-Publication Data

Sandler, Corey, 1950–
    Econoguide '96—Las Vegas, Reno, Laughlin, Lake Tahoe / Corey
Sandler.
       p.   cm.
    Includes index.
    ISBN 0-8092-3323-1 (alk. paper)
    1. Nevada—Guidebooks.   2. Las Vegas (Nev.)—Guidebooks.
3. Reno (Nev.)—Guidebooks.   4. Laughlin (Nev.)—Guidebooks.
5. Tahoe, Lake, Region (Calif. and Nev.)—Guidebooks.   I. Title.
F839.3.S26   1995
917.93—dc20   95-30905
                                                   CIP

To Janice, my fellow traveler

Copyright © 1995 by Word Association, Inc.
All rights reserved
Published by Contemporary Books, Inc.
Two Prudential Plaza, Chicago, Illinois 60601-6790
Manufactured in the United States of America
International Standard Book Number: 0-8092-3323-1
10   9   8   7   6   5   4   3   2   1

Contents

Acknowledgments

Dozens of hard-working and creative people helped move my words from the keyboard to the place where you read this book now.

Among the many to thank are editor Linda Gray and publisher Christine Albritton of Contemporary Books for working with me as we expand the Econoguide series and Dan Bial for his capable agentry. Thanks, too, to Eugene Brissie, our original champion, and to Bill Gladstone of Waterside Productions.

Dawn Barker of Contemporary Books gave the text a professional polish, and Kathy Willhoite managed the editorial and production processes with professionalism and good humor.

Several people were responsible for the production of the book. Thanks to Kim Bartko, Monica Baziuk, Dana Draxten, Matt Heavin, Ellen Kollmon, Laurie Liebewein, Todd Petersen, Audrey Sails, and Terry Stone.

Thanks to the hotels, casinos, restaurants, and attractions who opened their doors to us; special thanks to the companies who offered discount coupons to our readers.

Special thanks go to Janice Keefe who worked long and hard in the Word Association offices to collect and process the discount coupons.

And finally, thank you for buying this book. We all hope you find it of value; please let me know how we can improve the book in future editions. (Please enclose a stamped envelope if you'd like a reply; no calls, please.)

Corey Sandler
Econoguide Travel Books
P.O. Box 2779
Nantucket, MA 02584

Introduction to the Third Edition, 1996

Nevada is one of the most exciting places we know, from the man-made wonders of the Las Vegas Strip and Glitter Gulch to the concrete canyon of Hoover Dam to the almost indescribably beautiful natural splendors of Lake Tahoe and the Sierra Nevada mountains.

Nevada will probably always be the frontier. It is a place where things are different, where old assumptions are challenged, and where new ideas are tried.

That is, after all, why people come to Nevada. Although gambling has begun to spread across the nation, there is still no Las Vegas in Chicago or Boston or Los Angeles. There is no Lake Mead in New Jersey. There are no snow-capped mountains with ski runs that careen down to an alpine lake in Kansas. And, though Nevada is a relatively young state, there are few places we know that are as imbued with living history as Virginia City.

Welcome to the third edition of the Econoguide, completely updated with new information about Las Vegas and Reno, and with expanded coverage of Laughlin, Virginia City, and Lake Tahoe.

Before we go too far down the road, let's start with what this book is *not* about:

• It is *not* a rose-colored view of the world endorsed by the Chamber of Commerce. Not everything in Nevada is wonderful, a good value, or a worthwhile use of your vacation time. We'll try to help you get the most from your trip.

• It is *not* a guide for the cheapskate interested in sleeping in bus terminals (or motels that look like bus terminals) and eating exclusively at restaurants that use plastic forks. What we mean by "Econoguide" is this: helpful information so that you can get the most out of your trip to Nevada. We'll show you how to save time and money on travel, hotels, restaurants, and entertainment. Even if you choose to go for first class airfare, luxury hotels, and the most expensive restaurants in town, we'll help you spend your money wisely.

• It is *not* a guide to making money at the gambling tables. We will, though, offer a cautious guide to casinos, concentrating on how to have fun and not lose more money than you are prepared to donate in the name of fun.

Let's think a bit about the state of Nevada, a place of great contrasts.

The seventh-largest state in the union, it is 38th in population. It is today the fastest-growing state, though it is still very sparsely populated with 1.3 million people across 110,540 square miles—and almost all of the residents are concentrated around the urban areas of Las Vegas and Reno.

Winters are extremely cold in the north and west; summers in the south are oven-like. Nevada's highest point is a lofty 13,143 feet at Boundary Peak on the snowy border with California; the lowest is along the Colorado River as it enters the hot and dry desert in the southern tip of the state.

Nevada's economy is focused on mining: mining minerals out of the ground and mining gold and silver out of the pockets of tourists who come to visit in great droves. Las Vegas alone draws more than 20 million visitors annually. Fully half of the workers in the state are in the service trades, with 25 percent directly employed by a casino or hotel. In Las Vegas alone, casinos provide more than a hundred thousand jobs.

One of the great, uncelebrated things about Nevada's tourist centers of Las Vegas, Reno, Laughlin, and Lake Tahoe is that you can find a bathroom, telephone, change booth, or restaurant at any hour of the day or night, any day of the year. You can also find a casino open at any time. Usually in the same place, of course.

Let's head out on an exploration of all sides of Nevada, from the oasis in the desert at Laughlin to the mirage at Las Vegas to the Great Western Rest Stop at Reno to the honeycombed mountains of Virginia City and the Comstock Lode to the breathtaking beauty of Lake Tahoe.

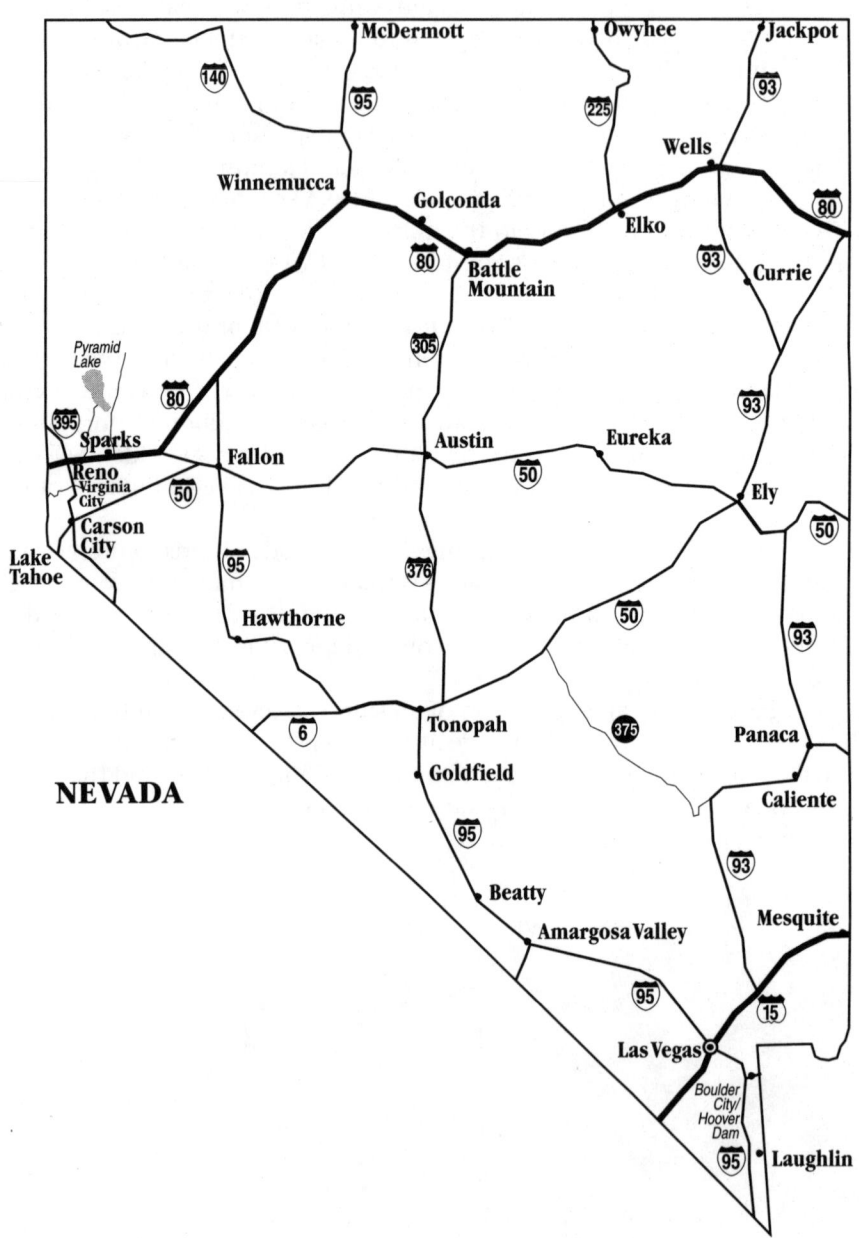

NEVADA

I
Nevada Bound

Chapter 1
A Short and Irreverent History of Nevada

When they spoke of the "Wild West," it was often Nevada they had in mind.

Wild, as in a nearly virgin land when the first white explorers set foot there about the time of the American Revolution.

Wild, as in the extremes of weather from the arid deserts of the eastern part of the state to the high, snowy mountains of Sierra Nevada in the west.

Wild, as in the heady days in the 1850s and 1860s when gold and then silver were discovered south of Reno, and when for a short period of time Virginia City was the richest place on earth.

Wild, as in the early days of Las Vegas at the start of the 20th century when the "anything goes" atmosphere of the railroad town laid the foundation for what would become Glitter Gulch and then the Strip.

Wild, as in the State of Nevada of today, a place that is just slightly ahead of, or behind, or off to one side of, anywhere else we know.

Throughout all of its history, Nevada has been looked upon as a colony for outside interests to exploit. First came the Spanish, then the British and their Canadian surrogates. When the land came under control of the young United States, Nevada was considered little more than a rest stop on the highway to California. When gold and silver were discovered in great quantities in and around Virginia City, much of the wealth was exported out of the state to California and even as far away as England.

The interests that developed much of the early commercial properties of Nevada were the railroads, and they, too, sent their money west and east. And finally, there was gambling, Nevada's one major homegrown industry. The casinos took off in the 1940s only after organized crime capitalists from New York, Chicago, Miami, Los Angeles, and elsewhere came in and exerted control. Today, the gangsters are mostly gone, but control of nearly all of the major casinos and hotels rests in the hands of huge stateless corporations.

The River to the Pacific
The region that would one day be Nevada was originally part of the Spanish

Empire in the New World. Father Francisco Garcés is believed to have entered the Las Vegas Valley in 1776. Garcés and other priest-explorers were expanding the Old Spanish Trail, which led from the commercial centers of Santa Fe (now in New Mexico) to the Spanish missions in southern California. Along the way, they sought to make converts if they could; more than a few Native Americans were killed in skirmishes and by disease.

There was, of course, a significant problem faced by the Spanish: getting through deserts and high mountain passes that stood between New Mexico and California. Sierra Nevada is a Spanish phrase meaning "snowy mountains." Garcés and others of his time followed the Colorado River into Nevada and did not fully explore the region geologists now call the Great Basin. And in the process, they made some significant errors on their maps and created the myth of what they called the San Buenaventura River, a great waterway that was supposed to cross the Great Basin and empty into the Pacific Ocean. In other words, they were claiming that there was an easy route from east to west that did not require crossing the high mountains. For much of the next half-century, trappers and explorers searched in vain for the San Buenaventura.

In 1825, Peter Skene Ogden explored parts of Nevada from the other direction, on an expedition south from Canada. Working for the Hudson's Bay Company, he discovered the Humboldt River in northwest Nevada in that year. A year later, Jedediah Strong Smith, an explorer and fur trader, followed the Colorado River into southern Nevada—the same entry Garcés took 50 years earlier—and soon thereafter the 1,200-mile-long Spanish Trail became firmly established.

Smith, born in 1798 in Bainbridge, New York, went to the West as a young fur trapper and became one of the great pathfinders of our country. His group of 17 set out from the Great Salt Lake in 1826 looking for fur trade routes to California and the Northwest. He crossed the Mojave Desert to Mission San Gabriel, California, near what is today San Diego, and may have been the first nonnative to enter California from the East. Returning eastward the next year, he crossed the Great Salt Lake Desert on an epic journey through the inhospitable, waterless sands.

Another group of explorers was seeking a way to link the Mormon settlements of Salt Lake City and California, and the trailblazers sought a way to avoid the highest of the Sierra Nevada mountain passes by going south.

In 1829, Rafael Rivera, a young scout for Spanish traders, entered a valley with a patch of tall grass about two miles long and half a mile wide—a desert oasis with a small amount of drinkable water. That valley, called *las vegas* (Spanish for "the meadows") became a regular stopping-off point for travelers on the westward trail.

John C. Frémont, a U.S. Army officer, conducted extensive explorations in 1843 and 1845. In 1848, at the end of the Mexican War, the territory that included what would become Nevada was acquired by the United States from Mexico for $15 million in the Treaty of Guadalupe Hidalgo.

But it took the discovery of gold at Sutter's Mill near Sacramento, California, in 1847 to begin mass migration to the West Coast, and much of the traffic passed through Nevada; over the next seven years, the population of California grew from about 15,000 to 300,000.

In 1849, Mormon settlers established a trading post at Mormon Station (now known as Genoa) in the Carson River Valley, at the base of the Sierra Nevadas. In 1855, a colony of Mormon evangelists arrived in the Las Vegas Valley and established the Las Vegas Mission in an attempt to bring their religion and knowledge to the Paiute Indians. They built a fort—importing some of the wood from mountains as far as 20 miles away—and planted crops. Although they apparently had some success in their assignments, in 1857, the settlers were recalled to Salt Lake City by Brigham Young after the church government had a dispute with the U.S. government, and the mission was abandoned.

In the late 1850s, the area around Virginia City, Carson City, and Genoa served as a staging area for settlers about to head over the Sierras to California. The Mormon Station had become a thriving commercial operation after a simple log cabin store was erected in 1851. Genoa was also the first home of the *Territorial Enterprise* newspaper, which was to become an important element of the developing Western culture.

The relatively quiet status of Nevada as a rest stop on the highway west changed mightily about this time. There had been some minor gold finds in Gold Canyon in about 1850, but the quantity was so relatively small as to be lost in the excitement over the California discoveries.

But in January of 1859, gold and then silver—the Great Comstock Lode—were found on the slopes of Mt. Davidson between Reno and Carson City. By the spring of 1860, a full boom was underway at Virginia City. (One of the miners, James "Old Virginny" Finney, bestowed his name on the rough settlement of tents and cave dwellings of the first miners.)

In 1862, the U.S. Congress granted a charter to the Union Pacific Railroad to build the first transcontinental railroad, stretching from near Sacramento, California, to Missouri, where it would connect to eastern systems.

The mines in and around Virginia City had a lasting impact on the nation, bringing Nevada Territory into the Union as a source of wealth at the start of the Civil War in 1861. Many local mine owners were opposed to statehood, fearing their riches would be taxed to support the war; President Lincoln, who sought Nevada's support in Congress, pushed its statehood, which took place in 1864. Along the way, the riches of the Comstock provided much of the capital for the development of San Francisco.

After the Mormons abandoned their fort in Las Vegas in 1857, a local farmer, Octavius Decatur Gass, acquired the water rights in the valley and moved into the old Mormon fort. Gass, who went on to become a major political force in the area, had come from Ohio in search of gold.

The 640-acre site, now referred to as the Las Vegas Ranch, occupied what is now the entire downtown area. A section of the old fort still stands in a city museum.

The next driving force in Nevada was the coming of the railroads. Though the Civil War held most of the attention of a war-weary America, citizens also watched as the Central Pacific and Union Pacific Railroads raced east and west toward each other in the construction of the first transcontinental railroad. The CP began on January 1, 1863, in Sacramento, California; the UP broke ground on December 2 of the same year in Omaha, Nebraska. The Central Pacific tracks passed through northern Nevada (Reno, Winnemucca, and Elko) to the meeting point at Promontory Point, Utah, where the Golden Spike was driven on May 10, 1869.

The main line became the lure to additional railroad construction in the state. The Virginia & Truckee Railroad, which serviced the silver and gold mines of Virginia City, was extended from Carson City to the east-west tracks at Reno.

At the start of 1905, the final spike connecting a southern railroad route between Los Angeles and Salt Lake City was driven into the desert floor about 20 miles south of what would become Las Vegas. The Tonopah & Las Vegas Railroad sprang up to link mining and ranching operations to the southern tracks.

The former Mormon ranch, which covered much of what is now down-town Las Vegas, came into the ownership of the Stewart family in 1882. Twenty years later, they sold the property for $55,000 to copper and railroad magnate William Clark, who was also U.S. Senator from Montana. He decided to make Las Vegas a division point for his San Pedro, Los Angeles, and Salt Lake Railroad and not incidentally drive up the value of his land holdings.

And so, on the morning of May 15, 1905, Clark's railroad and the closely linked Las Vegas Land and Water Company banged the opening gavel for an auction of the Las Vegas Ranch and surrounding lands. The sale was conducted from a temporary structure near the railroad station; the site today is roughly the location of the Union Plaza Hotel at the head of Fremont Street in down-town Las Vegas.

A crowd of more than one thousand bid feverishly on some twelve hundred lots; the action continued into a second day. Spots considered prime property brought as much as $1,750, and the total net was about $265,000.

The Las Vegas Rest Stop

The first through train from Salt Lake City to Los Angeles passed through the growing town of Las Vegas in 1906, and a year later a second railroad line was installed from Las Vegas northwest to Tonopah.

For most of the next quarter-century, the town thrived as a rest stop for travelers on the railroads and also as a commercial center for outlying mining operations.

The wants and needs of the miners were by most sensibilities a bit on the rough side. Many visited what passed for a town to buy basic supplies, obtain a hot bath, visit a saloon for some drinking and gambling, and find a woman for sex; the priorities were not necessarily in that order, either.

As a frontier town, Las Vegas included its share of illegal gaming parlors and a red-light district almost from the start. When the planners for the San

Pedro, Los Angeles, and Salt Lake Railroad divvied up the Las Vegas Ranch, they named the area that is now between First and Second and Ogden and Stewart Streets (one block in from the main drag of Fremont Street) as Block 16. It was here that the first saloons—many with "cribs" out back—were located.

The Arizona Club was one of the first brick buildings in town and generally considered the class of Las Vegas. An old photograph shows the tiny saloon along a very rough dirt road with a 50-foot-long boardwalk. The sign outside read, "Arizona Club. Headquarters for Fully Matured Reimported Straight Whiskey."

Town officials and the police turned a blind eye to the drinking, entertainment, prostitution, and gambling that took place in Block 16, which soon became known more simply as "The Block." These vices were not exactly legal, existing in a political netherworld for decades. In fact, the operators of the whorehouses were required to purchase an annual license for their operations, and the employees were subject to weekly medical examinations.

Gambling had been legal in Nevada from the time of its statehood until 1911, when reacting to a developing conservatism in the country, the legislature outlawed betting. Eight years later, the U.S. Congress instituted Prohibition, outlawing consumption of alcoholic beverages.

But that seemed to matter very little in the Wild West of Las Vegas, particularly in Block 16. Bootleggers supplied alcohol, prostitution flourished, and unregulated games of chance continued for the next 20 years.

A Dam Site

The next important event in local history came courtesy of the Federal Bureau of Reclamation when it authorized the construction of the Boulder Dam on the Colorado River about 30 miles southeast of Las Vegas. The dam was deemed necessary to control the Colorado, which regularly flooded the Imperial Valley in California and the Yuma Valley in Arizona when mountain snows melted each spring and dried to a near trickle in the summer.

Bureau of Reclamation engineers investigated more than 70 sites along the Colorado River before choosing the site of Black Canyon for the Boulder Dam.

The dam was to create the 110-mile-long Lake Mead reservoir upstream and allow the controlled release of water down the Colorado River. (During the construction period, the Colorado River was diverted around the site by four huge tunnels, each 50 feet in diameter.)

Construction began in 1930 and took five years to complete. More than 5,000 workers, many of them with families, moved to the area, and Las Vegas once more was the attractive rest stop in the desert.

Not at all coincidentally, the Nevada legislature reestablished legalized casino gambling in 1931, and small casinos began catering to the construction workers. Included in the same session was a liberalization of divorce laws, requiring a short six-week residency for out-of-staters seeking to cast asunder their marriage vows.

And also not incidentally, the huge generators at the dam—renamed Hoover

Dam—produced plentiful, cheap electricity that was essential to the neon signs of Glitter Gulch and the Strip and the air-conditioning within the huge hotels.

The first Las Vegas gaming license was issued in 1931 to the Northern Club at 15 East Fremont Street. Two years later, Prohibition was officially ended throughout the nation, and the consumption of alcohol became legal again.

Block 16, which continued to thrive even when most of its vices became legal, was finally killed off by a different sort of national urgency—World War II. The commander of the Las Vegas Aerial and Gunnery Range, where many thousands of soldiers were training, feared outbreaks of disease and lack of discipline among his troops. Las Vegas officials were informed that unless they cracked down on The Block, the Army would declare the whole city off-limits to servicemen. Almost immediately, the liquor and slot machine licenses of The Block were revoked. Prostitution, which operated as an adjunct to the other forms of entertainment, died off as an organized operation soon afterward.

Prostitution receded into the underworld again for the next few decades, reemerging as a legal industry in 1973 when the Nevada Supreme Court upheld the right of the state's counties to permit the activity. Brothels are legal in several Nevada counties today, and several major brothels operate outside of Las Vegas, Reno, and Carson City.

The first major casinos were established in downtown Las Vegas along Fremont Street, which eventually became known as Glitter Gulch. Joining the Northern Club in 1932 was the Hotel Apache, with 100 rooms and the first elevator in town. With the exception of the dam workers—most of whom departed by 1936—the attraction of the casinos was almost entirely regional.

The war contributed to the growth of the area, with the establishment of the Aerial Gunnery School and a huge magnesium processing plant, Basic Magnesium, that brought ten thousand workers to Pittman (now Henderson) between Las Vegas and Boulder City. Magnesium is a component of incendiary bombs.

It was in the 1940s, however, that Las Vegas gained national notoriety, and much of the impetus came from organized crime, led by Benjamin "Bugsy" Siegel, Charles "Lucky" Luciano, Meyer Lansky, and others.

Clever businessmen, the gangsters forged links right from the start with Hollywood. This is not to say that the movie stars of the era were directly involved with the gangsters, but there was a definite synergy between the needs of the stars and the operators of the casinos.

Clara Bow (the "It girl") and Rex Bell, film stars of the 1920s and '30s, were early adopters of Las Vegas glitz. They built a ranch and were hosts of the town; they brought many later stars, including Clark Gable, Errol Flynn, the Barrymores, and others to town for visits.

Gamblers Get Out of Town

The El Rancho Vegas was founded miles from downtown in 1941, on U.S. 91, then called the Los Angeles Highway. The hotel included 63 bungalow-like rooms and included riding stables, a showroom and, of course, a casino.

Five years later on the highway (renamed as Las Vegas Boulevard and soon to become known as the Strip) the famous Flamingo hotel opened, and the seeds of modern Las Vegas were sown.

If there is a true civic father to Las Vegas, it would be Benjamin Siegel; you didn't call him "Bugsy" to his face. Born in Brooklyn, Siegel was a major operator in East Coast organized crime. He was sent out West in the 1930s to run a bookmaking wire service and to look after other interests there; among other things, he also owned and operated a fleet of offshore gambling ships that served Californians.

The Flamingo was Siegel's lavish dream; at the time of its opening on December 26, 1946 (with Jimmy Durante and Abbot & Costello as opening acts), the hotel was the southernmost hotel on the Strip. Siegel saw that building an expensive pleasure palace would draw rich—and unprofessional—gamblers.

Siegel was martyred for his cause, too. He was executed by business associates in 1947, allegedly because of claims he siphoned money from the building fund for the Flamingo.

The second big resort out of town was the Last Frontier, which used an Old West theme; guests who flew into town were picked up at the airport in a stagecoach.

One after another, hotels and casinos were built on the Strip, moving farther southward.

The Desert Inn opened in 1950 and made its mark with its featured showrooms with some of the biggest stars of the time. The Stardust brought another staple of Las Vegas in 1958, the fancified girlie show: the Lido de Paris was a spectacular stage show that (almost) incidentally included a stageful of topless dancers.

In 1966, Caesars Palace opened and launched the era of the opulent gambling palace, and Las Vegas as we know it was born. The idea of Las Vegas as a "family" resort accelerated in 1993 and 1994 with the opening of the MGM Grand Adventures theme park and hotel (with a casino, of course) as well as the spectacular Luxor and Treasure Island pleasure palaces.

The Biggest Little Second City of Nevada

Across the state, Reno began as a toll booth over the Truckee River, a private bridge known as Lake's Crossing. And, of course, as a rest stop for travelers heading somewhere else: to California over the Sierra Nevadas and to the wild mining towns of Virginia City and the rest of the Comstock.

Today, though Reno depends upon casinos and tourism for much of its income, it has a more diversified economy than Las Vegas.

Chapter 2

How to Buy the Lowest-Cost Airline Tickets and Protect Yourself from the Uncertainties of Modern Travel

The agent at the gate will smile at you and take your ticket, and the flight attendant will point you to your seat without knowing that you paid just $300 for your round-trip ticket from Boston to Las Vegas.

The businessman across the aisle will suffer through the same mystery meal, watch the same crummy movie, and arrive at McCarran Airport at the same millisecond you do—and pay $804 for his ticket.

But wait: the couple in front were happily bumped off the previous flight because of overbooking and are discussing where to use the two free round-trip tickets they received in compensation. And up front in first class—where the food is ever-so-slightly better—a family of four is traveling on free tickets earned through Mom's frequent flyer plan.

As for me, I've got a cut-rate ticket *and* I'm due for a 5 percent rebate on airfare, hotel, and car rental arranged through my travel agent. And on my trip back home, I will get on the flight I really wanted to take instead of the less-convenient reservation I was forced to sign up for when I bought that cut-rate ticket.

In today's strange world of air travel, there is a lot of room for maneuvering for the dollarwise and clever traveler. You can pay an inflated full price, you can take advantage of the lowest fares, or you can play the ultimate game and parlay tickets into free travel. In this section, we'll show you how to do each.

The Econoguide Golden Rules of Travel

There are three golden rules and a handful of corollaries to saving hundreds of dollars on travel: be flexible, be flexible, and be flexible.

• Be flexible about when you choose to travel, and visit Nevada during the off-season or low-season when airfares, hotel rooms, and other attractions offer substantial discounts.

The best policy. If any significant portion of your trip is nonrefundable, consider buying trip cancelation insurance from a travel agency, tour operator, or directly from an insurance company (ask your insurance agent for advice). The policies are intended to reimburse you for any lost deposits or prepayments if you must cancel a trip because you or certain specified members of your family become ill. Read the policy carefully to understand the circumstances under which the company will pay.

Take care not to purchase more coverage than you need; if your tour package costs $5,000 but you would lose only $1,000 in the event of a cancellation, then the amount of insurance required is just $1,000. Some policies will cover you for health and accident benefits while on vacation, but your existing health policy will probably handle such an emergency as well. In any case, travel insurance usually excludes any preexisting conditions.

• Be flexible about the day of the week you travel. In many cases, you can save hundreds of dollars by changing your departure date one or two days in either direction. Ask your travel agent or airline reservationist for current fare rules and restrictions.

• Be flexible on the hour of your departure. There is generally lower demand—and therefore lower prices—for flights that leave in the middle of the day or very late at night.

• Be flexible on the route you will take, or your willingness to put up with a change of plane or stopover. Once again, you are putting the law of supply and demand in your favor. Don't overlook the possibility of flying out of a different airport, either. For example, metropolitan New Yorkers can find domestic flights from La Guardia, Newark, or White Plains. Suburbanites of Boston might want to consider flights from Worcester or Providence as possibly cheaper alternatives to Logan Airport. Suburbanites in California have similar choices with Orange County or Ontario airports.

• Plan way ahead of time and purchase the most deeply discounted advance tickets, which usually are noncancelable. Most carriers limit the number of discount tickets on any particular flight; although there may be plenty of seats left on the day you want to travel, they may be offered at higher rates.

In recent years, most airlines modified nonrefundable fares to become noncancelable. What this means is that if your plans change or if you are forced to cancel your trip, your tickets retain their value and can be applied against another trip, usually for a fee of about $35 per ticket.

• Or, conversely, you can take a big chance and wait for the last possible moment, keeping in contact with charter tour operators and accepting a bargain price on a "leftover" seat and hotel reservation. You *may* also find that some airlines will reduce the prices on leftover seats within a few weeks of departure date; don't be afraid to check regularly with the airline, or ask your travel agent to do it for you. In fact, some travel agencies have automated computer programs that keep a constant electronic eye on available seats and fares.

• Consider booking a package tour through an airline or a travel agency. There are enough people traveling to Las Vegas or Reno almost any week of the year to permit companies to buy and resell at a discount blocks of space on scheduled airlines and blocks of rooms at major hotels. There are some very good deals to be had by purchasing a package. However, it is worth the time to deconstruct the package to its various parts: airfare, car rental or bus transfer, hotels, and any meals or entertainment included. Could you do better booking your own trip?

• Take advantage of special discount programs like senior citizens' clubs, military discounts, or offerings from organizations to which you may belong. If you are in the over-60 category, you may not even have to belong to a group like AARP; simply ask the airline reservationist if there is a discount available—you may have to prove your age when you pick up your ticket or boarding pass.

• Consider doing business with discounters, known in the industry as consolidators or, less flatteringly, as "bucket shops." Look for their ads in the classified sections of many Sunday newspaper travel sections. These companies buy the airlines' slow-to-sell tickets in volume and resell them to consumers at rock-bottom prices. Be sure to study and understand the restrictions; if they fit your needs and wants, this is a good way to fly.

• A bit more in the shadows are ticket brokers who specialize in the resale of frequent flyer coupons and other free or almost-free tickets. Are you willing to take a small financial risk to save hundreds or even thousands of dollars on a long trip?

Although most airlines attempt to prohibit the resale or transfer of free tickets from the original "owner" to a second or third party, the fact is that very rarely are they successful in preventing such reuse. (When is the last time you were asked for some proof of identity in boarding a domestic air flight?)

Still, you do run the risk of losing your ticket *and* being forced to buy a full-fare replacement en route. Be sure to read and understand the terms

Low-season in most of Nevada is generally the late fall to early spring, with the quietest time of the year the weeks around Christmas and New Year's, but not including those holidays themselves.

Watch out for the huge conventions that descend on Las Vegas and grab the premium rooms and drive up the prices of all the rest.

In Reno, the winter is the offest of off-seasons, although the new bowling stadium in downtown will eat up some of the rooms. The ski-oriented resorts around Lake Tahoe are busy in the winter and sometimes sold out on weekends and holidays, but rooms are usually available during the week except in holiday periods.

Light air. Planes are usually least crowded in midweek and on Saturday afternoons and Sunday mornings.

In general, you will receive the lowest possible fare if you include a Saturday in your trip, buying what is called an **"Excursion Fare."** Airlines use this as a way to exclude business travelers from the cheapest fares, assuming that business people will want to be home by Friday night.

Funny hat fares. You may not have to have any affiliation at all with a convention group in order to take advantage of special rates, if offered. All the airline will ask is the name or number of the discount plan for the convention; the reservationist is almost certainly not going to ask to see your union card or funny hat.

Check with conventions and visitors bureaus at your destination to see if any large groups are traveling when you plan to fly. Is this sneaky and underhanded? Yes. But we think it is sneaky and underhanded for an airline to charge hundreds of dollars more for the seats to the left and right of the ones we are sitting in.

Finding a bucket shop. Look for ads for ticket brokers and bucket shops in places like the classified ads in *USA Today,* the "Mart" section of the *Wall Street Journal* or in specialty magazines like *Frequent Flyer.*

of your contract with the broker, and pay for your ticket with a credit card, if possible.

Standing Up for Standing By

One of the little-known secrets of air travel on most airlines and most types of tickets is the fact that travelers with valid tickets are allowed to stand by for flights other than the ones for which they have reservations; if there are empty seats on the flight, standby ticketholders are permitted to board.

Some airlines are very liberal in their acceptance of standbys within a few days of the reserved flight, while others will charge a small fee (usually $25 to $50) for changes in itinerary. And some airline personnel are stricter about the regulation than others.

Here's what I do know: if I cannot get the exact flight I want for a trip, I make the closest acceptable reservations available and then show up early at the airport and head for the check-in counter for the flight I really want to take. Unless you are seeking to travel during an impossibly overbooked holiday period or arrive on a bad weather day when flights have been canceled, your chances of successfully standing by for a flight are usually pretty good.

One trick is to call the airline the day before the flight and check on the availability of seats for the flight you want to try for. Some reservation clerks are very forthcoming with information; many times I have been told something like, "There are 70 seats open on that flight."

Be careful with standby maneuvers if your itinerary requires a change of plane en route; you'll need to check availability of seats on all of the legs of your journey.

And a final note: be especially careful about standing by for the very last flight of the night. If you somehow are unable to get on that flight, you're stuck for the night.

My personal strategy usually involves making a reservation for that last flight and standing by for one or more earlier flights on the same day.

About Travel Agencies

Here's my advice about travel agents in a nutshell: get a good one or go it alone.

A good travel agent is someone who remembers who he or she works for: You. Of course, there is a built-in conflict of interest here, since the agent is in most cases paid by someone else. Agents receive a commission on airline tickets, hotel reservations, car rentals, and many other services they sell you. In most cases, the more they sell (or the higher the price) the more they earn. A major upheaval in the travel business came at the start of 1995 when several major airlines—led by Delta—declared that they would no longer pay an automatic 10 percent commission to agents but would instead cut off the commission at a flat $50 for a $500 ticket. It remains to be seen whether this one-sided renegotiation of business will hold or whether some airlines will seek to buy the hearts of travel agencies by putting more cash in their pockets.

In any case, I recommend you start the planning for any trip by calling the airlines and a few hotels and finding the best package you can put together for yourself. *Then* call your travel agent and ask them to do better.

If your agent contributes knowledge or experience, comes up with dollar-saving alternatives to your own package, or offers some other kind of convenience, then go ahead and book through the agency. If, as I often find, you know a lot more about your destination and are willing to spend a lot more time to save money than will the agent, do it yourself.

There is one special type of travel agency worth considering. A number of large agencies offer rebates of part of their commissions to travelers. Some of these companies cater only to frequent flyers who will bring in a lot of business; other rebate agencies offer only limited services to clients.

I use an agency that sends me a check after each trip equal to 5 percent of all reservations booked through them. I have never set foot in their offices, and I conduct all of my business over the phone; tickets arrive by mail or by overnight courier when necessary. (It remains to be seen if the change in agency fees will affect the amount of rebate.)

You can find discount travel agencies through many major credit card companies (Citibank and American Express among them) or through associations and clubs.

And if you establish a regular relationship with your local travel agency and bring them enough business to make them glad to see you walk through their door, don't be afraid to ask them for a discount equal to a few percentage points.

Your Consumer Rights

The era of deregulation of airlines has been a mixed blessing for the industry and the consumer. After a period of wild competition based mostly on price, we now are left with fewer, huge airlines and a dizzying array of confusing rules.

The U.S. Department of Transportation and its Federal Aviation Administration still regulate safety issues, overbooking policies, baggage limits, and no-smoking rules. Almost everything else is between you and the airline.

Policies on fares, cancelations, reconfirmation, check-in requirements, compensation for lost or damaged baggage, and for delays all vary by airline. Your rights are limited and defined by the terms of the contract you make with an airline when you buy your ticket. You may find the contract included with

Checking in again. Having a boarding pass issued by a travel agent is not the same as checking in at the airport; you'll still need to show your ticket at the counter so that the agent knows you're there.

the ticket you purchase, or the airlines may "incorporate terms by reference" to a separate document which you will have to request to see.

Whether you are buying your ticket through a travel agent or dealing directly with the airline, here are some important questions to ask:

• Is the price guaranteed or can it change from the time of the reservation until you actually purchase the ticket?

• Can the price change between the time you buy the ticket and the date of departure?

• Is there a penalty for cancelation of the ticket?

• Can the reservation be changed without penalty or for a reasonable fee?

And, ask your travel agent the following:

• Is there anything I should know about the financial health of the airline offering me this ticket?

• Are you aware of any significant threats of work stoppages or legal actions that could ruin my trip?

Overbooking

Overbooking is a polite industry term that refers to the legal business practice of selling more than an airline can deliver. It all stems, alas, from the unfortunate habit of many travelers of neglecting to cancel flight reservations that will not be used. Airlines study the patterns on various flights and city pairs and apply a formula that allows them to sell more tickets than there are seats on the plane in the expectation that a certain percentage will not show up at the airport.

But what happens if all passengers holding a reservation do show up? Obviously, the result will be more passengers than seats, and some will have to be left behind.

The involuntary bump list will begin with the names of passengers who are late to check in. After them, airlines must ask for volunteers before bumping any passengers who have followed the rules. Assuming that no one is willing to give up his or her seat just for the fun of it, the airline will offer some sort of compensation—either a free ticket or cash, or both. It is up to the passenger and the airline to negotiate an acceptable deal.

The U.S. Department of Transportation's consumer protection regulations set some minimum levels of compensation for passengers who are bumped from a flight due to overbooking.

If a passenger is bumped involuntarily, the airline must provide a ticket on its next available flight. Unfortunately, there is no guarantee that it will arrive at your destination at a convenient time.

If a passenger is bumped involuntarily and is booked on a flight which arrives within one hour of the original arrival time, no compensation need be paid; if the airline gets the bumpee to his or her destination more than one hour, but less than two hours after the scheduled arrival, the traveler is entitled to receive an amount equal to the one-way fare of the oversold flight, up to $200; if the delay is more than two hours, the bumpee will receive an amount equal to twice the one-way fare of the original flight, up to $400. The compensation is often in the form of credits for future flights; most are transferable.

It is not considered "bumping" if a flight is canceled because of weather, equipment problems, or the lack of a flight crew. You are also not eligible for compensation if the airline substitutes a smaller aircraft for operational or safety reasons, and if the flight involves an aircraft with 60 seats or less.

How to Get Bumped

Why in the world would you *want* to be bumped? Well, perhaps you'd like to look at missing your plane as an opportunity to earn a little money for your time instead of an annoyance. Is a two-hour delay worth $100 an hour to you? How about $800 for a family of four to wait a few hours on the way home—that will pay for a week's hotel plus a meal at the airport.

Double indemnity. Your homeowner's or renter's insurance policy may include coverage for your possessions while you travel, making it unnecessary to purchase a special policy. Check with your insurance agent.

Second chance. Tour cancelations are rare. Most tour operators, if forced to cancel, will offer another package or other incentives as a goodwill gesture. If a charter flight or charter tour is canceled, the tour operator must refund your money within 14 days.

If you're not in a tremendous rush to get to Nevada—or to get back home—you might want to volunteer to be bumped. We wouldn't recommend doing this on the busiest travel days of the year, or if you are booked on the last flight of the day, unless you are also looking forward to a free night in an airport motel.

Tour Packages and Charter Flights

Tour packages and flights sold by tour operators or travel agents may look similar, but the consumer may end up with significantly different rights.

It all depends on whether the flight is a scheduled or nonscheduled flight. A scheduled flight is one that is listed in the *Official Airline Guide* and available to the general public through a travel agent or from the airline. This doesn't mean that a scheduled flight will necessarily be on a major carrier, or that you will be flying on a 747 jumbo jet; it could just as easily be the propeller-driven pride of Hayseed Airlines. In any case, though, a scheduled flight does have to meet stringent federal government certification requirements.

In the event of delays, cancelations, or other problems with a scheduled flight, your recourse is with the airline.

A nonscheduled flight is also known as a charter flight. The term charter is sometimes also applied to a complete package that includes a nonscheduled flight, hotel accommodations, ground transportation, and other elements.

Lug-it-yourself. If you are using a scheduled airline to connect with a charter flight, your baggage will not be automatically transferred. You must make the transfer yourself.

Delays may be costly. Charter and tour flights operate independently of other flights. If you are on a trip that combines scheduled and non-scheduled flights, or two unrelated charter flights, you may end up losing your money and flight because of delays.

It may make sense to avoid such combinations for that reason or to leave extra hours or even days between connections.

Some tour operators offer travel delay insurance that pays for accommodations or alternative travel arrangements necessitated by certain types of delays.

Charter flights are generally a creation of a tour operator who will purchase all of the seats on a specific flight to a specific destination, or who will rent an airplane and crew from an air carrier.

Charter flights and charter tours are regulated by the federal government, but your rights as a consumer are much more limited than those afforded to scheduled flight customers.

Read the Fine Print

You wouldn't buy a hamburger without knowing the price and specifications (two all-beef patties on a sesame seed roll, etc.). Why, then, would you spend hundreds or even thousands of dollars on a tour and not understand the contract that underlies the transaction?

When you purchase a charter flight or a tour package you should review and sign a contract that spells out your rights. This contract is sometimes referred to as the "Operator Participant Contract" or the "Terms and Conditions." Look for this contract in the booklet or brochure that describes the packages; ask for it if one is not offered. The proper procedure for a travel agent or tour operator to follow requires that they wait until the customer has read and signed the contract before any money is accepted.

Remember that the contract is designed mostly to benefit the tour operator, and each contract may be different from others you may have agreed to in the past. The basic rule here is: **if you don't understand it, don't sign it.**

Depending on your relative bargaining strength with the provider, you may be able to amend the contract so that it is more in your favor; be sure to obtain a countersignature from an authorized party if you make a change in the document, and keep a signed copy for yourself.

The Best Way to Book a Package or Charter Flight

If possible, use a travel agent—preferably one you know and trust from prior experience. In general, the tour operator pays the travel agent's commission. Some tour packages, however, are available only from the operator who organized the tour; in certain cases, you may be able to negotiate a better price by dealing directly with the operator, although you are giving up one layer of protection for your rights.

Pay for your ticket with a credit card; this is a cardinal rule for almost any situation in which you are prepaying for a service or product.

Realize that charter airlines don't have large fleets of planes available to substitute in the event of a mechanical problem or an extensive weather delay. They may or may not be able to arrange for a substitute piece of equipment from another carrier.

If you are still willing to try a charter after all of these warnings, make one more check of the bottom line before you sign the contract. First of all, is the air travel less expensive than the lowest nonrefundable fares from a scheduled carrier? (Remember that you are, in effect, buying a nonrefundable fare with most charter flight contracts.)

Have you included taxes, service charges, baggage transfer fees, or other charges the tour operator may put into the contract?

Is the savings significantly more than the 10 percent the charter operator may boost the price without your permission? Do any savings come at a cost of time? Put a value on your time.

> **Drop us a card.** Keep in touch with your travel agent or tour operator. In many cases they can anticipate major changes before departure time and will let you know. And, many operators will try hard to keep you from demanding a refund if you find a major change unacceptable. They may offer a discount or upgrade on a substitute trip or adjust the price of the changed tour.

And finally, don't buy a complete package until you have compared it to the a la carte cost of such a trip. Call the hotels offered by the tour operator or similar ones in the same area and ask them a simple question: "What is your best price for a room?" Be sure to mention any discount programs that are applicable, including AAA, airline frequent flyer programs, or other organizations. Do the same for car rental agencies and any other attractions you plan to visit to get current prices.

And, of course, don't overlook the discount coupons for hotels, motels, restaurants, and attractions that are included in this book—that's why they're there.

McCarran International Airport

Las Vegas' airport is within a chip's throw of the Strip, about a mile from the top end of the casino district and five miles from downtown. McCarran is the 11th busiest airport in the world, ahead of even Orlando, Boston, and New York's La Guardia.

Construction was underway on an extension to the main runway that will give McCarran the second longest civilian runway in the United States, just 66 feet shorter than the one at Kennedy Airport in New York.

More than a dozen major commercial carriers and three dozen charter companies serve the airport, with an average of more than 750 flights per day. In 1994, about 24 million passengers used the airport.

At the start of 1995, work was completed on the $200 million Airport Connector and Runway System, which provides a direct connection from McCarran to I-15, including a half-mile-long tunnel beneath two of the airport's runways. Future plans call for the airport connector to tie into the proposed Las Vegas Beltway that will circle the valley.

Construction is due to begin soon on a new 3,000-space parking garage, with completion due in 1997.

Airlines Serving Las Vegas

Phone numbers are in area code (702) unless indicated otherwise.

National Carriers

America West Airlines. 798-1715, (800) 247-5692
American Airlines. (800) 433-7300
Continental Airlines. 383-8291, (800) 525-0280
Delta Air Lines. 731-3111, (800) 221-1212
Northwest Airlines. (800) 225-2525
TWA. 385-1000, (800) 221-2000
United Airlines. 385-3222, (800) 241-6522
USAir. 382-1905, (800) 428-4322

Regional Carriers

Aero California. (800) 237-6225
Air Nevada. 736-8900
Air Vegas. 736-3599
Alaska Airlines. (800) 426-0333
Hawaiian Airlines. 796-9696, (800) 367-5320
Skywest Airlines. (800) 453-9417
Southwest Airlines. (800) 435-9792

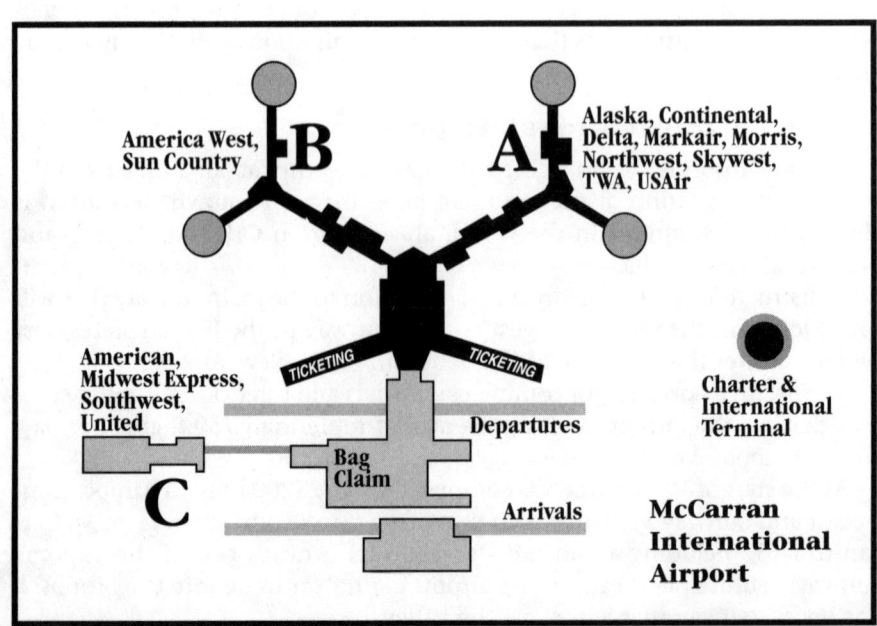

Chapter 3
How to Sleep for Less

Negotiating for a Room

Notice the title of this section: I didn't call it "buying" a room. The fact of the matter is that hotel rooms, like almost everything else, are subject to negotiation and change.

Here is how to pay the highest possible price for a hotel room: walk up to the front desk without a reservation and say, "I'd like a room." Unless the "No Vacancy" sign is lit, you may have to pay the "rack rate," which is the published maximum nightly charge.

Here are a few ways to pay the lowest possible price:

1. Before you head for your vacation, spend an hour on the phone and call directly to a half dozen hotels that seem to be in the price range you'd like to spend. (I recommend membership in AAA and use of their annual tour books as *starting points* for your research.)

Start by asking for the room rate. Then ask them for their *best* rate. Does that sound like an unnecessary second request? Trust us, it's not: I can't begin to count the number of times the rates have dropped substantially when I ask again.

[True story: I once called the reservation desk of a major hotel chain and asked for the rates for a night at a Chicago location. "That will be $149 per night," I was told. "Ouch," I said. "Oh, would you like to spend less?" the reservationist said. I admitted that I would, and she punched a few keys on her keyboard. "They have a special promotion going on. How about $109 per night?" she asked.

Not bad for a city hotel, I reasoned, but still I hadn't asked the big question. "What is your best rate?" I asked. "Oh, our best rate? That would be $79," said the agent.

But, wait: "I'm a member of AAA, by the way." Another pause. "That's fine, Mr. Sandler. The nightly room rate will be $71.10. Have a nice day."]

When you feel you've negotiated the best deal you can obtain over the phone, make a reservation at the hotel of your choice. Be sure to go over the dates and prices one more time, and obtain the name of the person you spoke with and a confirmation number if available.

Showing your card.
Membership in AAA brings some important benefits for the traveler, although you may not always be able to apply the club's usual 10 percent discount on top of whatever hotel rate you negotiate. (It doesn't hurt to ask, though.) Be sure to request a tour book and Nevada maps from AAA even if you plan to fly there; they are much better than the maps given by car rental agencies.

Room safety. The small safes available in some hotels can be valuable to the traveler; be sure to inquire whether there is a service charge for their use. We've been in hotels that apply the charge regardless of whether we used the safe or not; look over your bill at check-out and object to any charges that are not proper. In any case, we'd suggest that any objects that are so valuable that you feel they should be locked up should probably be left home.

2. When you show up at your hotel on the first night, stop and look at the marquee outside; see if the hotel is advertising a discount rate. Here's where you need to be bold. Walk up to the desk as if you *did not* have a reservation, and ask the clerk: "What is your best room rate for tonight?" If the rate they quote you is less than the rate in your reservation, you are now properly armed to ask for a reduction in your room rate.

Similarly, if the room rate advertised out front on the marquee drops during your stay, don't be shy about asking that your charges be reduced. Just be sure to ask for the reduction *before* you spend another night at the old rate, and obtain the name of the clerk who promises a change. If the hotel tries a lame excuse like, "That's only for new check-ins," you can offer to check out and then check back in again. That will usually work; you can always check out and go to the hotel across the road that will usually match the rates of its competitor.

3. Are you planning to stay for a full week? Ask for a weekly rate. If the room clerk says there is no such rate, ask to speak to the manager: he or she may be willing to shave a few dollars per day off the rate for a long-term stay.

Welcome, Conventioneers

Not all of the visitors to Las Vegas have chosen to go there for recreation. Each year, millions are drawn to the spectacular facilities of the Las Vegas Convention Center or the Sands Expo & Convention Center as well as the relatively smaller facilities at many of the major hotels in town.

The conventioneers come to town because of the lure of the casinos and entertainment, but even more importantly, they come because Las Vegas is one of the few places in the country with a huge capacity for shows as well as an available bank of hotel rooms for attendees.

The biggest Las Vegas conventions include the annual visits of CONEXPO (the Construction Industry Manufacturers Association) in March; the Consumer Electronics Show usually in January; the National Association of Broadcasters in April; Comdex (the computer industry show) in November; and the International Council of Shopping Centers in May.

Of course, we mustn't overlook the National Pizza and Pasta Association, the American Concrete Pumping Association, the Coca-Cola Collectors Club International, the International Carwash Association, and, obviously, the American Ostrich Association, which draws 2,000 people (and, we presume, a few big birds).

The leading convention facility is the Las Vegas Convention Center, at 3150 Paradise Road, about three blocks east of the Strip and adjacent to the huge Las Vegas Hilton Hotel.

The 1.3 million-square-foot facility includes 880,000 square feet available for exhibit space, plus 89 meeting rooms with seating for from 50 to 7,500. Kitchen facilities can serve a banquet for up to 12,000 close friends. The surrounding parking lots can hold as many as 4,000 cars.

Some of the larger conventions need even more space and spill over into the several large halls of the Hilton next door and from there to convention spaces around town.

The Sands Expo & Convention Center, at 201 Sands Avenue, is used primarily as the second hall for one show, the annual Comdex computer convention, the largest annual trade show in the U.S. (There's a bit of special interest here: the Sands Center is part of the Sands Hotel, which is itself owned by the Interface Group, which puts on the Comdex show.)

Phone bills. Be sure you understand the telephone billing policy at the hotel. Some establishments allow free local calls, while others charge as much as 75 cents for such calls. (We're especially unhappy with service charges for 800 numbers.) Be sure to examine your bill carefully at checkout and make sure it is correct.

We strongly suggest you obtain a telephone credit card and use it when you travel; nearly all hotels tack high service charges on long-distance calls, and there is no reason to pay it.

The first phase of construction at the Sands put about 615,000 square feet of convention space on one level, plus an underground parking lot for 1,100 cars; future plans call for enlarging the center to 1 million square feet, which would make it the world's largest single-level convention facility.

Another facility that is used for smaller conventions and for occasional special events from the mega-gatherings is the Cashman Field Center, at 850 Las Vegas Blvd. North, just outside of downtown Las Vegas.

Cashman Field Center includes a 1,954-seat auditorium/theater and a pair of exhibit halls that total 100,000 square feet of space. Outside is a stadium that is home to the AAA Las Vegas Stars baseball team April through September.

How to Get a Room During a Convention

For most of the year, finding a place to stay in Las Vegas is not difficult. However, the very largest of the conventions will soak up most of the rooms at the major hotels.

If you are coming to Las Vegas as part of a convention, check with the organizers to see which hotels they may have made special arrangements with. Or, the convention may use the services of the Las Vegas Visitors' Bureau to book rooms.

The advantage of using a group's services include these:

There *may* be less expensive rooms available through the convention group.

The "official" hotel may be the location of the convention itself or on the bus route for shuttle service to the convention hall.

However, there are times when you can obtain a less expensive or more convenient place to stay by booking directly. Most major conventions, for example, only reserve blocks of rooms at the largest hotels, and there may be some rooms available directly; smaller hotels right near the convention halls are sometimes overlooked.

When the town is completely packed because of a convention, you may be able to sweet-talk your way into a room by contacting the lodging bureau handling the group. You don't have to be so bold as to lie, but you may be able to allow them to assume you are with the convention and in dire need of a room.

On the other hand, don't always assume that convention groups will be offered the lowest prices at hotels. On more than one occasion, I have obtained a cheaper price by calling a hotel directly to book a room rather than going through the lodging bureaus.

In addition, though the official hotels for a convention may be packed—and may be charging peak or even above-peak rates—nonconvention hotels may have rooms at low-season bargain rates. For example, during one of the research trips for this book, all of the major official hotels were sold out for the CONEXPO show, and the few that had rooms were asking $150 to $200 per night. Yet the huge Circus Circus hotel, which was not affiliated with the convention, had plenty of rooms at $39; up the Strip, the independent Center Strip Inn had deluxe rooms with Jacuzzi tubs for $49.

One safe bet in Las Vegas is that downtown hotels will often have available rooms, even during major conventions. Of course, all bets are off during peak Christmas and other holiday times.

Chapter 4
Cars, Trains, and Buses

Mileage to Las Vegas

Atlanta	1,964	Barstow	153
Boston	2,725	Boulder City	24
Carson City	430	Chicago	1,772
Dallas	1,221	Death Valley	160
Denver	777	Flagstaff	275
Grand Canyon	288	Henderson	13
Hoover Dam	25	Jackpot	488
Kingman	103	Lake Havasu City	145
Lake Tahoe	470	Laughlin	93
Los Angeles	282	New York City	2,548
Palm Springs	280	Philadelphia	2,468
Phoenix	298	Reno	440
Salt Lake City	433	San Diego	337
San Francisco	564	Sparks	207
Washington, D.C.	2,393	Zion National Park	156

From the Airport to the Strip and Downtown

You'll know you're in Las Vegas and not Atlanta or Dallas or Podunk the moment you get off your plane. Yep, those are slot machines in the boarding lounge waiting to suck up your first (or last) quarters.

McCarran International Airport is just over a mile from the top of the Strip and about five miles from downtown Las Vegas.

Taxis cost about $7 to $10 to the Strip or $10 to $15 to downtown, plus tip. Cabs are usually plentiful outside the baggage area of the airport, although long lines may build when there is a major convention in town.

An alternative is to take one of the shuttle services. For about $3 to $4 to the Strip or $4 to $5 to downtown per person, you'll share the minibus with as many as a dozen or so others, and the driver will choose the order of the stops. The shuttle service may be appropriate if you are traveling alone and are not in a hurry; otherwise a taxi makes more sense.

Credit cars. Although it is theoretically possible to rent a car without a credit card, you will find it to be a rather inconvenient process. If they cannot hold your credit card account hostage, most agencies will require a large cash deposit—perhaps as much as several thousand dollars—before they will give you the keys.

Simple code. All of Nevada lies within the 702 area code.

Frequent drivers. Don't let it force you to pay too much for a rental car, but all things being equal, use a rental agency that awards frequent flyer mileage in a program you use.

A third choice is CAT bus route 20, which leaves the airport and then heads down the Strip. The bus does not enter into the driveways of the hotels, and you may end up on the wrong side of the Strip and have to lug your bags across the road.

Renting a Car

Tens of millions of people come to Las Vegas and other Nevada magnets each year, about half of them by plane. This means, of course, that the other half arrive by car, bus, or train.

This makes Nevada one of the most competitive markets for car rental agencies in the country. You will find, of course, the major rental companies like Avis, Budget, Hertz, and National. You will also find very large operations by companies like Alamo and General. And there are also more than a few rental agencies that operate only in Nevada or even just in one of its major cities.

Your travel agent may be of assistance in finding the best rates; you can make a few phone calls by yourself, too.

Be aware that the least expensive car rental agencies usually do not have their stations at the airport itself. You will have to wait for a shuttle bus to take you from the terminal to their lot, and you must return the car to the outlying area at the end of your trip. This may add about 20 to 30 minutes to your arrival and departure schedule.

One more last-minute note: as you fly into Las Vegas, read the airline's frequent flyer magazine in the seatback pocket. There are often special car rental rates advertised for destinations served by the airline. It may be worthwhile to cancel your reservation at a higher rate; or you can take the ad with you to the rental counter and show it to the clerk and ask for a better rate.

In 1995, several major car rental companies announced tests of programs that would charge a penalty to renters who cancel reservations on short notice. It remains to be seen whether this practice will take hold; be sure you understand any cancelation policies before you make a reservation.

Pay attention, too, when the rental agent explains the gas tank policy. The most common plan says that you must return the car with a full tank; if the agency must refill the tank, you will be billed a service charge plus what is usually a very high per-gallon rate.

Other optional plans include one where the rental agency sells you a full tank when you first drive away and takes no note of how much gas remains when you return the car. Unless you somehow manage to return the car with the engine running on fumes, you are in effect making a gift to the agency with every gallon you bring back.

We prefer the first option, making a point to refill the tank on the way to the airport on getaway day.

Car rental companies will try—with varying levels of pressure—to convince you to purchase special insurance coverage. They'll tell you it's "only" $7 or $9 per day. What a deal! That works out to about $2,500 or $3,330 per year for a set of rental wheels. And the coverage is intended primarily to protect the rental company and not you.

Check with your insurance agent before you travel to determine how well your personal automobile policy will cover a rental car and its contents. And we strongly recommend you use a credit card that offers rental car insurance; such insurance usually covers the deductible below your personal policy. The extra auto insurance by itself can usually more than pay for an upgrade to a "gold card" or other extra-service credit card.

The only sticky area comes for those visitors with a driver's license but no car, and therefore no insurance. Again, consult your credit card company and your insurance agent.

And finally, check with the rental company about its policies on taking the car out of the state. Some companies will charge you extra if you are planning to take the car across a state line. In Las Vegas, this can become an issue if you travel south to Hoover Dam; the far side of the dam is in Arizona. Similarly, in Laughlin, the bridge across the Colorado River begins in Nevada and ends in Arizona.

At Reno, the California state line is nearby on the west side of the Sierra Nevadas and the popular destination of Lake Tahoe is on the line; restrictions on interstate travel are less common there.

The following are among companies serving McCarran Airport, the Strip, and downtown; check with them for the office nearest where you want to pick up a car. (Where there is more than one office, we have listed the direct phone number for the airport location.) Local phone numbers are in area code (702).

Abbey Rent-A-Car. 736-4988
Action Auto Rental. 369-1510
Advantage Rent-A-Car. 386-5775, (800) 777-5500
Agency Rent-A-Car. 798-7795, (800) 321-1972
Airways Rent-A-Car. 798-6100, (800) 777-9377
Ajax Rent a Car. 798-7200
Alamo Rent a Car. 737-3111, (800) 327-9633
Allstate Car Rental. 736-6147, (800) 634-6186
Avis Rent A Car. 261-5595, (800) 331-1212
Budget Car & Truck Rental. 736-1212, (800) 527-0700
Dollar Rent A Car. 739-8408, (800) 800-4000
Enterprise Rent-A-Car. 795-8842, (800) 325-8007
General Rent-A-Car. 739-1954, (800) 327-7607
Hertz Rent A Car. 736-4900, (800) 654-3131
Montgomery Ward. 736-2279, (800) 367-2217
National Car Rental. (800) 227-7368

Nevada Commission on Tourism, Capitol Complex, Carson City, NV 89710; 687-3636 or (800) 638-2328.
Lake Mead National Recreation Area. 601 Nevada Hwy., Boulder City, NV 89005; 293-8907.
Nevada Division of State Parks. Capitol Complex, Carson City, NV 89710; 687-4387.

Payless. 739-8488, (800) 729-5377
Rebel Rent-A-Car. 597-1683, (800) 336-4222
Rent-A-Vette. 736-2592, (800) 372-1981
Sears Car & Truck Rental. 736-8006, (800) 527-0700
Thrifty Car Rental. 736-4706, (800) 367-2277
Value Rent-A-Car. 733-8886, (800) 468-2583

Getting Around in Las Vegas

On the one hand, navigating in Las Vegas is pretty simple. Almost every major hotel and casino is found along Las Vegas Boulevard (better known as the Strip), along Fremont Street in downtown Las Vegas, or on a cross-street to one of those two roads.

Except when there is a large convention in town, taxis are plentiful at the airport and along the Strip, and bus service is adequate. And, although it is not as common as it should be, it is quite possible to walk between and among the clusters of casino/hotels on the Upper Strip and Center Strip.

On the other hand, as you find in reading this book, there is a lot more to Las Vegas than the Strip and Fremont Street. If you've got the time, we strongly recommend you rent a car or take a guided tour to visit some of the great natural and man-made sights of the region.

Personally, we find it mind-boggling that a visitor to Las Vegas who will ogle The Mirage or The Luxor or Excalibur can come and go without seeing even more amazing sights like Hoover Dam or Red Rock Canyon. (And, as you will find later in this book, we cannot imagine a trip to Reno that does not include a visit to Lake Tahoe and Virginia City.)

Taxi Services

Cabs, cabs everywhere—except when there is a big convention in town, anytime you are in a hurry, or during one of Las Vegas' rare rainstorms. There are two major taxi companies that all but control the market: Yellow Cab and Whittlesea Blue Cab.

Taxi dancing. Here's a tip for visitors unable to get a cab from the convention center: walk up Convention Center Drive to the Strip and wait for a car at one of the hotels there—with luck you will be able to snare a ride in a taxi that has brought a rider the few blocks you walked from the LVCC.

Taxis line up at McCarran Airport to meet most flights. During conventions, taxis usually arrive regularly at the front entrance to the Las Vegas Convention Center. Your next best bet is to wait at the main entrance at one of the major hotels.

Here are the phone numbers of the major local cab companies:
ABC. 736-8444
Ace. 736-8383
Desert Cab. 386-9102
Henderson Taxi. 384-2322
Western. 382-7100
Whittlesea Blue Cab. 384-6111
Yellow-Checker-Star. 873-2000

Busing to the Tables

Las Vegas Transit operates bus routes serving much of the metropolitan area. Call 228-7433 for information.

The Downtown Transportation Center, at Stewart Avenue and Casino Center Blvd., is the transfer point for many routes, open from 6:15 A.M. to 10 P.M. daily. Riders must request and pay 15 cents for a transfer at the time of paying the first fare.

Fares in 1994 were $1 for adults, 50 cents for senior citizens 65 years and older, and 50 cents for children 6 through 17 years of age.

Sin-less City. Boulder City was born as a boom town for construction workers on what was then called Boulder Dam, now called Hoover Dam. As a vestige of its former status as a government owned and operated facility, it is the only town in Nevada that prohibits gambling.

Here are a few bus routes that service the major tourist areas. Be sure to call to check on hours of operation and possible changes in route:

Strip/Downtown (Route 6). From the Downtown Transportation Center across Stewart Avenue to Las Vegas Blvd. (the Strip) and south to the Hacienda at the top end of the road where it turns around and makes its way down the Strip to downtown.

The Strip Express. Makes express stops only ($1.25 exact fare), Outbound: Downtown Transportation Center, Circus Circus, Caesars Palace, and Excalibur Hotel (rear entrance). Inbound: Tropicana Hotel, Flamingo Hilton, Riviera Hotel, Downtown Transportation Center.

The Strip Shuttle (Route 13). Connects the Las Vegas Convention Center and the Las Vegas Hilton to the Fashion Show Mall and eventually the top of the Strip at the Hacienda Hotel. The bus goes from the Hilton north on Paradise Road to Sahara, west to the Strip and then south to the Hacienda where it turns around for the return.

The Mall Hopper (Route 14). Connects the west entrance of the Fashion Show Mall on the Strip to the Meadows and Boulevard Shopping Malls. The bus runs in an S-curve from the Boulevard Mall on Maryland Parkway across Twain and Sands to the Strip and the west entrance of the Fashion Show Mall, continuing north on the I-15 freeway to the Meadows Mall west of downtown.

The privately run **Strip Trolley** makes runs about every 20 minutes up and down the Strip. Its northern terminus is the Las Vegas Hilton and the Sahara; at the south end it goes to MGM Grand, Tropicana, Excalibur, Luxor, and the Hacienda. Exact fare of $1.10 is required. For information call 382-1404.

Train Service

Amtrak. The most popular train route into Las Vegas is the **Desert Wind**, which connects to Los Angeles. National information: (800) 872-7245. Reno: 329-8638. Truckee: (916) 582-1623.

II
Las Vegas

Chapter 5
Welcome, Pilgrim

As far as we are concerned, there are two types of visitors to Las Vegas:

　1. Those who have never been there before and are anxious to see if all of the strange and wonderful things they have heard are true.

　2. Those who are returning to Las Vegas to see if things are really as strange and wonderful as they remember.

Either way, Las Vegas is unlike any other place on earth, with the possible exception of those other fantasy zones called Walt Disney World and Disneyland.

Coming in to Las Vegas

The best way to approach Las Vegas is to fly in on a moonlit, clear night. As your plane descends from points east, you cross hundreds of miles of barren desert that seem as lifeless as the moon. Suddenly, you'll come upon a huge oddly-shaped lake in the desert held back by a tremendous dam, a pale white saucer set on end in a canyon.

Just minutes later you will see on the horizon an island of light, an electric oasis in the desert. About the time the pilot brings down the landing gear, you should be able to pick out some of the elements of a skyline like nowhere else on earth: a huge Egyptian pyramid, a Roman garden and amphitheater, a pirate ship, and a gaudy castle constructed of gigantic toy blocks.

Coming in from California and points west, your jet will cross the last wall of mountains and then drop into the Las Vegas Valley. The pilot will hang a right turn over the Vegas World Tower and proceed up the length of the Strip to the airport.

Welcome to Las Vegas, pilgrim.

Las Vegas Climate

Las Vegas has two basic weather patterns: sunny and moderate and sunny and hot.

Las Vegas averages 320 days of sunshine per year and only 4.19 inches of rain. In the summer months from June to September daytime temperatures may top 100 degrees. In the short spring and fall seasons, they usually reach the 70s during the day. In the winter, high temperatures may drop all the way down to the 50s.

Average high temperature in January	56 degrees
Average low temperature in January	33 degrees
Average high temperature in July	104 degrees
Average low temperature in July	75 degrees
Annual average relative humidity	24 percent
Annual average rainfall	4.19 inches
Annual average snowfall	1.5 inches
Annual days with precipitation	26 days

Chapter 6
The Best of the Strip

MUST-SEE Caesars Palace

Depending on your point of view, this is either one of the unnatural wonders of the world or one of its greatest exercises in gaudy excess. Either way, Caesars Palace is surely one of the must-see attractions of Las Vegas.

The inside of this sprawling hotel and casino complex includes an incredible amount of detail; the detail may not be accurate, but it certainly is interesting. Think of Caesars Palace as a realization of Hollywood's vision of ancient Rome as seen through the jaded eye of a Las Vegas decorator.

Everything about this place is grand. The Roman Forum casino is a riot of red and gold. The sports book is among the most spectacular theater-like settings at any casino. The various restaurants, including the aptly named Bacchanal, include some of the most opulent settings on the Strip. And the casino employees offer equal-opportunity gawking for both sexes: there are gods and goddesses in short, short togas at most every turn.

And the spectacular **Forum Shops at Caesars** feature more than 70 specialty retailers and restaurants set in a re-creation of the skies of ancient Rome. *See the section about shopping in Las Vegas for full details on this must-see shopping mall.*

It is also an interesting spectator sport to observe the continuing competition between Caesars Palace and its next-door neighbor, the Mirage; this is a case of "keeping up with the Joneses" taken to the extreme.

A real fake. The Brahma Shrine on the north lawn of Caesars Palace is an authentic replica of one of the most popular Buddhist shrines in Thailand. The original was installed more than 30 years ago at the Erawan Hotel in Bangkok to ward off bad luck after the hotel suffered various mishaps during its construction. The statue is credited with fixing the problem.

The Las Vegas version was a gift to the hotel from a Thai newspaper and Hong Kong high roller in 1983. Cast in bronze and plated in gold, the statue is housed in concrete covered with tiny pieces of beveled glass.

Thai-Buddhist tradition associates Brahma with creation. The four faces of the shrine represent the Four Divine States of Mind: loving kindness, compassion, sympathy, and equanimity.

Since its formal dedication, many visitors have made various offerings—from flowers to joss sticks (incense) to money—in search of a divine state of mind, or at least good luck at the tables.

By the way, although Caesars Palace rakes in the coins regularly, this is one small area where Caesars Palace does not hold a house advantage. The money tossed into the shrine is returned to charities in Thailand.

When Caesars Palace was built in 1966, it was set far back from the Strip, partly for zoning reasons in the second wave of construction and partly because at the time it was believed that the new hotels would be destinations in and of themselves and that visitors would drive up the grand driveway to a parking space. The front yard of the hotel is filled with a mind-boggling collection of strange stuff, including a 20-foot-tall statue of Julius himself, almost two dozen spouting fountains, and a lucky Brahma.

There are also several lengthy people-mover sidewalks intended to suck pedestrians from the curbside of the Strip all the way back to the entrance of the hotel; in 1989 an additional people mover was installed at the far northern corner of Caesars' property. Coincidentally, of course, that put the Caesars moving walkway right next to the moving sidewalk for the new Mirage hotel next door. By the way, the sidewalks move only one direction—into the casino. When you are ready to leave, you'll have to walk to the Strip, or you can call a cab if you have any money left in your pockets.

Hidden from view of casino guests is the Garden of the Gods pool area. It includes, naturally, an Olympic-size swimming pool that is the centerpiece of the Caesars Garden of the Gods. The garden design was inspired by the Pompeii Baths of Rome.

The bottom and sides of the main pool are covered with imported Carrara marble tiles. On the upper level, a second pool includes three large "lounging islands" installed just below the water's surface so that sunbathers can be cooled by the water while they tan. Fountains spray water to the corners of the pool.

We'll start with the hotel and move on to the casino, restaurants, shops, and entertainment.

Basic room rates start as low as $95 for a single and $110 for a double room at ordinary periods of the year. Deluxe rooms start at $135 for a single and $150 for a double; superior at $160 and $175. One-bedroom suites begin at $475; two bedrooms start at $610. However, during the quietest times of the year, prices drop into double digits for basic and deluxe rooms. At peak times, prices can double.

Like most other Las Vegas hotels, the quietest time of the year is usually around Christmas, excluding the holiday itself and New Year's Eve. Available rooms at that time are often offered at significantly less than the rack rate. However, Caesars Palace has been working hard to fill up its rooms during slack periods with guests from Asian locations, including Hong Kong.

Olympic Tower. The main tower includes dozens of room types. A typical standard room is the Olympic Square King, which includes marble and mirrors and a Jacuzzi in each room. Round Kings—featuring round beds—are also available. Standard rooms in the Roman Tower have a rack rate of about $145 per night.

Regular suites rent in the range from about $850 to $1,000 per night, depending on the number of bedrooms. The largest suites can link together eight bedrooms, perfect for the large family or the high roller traveling with a nanny, bodyguard, chef, or other staff.

Fantasy Suites. It's not that they are free; Caesars prefers to call them "priceless." Suffice it to say that they would cost a small fortune if you were in fact able to rent them; they are offered without charge to invited guests including celebrities, members of royal families, and (of course) the highest of the high rollers visiting Caesars Palace.

We visited a few of the two-story extravaganzas, including the 4,000-square-foot Jupiter Suite, which featured a laser light show in the domed ceiling of the central alcove, glass curtain walls, two bedrooms, five TVs, a karaoke music system, and a pair of servants. The slightly skewed wall sconces were designed by the studio of the extremely skewed Salvador Dalí.

There are a total of 10 Fantasy Suites: two in Roman decor, three with Egyptian themes, and five as Las Vegas re-creations of ancient Pompeii. As guests arrive on their interior balconies, they are greeted by a laser show and a fiber optics sky depicting the night sky as it is believed to have looked on the evening of the birth of Caesar Augustus.

Armless in Vegas. The grounds around Caesars Palace include replicas of some of the most famous statues of antiquity. In front of the fountains at the main entrance of the hotel is a re-creation of the famous *Victory at Samothrace* statue, sculpted about 300 B.C. by an unknown artist; the original is in the Louvre Museum in Paris.

In front of the elliptical pool at the entrance is a copy of the *Rape of the Sabines*; the original was done by Giovanni da Bologna in 1583.

Elsewhere, you'll find reproductions of Michelangelo's *David* and *Bacchus*. On a more contemporary note, at the entrance to the Olympic Casino stands a statue of the boxer Joe Louis, who worked for the casino as a greeter after he retired from the ring.

Airborne breakfast. Caesars Palace has a "flying kitchen" in one of the tower service elevators permitting delivery of a standard continental breakfast to almost any room in the hotel within eight minutes of a phone call.

Unlike father. On December 31, 1967, daredevil Evel Knievel attempted to jump over the Caesars Palace fountains on a motorcycle; 12 years later, his son Robbie Knievel avenged his father's unsuccessful attempt.

In 1981, an entire racetrack was created for the first of four Grand Prix auto races on site.

In 1991, Wayne Gretzky led the Los Angeles Kings to victory over the New York Rangers in the Palace's first ice hockey event, the NHL's first outdoor game since 1925.

Sport lights. The spectacular Race and Sports Book at Caesars Palace uses 60 panels made up of 1.5 million yellow, red, and green light-emitting diode (LED) panels that display computer-produced data including track conditions, horse and jockey names, and other information.

The largest of the video screens is 32 feet wide by 26 feet high.

An entire wall of each room is given over to an entertainment system that includes five video screens, two compact disc players, and a karaoke machine. A master control panel can send different music to different rooms. Each of the bedrooms includes an additional large-screen TV. In fact, there's more than two miles of wiring in each suite for entertainment, motorized bedroom and living room draperies, color wheel effects on the ceiling, and other lighting.

Casinos. The 85-acre site includes three casino areas. The main Olympic Casino has more than 1,400 slot machines, 31 blackjack tables, three craps tables, and various other enterprises including the spectacular Olympiad Race and Sports Book with seating for 650. Nearby is the Roman Forum Casino with 615 slots, 30 blackjack tables, 9 craps tables, and a keno area. Finally, there is the exclusive Palace Court Casino with 3 blackjack tables, 2 baccarat tables, a pai gow table, and a roulette wheel.

The World of Caesar is a presentation in the rotunda at the entrance to the central people mover. Designed to resemble a Roman temple, the World of Caesar includes a miniature city of Rome as it might have looked two thousand years ago. The hotel spent $2.5 million on just this little bit of decoration. The effect is enhanced with technology including video projection.

In fact, the world of Caesars Palace is so immense that the hotel/casino has begun offering **Guided Tours** on weekdays, with trips leaving at 9 A.M., 10:30 A.M., 1:30 P.M., and 3 P.M. Tickets are $5 per person, and are available at the Omnimax ticket booth.

Eating Your Way Through Caesars Palace

The hotel offers a world of fine dining, from one of the most opulent buffets to one of the most sybaritic and expensive feasts in town.

Palatium. One of the best buffets in Vegas. A lovely setting with open-air boundaries just off the spectacular Race and Sports Book. Buffet offerings change from day to day. One evening featured a mountain of crab legs and a huge bowl of shrimp. One indication of class: the shrimp comes prepeeled.

Palatium, Latin for palatine, takes its name from the second-century meeting place of Rome's first academy of chefs. The term was also used in naming the many royal residences and buildings in the vicinity of Rome's Palatine Hill.

Dining areas are arranged in semicircles around a doubleline service center. The buffet is open for breakfast, lunch, and dinner Monday through Friday; special brunches are served Saturday and Sunday. Dinner includes a variety of breads, an elaborate salad bar, vegetables, and entrees including carved meats and poultry. Ethnic dinners including Italian, Mexican, and Western themes are offered some nights. There is also a sinful dessert section. *See hours and prices in the section on buffets in this book.*

Palace Court. Classical French cuisine served in a museum-like setting. Guests arrive in a crystal and bronze round elevator or a spiral staircase under a crystal chandelier. The dining area sits beneath a domed stained glass ceiling. Tables are decorated with fine fabric and lit candelabras.

Pause for a moment and admire the glorious fruit basket in the glass case at the entrance. It's an edible work of art, constructed out of pulled sugar by a Caesars chef.

The Palace Court, open for dinner only, has entrees in the range of $20 to $40. Some menu items we have seen include: *bisque d'homard a l'armagnac* (lobster bisque flamed with Armagnac), *papillote de saumon aux asperges* (fresh salmon prepared in a paper pouch with asparagus and sun-dried tomatoes), *cote de veau roti* (veal chop served with roasted leeks and mustard sauce), *maigret de canard au poivre rose* (breast of duck with pink peppercorn sauce), *carre d'agneau roti a l'ail doux* (roast rack of lamb served with sweet garlic sauce), free-range chicken with roasted leeks and morels, and salmon in potato crust flambéed with lemon vodka.

Bacchanal. In ancient Rome, they eventually outlawed Bacchanalia, a festival in honor of Bacchus, the god of wine. It seemed that the drunken, licentious events were even too much for ancient Rome.

Of course, in modern Las Vegas, almost anything goes. And so there is Bacchanal, which is a re-creation of a Roman feast in the atmosphere of a private villa and a whole lot of fun.

The evening includes a seven-course prix-fixe feast of appetizers, soup, salad, pasta, entree, and dessert; included are three wines, splashed into your chalices by exotically clad "wine goddesses." There are also belly dancers, a smoke

Michelangelo's casino. At the top tier of the portico entrance to the World of Caesar is a marble statue of Apollo, the Greek and Roman god of sunlight, prophecy, music, and poetry. According to its makers, it is carved from stone taken from the same quarries that Michelangelo is believed to have used.

Somewhere to hang your hat. The large mural opposite the window wall at the Palace Court at Caesars Palace is entitled *Le Manoir du Chapeau;* it represents the countryside of the French province Bourbonnais.

Private bank. As you enter the Palace Court, note the small dark room off to the left: the Palace Court Gaming Room is a private casino within the casino for the highest of high rollers.

How fresh? The Caesars Palace chefs have an herb garden off the pool area where they grow some of the fresh herbs used in the gourmet restaurants.

Good reef. The coral reef in the aquarium at the Empress Court of Caesars Palace is a reproduction of an actual reef along the coast of Hong Kong.

and laser light show, and a guest appearance by Caesar and Cleopatra themselves. In the center of the two-tiered dining room is a bronze statue of a vestal virgin pouring water into a marble reflecting pool.

The menu changes with the seasons. One sample fall menu started with fresh vegetables with herb dip, shrimp, crab claws, and marinated scallops, cream of chickpeas with legumes, fettuccine Alfredo, and Caesar salad, tossed tableside. Choices of entrees included Cornish game hen, roast duckling with three-color peppercorn sauce, stuffed veal chop with pine nuts, filet mignon, and filet of sole with shrimp florentine.

A winter menu included rigatoni with sun-dried tomatoes in creamy pesto sauce; Caesar salad or Cleopatra salad with hearts of palm, celery root, and beets; choice of roast rock Cornish hen stuffed with wild rice, roast duck with Mandarin orange or peppercorn sauce, twin tournedos of seasoned beef with three-color peppercorn sauce, or pan-seared catch of the day with herbed butter. The seventh and final course is a flaming desert of strawberries and seared Hawaiian pineapple served over ice cream with petit fours.

Dinner only, Tuesday through Saturday. Seatings are 6 and 9:30 P.M. daily. The fare in 1995 was $67.50 per person, including wines, champagne, and dessert; not included are cocktails, tax, and tip. Reservations: 731-7731.

Empress Court. Named in *USA Today* as one of the top gourmet Chinese restaurants in the country, the kitchen concentrates on Hong Kong–style Cantonese cooking, although there are touches of Malay, Thai, and Indonesian cuisine.

Entrance is via a dramatic staircase that encircles a koi pond and leads to a coral reef aquarium at the restaurant's door. Within the kitchen is a more purposeful giant aquarium, stocked with live rock cod, Dungeness crab, lobster, and other seafood used in meals. The galley itself includes some extraordinarily hot grills used in preparation of specialties.

The Empress Court menu includes prix-fixe dinners at about $40 to $60 per person, as well as a la carte offerings. Appetizers include crabmeat seaweed rolls, minced squab in crystal wrap, and shrimp with taro. Entrees, generally in the range from about $20 to $48 each, include double-boiled shark's fin, braised abalone with sea cucumber, sautéed scallops with macadamia nuts, imperial Peking duck as well as other uncommon Chinese fare. Open for dinner only. Reservations: 771-7731.

Primavera. A favorite garden spot alongside the Garden of the Gods pool, the menu changes from casual fare for breakfast and lunch to formal Italian dining for dinner.

At various visits, the dinner menu included appetizers of *bresaola con parmigiano* (dried cured beef with Parmesan cheese and arugula) and *carpaccio di salmone* (raw salmon very finely sliced with a strawberry vinaigrette). Pasta entrees, in the range of $12 to $20, included *trenette nere ai calamari* (black noodles with calamari and clams in a natural juice sauce), and *mostaccioli all'amatriciana*. Other entrees, ranging from $20 to $30, included *filetto ai tre pepi* (beef tenderloin with black, green, and pink peppercorns); *pollo cacciatora con polenta* (chicken breast in a sauce of roasted peppers, mushrooms, tomato, and white wine with a side order of cornmeal), *costolette d'agnello colosseo* (lamb chops sauteed with garlic, rosemary, and balsamic vinegar) for $32.50, *gamberoni al rosmarino* (shrimps with rosemary and radicchio) for $29.50, or *zuppa di cozze* (New England mussels in a white wine, black olive, caper, and tomato sauce).

One of the specialties of the bar is the Casanova Cream Fizz, a rich combination of lemon and lime juice with cream and apricot brandy. Dinner is served nightly from 6 to 11 P.M.

Ah'So. Yet another restaurant, this one offering fine dining in a serene Japanese garden. Sushi and sashimi are available with dinners as well as to patrons at the cocktail lounge.

The restaurant offers a prix-fixe six-course menu of selections prepared and served in teppen yaki style at the table (the skills of the chef are part of the entertainment) or in shabu-shabu style (Chinese fondue-like cooking). Each was priced at about $50 in 1995.

Offerings include *miro shiru* (soy bean soup with tofu) or *sumashi* (clear chicken broth with long rice). Appetizer selections feature tempura (fried seafood and vegetables) and *sunomono* (a salad of marinated cucumbers with shredded crabmeat). The entree list includes lobster, beef tenderloin, and chicken breast, all served with *yasai* (assorted Japanese vegetables).

Open for dinner.

Cafe Roma. A 24-hour restaurant that draws its menu from all around the world. In fact, it's one of the only places we have ever heard of that offers Japanese *miso* broth, Mexican *quesadillas*, New York steak, spaghetti bolognese, Nova Scotia salmon, and more on the same menu. Appetizers range from about $5 to $12, salads

Flowery complement. The oil on canvas of Flora surrounded by flowers and classic statuary in the Primavera Restaurant at Caesars Palace is a hand-painted reproduction of *Garden of Armida,* by the 19th-century artist Eduoard Miller.

Burger palace. Feature films made at Caesars Palace include *Oh God! You Devil*, with the ageless George Burns; *The Electric Horseman*, starring Robert Redford, Jane Fonda, Willie Nelson, and Valerie Perrine, and Mel Brooks' *History of the World—Part 1.*

Parts of the 1988 Academy Award-winning *Rain Man* starring Dustin Hoffman and Tom Cruise were filmed in a suite at Caesars Palace. Hotel legend includes the story that star Hoffman used to order 200 or so hamburgers every night from the tiny **Post Time Snack Bar** off the Race and Sports Book for the crew. He apparently knows his chopped meat; the burgers are made from the trimmings of the filets from the hotel's butcher shop and are among the best values at Caesars Palace. Burgers are priced at $4, with deli sandwiches including pastrami and corned beef going for $4.25.

from $3 to $14, and entrees from $9 to $15. In keeping with the Las Vegas lifestyle, breakfast is offered around the clock.

But did we mention the all-day Chinese menu? The Cafe doesn't quite have the ambiance of the Empress Court, but we suspect the same kitchen and ingredients are used, and we have long ago learned not to judge a Chinese restaurant by its furnishings. There's an above-average selection of Oriental offerings ranging from $5 to $9 for appetizers and $10 to $28 for entrees.

Nero's. They don't fiddle around in this elegant seafood and steakhouse, open for dinner only. Appetizers can include avocado with lump crabmeat, Scottish smoked salmon, steamed clams, and frog legs Provençale, and range from about $7 to $17. Entrees, which range in price from $26 to $48, include Dover sole, grilled or seared tuna, lamb chops, and more.

La Piazza Food Court. A high-tone food court with offerings from Japanese ramen soups and bento boxes to Chinese stir-fry, Italian pasta and pizza, Mexican specialties, and an all-American deli. There are also ice cream, yogurt, candy, and bakery stands.

Cleopatra's Barge. A re-created boat set in a small pond; it'll never set sail, but when things really get rocking at this cocktail lounge, the place starts rolling.

And don't overlook the new group of restaurants that were added to the scene with the opening of the Forum Shops at Caesars, including Boogie's Diner of Aspen, Chang—Cuisine of China, La Salsa, Lombardi's, Spago, and the Stage Deli. *You'll discover more about these restaurants in the section of this book about shopping in Las Vegas.*

Caesars Entertainment

Omnimax Theatre. Go into space, under the sea, deep into the Grand Canyon, or into an atom in one of the highest-tech movie theaters anywhere. The 386 seats of the Omnimax recline to permit full view of the huge 10-story screen which showcases specially made films such as *To Fly, The Dream is Alive, Grand Canyon—The Hidden Secrets,* and *Africa: The Serengeti.* The films are shot on 70-mm film with a frame size 10 times larger than standard 35-mm media. A nine-channel "sensaround" system engulfs the audience in sound.

Ticket prices are about $6 for adults. Seniors (over 55), juniors (4–12), military personnel, and hotel guests pay $4. Show times vary, but shows typically run hourly from 2 P.M. through 10 P.M. during the week, and from 1 P.M. to 11 P.M. on Friday and Saturday.

Check your horse, sir? The Circus Maximus Showroom at Caesars Palace was used for the scene in the film *The Electric Horseman* when Robert Redford rode his horse down off the stage and into the casino.

Circus Maximus Showroom. The main showroom at Caesars Palace is used for headliner acts and an occasional Broadway production or television show. It is typically set up with more than a thousand seats; booths are designed in the shape of Roman chariot seats. In a change from Las Vegas protocol of the past, tickets are sold in advance for reserved seats—there is no need to grease the palm of the maitre d' to get a prime spot. However, it is fair to assume that the very best seats will be held by the casino for its "invited guests."

A Brief History of Caesars Palace

The original proposed name for Caesars Palace was Cabana Palace, after developer Jay Sarno's successful Cabana Hotel in Palo Alto, California. Once the design began to take shape, the hotel was renamed as Desert Palace, but it finally opened as Caesars Palace on August 5, 1966.

Sarno considered the oval to be a magic shape, believing it was conducive to relaxation. The central casino and a number of other rooms took that shape at his suggestion.

The first entertainer at the Circus Maximus Showroom was singer Andy Williams.

In 1969, Caesars Palace was bought by Lum's, a Florida-based fast-food restaurant chain known for, among other things, its hot dogs. In 1971, the tail wagged the dog when Lum's became Caesars World, Inc. And in 1994, the company was sold to ITT, the corporate parent to the Sheraton hotel chain among other holdings.

Down to the sea in chips. Haven't dropped enough at the tables? The folks at Caesars Palace have come up with a way to put its patrons to sea, aboard the Los Angeles–based luxury liner *Crystal Harmony*. The Japanese ship, which carries 960 guests, includes the Caesars Palace at Sea casino as well as Japanese and Italian restaurants, an indoor-outdoor pool with swim-up bar and a large lap pool, a 270-seat cinema, and a shopping arcade. Information on itineraries is available through travel agents.

Caesars World includes three gaming resorts: Caesars Palace in Las Vegas, Caesars Tahoe in Lake Tahoe, and Caesars Atlantic City in Atlantic City, New Jersey. The company also operates four resorts in the Pocono mountains of Pennsylvania: Caesars Cove Haven, Caesars Paradise Stream, Caesars Pocono Palace, and Caesars Brookdale.

Plans have been announced to expand the hotel with new restaurants and three theaters for magic acts.

Caesars Palace. 3570 Las Vegas Blvd. South; 1,518 rooms; 731-7110, (800) 634-6661.

MUST-SEE ● Circus Circus

From the sublime to the ridiculous: another must-see attraction.

For many of us, our expectations of Circus Circus were molded by the lurid account of Hunter S. Thompson in his gonzo classic, *Fear and Loathing in Las Vegas*. Just about everything Thompson wrote about in that book, including the acrobats tumbling overhead, the motorcyclists roaring around within a ball, and the general atmosphere of a Roman Circus, is true—although not quite as wild as he made it out to be.

In any case, Circus Circus is one of the great grind joint successes of Las Vegas. It has cheap rooms (including an RV park), cheap meals, and lots and lots of low rollers at the tables. The hotel obviously makes its money on the quantity of action, not the size of the bankrolls at play. (Some wags have called Circus Circus the K-mart of gambling establishments.)

The proprietors were way out in front of a current Las Vegas trend in their

Eight-ring circus. The Circus Circus empire has expanded wildly, now including the huge Excalibur Hotel and the Luxor pyramid further up the Strip. The same company also owns Slots-A-Fun, a neighboring coin palace on the Strip, and the Silver City Casino across the road. Other properties include Circus Circus/Reno, Edgewater Hotel & Casino in Laughlin, and the Colorado Belle in Laughlin.

attempts to lure the entire family. Upstairs over the casino floor is an indoor carnival, midway, and video arcade that will entertain (and draw allowance money) from the kids while their parents drop the rent money downstairs.

Most of the rooms are located in two separate towers, connected by a shuttle tram to the main building. Circus Circus often has the least expensive major hotel rooms in town; the rooms, especially in the main tower, are quite acceptable.

In 1993, Circus Circus opened **Grand Slam Canyon**, a five-acre entertainment park that presents a Las Vegas-eye view of the Grand Canyon, including 140-foot man-made peaks, a 90-foot re-creation of Havasupai Falls, and a river. The entire park is covered by a pink dome called an Adventuredome. *See the description of Grand Slam Canyon in Chapter 10 of this book.*

Parts of Circus Circus give new meaning to tacky, but it's all part of the peculiar charm of the place. You are sure to want to visit the mezzanine of coin-sucking machines, including pinball, a video arcade, bowling machines, and carnival attractions including coin tosses, dart games, and more.

Restaurants include a **McDonald's.** A food court includes the Circus Circus Pizzeria, which offers 10-inch individual pies for about $2 and unusual offerings like a chicken fajita pizza for about $3.

The **Buffet** is served beneath a red-and-white circus tent ceiling, an assault on the eyes, even by Las Vegas standards.

The **Steakhouse**, open for dinner only from 5 P.M. to midnight, has entrees in the range of $15 to $20 and is generally considered one of the better cuts-of-meat palaces in town. In addition to steaks, you can chow down on lamb chops or broiled lobster tail. And even nicer, it's a dark, quiet, and private sanctuary from the circus.

Exactly the opposite is the garish **Pink Pony** coffee shop just off the casino level. And finally, there is the **Skyrise Dining Room**, serving breakfast, lunch, and dinner, with specialties including French toast or prime rib for $3 to $10. At a recent visit, the Skyrise offered a steak dinner for $6.95 from 5 to 11 P.M.

Circus Circus Hotel/Casino. 2880 Las Vegas Blvd. South; 2,800 rooms; 734-0410, (800) 634-3450.

★ MUST-SEE ★ Excalibur

To truly enjoy this place, you've got to buy into the concept: King Arthur's Castle on the Strip. Part of the Circus Circus empire, Excalibur looks as if it were constructed out of a child's toy blocks. It's a place where the staff is drilled to finish conversations with, "Have a royal day."

The best approach to the Excalibur is by night. The colors of the 265-foot-tall bell towers and the castle's fairy tale shape are amazing enough, but even weirder when looked at between the Egyptian pyramid of the Luxor and the tropical gardens of the Tropicana. What a city!

If anything, Excalibur is even more overwhelming inside. The designers seem to have collected all of the missing high ceilings from the older casinos on the Strip and taken them to Nevada extremes. More so than at most other places in Vegas, the Arthurian theme is carried through in almost every detail—the decorations, costumes, restaurants.

In keeping with its orientation toward family visitors, the Excalibur is one of the few casinos in Las Vegas that welcomes cameras: still, movie, and video. (In keeping with state law, though, you must keep children under 21 away from slot machines and gambling tables.)

There are, though, no windows within the cavernous interior; one of the only ways to tell the time of day inside a dark casino like this is to listen to the cocktail waitresses. As dawn breaks, they add orange juice to their offers of coffee and cocktails.

> **Testing the metal.** The swords in King Arthur's Tournament are made of lightweight titanium metal; try as they might, the designers could not find a way to fake the sound of metal hitting metal.

> **Horse track.** The Excalibur stables are located at the back of the parking lot. The horses for the King Arthur's Tournament are walked to work for the evening show each evening sometime between 5 and 5:30 P.M.

The Excalibur was holder of the title as the world's largest resort hotel for several years, with 4,032 rooms in four 28-floor towers. Today, it is certainly the world's largest resort hotel set inside a castle with a moat, a drawbridge, a jousting tournament, and a western dance hall.

How big is this place? The Excalibur serves an average of about 136,032 guests and 751,388 meals per month, including 330,000 bread rolls, 44,100 Cornish game hens, and 24,000 watermelons.

There are four levels to the hotel; you will enter from the main parking lot or front entrance to Level I, which is, of course, the casino floor and registration desk. An escalator descends to the lower level **Fantasy Faire**, home of **King Arthur's Arena**, the **Magic Motion Machines**, and **Fantasy Faire** games. Or, you can take an escalator up to Level II, the Medieval Village, home of the **Roundtable Buffet, Wild Bill's Saloon & Steakhouse, Lance-A-Lotta Pasta, Sir Galahad's, Robin Hood's**, and the **Sherwood Forest Cafe.** One more level up takes you to Level III, which includes the **Canterbury Wedding Chapel**, banquet rooms, and the **Camelot** restaurant.

There is, of course, a casino, and it's a whopper: 2,600 slot machines, 68 blackjack tables, six craps tables, six roulette wheels, and more, spread out over 105,000 square feet. The casino includes a central pavilion for high-rolling slot players. The poker room features 18 regular poker tables and two pai gow poker tables.

Excalibur has also opened a no-smoking casino area, called **Lady Guinevere's Gold.**

Also featured in the casino is Circus Bucks, a progressive slot game that is specific to Circus Circus properties in Nevada; its claim to fame is that it pays off all at once rather than as an annuity over 20 years. We have seen the jackpot as high as $2 million.

The Sports Book at Excalibur is obviously not a priority at this K-mart of a casino; bettors are seated on ordinary metal banquet chairs, with only a dozen or so medium-sized monitors scattered about.

The Excalibur's 900-seat showroom is unlike any other in Las Vegas. To begin with, the floor of the stage is dirt rather than polished wood, and many of the stars have four legs.

The evening program at 6 or 8:30 P.M. is **King Arthur's Tournament**, an original musical production based on the legend of King Arthur. You've got your basic knights in armor, fair maidens in less, and events including a jousting tournament.

The story begins when Merlin the magician satisfies a young boy's wish to be a knight by transporting him back to the Middle Ages and transforming him into Jeffrey, the White Knight. Jeffrey will meet the King, of course, as well as Queen Guinevere, before he battles the treacherous Dark Knight and wins the hand of the beautiful princess. Tickets are $29.95, which includes dinner and tip; they can be purchased up to six days before the show. Check with the hotel for dark days and hours; there are generally two shows per night.

When you buy your ticket, you will be assigned to a reserved place. According to insiders, the best seats are up high in the center; in football terms, at the 50-yard line. Avoid the end zones and stay up high to avoid the dust from the horses.

The meal, served on pewter plates, includes a Cornish hen. By the way, they didn't use silverware in medieval times, and neither will you.

During the afternoon, the hotel presents family-oriented animal acts including a Lippizaner horse show and "Sooper Dogs."

The **Fantasy Faire** level offers carnival games as well as a pair of "dynamic motion simulators" called **Merlin's Magic Motion Machines** that can take riders on a wild ride without ever leaving the room. There are six different "rides," changing during the course of a day, shown in a pair of identical 48-seat theaters. Rides include "Space Race," an outer-space demolition derby directed by George Lucas and "Devil's Mine Ride," a wild and crazy journey through underground caves and caverns. Other experiences include "Desert Duel," a bone-jarring desert race over dirt trails; "The Revolution," a simulation of one of the wildest roller coasters at the Magic Mountain amusement park, and "Runaway Train," a breakneck plunge through tunnels and steep mountain passes on a train with no brakes. Ticket prices are about $3 per ride. Note: You must be at least 42 inches tall and in good health to ride the simulator.

The **Medieval Village** re-creates one vision of an ancient village, with shops, restaurants, strolling magicians, jugglers, and singers. Free 10-minute shows are presented every half hour on the Court Jester's Stage from 10 A.M. to 10 P.M. Many are a bit on the corny side but fun for the youngsters.

The **Fantasy Faire** itself is an unusual mix of modern video arcade and pinball machines with medieval theme carnival games. If you're into shooting galleries, be sure to check out the Electronic Crossbow (20 shots for 50 cents) with animated, moving figures in the line of fire.

Wedded Biz

Apparently, there are a lot of people who dream of getting married wearing long, flowing velvet robes with swords at their sides and heavy crowns on their heads. There are as many as 50 or 60 weddings a week in the **Canterbury Room** and **Canterbury Gardens**, a small outdoor-like garden. You don't have to dress like King Arthur and Guinevere, either; suit and gown are acceptable. According to the hotel, one of the most memorable weddings took place on Halloween, with all guests in costume.

Excalibur Beds and Breakfasts

Room rates start at $39 for weekdays and $65 to $75 on weekends. The basic rooms are comfortable but a bit garish in decor and inexpensive in appointments. There are two pools, one at each tower; plans for expansion include construction of a wall with water slides.

Each of the restaurants at Excalibur is a spectacular exercise in decoration and theme. Some of the food is decent, too.

The **Round Table Buffet** is one of the biggest, if not the biggest, buffet room in Las Vegas with 1,446 seats. Breakfast, lunch, and dinner rates are $3.99, $4.99, and $5.99 for adults.

Camelot has just 144 seats, so reservations are recommended. Open for dinner from 6 to 10 P.M. Sunday through Thursday, and from 5 to 11 P.M. on Fridays, Saturdays, and holidays. Gourmet entrees range in price from about $13 to $19. The menu includes such items as chicken Guinevere (braised breast of chicken, young potatoes, fresh tomatoes, artichokes, and fresh herbs in a tangy sauce). Also available on one visit was rack of lamb Black Knight (lamb basted with dijon mustard and finished in the oven with crisp garlic brioche crumbs), and sea bass florentine (poached fresh Pacific sea bass stuffed with cream spinach laced lightly with white wine).

Wild Bill's Saloon and Steakhouse is a large, lively, and loud room that makes mealtime an adventure (it sounds somewhat like supper at home).

This explains a lot, doesn't it? As if Las Vegas wasn't already one weird place, consider the fact that 50 or so miles north and west of town is the neighborhood nuclear test site.

From its start in the depths of the Cold War in 1951 through today, there have been nearly 700 tests of nuclear bombs. At first, the explosions were conducted in the atmosphere and it was not an unusual sight to see a mushroom cloud cresting over downtown Las Vegas. Since the 1960s, the explosions have taken place underground.

The Nevada Test Site at Yucca Flat is part of the huge Nellis Air Force Range. The test site is 1,350 square miles, about the size of the entire state of Rhode Island. In case you had your heart aglow in anticipation of a tour, though, we're sorry to disappoint you: the entire area is off-limits.

Appetizers include chili and fried onions with hot sauce. Entrees, priced from about $10 to $17, include barbecued ribs for $10.95, grilled shrimp for $16.95, steaks, filet mignon, a rodeo burger for $5.95, roasted chicken, and a grilled vegetable platter.

Lance-a-Lotta Pasta is a favorite for lunch and light dinner, open from 11 A.M. to 2:30 P.M. daily, and from 5 P.M. nightly. Typical offerings include salads, sandwiches, and Italian sausage heros. Entrees such as lasagna or ravioli and small pizzas are priced from about $5 to $10. Pizza toppings for plate-sized pies include bianca (white sauce), scampi shrimp, vegetali (broccoli, sun-dried tomatoes, green peas, and sweet peppers), Philadelphia (marinated steak, smothered onions, peppers, and sun-dried tomatoes), and Caliente (a flour tortilla with chili meat, tomatoes, bell peppers, jalapenos, avocados, green onions, cilantro, and Monterey Jack and cheddar cheeses).

Sir Galahad's Prime Rib House. Open every night for dinner at 5 P.M., the specialties include prime rib from the Traditional English cut to the whopping King Arthur cut, priced from about $10 to $15. Seafood and poultry dishes are also available. On one visit we were enticed by breast of capon Harlequin, simmered in red wine sauce and garnished with pearl onions and mushrooms. Reservations are recommended for the 234-seat eatery.

The Excalibur's 24-hour coffee shop is the **Sherwood Forest Cafe.** Offerings extend to some vegetarian dishes, including omelettes. Entrees and salads range from about $6 to $12 and have included items such as a barbecue platter, ribs, chicken-fried steak, orange roughy, and turkey steak.

Excalibur Hotel & Casino. 3850 Las Vegas Blvd. South; 4,032 rooms; 597-7777, (800) 937-7777.

Hard Rock Hotel & Casino

It's rock in a hard place, but hopes are high for the new Hard Rock Hotel & Casino which opened in Las Vegas in 1995.

The 14-story, 325-room hotel is located next to the successful Hard Rock Cafe on Paradise Road a few blocks in from the Strip. And, of course, there is a casino, a 28,000-square-foot room decorated with musical memorabilia, guitar-shaped roulette tables and a general rock 'n' roll theme. A showroom will feature live concerts.

The hotel includes the first **Hard Rock Beach Club** with a sandy beach and a lagoon where the music even plays under water. The **Hard Rock Athletic Club** offers personal trainers and a New York-style steam room.

Mr. Lucky's Twenty Four/Seven is billed as the hippest coffee shop in Las Vegas. The signature restaurant is an Italian eatery called **Mortoni's,** which draws its name from Hard Rock founder Peter Morton.

The hotel also offers a babysitting service for guests and a retail store with Hard Rock Cafe merchandise. You'll also find an interactive television network that allows guests to shop without having to leave the room—kind of an away-from-Home Shopping Network.

The hotel is a joint effort of Hard Rock and Harveys Casino Resorts, the first casino for Hard Rock and the first operation in Las Vegas for South Lake Tahoe–based Harveys.

LAS VEGAS STRIP

1 Vacation Village
2 Hacienda
3 Luxor
4 Excalibur
5 Tropicana
6 MGM Grand
7 Aladdin
8 Bally's
9 Barbary Coast
10 Caesars Palace
11 Flamingo Hilton
12 O'Shea's
13 Imperial Palace
14 Mirage
15 Harrah's
16 The Sands
17 Treasure Island
18 Desert Inn

19 Frontier
20 Stardust
21 Westward Ho
22 Riviera
23 Circus Circus
24 Sahara
25 Vegas World

Near the Strip

26 San Remo
27 Alexis Park
28 St. Tropez
29 Bourbon Street
30 Maxim's
31 Continental
32 Rio Suites
33 Gold Coast
34 Debbie Reynolds'

35 Las Vegas Hilton
36 Showboat

Downtown

37 Plaza
38 Las Vegas Club
39 Binion's Horseshoe
40 Fremont
41 Golden Gate
42 Pioneer
43 Golden Nugget
44 Four Queens
45 Fitzgerald's
46 El Cortez
47 Gold Spike
48 Lady Luck
49 California

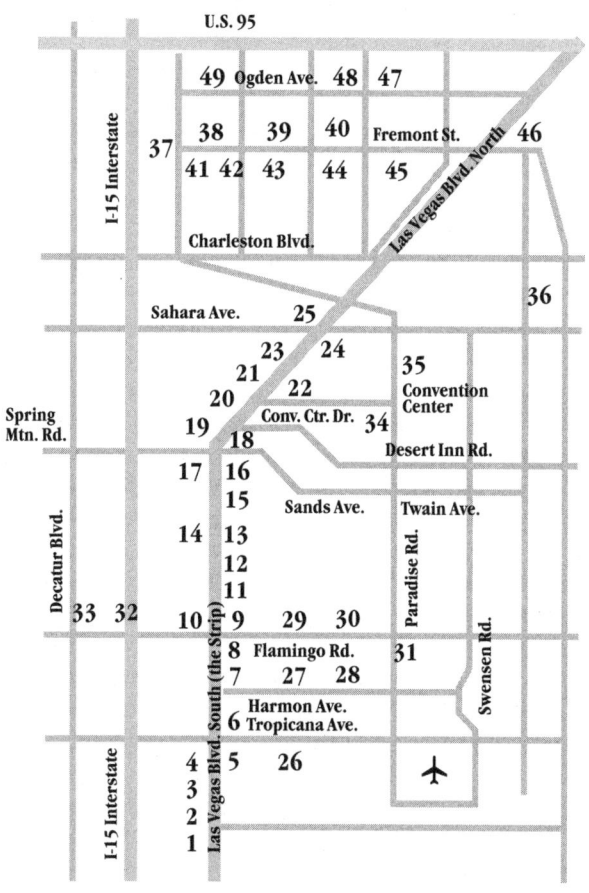

Hard Rock Hotel and Casino. 4475 Paradise Rd.; 325 rooms; 693-5000.

MUST-SEE **Las Vegas Hilton**

Elvis slept here! In fact, this place is so large that he may still be roaming the halls somewhere, looking for the elevator.

Opened as the International Hotel in 1969, it was for a while the largest hotel in town and still claims the title as the largest convention hotel in the world. In 1994, it reached for another record with the installation of what is said to be the world's largest and tallest freestanding sign, at 362 feet tall. The Hilton is directly next to the Las Vegas Convention Center and its own 220,000-square-foot convention facilities and meeting rooms are often used for spillover from shows like the Comdex computer exposition. Its rooms are among the first to sell out for major conventions, too.

The hotel is now so large that they have to run shuttle buses from the outlying parking lots to the front door.

The hotel's showroom was the site of the late-model Elvis Presley's glitter-era performances from 1969 until his reputed death in 1977. It also served as the showcase for another Vegas icon, Wayne Newton.

In 1994, the 1,600-seat theater underwent a $9 million renovation to become the home of a production of Andrew Lloyd Webber's *Starlight Express*, a musical extravaganza on roller skates. Lloyd Webber is also the composer of *Cats*, *Jesus Christ Superstar*, and *Sunset Boulevard*, among other shows. *Starlight Express* features a cast of 38, who are outfitted in spectacular costumes and skate in and around the audience including those seated in the center of two "roller-bowls" and others perched on seats directly above the stage.

The special seats offer a real up-close view of the goings-on, but you may miss some of the overall pageantry. The view from the "cheap" seats in the balcony is fine, but the skaters do not come up ramps to visit you as they do in the original London production.

In 1996, the Hilton is expected to open an interactive adventure based on *Star Trek*. Visitors will take on the roles of *Star Trek* characters and participate in a re-created episode from the popular show.

The three 30-story towers include 3,174 rooms and suites. The 1,500-seat showroom, now used for major shows and boxing matches, has one of the largest stages in Las Vegas. Recreational facilities include a large pool (it actually sits above the ceiling of the main casino), tennis courts, a health club, and a nine-hole putting green.

Elvis sighting number one. Elvis Presley made 837 sold-out appearances in 15 engagements at the Hilton from 1969–1977. From time to time, the hotel has exhibited various pieces of Elvis memorabilia.

Parents may be excited to learn about the Hilton's **Youth Hotel,** a separate camp-like setting for children from 3 to 18. Supervised by a licensed and professional staff, the Youth Hotel offers indoor and outdoor activities and meals. Overnight accommodations are also available.

The facility is designed to handle up to 101 guests, with overnight accommodations for 24 children in separate dorms for boys and girls, kind of like a large slumber party. The hotel is available to registered guests of either the Las Vegas Hilton or the Flamingo Hilton. Rates per kid are $4 an hour or $25 overnight. The busiest night of the year is New Year's Eve; a recent celebration brought 325 youngsters to the Youth Hotel on that special occasion.

Separate recreation rooms include Ping-Pong, pool, air hockey, Foosball, shuffleboard, a playground, and art supplies. Electronic diversions include movies and the latest video games.

Kid-tested meals include such haute cuisine as hot dogs, hamburgers, French toast, waffles, and grilled cheese.

Contact the Youth Hotel directly at 732-5706.

There is, of course, a casino, and it provides a large and attractive field in which to dream. Recent renovations have upgraded the chandeliers throughout. There are 65 game tables and 1,200 slot machines. A Sports and Race Book with more than 50 television monitors and projection screens is one of the most spectacular in town.

Standard room rates start at $85 but can climb sharply—if space is available at all—during conventions. The best rates can be obtained at Christmastime, with the exception of New Year's Eve. **Classic Suites** on the upper floors are for high rollers only.

> **Elvis sighting number two.** Elvis had his own intimate 5,000-square foot hideaway on the 30th floor of the hotel, used during his appearances at the Hilton. After Elvis' death, the maintenance staff at the Hilton filled in two bullet holes in the walls and actually redecorated the place! Obviously, they had no sense of history.
>
> In 1994 the entire place was gutted and incorporated into one of three spectacular new suites, each 10,000 to 15,000 square feet in size and costing a cool $45 million to build.
>
> As with most of the super-suites in Las Vegas, we mere mortals cannot rent the rooms; they are available only to high rollers and guests of the hotel.

In 1994, the hotel spent some $30 million to create three fabulous "sky villas" at the top of the Hilton. They include the 12,600-square-foot **Villa Conrad**, a two-story home away from home decorated in French style; the larger **Villa Tuscany** with a private garden, and the 15,400-square-foot **Villa Verona**, modestly modeled after the Palaces of Versailles.

The fanciest restaurant in the building is **Le Montrachet**, which is very French. A wine cellar offers more than 400 varieties. Check out the beautifully sculpted pear in a sugar cage at the entrance. Among the specialties, priced from about $32 to $36, is *le filet de Saint Pierre* (poached filet of John Dory with leek pasta in a creamy saffron, wild mushroom, and tomato sauce), *l'entrecote grillee, beurre noisette au poivre vert* (broiled New York cut steak in *noisette* butter with green peppercorns and a dash of cognac), roasted double breast of chicken with morels, filet of brill (a European flounder) poached in champagne sauce and lobster coral, and grilled veal chops stuffed with wild mushrooms and a port wine sauce with truffles.

Barronshire features prime rib in a traditional English setting. Open from 6 to 10:30 P.M. every day except for Tuesday, it offers three prime rib cuts:

English, Barronshire, and the Barron, for $21 to $25. The meat is served with Yorkshire pudding, mashed potatoes, and creamed horseradish. Barronshire Platters include petite filet mignon and shrimp for $32.50 and sautéed veal medallions for $20. Other offerings include grilled filet of fresh salmon and grilled breasts of chicken Dijon. Dessert on one visit included English trifle, a crystal glass filled with layers of pound cake, strawberries, blueberries, and peaches topped with sauce melba and a dash of sherry with whipped cream.

Andiamo is the home of Northern Italian specialties and homemade pasta, offered daily for dinner from 6 P.M. to 11 P.M. There's an impressive espresso and cappuccino counter at the entrance, and diners can see the chefs at work behind a glass wall. Specialties include *medaglioni di vitello andiamo* (two veal medallions sautéed and served with creamy rosemary sauce and asparagus) for $21, and *costoletta di vitello con spugnole* (Provini veal chop sautéed with morel mushrooms and pine nuts in marsala sauce) for $24.

Benihana Village features two traditional Japanese restaurants, **Hibachi** and the **Seafood Grille.** At Hibachi, chefs chop, slice, and grill your food at your table. Offerings include hibachi chicken for $15, swordfish for $21, and combination dinners including the Samurai (hibachi steak and salmon) for $28.50, and the Benihana (hibachi steak and lobster tail) for $37.50.

The Seafood Grille offers sushi appetizers and barbecued dishes, such as halibut steak for $17.75, tuna for $23, and red snapper for $19. Combinations include the *Takara* (steak and Gulf prawns) for $29, and the Grille Special (choice of two from calamari steak, chicken teriyaki, Norwegian salmon, or Pacific swordfish) for $24.50. Also available are tempura (batter fried) vegetable or seafood platters, and sashimi. Dinner is complemented by the animated musical show "Jambirdee" and a fireworks display over the Benihana Musical Waters.

The **Garden of the Dragon** features gourmet Chinese dishes from 6 to 11 P.M. In addition to basic Chinese fare, you'll also find some unusual offerings such as sizzling lamb (tender lamb loin sliced with Chinese fresh vegetables, served sizzling at the table), lobster Peking style (lobster tail dipped in special batter, served with sweet and sour sauce), and steamed whole flounder (whole flounder steamed in the Cantonese style and garnished with scallions, ginger, and soy sauce).

The **Hilton Steakhouse** offers charbroiled steak, ribs, fish, and chicken. Open 5 to 11 P.M. and closed Thursdays. Offerings include several cuts of steak, such as a 36-ounce double New York strip sirloin for two, priced at $58; center-cut pork chops for $22; and large-cut filet mignon for $28. Other entrees include fresh swordfish steak for $25, skewer of Tiger shrimp for $25, and lemon oregano chicken for $19.

Also available is **MargaritaGrille**, a casual Mexican restaurant. Offerings include *albondigas* (Mexican vegetable soup with meatballs), *chili con queso,* fajitas, chimichangas, *flautas,* and burritos. Combination dinners include a choice of two ($8.95) or three ($9.95) from tamales, enchiladas, tacos, *chili relleno*, and tostadas.

Socorro Springs is a 24-hour coffee shop named for the birthplace of hotel chain founder Conrad Hilton.

The **Buffet of Champions** is open for breakfast during the week from 7 to 10 A.M. for $6.25; lunch is served from 11 A.M. to 2:30 P.M. for $7.25; dinner is from 5 to 10 P.M. for $8.99. A champagne brunch is offered Saturdays, Sundays, and holidays for $8.99.

Las Vegas Hilton. 3000 Paradise Rd.; 3,174 rooms; 732-5111, (800) 732-7117.

MUST-SEE Luxor

The real and imagined treasures of another desert empire come to near life in the fabulous Luxor, a 2,521-room, 30-story, $300 million pyramid-shaped complex.

Located just south of the Excalibur at the top end of the Strip, the hotel is the latest in a string of Circus Circus resorts. The interior of the hotel—a vast hollow pyramid—is about as spectacular a sight as you'll see on the Strip.

The designers of the Luxor conceived of it as a simulation of a vast archeological dig where the mysteries of ancient Egypt are revealed as though the interior was a vast excavation site. Replicas of Egyptian artifacts, including a full-sized reproduction of King Tut's tomb, are on display.

As you approach, the hotel appears to be a huge sand-colored pyramid; the rooms of the hotel occupy the exterior steps of the structure. Out front is a huge replica of the Sphinx, the mythical Egyptian creature with a human head and the body of a lion. The figure was often meant to symbolize the pharaoh as an incarnation of the sun god, Ra. Blazing out of the top of the pyramid is a 40-billion-candlepower light—claimed to be the most powerful beam of light in the world; orbiting Space Shuttle crewmembers fulfilled a PR person's dream when they reported seeing it from space. The light is actually 47 separate xenon units mounted in the top of the pyramid.

The central obelisk in the casino lights up, with the aid of fiber optics, to reveal hieroglyphics and cartouches.

The pyramid, a symbol of eternal life believed by the Pharaohs to be a "stairway to the stars," offers three levels of entertainment. The Hanging

Something to glow about. Another improvement to the Nevada economy—if not its environment—is the Nevada Nuclear Waste Repository at Yucca Mountain about 100 miles from Vegas. Due for an off-limits opening sometime around the year 2000, the repository is planned as a waste dump for the radioactive garbage from nuclear weapons, power plants, and other assorted reactors around the nation.

This permanent improvement has to be able to remain untouched for 10,000 or so years, which just may outlast the Strip.

The big top. If you have any doubts about the financial viability of the super resorts of Las Vegas, consider this: according to Circus Circus, the new Luxor's $300 million construction cost was funded entirely by cash flow from the company's various resorts. There is no mortgage.

The real thing. Luxor, on the east bank of the Nile about 315 miles southeast of Cairo, is near the site of Thebes, the capital of ancient Egypt. The temple at Luxor was built by Amenhotep III and dedicated to Amon-Re, king of the gods, the sun god. Nearby are the Valley of the Kings, where the tomb of Tutankhamen was discovered in 1922; the Valley of the Queens; and the magnificent monuments of Karnak.

Boat shop. Across from the check-in desk is an overlook to the boat ride. Note the camouflaged overhead track and the hidden slab beneath. This is not the true secret of the Nile, but actually the entrance to a hidden work area for repair of boats. The slab is lifted and put aside, and then a boat is carried into the work area.

Gardens of Babylon occupy the front entrance, while lagoon-like pools and a beach are at the rear entrance.

The main level of Luxor includes the "River Nile" flowing along the perimeter, separating the hotel rooms from the casino. Guests and visitors can take a narrated voyage on the river to view architectural scenes of ancient Egypt. (The original concept had been for the boats to transport guests from the registration desk to the hotel tower elevator lobbies located in the four corners of the pyramid.)

Guests are transported to their floors on unusual inclined elevators moving at a 39-degree angle up the sides of the pyramid, or on more conventional vertical lifts.

The rooms themselves have an unusual feature that may be a bit disconcerting to some visitors; the outside window wall is slanted sharply since it is part of the exterior of the pyramid. Other visitors may find the view of the interior atrium a bit dizzying; the interior balconies extend all the way up to the 27th floor, while the top three floors—mostly suites—have interior hallways. And residents of one of the first few floors of the hotel may find a great deal of pedestrian traffic right outside their doors.

The rooms are nicely appointed, from the standard guest room (as low as $59 in off-season and more than twice that during conventions and at peak times) to the Jacuzzi Suites (starting at $150) and the spectacular upper-level rooms including the Presidential Suite that rents for several thousand dollars per night.

Within the 90,000-square-foot casino area— about twice the size of most of the Strips' gambling rooms—the Egyptian theme is carried through with reproductions of artifacts, columns, and tombs found in the temples of Luxor and Karnak.

The **Sacred Sea Room**, an attractively decorated hideaway, includes entrees priced from about $12 to $26, with dishes including linguine and clams, New York steak, and veal chops. Fresh vegetables complement each meal, with a lazy Susan salad bar at each table.

More adventurous dishes are offered at **Papyrus**, including Polynesian, Pacific Rim, Szechwan, and Cantonese fare. Dishes on a recent visit, priced from about $11 to $21, included spicy Thai shrimp scampi, paniolo steak (grilled pineapple, toasted coconut, and teriyaki sauce), and wok-seared rare salmon with a basil ginger sauce. Also offered is the Otemanu Hot Rock Sampler, Pacific basin hot rock grilling at your table. A replica of a wall in a Mayan ruin stands at the rear of the dining room, which is open to the atrium's height.

The **Pyramid Cafe's** menu offers a wide range of salads, priced from about $2 to $9, plus entrees including burgers, grilled Pacific salmon, and fried chicken, priced from about $6 to $14.

The **Millenium High Energy Cafe** is a bright and cheerful open space offering burgers, fajitas, pizzas, and sandwiches, with entrees priced from about $5 to $10.

> **Family tree.** Luxor is the third "entertainment mega-store" owned and operated by Circus Circus on the Strip. The company operates Circus Circus in Las Vegas and Reno, Excalibur in Vegas, the Colorado Belle and Edgewater in Laughlin, and Slots-A-Fun and Silver City casinos on the Strip.

The **Nile Deli** is sort of a New York Jewish delicatessen on the banks of the Nile. Large sandwiches, Philly cheesesteaks, reubens, lox on a bagel, and other delicacies are priced from about $5 to $10.

The **Manhattan Buffet** is an open-air buffet set in a metropolitan downtown setting. For hours and rates see the section on buffets.

The gourmet room is **Isis**, which serves continental fare as well as seasonal specialties. Guests enter along a colonnade walk of caryatid statues and through glass doors with gold-embossed "wings of Isis." Within the restaurant is a vaulted ceiling decorated with gold Egyptian stars.

At **Nefertiti's Lounge** you can get up close and personal with human clones of musical stars. The American Superstars show moved to the Luxor in 1995 from its former home at the Flamingo Hilton. Impersonators do their best at Elvis, Cher, Little Richard, the Blues Brothers, the Temptations, and other entertainment icons. Heidi Thompson's imitation of Cher is complete down to the tattoo on her derriere. Men: unless you have an unfulfilled urge to play Sonny Bono, you are advised to stay out of the front rows of the theater. The show is free with a two-drink minimum and is performed nightly except Sundays at 7:30 and 9:30 P.M.

And there is, of course, an ancient shopping bazaar. The hotel features a 1,200-seat oval showroom for a nightly special effects production show; the entrance to the arena is decorated to resemble the ancient tombs of the pharaohs in the Valley of the Kings.

The third level offers three attractions created by special effects designer Douglass Trumbull (also responsible for the spectacular *Back to the Future* ride at Universal Studios in Orlando, Florida). *For details, see the section on Las Vegas attractions in Chapter 10.*

The 1,100-seat Pharaoh's Dinner Theater presents "Winds of the Gods," your basic chariot-race-exotic-animal-Egyptian-theme entertainment.

Luxor Hotel/Casino. 3900 Las Vegas Blvd. South; 2,521 rooms; (800) 288-1000.

MUST-SEE **MGM Grand**

The MGM Grand claimed the mantle as the World's Largest Hotel, Casino, and Theme Park when it opened early in 1994.

It could also advertise itself as the World's Only Hotel Where Guests and Visitors Will Enter Through an 88-Foot-Tall MGM Lion into a Seven-Story Replica of Emerald City, Complete with Yellow Brick Road. It is a decidedly strange and somewhat wonderful place, Las Vegas' version of Oz for adults and children of all ages.

The hotel and theme park is located on 112 acres at the northeast corner of Las Vegas Boulevard South and Tropicana Avenue, the former site of the Marina Hotel-Casino and the Tropicana Country Club. The $1 billion project is the largest in the history of Nevada and added 5,009 rooms, including 744 suites, in a set of 30-story towers.

The biggest lure of this grand experiment is **MGM Grand Adventures**, a 33-acre theme park including rides, shows, themed streets, entertainment, restaurants, and shops. It is all lorded over by King Looey, the lion ambassador of the park.

For details on MGM Grand Adventures, see the section on Las Vegas attractions in Chapter 10.

And speaking of grand experiments, the spectacular **EFX** show opened at the 1,700-seat **MGM Grand Theatre** in the spring of 1995 after more than a year of preparation.

The $41 million production, which boasts a 70-person cast and more special effects than much of the rest of the Strip combined, features Michael Crawford, star of Andrew Lloyd Webber's *The Phantom of the Opera* in London, New York, and Los Angeles. Crawford takes the role of the EFX Master, a mysterious character whose mission is to shepherd the audience on a trip to strange

MGM Grand, Las Vegas

new worlds. He introduces the audience to the Master of Time, the Master of Magic, the Master of the Spirit World, and the Master of Laughter.

Crawford also takes on the roles of Merlin, the wise man and sorcerer of the Arthurian legend; P. T. Barnum, the legendary circus entrepreneur; magician Harry Houdini; and H. G. Wells, the English science fiction writer. Also featured is the Kagonovich Russian trapeze team.

EFX is presented twice nightly except Tuesdays.

The hotel and casino are certainly grand and worth a visit, but the overall tone is down a notch from places like Caesars Palace or the Mirage. It is also one of the few hotel complexes we know of that requires the use of a map; we suspect some of the bellhops keep copies in their back pockets, too.

There are two main entrances to the hotel. The most dramatic is the **Lion Entrance**, which is mostly for use by pedestrians; visitors arriving by car or taxi will probably enter beneath the more formal canopied porte cochere, a fancy term for carriage entrance.

The Lion Entrance must be seen to be believed. You'll walk between the golden paws of a huge MGM lion; bright lights behind his eyes radiate toward the Strip. An elevated pedestrian crosswalk at the corner connects to the nearby Tropicana, Excalibur, and Luxor. When you walk through the door, you'll be in **Emerald City**, home of a strange little magic show and near the **Oz Buffet.** You're also within one of four casino areas, one watched over by an animated Good Witch in pink, bestowing a blessing on the slots below. The slots, by the way, can accept folding money as well as tokens; they will eat bills as large as $100.

Oz, MGM Grand, Las Vegas

Door number 18,000.
Construction began with
ground breaking on
October 7, 1991, and
more than 1,500 workers
were on the job soon
thereafter. Building
materials included
18,000 doors, 93 eleva-
tors, 100,000 square feet
of marble, and enough
air-conditioning to cool a
town of 5,500 homes.

**Some may still be mov-
ing east.** The first big
event at the MGM
Grand took place a year
before its opening when
the hotel/casino/theme
park threw a party to
celebrate the "topping
off" of the hotel. As a
crane lifted the final
panel into place on the
four emerald green tow-
ers, 5,009 balloons—
representing each of the
rooms in the hotel—
were released. Each bal-
loon contained a certifi-
cate good for one free
night's stay.

If you come in through the porte cochere, you'll
be at the registration desk, which is also worth
seeing; a bank of some 60 video monitors behind
the clerks displays some spectacular images from
sporting events and movies. We enjoyed watching the speeded-up baseball game.

The **Grand Theatre** is a handsome Vegas showroom, wider than deep with a stage about three
city buses wide and decorated in red and black.
The tables and booths seat about 1,700. The relatively cozy **Hollywood Theatre**, with 630 seats,
features headliners.

The **Sports Book**, to the left of the Grand Theatre, has a gigantic screen capable of handling a
single event like the Super Bowl, or being split
into as many as 12 separate images for various
sporting events.

We also mustn't overlook (as if we could) the
MGM Grand Garden special events center. This
arena, modeled after New York's famed Madi-
son Square Garden, offers seating for up to 15,200
for championship boxing. There's nothing
very grand about the arena itself, except for its
ability to change its configuration for events from
ice shows, hockey games, and basketball games
to prize fights and concerts. According to the
designers, it can be transformed from a major
exhibition hall to an arena for sporting events
or concerts in four hours. The Garden was the
site of the much-publicized opening night concerts by Barbra Streisand.

In the hotel, standard rooms are about 446 square
feet in size; 744 suites range in size from 675 to
6,000 square feet. (A bit of perspective here: a typical three- or four-bedroom home is 2,000 square feet or less.)

Standard rooms are decorated in Wizard of Oz, Hollywood, Southern, and
Casa Blanca styles. They are larger than average and fairly quiet. Suites include
traditional, Marrakech, Oriental, Bahamian, and Las Vegas designs.

One of the disadvantages of the MGM Grand is that the parking garage is
at some distance from the hotel and not connected with an indoor passage
to keep you out of the sun, rain, or cold. There is a 1,200-spot underground
lot beneath the porte cochere for valet parking, which may be worth the extra
expense at check-in or check-out.

The huge casino encompasses a total of 171,500 square feet, including about
3,500 slot machines, 165 gaming tables, and a Race and Sports Book. The casino
is divided into four themed areas: Emerald City, Hollywood, Monte Carlo,

and Sports. The Emerald City dome includes 75-foot-tall emerald crystal spires, a Yellow Brick Road, Wizard of Oz characters, and The Wizard's Secret special effects and magic show.

At the very center of it all is **Wolfgang Puck's Cafe,** a Nevada outpost of the successful California chef's unusual restaurants. You can buy a plain wood-fired pizza for about $7.50, but why would you when you could order a pie with shrimp or with chicken and anchovies. We were drawn to the pizza with smoked salmon and red onions for $14.50.

Most of the other restaurants are clustered in a corridor that leads from the casino to the MGM Grand Garden and the MGM Grand Adventures area. **Leonardo's** serves entrees ranging from about $7 to $12 for lunch and about $10 to $20 for dinner. They include pasta dishes and regular-to-extraordinary pizza.

Across the corridor is the **Coyote Cafe,** a transplant from Santa Fe, serving tacos, tortillas, quesadillas, soups, and salads; entrees range from about $7 to $12. The bar boasts 26 different types of tequila.

Sir Reginald's Steakhouse offers meat-eater delights including steaks, prime rib, and chicken, priced from about $18 to $30. A signature dish is hobo steak in salt crust, priced at about $45 for a two-person serving.

The Ocean Grille is a small seafood eatery near the Fast Food Court, with entrees priced from about $14 to $25. Outside the doors of the restaurant is a small, pricey seafood bar called **Crack Crab** with offerings including oysters, crabs, and mussels.

Dragon Court is a high-tone Chinese eatery, quiet and off the busy track. The small menu includes braised shark fin and chicken in brown sauce for $30, as well as more ordinary offerings such as beef with oyster sauce for $13.50 and pork chop with black pepper sauce for $15.

The **One-Liners Fast Food Court** features a **Nathan's,** a **McDonald's,** and **Hamada Oriental Express.**

Make sure you check out the robotic version of comedian Foster Brooks doing one of his routines at the bar near the elevators to the hotel rooms. It takes a while before you realize that the guy sitting at the bar telling stories is not just your ordinary drunk. He is a professional electronically operated drunk.

The Grand Oasis includes a swimming pool with beach. Nearby is the **Grand Health Club & Spa,** a fitness center including six Jacuzzis.

Wolfgang Puck's Cafe,
MGM Grand, Las Vegas

For children, the MGM Grand features **King Looey's Youth Activity Center**, Las Vegas' second "youth hotel" (the other is at the Las Vegas Hilton) offering supervised activities for children. The center will accommodate children from ages 3 to 12 at its location near the theme park; rates are about $5 per hour for guests of the hotel and $7 per hour for others. The activity center also offers supervised tours of the MGM Grand Adventures theme park. Departing at 11 A.M. and concluding at 5 P.M., the tour is for children from ages 6 to 16 for a fee of $70 for guests and $80 for others.

Also available is the **Wizard's Midway & Arcade**, a 30,000-square-foot center including 33 games of skill and the latest video games. If you've got any stomach left after gambling or visiting the theme park, you may want to try the **G360** virtual reality arcade game; you'll "fly" your craft into a dogfight and then come back to a carrier landing. If you're anything like the pilots I saw, you'll spend most of the time upside down trying to figure out which way is up.

Bars and lounges include the **Center Stage Lounge**, **Turf Club Lounge**, **Flying Monkey Bar**, **Betty Boop Bar**, and the **Margarita Bar.**

In 1995, construction is due to be completed on a privately financed monorail system that connects the MGM Grand to Bally's a few blocks away. At the MGM, the station will be between the garage and the main building. The **MGM Grand–Bally's Monorail** is a $25 million joint venture, privately funded by the two casinos. The 1.6-mile route runs north-south along Audrie Lane on Bally's property, crossing Harmon Avenue and proceeding along an internal boulevard on MGM Grand property.

Two trains of six 40-passenger cars each run on the line at top speeds of up to 50 miles per hour.

The companies believe the line may turn out to be the first leg of a system that will one day link downtown, the Strip, the Las Vegas Convention Center and McCarran International Airport, although there are no indications of movement in that direction.

The monorail links what is now the top end of the Strip—MGM Grand, Tropicana, Luxor, Excalibur, and the new New York, New York—to the Center Strip. Bally's is next door to the Aladdin Hotel on one side and the Imperial Palace on the other, and a few blocks away from Caesars Palace and the Mirage. The Mirage, of course, is linked by its own trolley system to its neighbor, Treasure Island.

Dragon Court Restaurant,
MGM Grand, Las Vegas

The owners of the MGM Grand and

Bally's believe that anything they do to increase traffic through their casinos will result in more and more dollars fed into their slot machines or pushed across the felt at the gaming tables, even if some of the passengers will use the monorail as a way to get to other casinos or to the Las Vegas Convention Center at mid-Strip.

A Bit of History

MGM Grand, Inc., is a publicly traded hotel, casino, and travel company based in Las Vegas. The company also operates MGM Grand Air, a luxury charter airline.

The company's majority shareholder, Kirk Kerkorian, opened his first Las Vegas property, the International Hotel, in 1969. At the time, it claimed the title as the largest hotel in the world with a mere 1,517 rooms. The hotel, considerably expanded, is now owned by Hilton Hotels and called the Las Vegas Hilton.

The first MGM Grand Hotel opened in 1973 at Flamingo Road, and once again claimed top honors as the largest hotel. After a massive reconstruction following a tragic fire, it was sold to Bally's. Over the years, MGM Grand, Inc., bought—and quickly sold—the Sands Hotel. It also bought the Desert Inn and later sold it to Kerkorian's private holding company.

The latest expansion began with the 1989 and 1990 acquisition and subsequent demolition of the Marina Hotel-Casino and the Tropicana Country Club. In 1991, construction of the new MGM Grand hotel, casino, and theme park commenced at that site.

MGM Grand. 3799 Las Vegas Blvd. South.; 5,000 rooms; 734-5110, (800) 929-1111.

New York, New York

New for 1996 will be a major casino at the top end of the Strip, on the corner across from the MGM Grand and Excalibur. The hotel will include replicas of Big Apple icons including the Statue of Liberty, the Empire State Building, and a Coney Island roller coaster. Early plans call for integration of the walkway across the road directly into the new hotel/casino.

The 2,200-room hotel project is a joint venture of the MGM Grand and Primadonna Resorts.

MUST-SEE The Mirage

Every desert needs a mirage, although few are quite so phantasmagorical as this one.

The Mirage is a sight to behold inside and out, but any description of the hotel has to start with the live volcano out front that spews smoke and fire a hundred feet in the air from an artificial lagoon.

When the hotel first opened in 1989, locals were unsure which was more entertaining: the aerial show from the volcano or the continuous fender benders it caused on the Strip out front.

The man-made, computer-controlled 54-foot-tall volcano puts on a three-minute show every half hour from dusk to midnight, spitting steam, gas-fed flames, and "lava" created with the aid of a sophisticated lighting scheme. The pumping system moves 5,000 gallons of water per minute during the show. As part of the construction, 1,000 real palm trees were moved to the site; some of the trees nearest the flames, though, are constructed of steel and concrete.

An elevated tram connects the Mirage to its neighboring cousin, Treasure Island.

The $630 million, 100-acre site has three 30-story towers with 3,049 rooms including one- and two-bedroom suites, eight villa apartments, and six lanai bungalows with private gardens and pools. The top five floors of each tower are reserved for tower and penthouse suites.

The driveway delivers visitors to a white porte cochere with full-length louvered shutters that suggest arrival at a colonial government house. Entering through the main doors, you walk into a 90-foot-high indoor atrium with 60-foot-tall palm trees; a central forest includes tropical orchids and banana trees, an indoor waterfall, and lagoons.

Behind the hotel's registration desk is a huge 53-foot-long, 20,000-gallon coral reef aquarium stocked with sharks, rays, and other sea life from the Caribbean, Hawaiian Islands, Tonga, Fiji, the Marshall Islands, Australia, and the Red Sea. The aquarium really is worth a look, if you can find the check-in area in the complex maze of the casino.

Public areas are decorated in high-tone marble, teak, and rattan. In the atrium, the bent palm trees are necessarily fake, but they are covered in real bark. Almost every other piece of greenery is real.

The Mirage, Las Vegas

The tropical theme is carried through in most of the rooms at the Mirage, featuring lush colors, rattan, and cane. The highest of the high rollers can rent one of six lanai bungalows, each with its own private garden and pool.

The lowest room rates at the Mirage can usually be found bracketing Christmas, when rates fall to as low as $49 for standard rooms; those same rooms can go for as much as $239 at times of highest demand, including during conventions. Penthouse suites rent for $250 to $750.

The pool area includes a series of interconnected lagoons and two palm-tree islands.

The Mirage is one of just a few casinos in Las Vegas with $500 slot machines; there is a small nest of them in an alcove near the **Caribe Cafe**. The slots have a top payoff of $40,000 for a single coin. By the way, if you sit and play the $500 machines for a while, you'll be offered a free catered meal. Of course, they'll want you to eat it at the machines, feeding those expensive tokens all the while.

Nearby is the **Salon Privé**, a private gambling room for the highest rollers, where tens or even hundreds of thousands of dollars can hang on a single card in blackjack or baccarat, a roll of the dice in craps, or a spin of the roulette wheel. If you want to play, the casino will staff every table in the room in case you change your mind on which game to play.

Speaking of excesses in entertainment, the Mirage is the long-time home of Siegfried and Roy, who put on one of the most spectacular and expensive magic and stage shows anywhere. The boys appear 40 weeks per year—if you are determined to see their show, check with the hotel to avoid one of their vacation periods. They sell out almost every one of their 12 shows per week. *See the write-up on Las Vegas showrooms.*

The $30 million production premiered in February 1990 and grossed more than $80 million in the first two years. The show is presented in the **Theatre Mirage**, a 1,500-seat theater. The production was created and designed by John Napier, the Tony Award–winning artist responsible for English and American theatrical triumphs including *Cats, Starlight Express, Les Miserables,* and *Phantom of the Opera.*

There are 27 tigers in the Siegfried and Roy troupe. Not all of them appear in the show, and those that do are given regular times off for good behavior.

You can visit some of these beautiful creatures through the glass wall near the walkway entrance on the south side of the hotel. The re-creation of their native Himalayan world is open to the sky. There is a path that leads up almost to the roof; if you see an especially large pussycat outside your room one morning, don't open the door.

And there is a hallway that runs from the exhibit area to their cages and the showroom, allowing the animals to be walked to work. We'd suggest you avoid opening unmarked doors in the casino. (Just kidding . . . we think.)

Another interesting animal exhibit is the **Dolphin Habitat**, a 1.5-million-gallon tank for bottlenose dolphins located out back and open to the public for a nominal fee.

The Mirage also features a collection of some of the best and most attractive restaurants in Las Vegas.

Color scheming. The original color scheme for the Mirage was almost entirely drawn from a palette of muted earth tones—peach, beige, and green. The increasing influx of high rollers from Asia has brought about some redecoration to reds, blacks, and yellows—colors apparently more pleasing to Asian sensibilities. The registration desk—or the keepers of the comp rooms for the guests of the casino—will color coordinate rooms to appeal to the taste of individual guests.

Among our favorites is **Moongate**, a gourmet Chinese restaurant serving spicy Szechwan and subtle Cantonese cuisine in a lovely setting that includes a starfield ceiling, a live cherry tree, and tasteful jade objects and statuary; the hotel reportedly spent $2.5 million on decorations alone. Open for dinner only, from 5:30 to 11 P.M., Moongate offers entrees ranging from $10 to $38. Among specialties are jade pepper chicken for $15, Mongolian beef for $17.25, Mandarin pork cutlets for $17, scallops and shrimp with yellow leek for $31, and Peking duck for $41.

Next door, and sharing the starfield ceiling, is **Mikado**, set in a very elegant Japanese garden. Your chef can prepare teppen yaki dishes of chicken, steak, lobster, or vegetables at your table from about $20 to $43. Individual sushi pieces are priced from $4 to $8. Other offerings include a Japanese vegetarian delight for $16, a yakatori combo for $24.50, and chirashi (thinly sliced assorted raw fish and sushi) for $30. The restaurant is open for dinner only.

The smallest of the gourmet rooms at the Mirage is **Le Bistro**, with just 90 seats. The decor is very Parisian, with Toulouse-Lautrec-like murals and

Siegfried and Roy's Royal White tigers, the Mirage, Las Vegas

an attractive pressed-tin ceiling over most of the restaurant, except for an exquisite stained glass dome in the center. Specialties we found on one visit, priced from about $20 to $35, included venison tenderloin *chasseur;* tournedos Diane; breast of duck *au poivre*; sea bass *grenobloise,* sautéed with lemon, capers, vermouth, and butter for $23; and roasted rack of spring lamb for $33. Appetizing appetizers included escargot and wild mushroom crepes.

The **Ristorante Riva** was described for us by a hotel official as "an Italian restaurant without a Mob setting." Decorated in peaches and green, it is very Italian and very bright; entrees run from about $15 to $30. Pasta dishes we found included *agnolotti alla grafagnana* (halfmoon pasta with ricotta, spinach, and herbs with marjoram cream). Also offered are *zuppa di pesce cioppino* (shrimp, scallops, lobster, mussels, clams, and squid in a tomato-fish base) for $30, and *salmone con carciofi* (salmon with artichokes), *linguine con vongole* (linguine pasta with clams), *vitello saltimbocca,* and *scaloppina limone o marsala* for $25.

Kokomo is the only full-service restaurant open for lunch. It has an open-air feeling under the atrium. Offerings include burgers and sandwiches from $6 to $8 and steaks from $10 to $15.

An interesting alternative for lunch, or for dinner, is the **California Pizza Kitchen** located near the sports bar. They use wood-fired ovens to create some of the strangest—and tastiest—pizzas in town. Pies go for $10 for individual size; also available are salads and pasta dishes. No reservations are accepted, and lines can build during busy times.

The Mirage's **Buffet** is located in an attractive, bright room just off the casino floor. It is officially described as being set in an English garden at Bermuda, although we didn't quite see the connection. The food is good, but it is obvious that the Mirage feels it does not need the lure of a spectacular buffet to bring in the gambling visitors. Breakfast is served from 7 A.M. to 11 A.M. for $6.75, lunch is from 11 A.M. to 3 P.M. for $8.75, and dinner is from 3 to 9:30 P.M. for $10.75. A Sunday champagne brunch from 8 A.M. to 9:30 P.M. is priced at $13. Children under 10 eat for less.

The Mirage. 3400 Las Vegas Blvd. South; 3,049 rooms; 791-7111, (800) 627-6667.

Tiger, tiger. Two or three tigers are usually on display in the habitat at the Mirage at all times, with new groups moved in several times each day.

No dolphin served here. Several bouncing baby calves have been born in the Mirage's dolphin habitat. Each dolphin has its own signature whistle, and it is believed that the mother is able to recognize her own baby by listening for the sound.

By the way, don't feel guilty about ordering a tuna sandwich at the Mirage. The hotel has a "dolphin safe" policy for all of its restaurants. And the hotel also bars the sale of fur in any of its boutiques.

⬛MUST-SEE⬛ Rio Hotel & Casino

Hot, hot, hot! This is one fun place, a bit of Rio de Janeiro about a mile west

Inside joke. The "street" outside of Le Bistro and Ristorante Riva bears two authentic-looking European street signs: Via Stefano and Via Elena. They're not real, though: Stefano is named for Steve Wynn, the major-domo of the Mirage, and Elena for his wife Elaine.

of the Strip. It's a bright and cheery place of flowers, flowered shirts, and the hottest cocktail waitress uniforms in town, more of a swimsuit than an outfit, actually. Dancers in pink thong bikinis and dancers with trained birds parade through the casino from time to time.

The original building opened in 1990 and almost immediately was too small; construction of a new tower was completed in 1994. That same year work was begun on a third suite tower and a new parking garage. By mid-1995, the Rio had 1,400 suites. And who knows where it will all end—the 45-acre site is zoned for as many as 2,400 rooms.

For those who like to eat, though, the real news may be a doubling in the size of the **Carnival World Buffet.** This made one of our "Best" buffets even more of a best bet.

The Rio is only about a mile from the Strip, although it's not an easy walk because of the highways in the area; you'll need to use a car, cab, or the hotel's shuttle bus to get there.

The Rio's 430-seat showroom features ¡**Conga!**, an interactive multimedia dinner show.

All of the rooms at the hotel are considered suites, basically one 600-square-foot room with a large bathroom and dressing room. The sleeping area includes a couch. Standard rates in 1994 were about $85 for weekdays and $101 on weekends.

The small pool features a white-sand beach, complete with a volleyball court. The **Video Hut** arcade flanks the casino floor.

Our favorite part of this place, though, is the spectacular **Carnival World Buffet,** which is one of the best values in town at $7.95 for dinner. A pretty, bright room right off the casino floor, it offers cooked-to-order Brazilian stir-fry and other quality dishes. Breakfast features made-to-order omelettes, waffles, pancakes, sausage, bacon, fresh salsa, fruit, and a variety of fritters. Just when we were ready to waddle on out, we discovered the dessert section, which is the fulfillment of many a sweet tooth's wildest dream: a bakery where you can sample any food simply by pointing to it.

The expanded buffet added a sushi and teppen yaki bar, a fish and chips station, and a burger and fries joint—all included in the basic price. Also new is a spectacular "butcher shop" in the center of the buffet; here you can select a steak, chop, or piece of fish and have it cooked to order for an additional charge of about $3 to $5.

We especially enjoy the Brazilian stir-fry counter where you get to choose from vegetables including mushrooms, asparagus, onions, broccoli, bean sprouts, carrots, and tomatoes, plus herbs and spices including cilantro, garlic, and ginger; then you choose from pork, lamb, chicken, or beef and watch as a chef cooks it all with a special sauce. Other sections of the buffet include international offerings: American, Mexican, Chinese, and Italian.

The Rio's newest restaurant is the elegant **Fiore**, near the hotel's Beach Club. It's a quiet sanctuary down a glass-walled hallway; you can eat in the lovely dining room or move out onto the open-air porch. Entrees, priced from about $16 to $34, include pasta, veal, chicken, and beef dishes.

Another interesting restaurant is the **All-American Steakhouse**. Luncheon fare includes burgers for $5 to $7 and salads featuring lobster and avocado for $6 to $11. Dinner selections include pork ribs marinated in a secret sauce for 24 hours ($9.95), as well as chicken and shrimp dishes. The setting is a small, dark sports bar with pennants on the wall; the walls are open to the casino.

A small food court includes **Sonny's Deli**, **Pizza and Pasta**, and **Dreyer's** in a bright and airy room with metal chairs and counter service. Pizza by the slice goes for $1.50 to $2.50; whole pies are also available. Pasta with sauce is priced from $4.50 to $6.

Antonio's is a small, quiet eatery with an attractive light wood and marble decor and an impressive espresso machine at the entrance. Entrees include soup and salad and are priced from $15 to $25. A typical offering is *vitello al piccata* (scallops of veal sautéed with lemon, white wine, butter, and shallots). The restaurant is open every day for dinner from 5 to 11 P.M.

Old money. Be sure to check out the beautiful Caille Brothers Triple Upright slot machine, tucked away in a hallway near Antonio's restaurant at the Rio. This three-in-one machine also includes a music box. Built in 1907, less than ten are known to still exist.

Boob tube. The casino floor includes high-tech TV monitors advertising various promotions and offering some little bit of entertainment for visitors standing in line for the buffet. (At the time of our visit, the casino also offered one of our least favorite accommodations, a Next Day Tax Refund booth.)

The coffee shop facing the pool area is the **Beach Front Cafe**. Specials include T-bone steak and eggs with all the hotcakes you can eat for $2.99, served from 11 P.M. to 11 A.M. A dinner special, from 4 to 10 P.M., is steak and lobster tail for $6.49. A nice selection of pies and pastries is also offered.

We really like this place. Did we remember to mention the buffet and the cocktail waitress outfits?

Rio Suite Hotel & Casino. 3700 West Flamingo Road; 1,400 rooms; 252-7777, (800) 888-1808.

★MUST-SEE★ Treasure Island

Let's give credit where credit is due: extravagant casino developer Steve Wynn, already responsible for installing the town's only active volcano in front of his Mirage resort, was also the first person to realize that what Las Vegas was missing was its own pirate warship.

Treasure Island opened with a bang at the end of 1993, just north of its corporate cousin the Mirage; the two hotels are connected by an aerial tram.

The adventure begins with a boardwalk along the Strip and across a lagoon to the front entrance. The front of the resort has been designed as an outdoor theater modeled after Buccaneer Bay, the village in Robert Louis Stevenson's *Treasure Island* classic.

Each hour—depending on weather conditions—the British frigate HMS *Sir Francis Drake* sails around Skull Point to confront an 80-foot-long replica of the pirate ship *Hispaniola*. "In the name of His Royal Britannic Majesty, King of England and all that he surveys, I order you brigands to lay down your arms and receive a Marine boarding party," the British captain warns. "The only thing we'll receive from you is your stores, valuables, and whatever rum ye might have onboard, you son of a footman's goat," is the pirate's response.

Those are, of course, fighting words. The two ships engage in a cannon battle across the lagoon, complete with explosions, fire, and a spectacular sinking ship. Many of the 30 stunt players jump or fall from the rigging into the water below.

This is Las Vegas, after all: the pirates win. (The British captain goes down with his ship—or does he?)

The $430-million Treasure Island resort includes 2,900 guest rooms with 212 suites in three 36-floor towers. All rooms and suites have floor-to-ceiling windows. Standard room rates range from about $45 to $99 and suites are from about $150 to $300.

Other facilities include **Pirates Walk**, a glittering main street village lined with retail shops, two wedding chapels, and a lavish tropical pool with slide, two cocktail bars, and a snack bar. The shopping area includes our nominee for the worst pun in Las Vegas, a store called "Damsels in Dis Dress."

The hotel also has its own slightly more imaginative version of the photographic fantasy booth that is very common in Las Vegas. You can be pictured with Siegfried and Roy and some of the tiger cubs, in the middle of the set of Cirque du Soleil, collecting gold coins coming out in a waterfall from

Treasure Island, Las Vegas

a slot machine, or pulling up in front of the Treasure Island in a stretch limousine.

The **Buccaneer Bay Club** is a quiet, private room on the second floor off the casino with a view of the pirate battle out front. Offerings, priced from about $14 to $43, on a recent visit included duckling Grand Marnier, Chilean sea bass, spit roasted monkfish, and lobster *fra diavolo*.

The Plank is a very elegant and quiet hideaway, with a setting of an educated pirate's booty-filled library. Entrees range from about $13 to $32, including cioppino, mesquite-grilled salmon, and steak with crabmeat and béarnaise sauce.

Black Spot Grille. A bit away from the casino, it offers pasta, calzone, burgers, and other such fare, with prices from about $6 to $10.

The **Lookout Cafe** is a high-toned 24-hour coffee shop with dishes such as salmon, halibut, pot pie, and burgers. Prices range from about $5 to $13.

There are three themed buffets, in Italian, American, and Chinese flavors, presented in adjoining, attractive rooms. The food is a bit ordinary, though. Prices for breakfast, lunch, and dinner are $4.99, $6.99, and $8.99; Sunday brunch is $8.99.

For the non-gamblers, there is **Mutiny Bay**, a 15,000-square-foot arcade entertainment center set in an ancient Moorish castle. It includes Disney-like animated robots, including propositioning pirates, wisecracking wenches, and various automated animals. In addition to a state-of-the-art

> **Pirate Flambé.** A special treat at the 8:30 and 10 P.M. shows on Friday and Saturday is a pyrotechnic stunt. One of the high-diving pirates bursts into flame when a charge is detonated on his ship. The highly trained stunt performer is covered with a flame-retardant gel and dressed in special clothing which is soaked in a flammable solution.

collection of video arcade machines (including the most unusual, Ridge Racer, a racing simulator which puts the controls within a *real* red sports car), there is a collection of carnival games, complete with barkers. One favorite entertainment is Castle Climb, which pits three participants in a race to scurry up one of three twisting rope ladders.

There is, of course, a casino: a sprawling 90,000-square-foot affair.

Entertainment at Treasure Island is built around a permanent 1,500-seat home for the **Cirque du Soleil,** the decidedly strange French-Canadian circus troupe. Cirque du Soleil (French for "circus of the sun") is one of the youngest of the great circuses of the world, begun in 1984 in Montreal, Quebec. Its genesis stemmed from a group of street performers gathered by 24-year-old Guy Laliberte.

What we've got here is a one-ring human circus, without animals, air cannons, motorcycles, or the other high-tech trappings of other shows. The emphasis is on strange and wonderful human performances. "Mystère" is the current production.

Treasure Island. 3300 Las Vegas Blvd. South; 2,900 rooms; 894-7111, 800-944-7444.

Beau Rivage

We've got an Egyptian pyramid, an Arthurian castle, a Roman bacchanal, and a British man-of-war. But it's so obvious: what Las Vegas *really* needs is an artificial lake in the desert with a French Riviera beach.

That, more or less, is what the plan-

The Battle of Buccaneer Bay, Treasure Island, Las Vegas

ning committee at Mirage Resorts must have pondered. What they came up with was the Beau Rivage, a $1 billion, 3,000-room extravaganza to be built on the Strip. The French name (pronounced boh ree-vaj) means beautiful shore, and comes courtesy of a hotel overlooking a lake in the French Alps.

According to plans, 166 acres of the former Dunes property will be covered by a lake by the end of 1997. The shores of the lake will be three feet below the level of Las Vegas Boulevard South; pedestrians will look down at the lake.

In the middle of the lake will be a 17-acre island with a 46-story hotel tower in an S-shaped curve, with all rooms having a lake view. The design includes a parking lot on the "mainland" with a pair of bridges linking it to the island, which will be surrounded with beaches, waterfalls, and tropical foliage. Guests will be able to take paddleboats out on the lake, or swim from beaches along the lake.

There will, of course, be a casino as well as restaurants, shops, and theaters. Plans call for a 1,500-seat "water theater" with a water skiing show and an underwater monster; the theatrics were set to be developed by the zany and creative Cirque du Soleil company, in near-permanent residence at the Mirage's Treasure Island hotel in Las Vegas.

Another part of the hotel will be "Casablanca," themed after the classic movie and including a restaurant set in a Moroccan bazaar.

The hotel is not planned as an economy resort, with room rates expected to start somewhere around $200 per night.

The Plank restaurant, Treasure Island, Las Vegas

Chapter 7
The Rest of the Strip

Aladdin Hotel & Casino

A once-major hotel gone poof, the Aladdin is valiantly struggling to reinvent itself under new management.

Opened in 1966, the hotel at one time was renowned for its huge theater, the 7,500-seat Aladdin Theater for the Performing Arts.

Today, it is a sprawling and somewhat disorganized resort tottering on the edge of a descent into low rollerdom. New promotions include a "Country Tonite" show and Bingothons. The country show features a live band and a cast of 12 dancers.

The prime eatery at the Aladdin is the dark and relatively intimate

Aladdin Hotel, Las Vegas

Elvis sighting number three. The King married Priscilla Beaulieu at the Aladdin in May of 1967. They met in Germany while Elvis was in the Army. The Elvis Suite is available for rent, too.

No short jokes, please. Wayne Newton was a short-time owner of the Aladdin.

Bingo! The Club Bingo opened in 1947 across the road from the El Rancho Vegas and featured a 300-seat bingo parlor in addition to more ordinary games. It was remodeled and renamed as the Sahara in 1952.

Fisherman's Port. Specials on a recent visit, priced from about $15 to $30, included prime rib, steak *au poivre,* lobster *fra diavolo,* and fresh catches.

Wellington's Steak House offers beef, seafood, and chicken entrees, priced from $10 to $25. Open 5 to 11 P.M.

The **Market Place Buffet** serves breakfast, lunch, and dinner.

At the 24-hour **Oasis Coffee Shop**, the Late Nighters specials include eggs, sausage, and ham for about $3. Daytime specials on a recent visit included steak and lobster, prime rib, and orange glazed chicken.

Sun Sun features Chinese, Vietnamese, and Korean cuisine. A complete meal of soup, fried rice, egg roll, selected entrees, and fortune cookie goes for less than $10. Other entrees, priced from about $13 to $20, on one visit included sizzling short ribs with black pepper sauce, half Peking duck, and seafood with bean curd.

"Country Tonite" is presented nightly except Tuesdays at 7:15 and 10 P.M.

Aladdin Hotel & Casino. 3667 Las Vegas Blvd. South; 1,100 rooms; 736-0111, (800) 634-3424.

Alexis Park

This is one of the favorite hotels for visitors to Las Vegas who either don't want to visit the casinos, or who want to be able to find a better-than-decent hotel room without having to navigate through a quarter-mile of flashing neon and jangling slot machines.

The Alexis Park is half a mile east of the Strip, and any time you need to visit an Egyptian pyramid, a pirate galleon, or an Arthurian castle you can get there from here.

The hotel includes 500 better-than-average rooms, including many multiroom suites. Several small, pricey restaurants offer gourmet fare. Guests can use a fully equipped health spa and lighted championship tennis courts. Because the hotel does not have the casino to bring in profits, room rates are a bit on the high side for Las Vegas.

Alexis Park Resort. 375 E. Harmon Ave.; 500 rooms; 796-3300, (800) 582-2228.

Algiers Hotel

An old-style motor court with rooms centered around a pool, it is located across the Strip from Circus Circus. Nothing fancy but it's a decent place to stay and a good value; the inner courtyard is surprisingly peaceful.

If you're a guest, be sure to check out the black-and-white photos of the hotel in its heyday; they're located on the wall near the registration desk.

The venerable **Manfredi's Limelight** restaurant relocated to the Algiers Hotel, offering classical Italian fare.

Algiers Hotel. 2845 Las Vegas Blvd. South; 105 rooms; 735-3311.

Bally's

A high-quality joint, very well kept up but without much of an identity, Bally's includes a large convention facility often used for overflow exhibits from some of the larger trade conferences, so the place really jumps when a big show is in town.

Some of the function rooms and decorations still bear reminders of the former incarnation as the original MGM Grand, with names like the Garland and Gable ballrooms. The original 2,100-room hotel opened in 1973 with all of the hoopla of a Hollywood premiere; Cary Grant was master of ceremonies for the event, and the ribbon was cut by Fred MacMurray and Raquel Welch. An additional 732-room tower was added in 1981.

In 1994, the hotel underwent another major transformation with the construction of a $14 million dramatic moving walkway structure from the Strip to its front door and the installation of a mirrored-glass facade to the main building. Dramatically illuminated arches in changing colors beckon passers-by into the hotel; of course, there aren't that many pedestrians on this part of the Strip, but it's the principle of the thing, we guess.

By the end of 1995, a privately financed monorail will link Bally's to the MGM Grand at the top of the Strip.

Bally's, Las Vegas

The nearly 3,000 rooms at the hotel range from standard kings and doubles to Hollywood Suites and the extravagant Royal Penthouse Suites which rent for about $1,500 per night.

The **Big Kitchen Buffet** is one of Las Vegas' more attractive buffet rooms. The daily brunch-breakfast includes eggs, bacon, carved ham, shrimp, herring, and salads. Well isolated from the casino, the only reminder of where you are lies in the keno boards and runners. If one of your measures of class is whether the shrimp in the shrimp cocktail is peeled or not and whether the orange juice served at breakfast is fresh or not, Bally's Big Kitchen passes on both counts. By no means as impressive or large as the Rio, it is nevertheless one of the better buffets in town. Brunch is served from 7:30 A.M. to 2:30 P.M. for $5.95; dinner is from 4:30 to 10 P.M. for $10.95.

A special **Sterling Brunch Sunday** is served in Caruso's Restaurant from 9 A.M. to 2:30 P.M. for $22.95.

Bally's Steak & Seafood is a simple, elegant, large room, originally called Barrymore's, decorated in blacks and whites. Specialties include herb-marinated chicken breast for about $20. Steaks and filet mignon range from $23.50 to about $30 for about a pound-and-a-half of sirloin or porterhouse. If you are a fan of lamb chops, on a recent visit you could order a set for about $26 with your choice of sauce: béarnaise, hollandaise, green peppercorn, wild mushroom, horseradish cream, applesauce, or mint jelly. Broiled lobster tails went for about $37.50. Appetizers include black bean soup and oysters Rockefeller. Top off your meal with espresso, cappuccino, Irish coffee, or Spanish coffee.

The *especialidades de la casa* at the Mexican restaurant **Las Olas**, priced from about $10 to $25, include *tampiquena* (skirt steak marinated in spices, grilled in a cheese enchilada) and *zihuatenejo* (salmon broiled with jalapenos and topped with Mexican hollandaise) for $10.95. Also offered are burritos, tacos, enchiladas, tostadas, and fajitas for about $4 to $10. You can wash it all down with a variety of Mexican beers. Las Olas, by the way, is Spanish for "the waves."

The new **al Dente** restaurant offers light Italian specialties from pizzas (we were intrigued by the unusual *schiacciatina* with grilled potatoes, black olives, shaved red onions, imported prosciutto, and freshly chopped arugula for $11.50). Pastas range from $11 to $14, and include *linguine con gamberettie e funghi* (thin flat pasta with jumbo shrimp, mushrooms, tomato, and broccoli), and *rondelle d'anatra* (duck-filled ravioli with porcini mushrooms and blueberries). We also saw grilled chicken with garlic, mushroom, sausage, potatoes, and lemon for $17, and *pescespada salmorrigglio,* fresh swordfish lightly grilled with garlic, lemon, olive, and Italian parsley for $22.50.

A particularly interesting restaurant at Bally's is **Seasons**, with a wide range of American offerings. The menu on one visit included offerings from about $15 to $30 such as ballotine of rabbit in roasted pine nuts and sage, Pacific mahimahi in lobster sauce, roast rack of lamb in rosemary and garlic, or a grilled veal chop in chantarelle sauce.

Caruso's is a world of Roman/rococo columns and mirrors, more elegant than Rome itself. Specialties, priced from about $15 to $30, included on a recent visit *linguini alla Sangiovannino* (linguini with porcini mushrooms, sun-dried tomatoes and a dash of cream), *linguini con frutti del mare* (scallops, mussels, clams, and shrimp in a zesty sauce), *pollo Angelo* (breast of chicken with mushrooms, artichokes, and fresh herbs), and sautéed chicken breast in hazelnut crust for $21.50. The high end of the menu includes lobster filled with smoked salmon mousse and light crayfish sauce at $49.95.

The **Coffee Shop** is open 24 hours and includes a wide range of sandwiches, appetizers, and finger foods. Offerings, priced from about $5 to $15, include chicken wings, Cobb salad, veal cutlet Parmesan, and the self-declared Bally's Famous Reuben.

The "Jubilee!" show at the Jubilee Theater, one of the most expensive and elaborate stage shows ever produced, has been running for 14 years. You'll see such events as the sinking of the Titanic and the destruction of the temple by Samson. The 190-foot-wide stage is 15 stories high from the bottom of the pit to the roof; it includes

Faulty tower. The Landmark Hotel was a landmark of the rise and fall of Las Vegas fortunes.

You would think that this distinctive tower, with its rooftop showroom and prime location directly across the road from the bustling Las Vegas Convention Center where hundreds of thousands of conventioneers gather, would be a license to print money. However, the Landmark was never a success.

Begun in 1961, its developers ran out of money before it was completed, and it stood as a shell of a building for several years. It was finally finished in 1966, and in 1969 it was the sixth Las Vegas hotel purchased by Howard Hughes. Red ink continued to flow and after passing through several hapless owners, it was closed in 1991.

Conventioneers eyed its barricaded parking lots and boarded-up casino as they strolled to or from the convention center. In 1994, the property was purchased at auction by the owners of the Riviera; they announced plans to take down the tower, although they immediately ran into objections from some residents who consider the Landmark a landmark.

On the rocks. The drinking age in Nevada is 21, and in most of the state there are no closing hours for liquor sales or consumption. Visitors from states with more restrictive laws will be surprised to see other laxities including free drinks at casinos. You don't suppose the casinos (and their partner the state) are happy to see customers a bit loosened, do you?

The Chairman's first office. Frank Sinatra made his Las Vegas debut in 1951 at the Desert Inn; it was the Sands, though, that served as his performing home for many years.

five separate areas to accommodate the massive set pieces. There are three main elevators and eight smaller ones to move scenery. Special effects include dry ice fog, real flames, and a tank that drops 5,000 gallons of water for the last moments of the Titanic.

Bally's Las Vegas. 3645 Las Vegas Blvd. South; 2,832 rooms; 739-4111.

Barbary Coast

A small place, almost possible to overlook in the glare of its neighbors, but actually worth a look-see. The Barbary Coast is decorated in a turn-of-the-century San Francisco motif with lots of wood, stained glass, and chandeliers. Dealers wear garters on their arms; cocktail waitresses wear the adornments on their upper legs.

Except for the sign for the McDonald's in the basement, you could almost believe you had been transported back in time. Actually, even the McDonald's sign is constructed from stained glass.

The few rooms at the Barbary Coast are elegantly appointed if you can get a reservation for one; they are mostly kept aside for the regular clientele. There is no pool, no showroom, and few other amenities except for a pleasant ambiance—which is not a bad thing for a hotel/casino.

Barbary Coast. 3595 Las Vegas Blvd. South; 198 rooms; 737-7111, (800) 634-6755.

Desert Inn

Named after the considerably greener and officially gambling-free hotel in Palm Springs, California, the Desert Inn debuted in 1950. In typical Las Vegas fashion, the grand opening was a blast: ceremonies were made to coincide with the test of an atomic bomb outside of town. The Desert Inn's lure included its lush golf course, a regular stop on professional tours.

Its most famous owner was the reclusive Howard Hughes, who bought the resort in 1967, marking the start of a string of real estate purchases by Hughes.

The Desert Inn is now one of the smaller but more posh complexes on the Strip, with just 821 rooms including 92 suites, located across from the Fashion Mall. It was purchased by ITT Sheraton in 1993. The hotel includes a relatively small casino, five restaurants and the Crystal Room showroom.

There is, of course, a casino with somewhat distracting overhead lighting and mirrors. It is small enough, though, to ignore if you choose.

Rooms are nicely appointed; some near the pool have cabana entrances to the water.

The nice variety of restaurants includes **Howan**, a Szechwan eatery with prix-fixe meals at about $26 per person for appetizer, pot stickers, sweet and sour soup, and *kung pao*. Dishes ordered from the menu range from $10 to $35 for Peking duck. Shark's fin soup is offered for about $22.

La Promenade is a pool-view coffee shop featuring salads and sandwiches.

The two finest restaurants at the Desert Inn are **Portofino** and **Monte Carlo**, sharing the same grand glass elevator and marble foyer at the back of the hotel.

Portofino is a very elegant Italian restaurant. Pasta and other entrees range in price from about $10 to $30 and include *paglia e fieno* (green and white pasta with pancetta, peas, and mushrooms in a rosa cream sauce). Other specialties include *osso bucco Milanese con risotto* (braised veal shank with rice), *arigosta fra diavolo* (lobster in spicy red sauce over linguine), and *tonna alla griglia Adriatico* (fresh tuna with sweet pepper and a caper sauce).

Monte Carlo offers French cooking in a very elegant peaches and cream setting. Entrees range in price from $26 to $35, and include *le Vieux favori* (steak Diane flamed in wine sauce with fresh mushrooms) for about $26.

In 1994, Desert Inn owner ITT Sheraton announced and then canceled plans for a $750 million, 3,500-room hotel to be located alongside the existing property. The Desert Kingdom would have included a 3,000-foot river. Instead, ITT chose to put its money into acquisitions, including the purchase of Caesars World, which in turn owns Caesars Palace on the Strip.

Desert Inn Hotel & Country Club. 3145 Las Vegas Blvd. South; 821 rooms; 733-4444, (800) 634-6906.

The Dunes (Gone but Not Forgotten)

There were no (real) sand dunes in sight, but there was a heck of a golf course out back of this Strip veteran. The hotel and particularly the casino had a checkered past right from the moment of its opening in 1955, with numerous failures and near failures.

The Dunes is also revered among some aficionados of Vegas for its pioneering contribution to local art: the topless show.

In 1993, the Dunes finally sank beneath the oncoming wave of development by Mirage Resorts. Actually, the hotel collapsed in a spectacular implosion that was part of the grand opening ceremonies for Mirage's Treasure Island hotel and casino; the demolition itself became the dramatic conclusion to a perfectly dreadful made-for-TV movie to promote the Treasure Island (and its publicity-loving chairman Steve Wynn).

In mid-1994, Mirage Resorts and Gold Strike Resorts announced plans to build a 3,000-room, $250 million themed hotel and casino at one end of the 164-acre site; the new property is intended as a low-roller attraction, with room rates projected at between $40 and $50 per night at opening in mid-1996. The deal allows Mirage to go for the low end of the market, while giving Gold Strike—a traditional "grind" operator—its first access to the Las Vegas Strip.

At the other end of the property will be the Beau Rivage resort, which we discussed in Chapter 6.

Flamingo Hilton

Las Vegas is one of the only places in the world where present owners proudly promote the gangster roots of the founder of the enterprise.

The original Flamingo was the invention in 1946 of Benjamin "Bugsy" Siegel, among the first of many underworld figures to recognize that they could make money from legal gambling at least as easily as they could from illegal activities.

Siegel built his 100-room pleasure palace in a spot that was at the time in the middle of nowhere, six miles south into the desert. He spent an astronomical $6 million and in the process began the world of Las Vegas glitz, a style that has not yet stopped escalating.

Less well known, though, is the fact that Bugsy's Flamingo had a very short life: it closed in January 1947 after just 14 days in business. Bugsy may have been a terrific gangster and certainly was possessed of a showman's vision, but he apparently was not the best businessman.

The hotel reopened later that year under new management, including front men for a different leading light of the underworld, Meyer Lansky. Lansky held onto a hidden interest in the hotel until late in the 1960s.

Still standing well into the 1990s was the Oregon Building, a rather unassuming low structure that included the fourth-floor penthouse once occupied by Bugsy Siegel. Features of the apartment reportedly included a trap door exit to a basement tunnel that led to a neighboring building.

The Hilton Corporation became the first major hotel chain to "legitimize" the Las Vegas casino market when it purchased the Flamingo in 1971. Since then, the company has been adding to the hotel complex almost continuously, building a series of huge towers with a total of nearly 4,000 rooms.

Strike central. The unionized staff members of the Frontier Hotel have been off the job for several years. They've settled into what seems to be a fixture of the Strip with around-the-clock picketing and small huts on the sidewalk. The hotel has remained open through it all; be aware of the situation if your travel agent offers you a special deal there.

Is that a deed in your pocket? Mae West was not only a successful entertainer, but she had a way with real estate, buying half a mile of undeveloped land on the Strip between the eventual site of the Dunes and Tropicana.

Like mother. Liza Minelli's first contractual appearance in Las Vegas occurred in 1965 at the Sahara; eight years earlier, her mother Judy Garland had brought her onstage during an appearance at the Flamingo.

The "final" stage in the expansion of the Flamingo Hilton is a 612-room tower plus 201 interval ownership suites at the rear of the property. A 15-acre pool expansion includes four pools, water slides, waterfalls, and an island of live flamingos.

The new construction, alas, required the demolition of Bugsy's suite and the other low-rise garden buildings. According to the Hilton publicists, earlier hopes to make a "historical area" of the Oregon Building's Bugsy Suite had to be scrapped because of architectural complications.

Before the addition, the 50,000-square foot hall included 1,649 slot, video poker, and other gambling machines; 49 blackjack tables; 7 craps tables; 2 roulette and Big-Six wheels; 2 mini baccarat, 1 pai gow poker, and 1 sic bo table. Table stakes run from $1 to $2,000. The Flamingo Hilton also offers 6 poker tables including Texas Hold 'em and 7-card stud. The Race and Sports Book offers bets on baseball, football, basketball, hockey, and horse racing.

Flamingo Hilton. 3555 Las Vegas Blvd. South; 3,530 rooms; 733-3111, (800) 732-2111.

Dino and the kid. Dean Martin and Jerry Lewis made their Las Vegas debut at the Flamingo in October of 1948; by 1952, their movies made them the top box-office draw in the country.

Gold Coast

A K-mart of a casino aimed at the low rollers, hidden behind a tremendous, blank stucco front wall, the Gold Coast features a sea of slot machines including an unusually large number of video poker machines. The Gold Coast sits next door to the Rio, a mile west of the Strip.

The main point of distinction for this hotel is the second floor 72-lane bowling alley (we can only imagine the noise level when all of the lanes are in use). There are also two movie theaters showing first-run movies and a bingo hall. At the back of the casino is a large dance hall featuring country and western high-kicking, with free classes offered. A liquor store sits directly off the casino.

Las Vegas high. The official elevation at McCarran International Airport is 2,174 feet, which is low by mountain standards but still nearly half a mile higher than coastal cities like Boston or New York.

Elevations range from 470 feet along the Colorado River in the southernmost section of the state to 13,143 feet atop Boundary Peak on the border with California. The approximate mean elevation is 5,500 feet.

There has been some attempt at creating an old California theme with pressed-tin ceilings and chandeliers, though not anywhere nearly as successfully as at the Barbary Coast on the Strip.

The **Buffet** is an unusually ordinary setting in one of the corners of the casino. Breakfast is served from 7 to 10:30 A.M. for $2.45, lunch is from 11 A.M. to 3 P.M. for $3.45, and dinner from 5 to 9 P.M. for $5.45. On Mondays and Tuesdays, the buffet features prime rib; the Friday seafood specialties are salmon, crab legs, and shrimp. A Sunday brunch is served from 8 A.M. to 3 P.M. for $4.45.

Mediterranean Room offers pasta, veal, and chicken with entrees ranging in price from $4 to $8 in an ordinary room with a keno display.

Finally, there is **Terrible Mike's** for burgers and hot dogs, and **Kate's Korner** for ice cream and malts.

Gold Coast Hotel & Casino. 4000 West Flamingo Road; 750 rooms; 367-7111, (800) 331-5334.

The Hacienda

When it was built in 1956 near McCarran Airport, this hotel was miles away from the rest of the Las Vegas action. Over the ensuing years, though, the

Room service. In Las Vegas, the average hotel room turns over every three or four days.

Strip has extended south to encompass the Hacienda; it now finds itself in the reflected gaudy glow of the Excalibur and the new Pyramid.

The Hacienda was, and is, a haven for low rollers. Among its pioneering efforts were some of the first gambling junkets; at one time it maintained its own fleet of 30 airplanes to bring the sheep in to be shorn.

Inside, though, the Hacienda is a pleasant world of southwestern arches and adobe. It is considerably quieter than its neighbors.

The **Charcoal Room** hides behind a massive wooden door, offering prime rib, steaks, veal chops, chicken, and other steakhouse specialties, priced from about $17 to $30.

The **New York Pasta Company** offers linguine, ziti, fusilli, farfalle, bucatini, and all sorts of other Italian inis and itis with sauce, with prices from about $7 to $13; also available are individual pizzas for $7 to $8.

The **Cactus Room** is an attractive coffee shop with burgers, chicken, and beef dishes priced from about $5 to $10.

The Hacienda's buffet room is an attractive room with a window wall facing the mountains.

Hacienda. 3950 Las Vegas Blvd. South; 1,140 rooms; 739-8911, (800) 634-6713.

Harrah's Las Vegas

What was once the largest Holiday Inn in the world is now one of the largest landlocked Mississippi riverboats, or at least so it would seem from the outside. The distinctive exterior covers an attractive hotel and, of course, a casino.

The hotel, which includes 1,725 rooms and suites, is based on a Bourbon Street and New Orleans French Quarter design, with its 450-foot-long Mississippi riverboat facade, complete with 20-story smoke stacks and a 5-story paddle wheel.

The casino offers 1,900 slot and video poker machines and a 200-seat bingo parlor with continuous games from 10:30 A.M. to 1 A.M.

Entertainment includes the 525-seat **Commander's Theatre** where "Spellbound—A Concert of Illusion" has settled in for a long run.

School's open. Harrah's is one of several major casinos that offer classes on how to lose more money. Actually, they call the classes casino education. Courses, taught by Captain Casino or the Riverboat Gambler, take place at various locations in the casino from Monday to Friday.

The **Galley Buffet** features at least 35 items. Breakfast is served from 7 to 11 A.M. for $3.79, lunch from 11 A.M. to 4 P.M. for $3.99, and dinner is from 4 to 11 P.M. for $5.49.

Claudines presents steak and fresh seafood in a turn-of-the-century setting for dinners from 5:30 to 10:30 P.M. Wednesday through Sunday.

All That Jazz offers low-priced breakfasts from 7 A.M. to noon and Southern-style dinners including ribs, shrimp, and catfish from 5 to 11 P.M.

Joe's Bayou features Cajun and Southern items

such as gumbo, jambalaya, blackened red snapper, frog legs, and catfish in a Louisiana bayou decor.

The Veranda Cafe is Harrah's 24-hour coffee shop.

A Bit of Harrah's History

Harrah's Casino Hotels is part of The Promus Companies, the only gaming firm that operates resorts in all five major U.S. casino markets: Las Vegas, Reno, Laughlin, Lake Tahoe, and Atlantic City. The company claims about a 10 percent share of the total U.S. gaming market.

Other hotels in the chain include Harrah's Laughlin, a 1,658-room establishment designed to look like a Mexican village, the only hotel-casino in Laughlin with a private soft sand beach. Harrah's also operates the 565-room Harrah's Reno, the 760-room Harrah's Atlantic City, the Harrah's Lake Tahoe Resort Casino, and Bill's Lake Tahoe Casino. Harrah's began operating two casino riverboats in Joliet, Illinois, and one in Vicksburg, Mississippi, in 1993.

Promus was created in 1990 as a spin-off of the Holiday Corp. Holiday sold its worldwide Holiday Inn Hotel chain to Bass PLC of Great Britain and established Promus as a gaming and lodging company. In addition to Harrah's, Promus also owns Embassy Suites, Hampton Inn, and Homewood Suites.

Harrah's Las Vegas Casino Hotel. 3475 Las Vegas Blvd. South; 1,725 rooms; 359-5000, (800) 634-6765.

Imperial Palace

An eclectic place with a vaguely Oriental theme, this deceptively large hotel (2,700 rooms) sprawls up, down, left, and right from its location at the heart of the Strip, across from the Mirage and Caesars Palace.

One reason for the chockablock disorganization of the place may lie in its origins as a one-man band, the dream of contractor Ralph Engelstad who began by buying the old Flamingo Capri Motel in 1971. Construction has gone on almost continually since then.

Today, by Las Vegas standards the IP is a bit on the ordinary side, although it has one distinction that is a secret to many visitors. Hidden away on an upper floor of a parking garage in back is an amazing collection of antique and unusual cars.

If you are a car buff, you don't want to miss this collection. Even if you are not the sort to gush over a classic 1928 Cadillac Dual Cowl Phaeton or an antique 1906 Ford Model K Touring Car restored to mint condition, there are other reasons to visit the museum. Concentrate instead on the history of vehicles used by world leaders, or come close to the transportation of some of the greatest stars of the 20th century. *Look for more details on the car collection in the section of this book about Museums in Las Vegas.*

There's a nominal admission charge for the museum, but you can often obtain free passes from casino employees stationed at the front entrance of the Imperial Palace. The museum is open every day, late into the night. *You will also find a free family pass in the coupon section of this book.*

Wild palms. The palm trees of Las Vegas are not from Las Vegas; in fact, they are not indigenous to the United States. They were imported by the early developers of the Strip to give some "class" to the somewhat barren desert. If it makes you feel any better, many of the palm trees of California and Florida are similarly out of place. Some of the palm trees close to the flames at the Mirage's volcano are not native to anywhere on this planet: they are made of fireproof concrete.

An able employer. The Imperial Palace has gone out of its way to be sensitive to the needs of the disabled, both in providing employment and in offering adapted accommodations for guests with special needs. The hotel's showroom includes infrared listening devices for guests with hearing difficulties. Available rooms include special features for visitors with a wide range of special needs.

The large casino is a busy place and you may need to drop bread crumbs to find your way back to your room. The best rooms can be found in the newer tower; the hotel features an Olympic-size swimming pool and health and fitness center. The long-running show at the Imperial Theatre Showroom is "Legends in Concert," which features re-creations of musical greats, including Elvis (surprise!), the Beatles, Buddy Holly, Liberace, Roy Orbison, Nat King Cole, Marilyn Monroe, and Judy Garland. Legends is presented twice nightly, except Sundays.

The Imperial Palace features a double-handful of restaurants, including the **Teahouse**, a 24-hour coffee shop, and the large **Emperor's Buffet**. Just to make things confusing, there is also a slightly more upscale buffet, for dinner only, called the **Imperial Buffet**, which is served in the Teahouse after 5 P.M.

Standard fare at the Teahouse Coffee Shop on one visit included a steak sandwich or chicken pot pie for about $6 to $8.

Embers, tucked away on the third floor, offers steak, seafood, and Continental dishes in an intimate setting; it is open 5 to 11 P.M. Wednesday through Sunday with reservations suggested. Menu offerings may include items such as orange roughy sautéed with macadamia nuts for about $15 and Alaskan king crab legs with lemon drawn butter for about $29.

Seahouse. A seminautical setting with offerings including stuffed mushrooms with crabmeat and shrimp fettuccine. Entrees range from about $10 to $20. Open 5 to 11 P.M. Friday through Tuesday with reservations suggested.

Other self-describing eateries include **Rib House** (5 to 11 P.M. Thursday through Monday), **Pizza Palace** (daily from 11 A.M. to midnight), and **Burger Palace**. **Betty's Diner** features ice cream, sandwiches, hot dogs, and snacks.

The **Ming Terrace** restaurant features Mandarin and Cantonese cuisine and is open daily from 5 P.M. to midnight. Among out-of-the-ordinary offerings are egg flower soup, black mushroom and sea cucumber stew, and sour cabbage with beef. Entrees range from about $10 to $20.

The various bars in the casino area each bear Japanese names: Geisha, Ginza, Kanpai, Mai Tai, Nomiya, and Sake. Probably the most unusual watering hole in the hotel is the **Duesenberg Lounge** in the Duesenberg Room of the Auto

Collection; aside from the decidedly unusual setting, you will also want to check out the antique western bar itself, which is straight out of the "Gunsmoke" era.

The Imperial Palace is located at the heart of the Strip, across from the Mirage and Caesars Palace. There is a small streetfront casino on the Strip with a set of escalators that can bring you under the hotel entrance driveway to the main casino. Look for various come-ons out front, including cheap popcorn and hot dogs, drink coupons, discounts on shows, and passes to the auto museum.

Imperial Palace Hotel & Casino. 3535 Las Vegas Blvd. South; 2,700 rooms; 731-3311, (800) 634-6441.

Maxim's

Only in Las Vegas would a place like this be overshadowed. Maxim's is on Flamingo Road, a half-block in from Caesars Palace and the Mirage and down the street from Bally's,

Maxim's Hotel/Casino. 160 E. Flamingo Rd.; 800 rooms; 731-4300, (800) 634-6987.

O'Shea's Hilton Casino

O'Shea's is a mecca for the low roller on the Strip, albeit at a pretty toney location. Now part of the Hilton family, it is located next to the Flamingo Hilton and across the road from Caesars Palace. The casino features nickel slots, offers cheap beer, and promises to cash out-of-state checks. It includes a mini food court with Burger King, Dunkin' Donuts, Subway, Orient Express, and Baskin Robbins stations.

Also within the casino is the **Magic & Movie Hall of Fame,** an exhibit of show business memorabilia and a magic store. A stage production, "That's Magic," is presented nightly at 7:30 and 9:30 P.M., with tickets priced at $14.95 per person.

O'Shea's Hilton Casino. 3555 Las Vegas Blvd. South; 697-2711.

Palace Station Hotel & Casino

The Palace is off the beaten track for most visitors, but it's a favorite of Las Vegas locals primarily because of its restaurants.

It's no small place, with more than 1,000 rooms and a large and lively casino with 2,200 slots and a 600-seat bingo parlor. Out-of-towners can use the hotel's shuttle bus for free transport to the Strip, about a mile east.

The hotel began simply named The Casino in 1976, the first area operation west of the Strip. It later took on the name Bingo Palace, concentrating on locals for business. In the 1980s, more expansion and a railroad theme was added, and the complex took on its present name.

Fisherman's Broiler was chosen as the best seafood restaurant in Las Vegas in a local newspaper's reader poll four out of five years. Offerings on a recent visit included mesquite broiled mahimahi, halibut, catfish, red snapper, and other fish for $11 to $15. Landlubbers can also order steak and chicken dishes, priced from about $14 to $18.

The Feast is called an "action buffet" by the management, because many

State your business.
Income from gambling
alone brought in more
than $2 billion per year
at the start of the 1990s,
with the industry grow-
ing rapidly. The casinos,
hotels, and nightclubs of
Las Vegas accounted for
two-thirds of the state's
gambling revenues.

**Odd Couple number
one.** Marlene Dietrich
and Louis Armstrong
appeared together at the
Riviera in 1962.

of the dishes are prepared for guests as they wait. These include breakfast omelettes made-to-order, stir-fry, broiled steaks, and grilled chicken. The Feast often wins "best" ratings from the locals, although on my visits it ranked in the second tier below spectacular offerings like those of the Rio, Caesars Palace, and the Golden Nugget.

The **Guadalajara Bar & Grille** offers authentic Mexican food along with Tex-Mex cuisine and Southwestern fare. Specialties, priced from as low as $5 all the way up to $40, include shrimp Guadalajara (shrimp stuffed with cheese, wrapped with bacon, and charbroiled) and crabmeat enchiladas. The Guadalajara Bar & Grille is also known for its cheap margaritas.

The **Iron Horse Cafe** offers coffee shop food 24 hours a day. The breakfast special is called the skillet breakfast, served in a cast-iron skillet containing three eggs, ham, sausage or bacon, home-fried potatoes, and all the toast or pancakes you can eat. Iron Horse also serves Chinese food from 11 A.M. to 5 A.M., with graveyard specials nightly from 11 P.M. to 5 A.M.

For lighter fare, there's the **Pasta Palace**, featuring pasta, scampi, veal, and pizza cooked in a woodburning oven. It's open daily for dinner from 5 to 11 P.M. Nightly specials include steak or lobster dinners.

Palace Station Hotel & Casino. 2411 W. Sahara Avenue; 1,041 rooms; 367-2411, (800) 634-3101.

Debbie Reynolds Hotel/Casino

Yes, *that* Debbie Reynolds, with her very own small hotel, casino, and museum, with a nightly show starring D.R. herself.

The 192-room hotel is between the Las Vegas Convention Center and the Strip, the former Paddlewheel Hotel. The hotel's marketing plans attempt to appeal to the mature visitor, presumably including the core of Reynolds' fans.

The **Hollywood Movie Museum** in the hotel includes Reynolds' private collection of memorabilia including treasures from *The Wizard of Oz,* Marilyn Monroe's "subway" dress from *The Seven Year Itch,* and Elizabeth Taylor's "entrance to Rome" costume from *Cleopatra.* Some of the decorations in the lobby are props from films.

Reynolds appears in the 500-seat **Star Theatre** Tuesdays through Sundays; on Fridays and Saturdays she hosts a musical and comedy jam session until deep into the night at the **Celebrity Cafe.** Her schedule of appearances in 1995 was expected to include at least half the year; if you are a serious Debbie-phile, be sure to check with the hotel before making plans. Her regular second banana is the wild and crazy Rip Taylor.

Debbie Reynolds Hotel/Casino/Hollywood Movie Museum. 305 Convention Center Drive; 192 rooms; 734-0711, (800) 633-1777.

The Riviera

A grand creation intended to bring a touch of the Côte d'Azur to the desert floor, the Riviera collapsed into bankruptcy almost immediately after its opening in 1955. A series of subsequent owners, including the Chicago mob, restored it to health and a tremendous spurt of new construction that culminated in another bankruptcy in 1983. Its latest new owners have given it a major spruce-up since.

The Riviera includes one of the largest casinos in town, at 125,000 square feet. Although there is not much pedestrian traffic on the Strip, the casino does have an open front like some of the downtown joints. Inside is a riot of reds and golds.

The **Rik Shaw** is an ordinary name for a lovely place to eat. A variety of entrees range in price from about $10 to $40. Specialties include abalone and black mushrooms for about $40, scallops with asparagus, and shrimp with pine nuts. Appetizers include crabmeat and asparagus soup, about $11, and abalone and chicken soup for about $28.

An overly simple name for another nice place is **Ristorante**, a classy Italian eatery decorated with brass, brick, and statuary with a fake skyline of Rome outside the painted "windows." It also has one of the more elaborate espresso machines in town. Specialties, priced from about $16 to $40, include calamari fritti, lobster fra diavolo, chicken vesuvio, veal piccata, and veal francaise. Pasta dishes include fettuccine Alfredo.

Filmography. Debbie Reynolds appeared in 32 major motion pictures, from classics like *Singin' in the Rain* and *The Unsinkable Molly Brown* to cult favorites including *Tammy and the Bachelor, How the West Was Won,* and even *The Singing Nun.* And for those who must know, Ms. Reynolds was born in 1932.

The chandelier was extra. Liberace opened the Riviera Hotel in 1955, with a record-setting contract paying $50,000 per week.

Citizen Welles. Orson Welles, a star of radio and cinema, appeared on stage at the Riviera in 1956 with a spectacular magic act.

Kady's Brasserie is a 24-hour coffee shop. Sandwiches and burgers range from about $6 to $8. At the time of our visit, an overnight special offered one pound of snow crab legs for $10, or steak and lobster for $8.88.

Kristofer's offers chicken or steak for about $20 and filet mignon and lobster tail for about $23.

Okay, we get the idea: they like simple names around here. The Riviera buffet is called the **Buffet** and breakfast is offered from 7 to 10:45 A.M. for $3.95, lunch is from 11 A.M. to 3 P.M. for $4.95, and dinner is from 4:30 to 11 P.M. for $6.95. Special themes are Mexican on Monday, Italian on Tuesday, Oriental on Wednesday, Hawaiian on Thursday, international on Friday and Saturday, and Western barbecue on Sunday.

Riviera Hotel & Casino. 2901 Las Vegas Blvd. South; 2,136 rooms; 734-5110, (800) 634-6753, (800) 634-3420.

The Sahara Hotel & Casino

Another golden Strip oldie, the Sahara opened in 1952 and was an immedi-

I wanna hold your cash. The Beatles put on a pair of concerts in 1964 under the sponsorship of the Sahara, but held at the large Las Vegas Convention Center. Tickets for the show averaged $4, and the Beatles were paid $25,000 for the appearance.

Country Mile. Plans have been afoot for several years for the conversion of the former El Rancho Hotel and Casino on the Strip. It may reopen as Country Land USA.

ate sensation for the size and gaudiness of its gigantic outdoor sign. Actually, it can draw its lineage back to the Club Bingo, which opened in 1947 and featured a 300-seat bingo parlor. It was sold, remodeled, and opened as the Sahara five years later. At the time, it was the first casino visitors would come to as they left downtown for the Strip.

The Sahara was designed with an African theme, including statues of camels out front. Plaster Arabs with camels are still out front, but today the once-grand Sahara seems a bit ground down by the sands of time although there are some signs of cosmetic spiffing-up here and there.

There's a sprawling casino, twisting and turning here and there and including a collection of old-style reel slot machines. The African theme is faintly echoed with waitresses in leopard-skin sarong-like outfits.

The current show at the Sahara is "Boy-Lesque," a female impersonation show starring Kenny Kerr; if this is the sort of thing you like, here is a fine example.

The showplace restaurant is **House of Lords**, a private and quiet room decorated in reds and blacks. Entrees, priced from about $21 to $30, include rack of lamb, chateaubriand, prime rib, and lobster tail.

The **Turf Club** offers a range of sandwiches from about $6 to $9 including the lox burger (lox, cream cheese, onion, and tomato on a bagel).

The **Caravan Coffee Shop** offers nightly specials such as New York strip steak and lobster for $8.88, or New York strip steak and eggs for $2.95.

The **Oasis Buffet** is upstairs and away from the bustle; the food, though, is spectacularly ordinary. Breakfast, lunch, and dinner go for $4.95, $5.95, and $7.95, with a $7.95 weekend brunch.

On the third floor is a **Mexican Village** eatery with entrees beginning at $5.95, plus the **La Terraza** with gourmet Italian cuisine.

Sahara Hotel & Casino. 2535 Las Vegas Blvd. South; 2,000 rooms; 737-2111, (800) 634-6411.

San Remo Casino & Resort

Part of the Ramada group, the San Remo began as a lure to the business traveler and as such delivers decent rooms and service. There is, of course, a casino, too. Recent expansions have added a bit more glitz and a lot more rooms.

The San Remo is located about a block east of the Strip, next door to its flashy corporate neighbor, the Tropicana.

The fancy restaurant at the San Remo is **Le Panache**. Closed Mondays and Tuesdays, gourmet dining is offered from 5 to 11 P.M. Specials, priced from about $16 to $25, included on a recent visit filet and lobster, porterhouse steak, *cotelette de veau maison* (veal chop stuffed with mushroom duxelles and topped with Montrachet cheese and concasse of tomato), and *crevettes kiev* (large prawns stuffed with herb butter and crab-meat). The specialty soup is *le bisque d'homard maison* (lobster bisque, seasoned with French cognac, garnished with lobster meat).

> **Elvis sighting number four/Odd Couple number two.** Elvis Presley posed on stage in 1956 in a gold lamé jacket at the Riviera piano while Liberace, wearing Elvis' rocker duds, whipped at a guitar.

Pasta Remo offers fine Italian dining from 5 P.M. to midnight. Lighter fare, including Italian subs and salads, is available at **Luigi's Deli.**

The **Ristorante dei Fiori** coffee shop and buffet is open 24 hours. At the time of our visit, a prime rib special for $3.95 had a small catch: you had to show a room key from any other Las Vegas hotel and register at the Money Club window. With such deals, though, there is no requirement you gamble.

The **Sushi Bar**, open from 6 P.M. to midnight, offers prix-fixe assortments for $16 to $22. Miso soup is priced at $1.50.

The **Buffet** is available for breakfast from 7 to 10 A.M. for $3.50, lunch is served from 11 A.M. to 2 P.M. for $5.95, and dinner is from 5 to 9 P.M. for $6.95. A Saturday and Sunday champagne brunch is offered 7 A.M. to 2 P.M. for $5.95.

San Remo Casino & Resort. 115 East Tropicana Avenue; 711 rooms; 739-9000, (800) 522-7366.

The Sands Hotel Casino

In this one hotel/casino can be seen a great part of the modern history of Las Vegas. The Sands has gone from a shady past to a Hollywood connection to Howard Hughes to a mega-corporation to its current ownership by the sponsor of the huge computer convention that descends on Las Vegas once a year.

The Sands opened in 1952 with 200 rooms. It had been built by Texas gaming entrepreneur Jakie Friedman and an assortment of alleged gangsters from around the country. Also among the owners were Frank Sinatra and Dean Martin, who each held significant minority interests. Their business involvement made it natural for them to make the Sands their stage for Las Vegas appearances, and also attracted their friends including the famous Rat Pack.

The hotel was purchased by Howard Hughes' Summa Corporation in 1966; soon thereafter there was a falling out with Frank Sinatra, who moved his act to Caesars Palace. In 1981, the hotel was sold to a new Texas owner, but two years later Summa regained control of the hotel. In 1988, it was purchased by Kirk Kerkorian's MGM Grand, Inc., but in one of the more interesting twists of ownership, two months later the Sands ended up in the hands of the Interface Group, the sponsor of the Comdex computer trade show that virtually takes over Las Vegas for a week each year. Interface added a giant convention center at the back of the Sands property.

The Sands Expo & Convention Center is used primarily for the annual Comdex convention. The first phase of construction put about 615,000 square feet of

Thank you for coming. About 50 percent of the state's workers are in the service trade, with 25 percent directly employed by a casino or associated hotel.

convention space on one level, plus an underground parking lot for 1,100 cars; future plans call for enlarging the Center to 1,000,000 square feet, which would make it the world's largest single-level convention facility.

In days past, the Copa Room was one of the hangouts for the famed Rat Pack of Frank Sinatra, Sammy Davis, Jr., Joey Bishop, Dean Martin, and Peter Lawford, each of whom also appeared on stage at the Sands.

Opening act. The Sands in 1952 featured Danny Thomas at its debut; also appearing were Billy Eckstine and Jane Powell.

The premier dining establishment is the **Regency Room**, open from 6 to 11 P.M. nightly; reservations are suggested. The room is elegantly paneled, with widely spaced tables. Its menu features specialties, priced from about $20 to $32, such as steak Diana, Long Island duckling, veal francaise, and lobster tail with filet mignon. Appetizers include oysters Rockefeller.

Odd Couple number three. Former President Harry S. Truman appeared at the piano with Jimmy Durante at the Sands in 1962.

The **Garden Terrace** is a California-theme coffee shop with a view of internal gardens, serving a breakfast buffet. A breakfast menu is also available, featuring selections including omelettes for about $5. Lunch offerings when we visited included tuna salad club with cucumbers, egg, and tomato for about $6. Dinner specials, priced from around $15 to $20, included lamb chops with mint jelly, and a whole Maine lobster buffet, including pasta, side dishes, and salads nightly except Saturday. (In case you're interested, and very hungry, you are limited to three lobsters per person.) Overnight specials included steak and eggs or ham and eggs from 11 P.M. to 5 A.M. for $2.99.

The **House of Szechwan**, an attractive, tiny room decorated with mirrors and lanterns, opens at 4 P.M. Appetizer specialties include *gee po gai* (paper-wrapped chicken). Entrees, about $12 to $18 each, include such dishes as *chow siong sin* Double Happiness (a combination of shrimp and scallops with fresh vegetables in wine sauce), and oyster beef (sliced beef sautéed with scallions, snow peas, sliced mushrooms, and Chinese oyster sauce). Early bird specials are available Monday through Friday.

Sands Hotel Casino. 3355 Las Vegas Blvd. South; 720 rooms; 733-5000, (800) 634-6901.

The Stardust

A venerable establishment, if you are somehow able to overlook an extremely checkered history of involvement by various factions of organized crime. For many years, the hotel was a semi-legit operation of the Chicago mob, a connection which ended with the discovery of a massive "skimming" scandal—the raking off of profits from gaming operations before they were recorded and subject to taxation.

The Stardust was famous for its reproduction of the "Lido de Paris" floorshow, which saved millions on costume expenses for its showgirls, many of whom were dressed only in, err, stardust. The Lido finally departed a few years back, after more than 30 years on stage. The current show is "Enter the Night," which features just a bit more glitz than sex.

There is a Stardust and a Stardust: the newer West Tower building is quite nice, the old strips of low motel buildings at the back of the hotel are generally not the sort of place you'd want to write home about, and the East Tower is somewhere in between.

The casino is a busy, intense floor with a sea of machines.

There is an interesting mix of middle-of-the-road restaurants, including several located along an attractive indoor street of shops.

The classy **William B's Steakhouse** is decorated like an old Chicago steakhouse in black and white. Entrees range from $15 to $20. Specialties include petite filet mignon for $16, king porterhouse for $20, and boneless double center cut pork chop for $16. Veal or chicken dishes are prepared with your choice of style, including Oskar, marsala, angelo, francaise, parmigiana, piccata, and William B (coated with flour and served with avocado and crab).

> **They could use a toll-booth.** According to the 1990 census, Nevada had a population of 1,201,833, an increase of 50.1 percent over 1980, making Nevada the fastest growing state in the nation.
>
> The average population density was 7 per square mile.
>
> The majority of the state population was concentrated in the Las Vegas and Reno metropolitan areas, with 88 percent of the population in urban areas. (The remainder of the state had fewer than 1 person per square mile.)
>
> The official number for the population of Las Vegas is listed at 232,370, with the total population of Clark County at 834,907.

The **Tres Lobos Mexican Restaurant and Cantina** is open for dinner only, from Wednesday to Sunday, with entrees priced from $5.95. Food is attractively presented in this lively room just off the casino floor.

On the menu at **Ralph's Diner**, they say: "If it is not on the menu—ask. We'll see." They don't say what they'll do, though. Options that are listed on the menu include burgers for about $5 and chili for a bit less.

There's a branch of the **Tony Roma's** chain, offering a full slab of baby back ribs, barbecue chicken and ribs combo, or a half barbecue chicken, priced from about $9 to $16.

Toucan Harry's is an attractive coffee shop. Dinner specials on a visit included half orange glazed chicken, fantail shrimp, and steak and lobster for $5 to $8. A 24-hour special is eggs with bacon or sausage for about $4.

The Stardust's **Warehouse Buffet** is one of the better buffets in town, set in a reproduction of a food locker, with huge cans of food stacked about. The food is, thankfully, fresher than that. Breakfast Monday through Saturday is served from 7 to 10:30 A.M. for $4.95, lunch is from 10:30 A.M. to 3 P.M. for $5.95, and dinner every night is from 4 to 10 P.M. for $7.95. A Sunday champagne brunch is offered 7 A.M. to 3 P.M. for $6.95.

Stardust Resort & Casino. 3000 Las Vegas Blvd. South; 2,340 rooms; 732-6111, (800) 634-6033.

Driven to come. About half of the visitors to Las Vegas arrive by car.

The Tropicana

An interesting mix of colorful Miami schmaltz and flashy Las Vegas glitz, the Trop is among the favorite "old" hotels on the Strip. First built in 1957, it has had its share of mob intrigue and corruption over the years. It was restored in recent years under the ownership of the Ramada Corporation.

Dear landlord. Nevada, which entered the Union on October 31, 1864, as the 36th state, covers 110,561 square miles, the seventh largest state in the country. As big as Nevada is, consider the fact that 86 percent of the land area is owned by the federal government.

Once all alone at the top of the Strip, now it is almost possible to miss in the flow of the flashy Excalibur, Luxor, and MGM Grand across the road. Recently, though, they added to the overdose at the corner with a tropical village facade complete with huge Easter Island–like statues and a new main entrance; in case you still miss the point, a nightly laser light show is presented.

Overhead walkways connect the Tropicana and the MGM and Excalibur hotels; there are escalators to take you up to the crossings, but the walkways themselves are exposed.

The leaded stained glass ceiling above the tables in the casino is worth a peek, and lovers of Miami staples such as dancing water fountains and chandeliers will not be disappointed. Machines sit under a blue sky in a forest of bamboo trees. Overall, it's a lively place, well kept up.

In keeping with its tropical theme, there is an emphasis on watery decorations including a five-acre water park with lagoons, spas, waterfalls, and what is claimed as the world's largest indoor/outdoor swimming pool. There are dozens of exotic birds and fish in surrounding cages and pools.

There is even a swim-up blackjack table. The entire area is carefully lit at night, including a laser light show.

Standard rooms are somewhat ordinary, jutting off long boring hallways.

The long-playing show at the Trop is the "Folies Bergere," which features $5 million in sets and costumes.

There's an attractive **Food Court** offering ice cream, pizza, hot dogs, and deli specialties.

The **Rhapsody Brunch** is in an elegant setting, which includes a sushi bar and a selection of smoked fish. Entrees range from about $18 to $30 and include duckling Chambord (Long Island duckling with black raspberry liqueur). The obligatory Las Vegas appetizer of oysters Rockefeller is available for about $10.

Mizuno is your basic tableside barbecue teppen yaki restaurant. The **Ristorante di Martino** offers Italian specialties in a simple and modern decor. And there is the **El Gaucho Steak House** for meat, chicken, and seafood.

The **Winners Coffee Shop** is a somewhat ordinary place, overly bright under fluorescent bulbs.

Tropicana Resort and Casino. 3801 Las Vegas Blvd. South; 1,910 rooms; 739-2222, (800) 634-4000.

Vegas World: New Weirdness Awaits

If P. T. Barnum was still alive, we think he'd have a little place on the Strip in Vegas. Barnum is long gone, but there's always Bob Stupak.

Bob Stupak's Vegas World was not the biggest, not the most spectacular, not the most famous—but Vegas World just may have been the loudest hotel and casino in town. Located at the bottom of the Strip, over the years it was one of the most iconoclastic casino operations in town. And the city has watched for half a decade as Stupak has slowly built his Barnumesque Stratosphere Tower from the ground . . . almost to completion.

In 1993, financial problems forced Stupak to sell much of his ownership of the property, but his new partners, Grand Casinos, had kept him in place as the front man.

The hotel was closed at the start of 1995 and was to be demolished. In its place—with completion expected sometime in 1996—was to be a new 1,500-room hotel with a 97,000-square-foot casino.

Have we mentioned Bob Stupak yet? Stupak grew up in a world of gambling; his father ran crap games in Pittsburgh for a living. According to his own autobiography—available at the casino—young Stupak began playing the numbers in third grade. He went on to run crap games in the army. He arrived in Las Vegas in 1972 with bigger dreams and parlayed a few small casinos into one big and splashy one. Stupak had his name on the hotel and on the carpet and his name and picture on the chips.

In addition to gambling, a preoccupation of Stupak is the space program. There were pictures of the planets and spacecraft on the exterior of the hotel and the casino was decorated in a space theme (including one area with replicas of spacecraft floating overhead).

At one time, the casino even displayed an actual piece of the moon in a case. The rock was mounted in a presentation trophy that was inscribed as a present from former President Richard Nixon to Anastasia Somoza, the former president and dictator of Nicaragua. The hotel was officially mum on how Stupak obtained the trophy, but we have to imagine there was a gambling debt involved.

In 1991, Stupak announced the Stratosphere Tower, a gigantic poured concrete structure. Construction began soon afterward, but proceeded in an on-again and off-again process. For a long time it seemed that Stupak was waiting until he had a few million extra dollars sitting around in his desk drawer before he ordered up a few more feet of the tower.

The tower was intended to reach to 1,012 feet when completed, which would have made it the tallest in America. Stupak told the world that it would be taller than the Leaning Tower of Pisa, the Tower of London, the Great Pyramids, the Washington Monument, Seattle's Space Needle, and the Eiffel Tower. Why, Stupak said, it will even be taller than the Tower of Babel; we haven't the slightest idea how he managed to calculate that particular piece of press release puffery.

Bigger than life. At various times, Vegas World claimed to offer more than 100 percent payout on some video poker machines. What does that mean? It means that if played properly, over the long haul, they would pay out more than they would collect from an individual player. It does not mean that a bad player—or even an average player—will win anything at all.

Some are more equal than others. At Vegas World, as at some other casinos, it is worth your while to pay attention to the payoff rates promised on slots and video poker machines. Some machines in the same casino will have different payouts. One way to check this is to look at the payout for a full house in poker; one bank of machines offered a standard 40:1, while another set of machines promised 50:1.

Construction, though, stalled in 1993; in 1994, Stupak and his new investors stunned Las Vegas with news that he planned to extend it 800 feet more to make it the tallest tower in the world at 1,825 feet, surpassing even the massive CN Tower in Toronto at 1,815 feet and 40 stories higher than the tallest building in the world, the puny 1,454-foot Sears Tower in Chicago.

But money, engineering, and concerns about planes landing at McCarran Airport a few miles away resulted in a compromise: the new peak of the Strip will be 1,149 feet high.

But wait: it gets weirder. At the top of the tower will be a revolving restaurant, a lounge, several wedding chapels, indoor and outdoor observation platforms, stores, and (surprise) a casino. However, we're looking forward to the debut of the **Space Shot**, a thrill ride that will allow 16 riders to circle at the top of the tower and drop a few hundred feet in free-fall before being reeled back in.

By the way, Las Vegas is subject to earthquakes, harsh desert winds, and the occasional underground nuclear test in the neighborhood. The designers assure us this has all been taken into account, including computer simulations and wind tunnel testing.

Check with us again next year; we'll fill you in on the next chapter in the stupendous Stupak story.

Bingo Parlors on the Strip and Downtown

Phone numbers are in (702) area code.

Aladdin Hotel. Games from 9 A.M. to 11 P.M. on the odd hours. 736-0111.

Arizona Charlie's. All day, on the odd hours. 258-5200.

Binion's Horseshoe. 8 A.M. to midnight on the even hours. 382-1600.

Ellis Island. 9 A.M. weekdays.

Gold Coast. 8 A.M. to 2 A.M. on the even hours. 367-7111.

Harrah's. Continuous from 10:30 A.M. to 1 A.M. 369-5232.

Palace Station. 9:45 A.M., then on the odd hours until 1 A.M. 367-2411.

Sam's Town. 7:30 A.M., then on the odd hours through 1 A.M., plus 2:45 A.M. 454-8063.

Santa Fe. 10 A.M. to 10 P.M. on the even hours. 658-4900.

Showboat. 11 A.M. to 7 A.M. on the odd hours. 389-9118.

Chapter 8
Glitter Gulch, Then and Now

Downtown Las Vegas was where it all started, and though the flashiest and largest of the casinos have moved south to the Strip, there is still a great deal of life and excitement on Fremont Street.

In fact, it was often the neon splash of Fremont—nicknamed Glitter Gulch—that was used as the picture to represent all of Las Vegas. The lights of the various signs were so bright in the narrow man-made canyon that pedestrians enjoyed electric noon at midnight.

The stretch was used as the setting for many movies, including *Honey, I Blew Up the Baby, The Stand,* and *Diamonds Are Forever.*

With this, the 1996 edition of the *Econoguide,* I've had to move all of the above into the past tense. At the end of 1995, Fremont Street went under cover. Think of it as the Glitter Gulch Theme Park and Indoor Gambling Mall and you'll get the idea.

The $63 million "Fremont Street Experience" put a five-block-long 100-foot-high cover over the main drag. Beneath the canopy is a 1.4 million-light "sky parade" and light show. The space frame drops behind the famous signs of Glitter Gulch.

Winding, landscaped paths meander through the pedestrian mall. At the head of Fremont Street is a new parking garage with 1,500 parking spaces, plus the Plaza Shops with 50,000 square feet of store space, and the Promenade Shops at Fremont Street, a blend of patio cafes and marketplace shopping in kiosks, street carts, and pavilions.

The canopy is being funded by a combination of redevelopment funds from the City of Las Vegas Downtown Redevelopment Agency, the Las Vegas Convention and Visitors Authority, along with an $18 million contribution by a consortium of downtown casinos. Hotel guests will pay an increased room tax in downtown as part of the package.

Along with the cover over Glitter Gulch, many of the downtown casinos will undergo renovations. Fitzgerald's Casino Hotel plans to add more rooms, restaurants, and parking. The Fremont Hotel plans to remodel its public areas including marble wall coverings, flooring, and facades. At the California Hotel, a new west tower will add 145 rooms. The Golden Gate Hotel will add land-scaping and wood to the exterior to enhance its San Francisco theme.

As a parting gesture, Fremont Street saw one last slow-speed parade of classic automobiles on the night of Sept. 8, 1994; following the salute, Las Vegas' first paved street was closed, possibly forever.

While the Strip is (mostly) opulent, Glitter Gulch is (mostly) wide open and a lot of fun. And, according to gambling experts, the downtown casinos pay off a bit better on their slots and many table games including blackjack.

Although some of the side streets of downtown are a bit scary, even to the locals, a visitor who parks in one of the casino parking garages is unlikely to be exposed to the seedier side of town. Most casinos offer free parking for several hours if you get your parking ticket validated inside; there is no requirement that you spend a dime at the tables or machines. With the completion of the Fremont Street Experience will come a new parking plaza off the top of what used to be Glitter Gulch.

✦MUST-SEE✦ Golden Nugget Hotel & Casino

Part of the Mirage dynasty, the Golden Nugget is the class of downtown. The lively casino is decorated with a San Francisco theme, painted in white and gold with ornate chandeliers and ceiling fans. The new tower at the hotel is a local landmark with its brilliant gold reflective glass; there are a total of 1,907 rooms including one- and two-bedroom suites, 27 luxury apartments in the Spa Suite Tower, and six Penthouse Suites in the North Tower.

Golden Nugget, Las Vegas

Be sure to walk deep into the casino to a display case near the registration desk to check out a few real golden nuggets. The most impressive is the Hand of Faith Nugget, which is claimed to be the world's largest piece of unrefined gold. Weighing in at 875 troy ounces (almost 62 pounds), it was discovered with a metal detector in 1980 by a young man prospecting behind his trailer home near Wedderburn, in Victoria, Australia.

As aficionados of the brewing art, we were most impressed with the central **38 Different Kinds of Beer Bar**, which delivers guess-how-many-kinds of guess-what. Actually, there may be more than 38 types at the time you visit; some beers are available in standard and light versions.

Each of the restaurants at the Golden Nugget is a small gem, too. They include:

Stefano's. A truly lovely small room, well insulated from the casino. Decorated like a real Roman hideaway, only much cleaner and newer. You'll be served by flocks of waiters in long aprons. A few sample offerings from one recent visit: *penne Bolognese* (fluted penne pasta served with veal meat sauce), or *zuppa de pesce "cioppino"* (shrimp, scallops, lobster, and squid in a light tomato fish broth) for about $22.

Lillie Langtrie's. Nearby is another quiet, lovely room, decorated in gold and mirrors and serving Cantonese fare by way of San Francisco. (Miss Lillie, also known as the Jersey Lily, was a famous English actress who made her name in the United States with a tour in the 1880s that included the Wild West; she was the Madonna of her day.)

Golden Nugget, Las Vegas

How many kinds? Available American brands at the 38 Different Kinds of Beer Bar on one visit included Coor's, Anchor Steam, Budweiser, Michelob, Miller, Pete's Wicked Ale, and Rattlesnake. Also available are Australia's Foster's and Red Back; Canada's Labatt's and Moosehead; China's Tsingtao; England's Bass Ale and Watney's Red Barrel; Germany's St. Pauli Girl, Beck's, and Hofbräu; Holland's Heineken, Amstel Light, and Grolsch; Ireland's Harp Lager and Guinness Stout; Italy's Peroni; Japan's Sapporo and Asahi; Mexico's Bohemia, Carta Blanca, Dos Equis, Corona, Simpatico, Pacifico, and Negra Modelo; the Philippines' San Miguel Pale; Scotland's McEwan's Ale, and Switzerland's Lowenbräu.

Sky high. North Las Vegas, a few miles beyond downtown, is the home of Nellis Air Force Range. The North Las Vegas Air Show takes place each fall, usually near the end of October, drawing tens of thousands of visitors. Events include all sorts of aircraft, hot air balloons, vintage autos, and various celebrations of Indian heritage.

California Pizza Kitchen. An outpost of the California-based wood-fired pizza chain (another location is within the Mirage on the Strip) it features more than 25 varieties of pizza ranging from the traditional to the unusual (BLT, barbecue chicken, duck sausage, Cajun, and goat cheese toppings among them) in personal sizes priced from about $7 to $10 on regular or honey-wheat dough. We were also intrigued by the possibility of a *moo-shu* chicken calzone.

Pasta offerings run from tomato and herb to Thai chicken and ginger-black bean sauce. The Pizza Kitchen is hidden away in a side room near the registration desk.

Golden Nugget Buffet. Breakfast Monday through Saturday from 7 to 10:30 A.M. for $4.75, lunch is 10:30 A.M. to 3 P.M. for $7.50, dinner is 4 to 10 P.M. for $9.50, and champagne Sunday brunch is 8 A.M. to 10 P.M. for $9.95.

Poker Parlor Snack Bar. Is this mix strange enough for a poker parlor? We think so: teriyaki chicken sandwich, assorted California sushi rolls, or grilled Spam with steamed rice, each for about $4.

Golden Nugget Hotel & Casino. 129 East Fremont Street; 1,907 rooms; 385-7111, (800) 634-3454.

Las Vegas Club

A lively, informal small club with a high mirrored ceiling, the Las Vegas Club holds a special attraction for baseball and blackjack fans. The Las Vegas Club opened in 1905 as the Overland Park Hotel, changing to its current name in 1931.

The casino claims the most liberal blackjack rules in the world; the somewhat complex rules do seem to reduce the house advantage, at least for experienced and knowledgeable players.

Among the special rules are these: you can double down on any of the first two or three cards; you can surrender your original two cards for half your bet; you can split and resplit aces up to two times; you can split and resplit any pair any time you choose, and any hand of six cards totaling 21 or less is an automatic winner. The Las Vegas Club somewhat compensates for its loose rules by dealing cards from a multi-deck shoe, reducing the edge for card counters.

But back to the atmosphere: you'll notice things are a bit different when you see the uniforms worn by the dealers; instead of white shirts and string ties, they are each decked out in baseball jerseys. The cocktail waitresses wear cheerleader outfits.

Take the hint and head toward the back of the casino to examine the great collection of old sports photos and memorabilia—mostly baseball and boxing—near the Dugout Restaurant. Photos on the wall date back as far as the 1920s.

Among the favorite sports stars is former speed-ster Maury Wills; you'll find his original 1950 minor league contract to the Hornell Baseball Association in upstate New York. He was paid a whopping $150 a month with a $500 signing bonus. Also on display are Wills' shoes from 1962, the year he set a major league record with 104 stolen bases.

(Wills, by the way, had a short career on stage in Vegas; among his appearances was in a show at the Sahara in 1969 where he played saxophone.)

Food service at the Las Vegas Club is better than at the ballpark:

The Dugout. At a recent visit, the All Star Special was eastern prime rib au jus for about $6. The three-egg Hall of Fame omelettes go for about $5 and are available in cheese, ham and cheese, spinach, and chili and cheese varieties.

Great Moments Room. Specialties, priced about $13 to $20, include *scaloné,* a combination of abalone and shrimp sautéed and finished with light white wine and garlic sauce, for about $14. Also offered on a recent visit was a julienne of grilled boneless breast of chicken over fresh garden greens with sesame oil and balsamic vinegar, and lemon chicken scallopini.

Las Vegas Club Hotel & Casino. 18 E. Fremont Street; 224 rooms; 385-1664.

Pawn Shop Plaza. How bad can things get? There is a group of pawn shops between the Golden Nugget and the Pioneer Club on both sides of Fremont Street. There is no *Econoguide* to using the services of a hock shop; there are no great deals for sellers and few bargains for buyers at such a place.

Truth in advertising. On the Strip heading into downtown, keep an eye out for the tiny Normandie Hotel on the left, a rather jarring pink stucco motor court. On one visit, the sign outside proclaimed, "Elvis Slept Here."

We suspect it was on an off night.

(By the way, the other side of the sign read, "Highly Recommended by Owner.")

Binion's Horseshoe Hotel & Casino

One of the eclectic oddities of Nevada, and worth a visit for that reason alone, Binions is a rambling, dim place semidecorated in dark browns, blacks, and reds.

Benny Binion was one of Las Vegas' old-time gambling men who ran a casino, which is quite a different thing from today's business people who own gambling casinos. However, it is worth noting that Steve Wynn, the flamboyance behind the Mirage and Treasure Island, was a protégé of Binion in his younger days.

Binion created his Horseshoe in the late 1940s out of two old downtown properties, the Apache Hotel and the Eldorado Casino. Today the casino has

Trivia question. Who is pictured on a $10,000 bill? The answer: Salmon Chase, Chief Justice of the U.S. Supreme Court under President Lincoln and a major political figure of his time.

Here's an even more obscure question: What is pictured on the back of a $10,000 bill? The answer: nothing. It says in big print: "The United States of America. Ten Thousand Dollars."

And for those of you whose minds run to investment strategies, consider this: if the million dollars in the Horseshoe's display was invested in a 10 percent account compounded monthly, it would be earning about $105,000 per year; at the same interest rate over the course of 10 years, the million would have grown to $2.7 million.

absorbed an entire city block, including the old Mint Hotel next door and the show is run by Benny's son Jack.

The casino is considered a haven for the "serious" gambler, with some of the highest limits in Las Vegas.

Work your way all the way in to the back of the casino and stand for a moment and gawk at the display of a cool million dollars in bills. There are 20 rows and five columns of $10,000 bills mounted between two sheets of thick glass. There's a guard and an alarm system, too. (Another million dollar display—made up of a jumbled mix of coins and bills—can be found at Bob Stupak's Vegas World between downtown and the Strip.)

You can also find the Poker Hall of Fame on the right wall of the casino, with pictures of the famous and infamous card players of all time.

Before you leave, go for a ride on the glass-walled elevator for a great view of downtown.

Coffee shop. The overnight special at the time of our visit was a 10-ounce New York strip steak with salad, potato, rolls, and butter for $2. Deeper into the night and into lunch, a chef's salad was offered for about $7.

Seafood Buffet. A downtown favorite, served from 4 to 10 P.M. for about $13, it includes giant shrimp, crab legs, salmon, oysters, mussels, a carving station for prime rib and seven hot entrees. Specials can include catfish and orange roughy.

Binion's Horseshoe Casino & Hotel. 128 E. Fremont Street; 354 rooms; 382-1600, (800) 937-6537.

Jackie Gaughan's Plaza

An attractive and well-kept hotel at the head of Fremont, it was for many years called the Union Plaza as a reminder of the former railroad interests that once controlled Las Vegas and of the railroad station that formerly occupied the spot. The hotel today is still connected to the Amtrak station at one end and the Greyhound terminal at the other.

The hotel was opened in 1971 on the spot where the land auction of 1905 took place. At the time, it had the largest casino in Las Vegas, a distinction that has since been passed up the Strip several times.

In late 1995, the Plaza will take on a new aura as the top end of the Fremont Experience in the new covered Fremont Street. Over the years it has thrown off some of its somewhat stodgy history, featuring rock and country music shows.

The Plaza offers a wide range of gambling opportunities, beginning with rarely seen penny slots and nickel progressive jackpot machines and moving upward from there.

The casino also occasionally features one of our least favorite come-ons: an instant tax refund stand. Why don't we like that? Even assuming you come to the desk with a professionally prepared tax return, what you are essentially doing is taking out a short-term loan at a very high interest rate; by some calculations, the cost of the loan can be the equivalent of as much as 100 percent in interest. If you are that hard up for an instant return of your tax refund, you might want to consider whether you really should be spending the money in a casino once you obtain it.

On the third floor of the hotel is an attractive Chinese and Thai hideaway restaurant with the unimaginative name of **Kung Fu Plaza.** Open for lunch and dinner, entrees range from about $8 to $20 and when we visited included spicy catfish, honey duck, moo goo gai pan, sweet and sour shrimp, and Mongolian beef.

We bet the tables are still busy. The Plaza has been the focal point of a Las Vegas tradition on New Year's Eve. Crowds lined Fremont Street to watch the fireworks set off behind the hotel. As we go to press, we don't know how the new celebration will fit in with Fremont Street under glass.

No day of rest. Sundays are surprisingly busy days at many casinos, bringing out the locals for brunches. It's also a common arrival day for big tour groups.

The signature restaurant at the Plaza is the **Center Stage**, on the second floor of the tower with a spectacular view up Glitter Gulch. The eatery is open from 4:30 P.M. to midnight, with dinners priced from about $10.

The **Plaza Diner** on the first floor serves breakfast, lunch, and dinner 24 hours a day.

John "Jackie" Gaughan's group also owns the **El Cortez Hotel** in downtown, the **Las Vegas Club, Western Hotel & Bingo Parlor,** and the **Gold Spike;** his son Michael owns and operates the **Barbary Coast** and **Gold Coast** hotels and casinos.

Gaughan's Plaza. 1 Main Street; 1,037 rooms; 386-2110, (800) 634-6575.

Lady Luck

One block in from Fremont on Ogden and Third streets, this is one of the livelier places in downtown. Queen of the Lady Luck Showroom at the time of our visit was Melinda, who puts on a magic show twice nightly. To be charitable, Melinda's act could be considered second-tier, not in the league with the huge production shows on the Strip. She is a bit prettier than former beau Rich Little, though.

The Lady Luck offers a few no-smoking tables, which we like to see, but the overall atmosphere is still pretty clouded.

One of our favorite slot machines in all of Nevada is the parking ticket validation machine at the Lady Luck. The sign reads: "Every 2000th ticket pays a $25 jackpot."

Elvis Sighting Number Five. The King's first Las Vegas appearance took place at the New Frontier in downtown in April of 1956, and it wasn't a smashing success. At the time, it seemed that the King of Rock 'n' Roll's appeal was to younger crowds than were coming to Las Vegas. In 1969, he returned and made the first of a long series of appearances at the International Hotel (now the Las Vegas Hilton).

Where do they get the coins? The Four Queens claims the title for the world's largest slot machine, duly noted in the *Guinness Book of World Records*. The Queens Machine is 9-feet, 8-inches tall and 18 feet long. Six people can play the slot, for $1 to $5 per pull, at the same time.

The **Burgundy Room** offers entrees such as tournedos *rossini* and fresh halibut. **Marco Polo's** features *osso bucco rissoto* and broiled salmon *alla Savoia.*

On Monday nights at the Lady Luck, you might want to check out **Lady Luck Luau,** a $12.95 all-you-can-eat luau and dance review with dinner beginning at 7 P.M. The **Brasserie** coffee shop offers specials including a broiled chopped sirloin with soup or salad for about $4, a prime rib dinner for about $5, and a New York steak dinner for about $10. On the lighter side, there is broiled skinless chicken breast or a pita pocket with chicken or beef, sprouts, tomatoes, and cucumbers, each for about $6.

The **Emperor's Room** offers a mix of entrees from about $7, including Asian specialties such as *kung pao* chicken and Mongolian beef.

The **Banquet Buffet** offers breakfast, lunch, and dinner.

Lady Luck Casino Hotel. 206 North 3rd Street; 796 rooms; 477-3000, (800) 523-9582.

Four Queens

By Las Vegas standards, the Four Queens is a relatively understated hotel decorated in blue and beige with mirrored ceilings and featuring a small but lively casino.

The hotel was first built in 1964 and supposedly drew its name from the fact that former owner Ben Goffstein had four daughters. Over the years, the hotel has expanded to 720 rooms with twin 19-story towers, and it occupies the entire block at Fremont and Third streets.

Check out **Hugo's,** one of the better eateries in Las Vegas. The meal begins with a make-your-own salad from a tableside cart laden with offerings from bay shrimp to roasted pine nuts to hearts of palm. Appetizers include the Hugo's Hot Rock Specialty for $21: diners are presented with a sizzling slab of granite along with plates of tenderloin medallions, marinated swordfish, breast of chicken, and jumbo shrimp with bowls of herbs and spices; you do the cooking to taste.

Entrees, priced from about $20 to $30 on a recent visit included filet of red snapper with crabmeat and shrimp sauce, *snapper en papillote,* chicken Hugo (in a basil and pine nut cream sauce), New York strip loin in petite and extra thick cuts, and tournedos Hugo (topped with a slice of *pate de foie gras,* artichoke hearts, and sauce béarnaise).

At the more casual **Magnolia's Veranda**, you can try the Four Queens' Dip, a pair of French rolls filled with sliced beef and swiss cheese, served au jus. Also available are a variety of omelettes in real and no-cholesterol versions. Entrees are priced from about $4 to $10. A complete prime rib dinner was offered for $3.95.

The Food Court offers a good selection of fast food.

Four Queens Hotel & Casino. 202 East Fremont Street; 720 rooms; 385-4011, (800) 634-6045.

Camp Las Vegas. Fremont Street is named after John Charles Frémont, a 19th-century American explorer who established a camp near Las Vegas Springs in 1844.

Sam Boyd's Fremont Hotel & Casino

One of the first "carpet joints" in downtown, it also featured one of the first block-long neon signs in the neighborhood. The joint is always jumping.

Paradise Buffet. The weekend Champagne Brunch, served Saturday and Sunday from 7 A.M. to 3 P.M., is one of the better deals in downtown. It includes breakfast omelettes and eggs cooked to order, herring, sour cream, smoked salmon, New York strip loin, ham, turkey, and salads. Diners are also offered specialty coffees including amaretto, chocolate mint, hazelnut, and mocha.

The buffet's Seafood Fantasy is served Tuesdays, Fridays, and Sundays from 4 P.M. for $11.95. (The "regular" dinner is offered other nights for $7.95.) The Seafood Fantasy includes swordfish, fried calamari, steamed clams, and mussels as well as ham, turkey, and roast beef. *See the section on buffets for hours and prices.*

The hotel includes a branch of the **Tony Roma's** chain, open for dinner from 5 P.M. to 11 P.M. Specialties include prime rib, steak, and chicken with prices starting about $8 for dinner.

The **Second Street Grill** offers American and Pacific Rim specialties priced from about $13 to $20. Offerings on a recent visit included seared ahi tuna steak with cucumber and plum wine vinaigrette, campfire grilled rib eye steak, bamboo steamed Hawaiian snapper, and grilled Szechwan rack of lamb with cabernet plum sauce.

The ground floor **Lanai Express** offers shrimp cocktail for 75 cents, hot dogs, and Chinese offerings.

The **Overland Stage Cafe** offers coffee shop fare including soup and sandwich for about $4. Breakfast is available from 11 P.M. to 11 A.M. , with $2 specials such as three eggs, two pieces of bacon or sausage, potatoes, toast, and jelly.

The Boyd Group also owns the **California Hotel and Casino** on Stewart Street in downtown, the **Main Street Station** on Main Street, the **Stardust Hotel** on the Strip, and the **Eldorado Casino** in Henderson.

Sam Boyd's Fremont Hotel & Casino. 200 East Fremont Street; 452 rooms; 385-3232, (800) 634-6182.

Fitzgerald's

If you have any question about whether this place intends to cater to the low

Las Vegas Chamber of Commerce. 711 E. Desert Inn Road, Las Vegas, NV 89109; 735-1616.
Las Vegas Convention and Visitors Authority. 3150 Paradise Rd., Las Vegas, NV 89109; 892-0711.

rollers or the high rollers, a quick glance at the ubiquitous advertisements for the hotel should tell you: a regular come-on at Fitzgerald's is a free burger at the McDonald's within the casino.

In the core of the casino is a world of Irish green, including what is claimed to be a piece of the Blarney stone, a collection of four-leaf clovers, and a gaggle of leprechauns. In other words, lots of luck.

The other come-on, if you can spot it in the neon glare of Glitter Gulch, is the hotel's 400-foot-tall skyscraper.

Molly's Country Kitchen and Buffet offers a champagne weekend brunch from 8 A.M. to 4 P.M. for $4.99.

Cassidy's offers a weekday luncheon special of soup and salad with bread sticks for about $5; a mix-and-match surf and turf dinner with a choice of prime rib, petite filet mignon, or New York strip sirloin and lobster tail, scampi, or orange roughy goes for about $20.

Fitzgerald's. 301 East Fremont Street; 650 rooms; 388-2400, (800) 274-5825.

El Cortez Hotel

A corner of this now-sprawling downtown casino and hotel, at the corner of Fremont and Sixth, constitutes the oldest continuously operating casino in Las Vegas. The El Cortez opened in 1941 as a western-themed casino and hotel with about 80 rooms. A 14-story, 200-room tower opened in 1983.

El Cortez. 600 East Fremont Street; 308 rooms; 385-5200, (800) 634-6703.

Street Casinos

Not all of the casinos in Las Vegas are billion-dollar enterprises with thousands of slot machines and spectacular settings. Some are small, full of character, and populated with characters. Some are so tacky you'll want to take a shower immediately after you make a break for the exit.

The best of the little places can be found in downtown along Fremont Street, which on a busy night becomes an outdoor block party with visitors strolling from one casino to the next.

(We would be remiss if we did not warn visitors against strolling too far off Fremont Street in downtown; like any big city, some places are safer than others. The casinos and city police concentrate their efforts on the main drag of downtown.)

Here are our four favorite street-level joints in downtown; you can stop in at all of them in a single visit.

Sassy Sally's Casino

Positively jumping with action and a lot of sassy women, this storefront casino is all slots, bouncy music, and special promotions and is one of our favorite places in downtown. You'll know you're there when you are accosted by a man on horseback handing out coupons; actually it's a man inside a walking horse costume, and boy does the horse feel silly.

Walk in to the back left corner for a decent snack deal at the **Belt-Bustin' Bar-B-Que.** Right out on the floor of the casino you can sit at a checkered tablecloth table and chow down on a plate full of ribs, sliced barbecue beef, or a T-bone steak with potato, all for $2 to $4.

Sassy Sally's Casino. 32 Fremont Street; 382-5777.

Pioneer Club

Another open-front downtown casino, it is notable for its frozen yogurt stand within. There's also a Carl's Jr. burger joint.

The Pioneer is the home of the huge animated neon cowboy sign on Fremont Street. Every few minutes he will announce, "Howdy Pardner. Welcome to Downtown Las Vegas." His name, at least among the locals, is Vegas Vic.

Pioneer Club. 25 E. Fremont Street; 386-5000.

Coin Castle

Not quite a castle, but surely a haven for coin players of all denominations. You will likely be accosted on the street with one of many come-ons for free drinks, sweepstakes, and other attractions.

Coin Castle. 15 E. Fremont Street; 385-7474.

Golden Gate Hotel & Casino

There's not much in the way of fancy accoutrements at the Golden Gate, although it is a lively street-front joint. Built in 1906 as the Hotel Nevada, the Golden Gate is the oldest hotel in Las Vegas; its rooms within have been recently remodeled in the style of the early 1900s. A new restaurant, the **Bay City Diner,** is set in 1930s San Francisco. At the very back is the **San Francisco Shrimp Bar and Deli,** which not surprisingly specializes in shrimp (99 cents for a cocktail) and overstuffed deli sandwiches for $2 to $3.

The first telephone in Las Vegas was installed at the office of Charles "Pop" Squires at the Hotel Nevada in 1907; the second phone was installed at his home four blocks east.

Golden Gate Hotel & Casino. 1 Fremont Street; 382-6300.

Outlying Areas

Boomtown Hotel Casino & RV Resort

A Western-theme casino and hotel modeled after a frontier mining town. The

Lost and found. In 1994, 28.2 million tourists came to Las Vegas. The tourist visits increased by nearly a third over 1992. The hotel and motel room occupancy was an astounding 89 percent.

Visitors left behind about $19.3 billion, which is about $683 per person.

No room at the casino. Las Vegas' 89 percent hotel and motel room occupancy figure is even more impressive when compared to the occupancy rates of other major convention and tourist cities. In 1991, for instance, New York City averaged a 66.5 percent occupancy rate; New Orleans, 68.1 percent; Los Angeles, 62.3 percent; and Houston, 63.5 percent. Nationally, the average was just under 61 percent.

A Thirst for Business.
When Las Vegas was first established soon after the railroad auction of 1905, there were only two types of businesses permitted to sell liquor: those in the red-light district of Blocks 16 and 17, and hotels. So the gambling clubs on Fremont Street, including the Las Vegas Club and the Northern, added a few rooms and called themselves hotels.

hotel includes 304 rooms; there's a 600-seat dinner theater and buffet.

Boomtown Hotel Casino & RV Resort. I-15 at Blue Diamond Highway; (800) 588-7711.

Sam's Town Hotel & Gambling Hall

Sam Boyd has built his own town six miles west of the Strip along the Boulder Highway. It's a lively place with 650 rooms in a tower somewhat hidden behind a false-front Western town, visible from I-93/95. Many of the visitors to the casino are locals, but visitors may want to visit the 25,000-square-foot Western Emporium where you can buy boots, belts, buckles, and more. Restaurants include **Billy Bob's Steak House & Saloon** and the Italian restaurant **Papamios.**

Sam's Town Hotel & Gambling Hall. 5111 Boulder Highway; 456-7777, (800) 634-6371.

Chapter 9
Las Vegas Showrooms and Nightlife

With a few notable exceptions, some of the best entertainment buys in America can be found in Las Vegas, with lavish stage shows, superstars, and fabulous music. Prices are as low as $15 or $20 for most shows; dinner shows or combination tickets with all-you-can-eat buffets are not much more expensive.

Why are the prices generally reasonable? In a word, gambling. Las Vegas, Inc., uses the shows and the buffets and anything else they can to try to lure you into the casino. You'll walk past every slot machine and gaming table they can possibly put in your way between the front door and the showroom; then you'll have to walk back past them on your way out.

But let's get one thing straight here: you are under no obligation to spend any more money than the price of your ticket. If you don't want to gamble, just stroll on by the tables and the machines and go to the show.

Before you buy your ticket, be sure you understand what's included. A common deal includes two drinks, usually from a selection of house brands; if you prefer a particular brand of alcohol, you'll have to pay extra. Both drinks are usually served before the show begins. Additional drinks and snacks are billed at lounge prices.

Some shows offer dinner, again usually from a limited menu (and rarely worth writing home about).

The final question is: does the ticket include gratuities for your servers?

Another important thing to know about Vegas shows: in the past, most of the shows did not offer assigned seating and you were at the mercy of the maitre d'. High rollers, and those who slipped the guy at the door $10 or $20 or more, got the best tables. Over the past few years, though, many of the showrooms have gone over to assigned seats, on a first-come, first-served basis; high rollers still get the very best places. In any case, there are very few really bad seats in the showrooms, which are most often designed to be wider than they are deep with a lot of front row tables across the very wide stage.

The least-preferred seats will put you at a long table perpendicular to the stage. You will share your evening with 10 or 12 strangers at the table. The best seats, although usually not the closest, are the first tier of couch-like booths.

The huge expense of creating, mounting, and promoting entertainment spectacles in Las Vegas generally means that shows will run for extended periods, sometimes for years. Be sure, though, to check with hotels for current schedules and prices.

The Econoguide to the Best Shows in Las Vegas

Cirque du Soleil. Treasure Island
City Lites. Flamingo Hilton
EFX. MGM Grand
Enter the Night. Stardust Hotel
Folies Bergere. Tropicana Hotel

Siegfried and Roy. The Mirage
Spellbound. Harrah's Las Vegas
Splash. Riviera
Starlight Express. Las Vegas Hilton

Production Shows

The major shows tend to settle in for long runs. Here is a list as of the spring of 1995. Be sure to call beforehand; you'll need a reservation for most shows, anyhow.

Call the hotels for information about special events and celebrity shows. All phone numbers are in the (702) area code.

Aladdin Hotel. Bagdad Showroom. "Country Tonite" country music comedy dance review. 7:15 and 10 P.M. nightly. Dark Tuesdays. Adults with Market Place Buffet $23.55. Children under 18, $12.85; with buffet $15.85. 736-0111.

Bally's. "Jubilee!" Singing, dancing (some topless), and fantastic production numbers including the sinking of the Titanic. Did we mention the topless dancers? Tuesdays through Thursdays and Saturdays at 8 P.M. and 11 P.M., and Sundays and Mondays 8 P.M. Dark Fridays. $42. 739-4567.

Debbie Reynolds Hotel. Debbie Reynolds, Rip Taylor, and the Uptown Country Singers. Tuesdays through Saturdays 8 P.M. and Sundays at 3 P.M. $29.95. 733-2243.

Excalibur. "King Arthur's Tournament." Production show about the Legend of Arthur. Two dinner shows nightly at 6 P.M. and 8:30 P.M. $29.95 with meal. 597-7600.

Excalibur. "Sooper Dogs." Mondays through Fridays 2 P.M., Saturdays and Sundays noon and 2 P.M. Dark Wednesdays. $4.95. 597-7600.

Flamingo Hilton. Flamingo Showroom. "City Lites" variety and comedy show with ice dancers. Dinner show 7:45 P.M. from $29.50, and cocktail show 11 P.M. $21.95, including two drinks. Dark Sundays. Minimum age is 7; children must be accompanied by an adult 21 years of age or older. 733-3333.

Golden Nugget. "Country Fever." Thursdays through Tuesdays. 7:15 P.M. and 10:15 P.M. $22.50. 386-8100.

Hacienda. "Lance Burton: World Champion Magician." Tuesdays through

Saturdays at 7:30 P.M. and 10:30 P.M. (adults only at late show); Sundays at 7:30 P.M. $21.95. 739-8911.

Harrah's Las Vegas. "Spellbound." Nightly 7:30 and 10 P.M. $22.95, including one drink. Dark Sundays. Minimum age 21. 369-5222.

Imperial Palace Hotel. Imperial Theatre. "Legends in Concert" impressions of legendary stars. 7:30 and 10:30 P.M. nightly. Dark Sundays. $23.50, including two drinks; children $11.75. 794-3261.

Jackie Gaughan's Plaza. "Hot Rock 'N Country" adults-only variety show. 7:30 and 10:30 P.M. Dark Tuesdays. $19.95, including one drink. 386-2110.

Lady Luck. "Melinda, First Lady of Magic and Her Follies Revue." Shows at 8 and 10:30 P.M.; late show for adults only. $27.45, including one drink; preferred seating $32.95. 477-3000.

Las Vegas Hilton. "Starlight Express." Dark Mondays. Tuesdays, Fridays, Saturdays, and Sundays at 7:30 and 10:30 P.M., Wednesdays and Thursdays at 9 P.M. Ticket prices vary; about $39.50, $42.50, and $45 for adults, $25 for children. 732-5755, (800) 782-7544.

Luxor. "Winds of the Gods." Chariot races, lavish costumes, and exotic animals on stage where they belong. 7:30 and 10:15 P.M. nightly. Dark Wednesdays. Dinner show $39.95, late cocktail show $24.95. (800) 778-0848.

MGM Grand. Grand Theatre. "EFX," a dancing, singing, and special effects spectacle with a cast of 70. 891-7777, (800) 929-1111.

The Mirage. Theatre Mirage. "Siegfried and Roy" magic spectacle. Twice nightly at 7:30 and 11 P.M. Dark Wednesdays. $78.35, including two drinks. Appearances 40 weeks of the year; other headliners appear during breaks. 792-7777.

Rio. Copacabana Showroom. "¡Conga!" dinner show. 6 and 8:30 P.M. Dark Sundays and Mondays. $38.95. 252-7776.

Riviera Hotel. Versailles Theatre. "Splash" musical variety. Nightly 7:30 and 10:30 P.M. $27.50, including two drinks. 794-9301.

Riviera Hotel. Mardi Gras Room. "An Evening at La Cage" female impersonators. Nightly 7:30 and 9:30 P.M. Late show 11:15 P.M. on Wednesdays and Saturdays. Dark Tuesdays. $16.95. Preferred seating $21.95. 794-9433.

Riviera Hotel. "Crazy Girls—Sensuous Passion & Pudgy" adult entertainment. Nightly 8:30 and 10:30 P.M. $14.95, including two drinks. Midnight show Fridays and Saturdays. Dark Mondays. 794-9433.

Sahara Hotel. "Boylesque" female impersonators. 8 and 11 P.M. nightly. Dark Wednesdays. $17.50. 737-2878.

San Remo. "Outrageous." Nightly 7:30 and 9:30 P.M.; Fridays and Saturdays 8:10 and 10:30 P.M. Dark Wednesdays. $17.95, including one drink. 597-6028.

Sands Hotel. "Viva Las Vegas" dance revue, 1 and 3:30 P.M. weekdays. $10, including one drink. 733-5453.

Stardust Hotel. "Enter the Night" stage spectacular and laser light show. Nightly 7:30 and 10:30 P.M. Wednesdays through Saturdays; 8 P.M. Sundays and Mondays. Dark Tuesdays. $24.90, including two drinks. 732-6111.

Treasure Island. Cirque du Soleil's "Mystère." 7:30 and 10:30 P.M. Dark Mondays. $52.80; children under 12, $26.40. 894-7722, (800) 392-1999.

Tropicana Hotel. Tiffany Theatre. "Folies Bergere" music and dance show, the longest-running stage production in Las Vegas. Dinner show 7:30 P.M., $26.95; cocktail show 10:30 P.M., $19.95, including two drinks. Dark Thursdays. 739-2411.

Tiffany Theatre. "ZaJi Chinese Acrobats." Wednesdays through Mondays 2 P.M., plus Saturdays and Sundays at noon. $7.95. 739-2411.

Comedy Shows

Bally's. "Catch a Rising Star" cabaret. Nightly 8 and 10:30 P.M. $12.50. Minimum age 18. 739-4111.

Maxim Hotel. Cabaret Showroom. "Comedy Max." Nightly 8 and 10 P.M. $12.95 with two drinks; $16.95 with buffet. 731-4300.

Riviera Hotel. "An Evening at the Improv." 8, 10, and 11:30 P.M. nightly. $13.95, including two drinks.

Tropicana Hotel. Monte Carlo Showroom. "The Comedy Stop." 8 and 10:30 P.M. nightly. $12.95, including two drinks. 739-2358.

Celebrity Shows

Caesars Palace. Circus Maximus Showroom. Tickets generally start at $40 to $45. 439-7110.

Desert Inn. Crystal Room. 733-4566.

Golden Nugget. Cabaret, Claude's. 386-8100.

Lady Luck. Cabaret. 477-3000.

Las Vegas Hilton. Showroom. 732-5755.

MGM Grand. MGM Grand Garden. Ice shows, sporting events, celebrity shows. 474-4000.

Off the Beaten Path

We're going to skip right over the strip joints, mud wrestling exhibitions, and table dancing bars. If you want 'em, there are more "adult" and "topless" night clubs in Las Vegas than you could shake a cocktail stick at. You will be assaulted with leaflets and advertisements and personal appeals as you walk along the Strip or downtown. The joints are every bit as crummy inside as they appear from outside, and Las Vegas police advise you to keep a close eye on your wallet and hotel key and anything else of value if you venture within.

There are, though, quite a few alternative and traditional nightclubs and cafes worth visiting in the Las Vegas area. Many of them cater to the locals rather than the tourists, which depending on your orientation, may be a real advantage.

Lounges

Café Copioh. A quirky dive across from UNLV. 4550 S. Maryland Parkway. 739-0305.

Café Espresso Roma. Another college joint, it features poetry nights on

Thursdays and comedy on alternate Saturdays. 4440 S. Maryland Parkway. 369-1540.

The Cave. Call beforehand to find out the weirdness du jour. Nights include erotica for women, hip hop, female impersonators, strippers, leatherware, and more. 5740 W. Charleston. 878-0001.

The Coffee Bar. Espresso, cappuccino, and desserts in a corner of the huge **Basset Book Shop.** Borrow a book from the shelf and give it a test read. 2323 S. Decatur. 258-0999.

Goodtimes. Disco fever, on what is claimed to be Las Vegas' only stainless steel floor—which sounds quite plausible. Thursday nights are for trash disco, in costume. 1775 E. Tropicana Avenue. 736-9494.

Nightclubs

Favorites. An eclectic mix—call for the latest—that can include an 18-piece brass band or punk rockers, or both. 4110 S. Maryland Avenue. 796-1776.

The Hard Rock Cafe. The Las Vegas outpost of the national chain, it's a loud place decorated with memorabilia of the rock 'n' roll pantheon. Go for drinks or dinner. 4474 Paradise Road. 733-8400.

Hurricane. Not for the sensitive of hearing or sensibilities. Call for scheduled events. 1650 E. Tropicana Avenue. 798-3883.

The Metz. An elaborate, multilevel dance club. 3675 S. Las Vegas Boulevard (between the Tropicana and Aladdin Hotels). 739-8855.

Shark Club. A high-tech club with a four-sided video screen and surrounding sound. 75 E. Harmon Avenue. 795-7525.

Cheyenne Saloon and Dance Hall. Country music and restaurant with a hardwood dance floor. 310 N. Rancho at Cheyenne. 645-4139.

The Country Club Music Hall. Dance hall and restaurant; open 24 hours. 3785 Boulder Highway. 641-5800.

Fremont Street Reggae and Blues. Live bands every night. 400 E. Fremont Street. 594-4640.

G.O. Nutz. Country fun saloon. 4424 West Spring Mountain Road at Arville. 368-6800.

Idle Spurs Tavern. Rodeo bar. 1113 S. Rainbow Boulevard at Charleston. 363-7718.

Play It Again Sam. Eat, drink, and be moody in a re-creation of Rick's Café Americain from *Casablanca*. 4120 Spring Mountain Road. 876-1550.

Babysitting Agencies

Need a night off from the kids? Many of the major hotels have arrangements for in-room babysitting; others can provide you with the names of babysitting agencies to call. In addition, there are several outside companies to try.

Follow the same sort of precautions you would at home: interview the company and the babysitter to be sure you feel comfortable with their professionalism; be sure to leave the phone number of your destination for the night, and don't leave valuables in the room.

Around the Clock Child Care. 365-1040.
Choice Care. 387-1103.
Four Season's. 384-5848.
Grandma Dotti's Baby Sitting Agency. 456-1175.
Nanny's & Granny's. 364-4700.
Precious Commodities. 871-1191.

Chapter 10

Mama Don't Allow No Gambling 'Round Here: Area Attractions

The Econoguide to the Best Places to Visit in Las Vegas

Grand Slam Canyon   MGM Grand Adventures
Hoover Dam   Red Rock Canyon
Imperial Palace Auto Museum

Okay, we know that Las Vegas *is* a show all by itself, but there is more to life than casinos, showgirls, neon lights, buffets, casinos, showgirls, shopping malls, exploding volcanoes, pirate ships, casinos, showgirls, and Egyptian pyramids.

Although you sometimes have to squint through a forest of slot machines and neon lights to see it, there is life outside of the casinos of Las Vegas.

Hidden to most visitors to Las Vegas is a wide variety of cultural and outdoor activities. With the developing role of the town as a lure for the entire family, the other attractions of the area will become more important.

Hardly qualifying as cultural highlights, but still fun are pleasure palaces such as **MGM Grand Adventures**, **Grand Slam Canyon**, and **Wet 'n Wild**.

MGM Grand Adventures

MGM Grand Adventures is without doubt the best theme park in Las Vegas. It's also the only one.

So, I won't devote a lot of space to comparing it to mega-parks like Walt Disney World, Disneyland, Universal Studios Hollywood, Universal Studios Florida, or even to the Disney-operated Disney-MGM Studios in Orlando—except to say that MGM Grand Adventures is one notch below the major leagues, but a lot better than most amusement parks.*

---

* If you're a fan of theme parks, you might want to pick up a copy of *Econoguide '96—Walt Disney World, Universal Studios Florida, Epcot, and Other Major Central Florida Attractions*, or *Econoguide '96—Disneyland, Universal Studios Hollywood, and Other Major Southern California Attractions*, both by Corey Sandler and published by Contemporary Books.

MGM Grand Adventures is worth a day or an evening, especially if you have children in tow. It's all part of the effort by many of the casinos in Las Vegas to give families a reason to come to town.

Surprisingly because of MGM's identification as a movie studio, there's not much of a cinema theme to the park. (A legal dispute with Disney over the Orlando park, which is very much based on movie themes, may be the reason.)

In any case, there are eight "areas" in the tightly packed park: **Casablanca Plaza, New York Street, Asian Village, French Street, Salem Waterfront, Tumbleweed Gulch, New Orleans Street**, and **Olde England Street.** Scattered around the park you'll find restaurants, including **Benninger's Gourmet Coffees, Hamada Orient Express, Mamma Ilardo's Pizzeria, Kenny Rogers Roasters, Hildegard's Ice Cream Parlour, The Cotton Blossom, Nathan's Famous**, and **Burger King**.

As you descend the escalator into the park from the MGM Grand, you'll arrive in Casablanca. Given a choice, most people go to the right, and that is the general flow around this park—a counterclockwise tour. Therefore, if the park is very busy you might want to go against the flow and head to the left. Our tour here, though, will discuss the rides as most people will approach them.

The first big ride is **Lightning Bolt,** an indoor roller coaster on an outer-space adventure. That certainly sounds like the famous Space Mountain ride at Disneyland and Walt Disney World, but the Disney touch is missing. There's almost no buildup to the adventure, and the space theme is merely hinted at; the ballyhooed ending which features a landing in Las Vegas at night is almost possible to miss. And the ride is very short, about a minute.

If you're in the mood to remember your trip forever, you can purchase a souvenir picture taken as you swooped about. We didn't.

Next up is **Deep Earth Exploration,** a more polished (and cinematic) simulator adventure that takes you aboard Gopher 1 for a voyage deep into the earth's core, and then back up out an erupting volcano. The ride includes high-tech audiovisual effects. Passengers "ride" in one of six 12-passenger vehicles; there are three scenes where the windows of the car will open and the passengers will be submerged into the animated scenery.

The **Backlot River Tour** is a very hokey simulation of a studio tour; there are no real production facilities at MGM Grand Adventures. Instead you'll see scenes sort of reminiscent of famous movies, including swamp creatures, a Vietnam War helicopter firefight, and other scenes. Bits and pieces of the outside world, including a nearby motel balcony, intruded on the view of some of the "sets."

What made our particular tour very enjoyable was the hitchhiker we picked up at the loading dock; an actress playing the part of Betty Boop sat down beside us and took the tour, staying in character all the way through. Try as we might—and we tried—we were unable to break her out of the role.

From the backlot tour, you'll move on to **Parisian Taxis,** which is a bumper car ride with a few French street signs.

Haunted Mine is, well, a haunted mine. It does a better job of setting up the atmosphere for the ride, but this is still no Disney Haunted Mansion—oops, there

MGM GRAND ADVENTURES, LAS VEGAS

I go again making comparisons. Let's just say that this is a PG-rated moving spook ride, a little bit better done than your local Jaycee Halloween Funhouse.

Are you ready to go **Over the Edge**? It's a pleasant little journey through a nostalgic old saw mill with quaint scenery and rustic charm. (Did someone say Thunder Mountain Railroad?) This log flume ride takes you up in the air over a corner of the park and down into two wet dropoffs.

You're now at the top of the map, and ready to visit **You're in the Movies**, a show familiar to veterans of studio tours but always amusing. Participants are drawn from the line about 15 minutes before the show and given small parts to play in a series of scenes from television and movie classics. Their actions are electronically combined with video and presented on the big screen for the rest of the audience to see. On the day of my visit a Rhett and Scarlet were chosen for a scene from a *Gone with the Wind*–like film (sort of Rhett meets the Three Stooges), a vampire was cast for a menacing pizza delivery, a Cleopatra and Anthony were selected for a romantic vamp, and various children and other monsters were cast.

Magic Screen Theatre turned out to be one of the most enjoyable spots in the park. The large theater alternates between presentations of **The Three Stooges**, a combination of live-action look-alikes and vintage video clips for an appropriately nyuk-nyuk show, and **Kaleidoscope**, a very entertaining black light puppetry and live performance show that should enthrall children of all ages.

Behind the Magic Screen building is the largest ride at the park, **Grand Canyon Rapids.** This is your basic raft ride (four to six per boat) through rapids and down a "blasting tunnel" drop; this is definitely a wet ride.

Nearby in **King Looey Theatre** is **The Cartoon Show**, a demonstration of the art of animation and based on the park's own theme character.

And then there is the **Dueling Pirates** show, a stunt performance that will entertain the kids pretty well. It does, though, suffer a bit by comparison to the (free) outdoor battle fought in the lagoon outside Treasure Island down on the Strip.

If you're on the lookout for souvenirs of MGM Grand Adventures or Hollywood collectibles, the park includes stores such as **Backstage Collectibles, Backlot Heirlooms,** and **Hollywood Clothiers.** Other shops include the **Behind the Scenes Craft Co.**, offering glass, leather, wood, pottery, and wax works. In Tumbleweed Gulch you'll find the **Old West Supply Company.** And at New Orleans Square, there is **Bayou Toys.**

You must be at least 36 inches tall to ride Parisian Taxis or the Backlot River Tour, and 42 inches or taller for Grand Canyon Rapids, Over the Edge, and Lightning Bolt.

The park is outdoors, and nights and winter days can be a bit chilly. Check with the park for operating hours. In the off-season, the park usually closes at 7 P.M.; in what was expected to be a busy summer, the park was scheduled to remain open until 10 P.M.

Admission prices will vary from season to season, in the range from about $15 to $20 for adults and $10 to $15 for children from 4 to 12. At the start of 1995, the park was also experimenting with a per-ride plan with individual tickets priced from about $1 to $3. The park may also offer discount rates for admission late in the day.

And finally, the park itself closed for a 10-day refurbishment in January of 1995. It's too early to see if this is going to be an annual down time; if you are traveling to Las Vegas in the winter and are promising the kids (or yourself) a day at the park, be sure to check with the theme park ahead of time for its schedule.

Luxor

The hollow interior of the Luxor pyramid houses three attractions created by special effects designer Douglass Trumbull (also responsible for the spectacular *Back to the Future* ride at Universal Studios in Orlando, Florida).

The theme for the mini-park is a three-part adventure more or less set in the time of King Tut and the more contemporary rediscovery of his tomb in Egypt.

Episode 1, **In Search of the Obelisk**, is a 15-minute simulation that includes a runaway elevator into the tomb (not quite as wild as the new Twilight Zone Tower of Terror at the Disney-MGM Studios theme park in Orlando) and then a frenzied chase sequence within a pyramid with some interesting special effects.

The second episode, **Luxor Live?**, involves guests in a 30-minute "live" broadcast that combines actors and video effects in a television studio setting.

Voyagers visit the future in a 17-minute cosmic time machine using high-tech movie and computer imagery for the third episode, **The Theater of Time.**

The attractions, presented as three separate shows, can be visited as part of a multiticket pass for about $15, including the river ride and the museum exhibit that replicates parts of King Tut's Tomb. The three episodes can be purchased on a single ticket for $12, or individually for $5, $4, and $4 each. The rides open at 9 or 10 A.M.

The Luxor attractions are entertaining for the technology they employ, but the story line is rather muddied. During 1994, some changes were made and more may be in the offing.

On the lowest level of the Luxor is **King Tut's Tomb and Museum**, a recreation of part of the treasure chamber found by explorer Howard Carter in 1922. And finally, there is the **Nile River Tour** by boat around the circumference of the pyramid; it's a pleasant break from the casino, although you can see it from the water.

Grand Slam Canyon

Only in Las Vegas could they come up with something like this: **Grand Slam Canyon**, a five-acre indoor entertainment park that presents a Las Vegas–eye view of the Grand Canyon, including 140-foot man-made peaks, a 90-foot recreation of Havasupai Falls, and a river. The entire park, attached to the **Circus Circus Hotel and Casino** is covered by a pink space-frame dome called an Adventuredome.

The park includes the world's only indoor double-looping roller coaster. If you're not already dizzy from the gambling, the neon, the buffets . . . then you are ready for the **Canyon Blaster** at Grand Slam Canyon. I'm not sure I was ready, but I went for a ride anyway; I survived, but I'm having a hard time reading the notes I took.

You'll know this is a serious ride as you walk around the Adventuredome; you'll feel the floor shake beneath your feet as the cars rumble by. The Canyon Blaster is a ride that emphasizes speed and twists and turns over height; its track circles in and around much of the sphere. There are two loops, two corkscrews, and some interesting views of the hotel and the Strip if you keep your eyes open.

The **Rim Runner** is a three-and-a-half-minute indoor water flume ride, with much of the raft ride in the dark. "This is a wet ride. You will get soaked," warn the signs. In case you are not fully prepared, the gift shop sells disposable ponchos for a dollar or two.

The first year for the park was a rough one, with its offerings greatly overshadowed by the excitement of the MGM Grand Adventures and Luxor; the new park underwent an almost immediate overhaul in 1994 with new attractions and a new pricing structure.

Here's your guide to the major attractions at Grand Slam Canyon:

Canyon Blaster. A double-looping, double-corkscrew indoor roller coaster. Riders must be at least 48 inches tall.

Rim Runner. Water flume ride. Minimum height 42 inches.

Hot Shots. Laser-tag adventure. Minimum height 42 inches.

Canyon Cars. Bumper cars. Drivers must be at least 52 inches tall; passengers must be at least 48 inches in height.

Sand Pirates. A swinging pirate ship. Minimum height 42 inches.

Children's rides include:

Thunderbirds. Airplane ride. Riders must be between 33 and 54 inches tall.

Miner Mike. Miniature roller coaster. Riders must be between 33 and 54 inches tall.

Road Runner. Miniature Himalayan ride.

Drifters. Balloon Ferris wheel.

Fossil Dig. Children's play area.

Cliff Hangers. Children's net climb and ball crawl.

Among the peaks and cascading waters, caves, and canyons are fully animated life-size dinosaurs in a representation of their natural habitat at the **Passage of Time**. Entertainment is presented on a regular schedule at the **Mystic Magic Theatre**.

Kids of all ages (and heights) can feed quarters into state-of-the-art video games at the **Sega Arcade** or at the game booths of the **Grand Slam Midway**.

Restaurants at the compact park include **The Cantina**, featuring Mexican dishes; the **Out Post Cafe;** and a snack bar and food carts.

Grand Slam Canyon is open every day and into the night; check with Circus Circus for operating hours. Various ticket plans have been in effect at different times of the year. In 1995, plans included an unlimited rides ticket priced at $13.95 for adults and $9.95 for youngsters ages 3 to 9 and limited to children's rides only. Also available was a $3 general admission ticket and individual ride tickets priced at $3 for adult rides and $1.50 for attractions aimed solely at children.

The busiest times at the park come weekends and holidays, with nighttime crowds larger than in the morning and afternoon.

Wet 'n Wild

For a cooling antidote to a hot day on the Strip, try Wet 'n Wild, located between the Sahara Hotel/Casino and El Rancho Hotel.

The park, which operates from about April 1 to October 1 of each year, added a pair of new wet and wild attractions recently: the **Bomb Bay** and the **Banzai Banzai.**

Bomb Bay is about as close as you are likely to get to a free-fall; think of it as a bungee jump without the bungee. One person at a time slips into a bomb-like capsule at the top of a 76-foot-high water slide which is then moved into a vertical position with the lucky occupant standing almost straight up inside. Then the bottom drops out and the rider drops nearly straight down the watery chute.

The Banzai Banzai is a double-slide water coaster, allowing a pair of riders to race each other down to a 120-foot-long runway pool at the bottom.

There are, of course, a few slightly less wild but just as wet rides, too.

Wet 'n Wild. 2600 Las Vegas Blvd. South; open in season; call 737-7873 for information. *You will find a discount in the coupon section of this book.*

Virtual World

As if Las Vegas was not already sufficiently otherworldish, now you can strap on a virtual reality helmet and take off on an interactive journey where your actions control the movie you see before you. Worlds include Battletech, where you will join warriors from all over the galaxy (and Las Vegas) on the desert planet of Solaris VII to test your skill at the control of 31st Century two-legged tanks called Battlemechs. Or, you can try the shuttered mines of the Red Planet where you can race a souped-up mining vehicle down the canals of Mars.

Virtual World. 3053 Las Vegas Blvd. South; 369-3583.

All American Family Sports Park

Due for its inaugural season in the summer of 1995, this amusement center across from the Sahara Hotel on the Strip includes batting cages, a golf driving range, go-carts, and an arcade.

Museums

Barrick Museum of Natural History. UNLV's collection includes a selection of lizards (chuckwallas, Gila monsters), snakes (rattlers, desert boas, red racers), and spiders (the poisonous brown recluse and black widow) guaranteed to make your skin crawl; there's also an impressive display of arrowheads. On the campus of UNLV at 4505 S. Maryland Parkway; open weekdays; 739-3381.

Boulder City Hoover Dam Museum. Historic artifacts of the construction of Hoover Dam. 444 Hotel Plaza in Boulder City; 294-1988.

Clark County Heritage Museum. A collection of area history, including railroad rolling stock and memorabilia; Heritage Street, a collection of historic homes in a park setting; and a time line from prehistoric to current times. Located in the former Boulder City railroad depot. Open daily except holidays, 9 A.M. to 4:30 P.M. 1830 South Boulder Highway; Henderson; 455-7955.

Guinness World of Records Museum. If Las Vegas is not quite weird enough for you, you might want to try out this strange collection. Part of an expanding chain of exhibits under license from the famous recorder of world records and strange accomplishments, the museum includes models and replicas that inform about such things as the largest number of hard-boiled eggs eaten at one sitting, the smallest ridable bicycle, the largest human being, the world's oldest man, and much more. Where else could you learn about the world's greatest shallow dive (from 28 feet into 12 inches of water), the world's loudest snorer, or the human lightning rod?

One of the more amazing facts on display is the demonstration of just how much detail the operators have been able to squeeze into the relatively small space of the museum.

The museum is open every day at 2780 Las Vegas Blvd. South, on the Strip north of Circus Circus and across from Wet 'n Wild and the Sahara Hotel/Casino;

call 792-3766 for hours and information. *You will find a discount in the coupon section of this book.*

Imperial Palace Antique Auto Collection. With more than 200 antique and classic cars, one of the most impressive collections anywhere. One corner of the museum is a room full of 25 or so Duesies worth more than $50 million; classic Duesenberg cars including Jimmy Cagney's 1937 Model J. More contemporary and a bit more flashy is Liberace's pale cream 1981 Zimmer Golden Spirit, complete with candelabra. There is, of course, an Elvis car: a pale blue 1976 Eldorado. Also on display is a 1938 Cadillac V-16 touring sedan (with backseat bar) owned by W. C. Fields.

Presidents Row includes John F. Kennedy's 1962 Lincoln Continental "Bubbletop," Lyndon Johnson's 1964 Cadillac, Dwight Eisenhower's 1952 Chrysler Imperial, Harry S. Truman's 1950 Lincoln Cosmopolitan, Franklin D. Roosevelt's 1936 V-16 Cadillac, and a 1929 Cadillac that transported Herbert Hoover.

From the darker side of history are vehicles including Al Capone's 1930 V-16 Cadillac, Adolf Hitler's 1936 Mercedes-Benz 770K, Benito Mussolini's 1939 Alfa Romeo, and Emperor Hirohito's 1935 Packard.

And in keeping with the generally offbeat atmosphere of Las Vegas, also on display is Howard Hughes' 1954 Chrysler, which comes equipped with an elaborate air purification system in the trunk intended to protect Hughes from the germs that afflict we mortals.

The oldest cars on display include an 1897 Haynes-Apperson, a two-cylinder, four-seat surrey that ran on naptha; and an 1898 LaNef, a three-wheeler with tiller steering. Rare cars include a few Tuckers, a 1903 Lenawee, and a 1913 Stanley Steamer bus.

There's a nominal admission charge for the museum, but you can often obtain free passes from casino employees who are stationed at the front entrance of the Imperial Palace. The museum is open every day, late into the night. Listed prices are $6.95 for adults and $3 for children from 5 to 12. *You will also find a free pass in the coupon section of this book.*

Open daily; 3535 Las Vegas Blvd., South; 731-3311.

Las Vegas Art Museum. Three galleries with displays of local and national artists changing monthly. The main building was constructed in the 1930s from wooden railroad ties. Within Lorenzi Park, 3333 Washington Avenue; free admissions; 647-4300.

Las Vegas Natural History Museum. Dinosaurs, wildlife, and an educational gift shop. A nice collection of dinosaurs, including the skull of a T-rex. Open daily; 900 Las Vegas Blvd. North; adults $5, children (4 to 12) $2.50; 384-3466.

Las Vegas Southern Nevada Zoological Society. Nevada's only public zoo, this small collection includes a Bengal tiger, a lion, a handful of monkeys, and indigenous wildlife; there's also a petting zoo. 1775 N. Rancho; 648-5955.

Liberace Museum. "Mr. Showmanship" is gone, but the glitter remains. Much of his collection of costumes, pianos, candelabras, and cars stands vigil in this museum, operated by The Liberace Foundation for the Performing and Creative Arts, which provides educational grants to schools and colleges.

Some of his outfits were wilder than those worn by showgirls on the Strip, including a suit made of ostrich feathers. There are some 15 Liberace-special pianos, five Liberacemobiles including a Rolls Royce covered with mirror tiles, and jewelry including a piano-shaped ring containing 260 diamonds in a gold setting with ivory and black jade keys.

The main museum includes the Piano, Car, and Celebrity Galleries; the annex includes the Costume and Jewelry Galleries and a recreation of Liberace's office and bedroom from his Palm Springs home. The library includes personal mementos and memorabilia including a lifetime's press clippings and photographs.

The museum is located in a shopping district, a bit out of the way, a mile or so off the Strip at 1775 E. Tropicana Avenue; 798-5595. The minimum tax-deductible donation is $6.50 for adults, and $2 for children under the age of 12. Open Monday to Saturday 10 A.M. to 5 P.M.; Sunday 1 to 5 P.M. *You will find a discount in the coupon section of this book.*

Lied Discovery Children's Museum. A hands-on place for kids, including Toddler Towers, a model of the Space Shuttle, a kid-operated radio station, a collection of computer toys, and more. Tuesday to Saturday 10 A.M. to 5 P.M.; open Wednesdays to 7 P.M.; Sunday from noon to 5 P.M. Closed Mondays except most school holidays. Across from Cashman Field, 833 Las Vegas Blvd. North; adults $5, juniors (12 to 18) $4, and children (4 to 11) $3; 382-3445.

Lost City Museum of Archeology. Artifacts and interpretations of Pueblo Grande de Nevada, the so-called Lost City of the Anasazi Indians, who occupied the area for about 1,200 years until the year 1150. Located in Overton, 60 miles northeast of Las Vegas via I-15, at 721 S. Highway 169; 397-2193.

Nevada State Museum & Historical Society. The history of southern Nevada from the dawn of native culture some 13,000 years ago to the present, including the Hoover Dam, Nevada's role as a nuclear test site, and its mining industry. Take I-95 to Valley View. 700 Twin Lakes Drive in Lorenzi Park; 8:30 A.M. to 4:30 P.M.; 486-5205. *You will find a discount in the coupon section of this book.*

Searchlight Museum. A small outpost of the Clark County Heritage Museum, it chronicles the history of the former mining town of Searchlight and the story of famed Hollywood fashion designer Edith Head and screen stars Clara Bow and Rex Bell, all of whom lived there. Searchlight Community Center, 60 miles south of Las Vegas; 455-7955.

Commercial Attractions

Bonnie Springs Ranch/Old Nevada. *See the section on Red Rock Canyon in Chapter 15.* Highway 159, 20 miles west of Las Vegas. Open 7 days a week, with tickets priced at about $6.50 for adults and $4 for children; 875-4191.

Cranberry World West. A celebration of the tasty-tart fruit including a multimedia video about cranberries, free samples, and a view of the state-of-the-art juice processing plant. Open daily from 9 A.M. to 5 P.M., except holidays; free. Gibson Road, Henderson; 566-7160.

Dolphin Habitat. Mirage Hotel, 3400 Las Vegas Blvd. South; open 9 A.M. to 7 P.M. daily; admission $3, children under 3 free; 791-7111.

Ethel M. Chocolate Factory. Free factory tour and botanical garden and cactus display. And, yes, there are samples. Ethel was the mother of candy bar magnate Forrest Mars, the family behind the Mars Bar, M&Ms, Milky Ways and much more. The cactus garden showcases more than 300 varieties of prickly plants.

In Henderson, between the Strip and Hoover Dam. 2 Cactus Garden Drive; call for hours; 458-8864.

Holy Cow Brewery Tour. Guided tours of this small brewery are conducted daily every two hours from 11 A.M. to 5 P.M.; self-guided tours are offered from 8 A.M. to midnight daily. 2423 Las Vegas Blvd. South; 732-2697.

Kidd Marshmallow Factory. Sweet satisfaction for the kid in all of us. Tour and sampling area. 8203 Gibson Road; open daily 9 A.M. to 4:30 P.M.; 564-5400.

Omnimax Theatre. A giant dome theater, just off the gambling floor and a better bet for families and adults than most other entertainment on the Strip. The theater has a continuous schedule of spectacular 70-mm films.

Caesars Palace, 3570 Las Vegas Blvd. South; 731-7900.

Vegas Chip Factory. Ever wonder where the casinos get their gambling chips? Not here; these are the kind that come in bags and are covered with salt. Free tours working days. 2954 N. Martin Luther King Blvd.; 647-3800.

White Tiger Habitat. Mirage Hotel. 3400 Las Vegas Blvd. South; open 24 hours; free admission; 791-7111.

Cultural Information

Allied Arts Council. 731-5419.

Arts Hotline (24-hour recorded information). 385-4444, enter code 2172.

Clark County Library. 382-3493.

Cultural Hotline: Southern Nevada Arts Hotline. 385-4444.

Las Vegas Cultural Community Affairs. 455-8200.

University of Nevada Las Vegas Performing Arts. UNLV is a center of culture just two miles from the Strip. Call 739-3801 for information on various events.

Charles Vanda Masters Series. A series of orchestra performances, ensembles, and soloists.

Nevada Symphony Orchestra.

Nevada Dance Theatre. (Traditionally puts on *The Nutcracker* around Christmas time.)

Nevada Opera Theatre.

Chamber Music Southwest.

University Dance Theatre.

UNLV's University Theatre.

The City of Las Vegas Cultural and Community Affairs Division. Puts on a variety of events from Shakespeare to jazz.

New West Theatre. A professional troupe, cosponsored by the City of Las

Vegas, putting on shows at the Charleston Heights Arts Center, 800 S. Brush Street; call 656-5000.

Actors Repertory Theatre. 1824 Palo Alto Circle, Las Vegas 89108; 648-1986.

Community Drama Workshop. 3402 Katmai Drive, Las Vegas 89122; 458-0069.

Las Vegas Community Theatre. 111 Las Vegas Blvd. South, Suite 214, Las Vegas 89104; 382-7225.

Las Vegas Little Theatre. 2566 Sherwood, #11, Las Vegas 89109; 731-5958.

New West Stage Company. 3540 W. Sahara, Suite 235, Las Vegas 89101; 396-6553.

Sign Design Theatre. 3933 Renate Drive, Las Vegas 89102; 873-7446.

Theatre Arts Group. 1612 Metropolitan, Las Vegas 89102; 877-6463.

UNLV Department of Theatre Arts. 4505 S. Maryland Parkway, Las Vegas 89154; 739-3666.

Dance

Academy of Nevada Dance Theatre. 4634 S. Maryland Parkway, #110, Las Vegas 89109; 794-2889.

Department of Dance Arts. 4505 S. Maryland Parkway, UNLV, Las Vegas 89154; 739-3827.

Las Vegas Civic Ballet Association. P.O. Box 159, Las Vegas 89125; 385-1630.

Nevada Dance Theatre, UNLV. 900 Las Vegas Blvd. North, Las Vegas 89154; 739-3838.

Nevada State Troupers. 900 Las Vegas Blvd. North, Las Vegas 89101; 457-2044.

Opus Dance Ensemble of Las Vegas. 1600 E. Desert Inn Road, #209D, Las Vegas 89109; 732-9646.

Simba Talent Development Center. 3280 Wynn Road, Las Vegas 89102; 367-6788.

Theatre Ballet of Las Vegas. 3265 E. Patrick Lane, Las Vegas 89120; 458-7575.

Chapter 11
Local Protocol: Sex, Marriage, Shopping, Comps, and Tipping

Sex, Sex, Sex

There, we got your attention, didn't we? That is the philosophy of Nevada, too, and especially Las Vegas. The casinos and hotels and just about everything else in town are tied to sex, from the costumes on the cocktail waitresses, the togas on the greeters at Caesars Palace, and the production shows to the more-directly-to-the-point topless bars.

Getting past the idea of sex as tease, there is also a small but apparently thriving industry in prostitution in much of the state.

Prostitution is perhaps no more common in Nevada than it is in most other parts of the country, and certainly on a par with most convention and entertainment centers. It is, though, legal in several parts of the state, and there are about 36 legalized houses or "ranches" in the state. The industry is centered just outside of Reno and up or down the road from Las Vegas. For the record, the Nevada Supreme Court upheld the rights of the counties to legalize and regulate brothels; Clark County, which includes Las Vegas, and Washoe County, home of Reno, are among the few that do *not* permit brothels.

In Las Vegas, though, the streets are littered with brochures from "escort" services that offer what they describe as "in-room entertainment" and other such euphemisms. And Reno is ringed by special service companies.

Many of the companies masquerade as massage services ("Cathy's College Girls of Reno Hotel Guest Massage Service"), entertainment bureaus ("Plato's Retreat"), or escort services.

Among the brothels are the Cherry Patch Ranch an hour out of Las Vegas, the Mustang Ranch 1, six miles east of Reno in Lockwood, and the Sagebrush Ranch just outside of the state capitol in Carson City.

In this day and age it would be remiss of us not to warn that using the services of a prostitute is a highly dangerous activity. A much safer diversion is to read the entertainment section of the *Yellow Pages* in your hotel room for a few dirty laughs.

Getting Hitched

Speaking of more socially acceptable forms of expression, the idea of Las Vegas as a wedding—and divorce—mecca dates back to the same "anything goes" mentality that gave birth to the gambling industry and other adventures. The more convoluted and time-consuming the regulations for getting hitched or unhitched in the other states of the union, the more Nevada appealed as a place of convenience.

Today, many states have relaxed their strictures, but Las Vegas and Reno continue to have a thriving industry in weddings, offering the added lure of the grand hotels and casinos. Today, more than 75,000 couples tie the knot in Las Vegas each year.

If you are the sort of person who is impressed by celebrity name-dropping, check out some of the ads or billboards for the various wedding chapels. According to the proprietors, among those who have done the deed at their establishments include Joan Collins, Mia Farrow, Eddie Fisher, Michael Jordan, Jon Bon Jovi, Demi Moore, Dudley Moore, Mickey Rooney, Frank Sinatra, Elizabeth Taylor, and Bruce Willis.

Most of the major hotels offer elegant chapels for ceremonies ranging from the ridiculous to the sublime. You can get married dressed as King Arthur and Guinevere at the Excalibur, in a toga at Caesars Palace, or as just about anything else at any of a number of chapels. And there are dozens of small establishments that do nothing else but service the needs of the betrothed.

The busier chapels will require advance reservations, but many of the chapels in Las Vegas can also deal with walk-in customers. There are (honest!) a drive-up wedding window and a chapel on wheels for those in a hurry.

If you are planning to get married in Las Vegas, check with the County Clerk's office for the current legalities; here is a summary of the rules as this book went to print.

Marriages

Application. The prospective bride and groom must appear together at the County Clerk's office to apply for a wedding license.

In Las Vegas, the County Clerk's Office is located in the Courthouse, in the 200 block of South Third Street in downtown. The office is open from 8 A.M. until midnight Monday through Thursday, and from 8 A.M. Friday straight through to midnight Sunday. In addition, the clerk is available 24 hours a day on all Nevada legal holidays. $35 fee.

Consent. If you can prove you are 18 years or older, you do not need parental consent. Persons between the ages of 16 and 18 must have the consent of either parent or a court-appointed guardian. Either parent must appear in person, or the applicants must bring a notarized affidavit of consent including the birthdate of the minor and stating the relationship of the party giving consent.

A person under the age of 16 must have a court order from the Nevada District Court as well as the consent of either parent or a legal guardian. The court order will be granted if the court determines that the marriage will serve the best interests of the minor. Pregnancy alone is not an automatic qualification.

Blood Tests and Waiting Period. Blood tests are not required and there is no waiting period.

Previous Marriages. Divorces must be final in the state where granted. The date of the final decree and the city and state where granted are required.

Clark County Marriage License Bureau. 200 3rd Street; 455-3156.

Civil Ceremonies

If you want to have a quick civil ceremony in Las Vegas you can hop over to the office of the Commissioner of Civil Marriages at 136 South 4th Street, one block from the Marriage License Bureau. You can walk in single and stroll out married during the same hours that the County Clerk is open. The fee for a ceremony is $25 Monday through Friday from 8 A.M. to 5 P.M., and $30 for late nights, weekends, and holidays.

You must have at least one witness besides the person performing the ceremony. You cannot count on finding an extra clerk in the office; people have been known to hire strangers from the street for a quick stand-in.

Chapel Ceremonies

For many visitors, though, a civil ceremony at the commissioner's office is not what it is all about. Instead, they want to do it up in grand (by Las Vegas standards) style at one of the dozens of wedding chapels. You can get just about anything you want, from a choir of Elvis impersonators to a chapel on wheels to a ceremony in King Arthur's Court. Rates vary and reservations are necessary at some—but not all—of the chapels.

Here is a listing of some:

A Chapel by the Courthouse. 203 Bridger Avenue; 384-9099.
Candlelight Wedding Chapel. 2855 Las Vegas Blvd. South; 735-4179.
Chapel of the Bells. 2233 Las Vegas Blvd. South; 735-6803.
Chapel of Love. 1431 Las Vegas Blvd. South; 387-0155.
Cupid's Wedding Chapel. 827 Las Vegas Blvd. South; 598-4444.
Graceland Wedding Chapel. 619 Las Vegas Blvd. South; 474-6655.
L'Amour Chapel. 1901 Las Vegas Blvd. South; 369-5683.
Las Vegas Wedding Gardens. 200 W. Sahara Avenue; 387-0123.
Little Chapel of the Flowers. 1717 Las Vegas Blvd. South; 735-4331.
Little White Chapel. 1301 Las Vegas Blvd. South; 382-5943.
San Francisco Sally's Victorian Chapel. 1304 Las Vegas Blvd. South; 385-7777.
Silver Bell Wedding Chapel. 607 Las Vegas Blvd. South; 382-3726.
Wee Kirk o' the Heather. 231 Las Vegas Blvd. South; 382-9830.

Here are some of the hotel chapels in Las Vegas:

Bally's Wedding Chapel. Bally's Casino Resort; 892-2222.
Circus Circus Chapel of the Fountains. Circus Circus Hotel/Casino; 794-3777.
Excalibur Hotel Wedding Chapel. Excalibur Hotel & Casino; 597-7260.
Little Church of the West. Hacienda Hotel; 739-7971.
Plaza Chapel. Union Plaza Hotel; 386-2110.
Riviera Royale Wedding Chapel. Riviera Hotel; 794-9494.

Shalimar Wedding Chapel. Shalimar Hotel; 382-7372.
We've Only Just Begun Wedding Chapel. Imperial Palace; 733-0011.

Money, Money, Money

We can't think of very many places on earth more oriented to finding ways to take money out of the pockets of visitors than Las Vegas. And so, the proprietors are also quite accommodating when it comes to helping visitors scratch out every possible penny from its hiding place.

Arriving with foreign currency? No problem. Every major casino will be glad to exchange your francs, pounds, yen, or whatever into cash—or gambling chips. They'll extract a fee in the form of a discount from the actual exchange rate; you will probably get the best deal at a commercial bank.

Travelers checks are no problem at hotels, casinos, restaurants, or stores in Las Vegas; some places may require a photo ID card.

Need to cash a check? No problem for guests at a major hotel, although some establishments may enforce a limit on the amount they will release each day. At the casinos, the cashier will often cash checks for clients known to the casino, or in some way guaranteed by a credit card.

Need a loan? Most casinos will extend "markers" (credit vouchers) to gamblers who apply for such a loan in advance of their visit. Unsecured loans on the spot are more difficult to obtain.

Need a cash advance? Most major casinos have installed automated teller machines that permit withdrawal of cash from bank accounts or as cash advances against credit cards. Bank machines generally work with one of the national syndicates such as Plus, Cirrus, or Instant-Teller. If you choose to take a cash advance, be sure to read the disclaimer on the machine carefully; some systems apply a hefty service charge to the amount of money you are withdrawing, over and above any interest the holder of your credit card will charge.

A notch down on the pecking order are check-cashing businesses which specialize in handling out-of-state personal checks, money orders, and even savings account passbooks. You'll need personal identification, and you can expect to pay a fee that will increase with the complexity of the verification and transfer of funds.

And then there are the pawnshops of Las Vegas, filled with jewelry, cameras, furs, and other items left behind to raise cash. There are more than four pages of listings in the current *Yellow Pages*. If you arc that desperate for cash, perhaps you should seek counseling of a different sort than is available in these pages.

Comprehending Comps

Let's get one thing out of the way: there is no such thing as a free lunch, not even in Las Vegas.

There are, however, "comp" lunches, breakfasts, dinners, drinks, hotel rooms, shows, airline tickets, and more. That's comp as in complimentary, but as we say, they're not quite free.

The distinction is this: almost all of the casinos in Nevada offer all sorts of freebies to gamblers. They do so because they know that, over the long haul, they will win and you will lose.

The system starts with free drinks for players, which is actually one of the more insidious come-ons in marketing. Not only does it encourage players to sit at the slot machine or at the gaming table, but alcohol dulls the senses, reduces inhibitions, and otherwise aids in the removal of cash from your wallet.

The next step up is the provision of free meals. At a smaller casino, the process might be as simple as this: the pit boss, perhaps alerted by the dealer to your consistent gambling, will drop by and hand you a card good for dinner. It might be a free pass to the coffee shop or the buffet, or you may be "comped" into the gourmet restaurant. Either way, it's a reward for playing at the casino, and it also keeps you on the premises before and after the meal.

At larger casinos, the process has become a bit more complicated. Ask the floor manager or the pit boss to "evaluate" your play; he or she may actually chart your bets or may consult with the dealer. Generally, a comp rating will be given based on several hours of play at a consistent level.

And major casinos have begun using various electronic means to track the play of visitors at slot machines; they will issue a magnetically coded card that is placed in readers attached to the slots to record the amount of action. The cards can be cashed in for free meals or shows after a certain amount of play.

Some casinos have a slightly less sophisticated means of tracking slot players, relying on records kept by change booths or strolling change attendants. There is, of course, more of an opportunity to cheat here; one scheme would be to change a few hundred dollars in bills into coins but only play a small portion of the silver.

It doesn't hurt to ask one of the supervisors about how you can be evaluated. If you don't like the answer, you can always take your business elsewhere.

It all comes down to the amount of "action" you will provide the casino. Action is the amount of money you will put at risk over a particular period of time. For example, if you bet $25 per hand in blackjack for four hours a day over a three-day weekend, you are giving the casino something like $7,500 in action; at most middle-of-the-road casinos that should be worth a free hotel room for the length of your stay.

There is no official rulebook to the distribution of comps. Smaller casinos more desperate to attract action may be more generous than the bigger places. However, the most spectacular casinos—places like Caesars Palace and the Mirage—offer the most spectacular comps to the highest of rollers. The two-story, 4,000-square-foot Fantasy Suites at Caesars Palace, for example, are described by the casinos as "priceless" because they cannot be rented by guests. They are offered as comps, along with free meals, room service, shows, limousine service, and other amenities to people for whom money must truly hold no meaning.

According to insiders, the serious freebies start at about the $25 per hand level for free rooms. "RFB" players, who receive rooms, food, and beverages, generally are $75 to $125 per hand gamblers. The penthouses, limousines, and other perks are usually offered at about the $150 per hand level.

Some hotels are more up front about their comp programs than others. For example, the Flamingo Hilton in Reno issues a rate card for players in its Club Flamingo slot system, which uses a magnetic card to record action.

At the Flamingo Hilton in Reno, players can earn rewards ranging from a pair of free passes to the buffet to meals at the coffee shop or food court to admission to the Heavenly Bodies showroom and, for the highest rollers at the slots, free meals at the Top of the Hilton gourmet restaurant.

Playing time is based on six handle pulls per minute (once every ten seconds) using the maximum number of coins for each machine. In other words, if you are playing at a $1 machine, the club payoffs are based on betting the maximum number of tokens—usually five—for that machine. Fewer coins bet or fewer handle pulls per minute will require more playing time.

The quickest way to freebies is to play a $5 machine where you can obtain a dinner buffet, coffee shop or food court pass for two for one hour of play. (At $30 per pull, six times a minute, this means you are risking $10,800 in hopes of obtaining $20 worth of food.)

More reasonable requirements apply to the 25 cent machines. The Reno Hilton will give the same meals described above to a player who puts in five hours. (That's $1.25 per pull, six times a minute—a mere $2,250 in action.)

By the way, you'd have to play for four and a half hours at the $5 machines or 25 hours at the quarter slots for a pass for two to the Top of the Hilton.

Of course, unless you are completely luckless, you should be able to avoid losing all of your money. Slot machines generally pay back something between 90 and 99 percent of money bet. Remember, though, that this percentage applies over the very long haul and includes the very rare huge jackpot payoffs.

For table players, the Flamingo Hilton Reno offers comp packages that begin with discounts on hotel rooms for visitors willing to put down $10 at a time for four hours a day; free rooms for bettors playing $35 a hand for four hours a day; free room and buffet or coffee shop meals and drinks for $75 bettors; and free rooms, gourmet meals, and drinks for a player betting $100 at a time for four hours a day. If you are willing to bet even more and establish your credentials beforehand, the hotel will offer reimbursements of your airfare to Reno.

If you want to earn comps, keep in mind a few pointers. It is against your own interests to move from casino to casino, since you are diluting your influence in this way. (And don't think that casinos don't know this. That's why they have all of those "clubs" for loyal patrons.) And, if you change from one area of the casino to another, be sure that whoever is evaluating you is aware of where you are going and can transfer supervision.

Note that we have not talked about winning versus losing here. At any particular moment, the casino doesn't really care whether a player is ahead or behind. They know which way the dollars will eventually flow; in fact, if you're ahead of the game, they very much want you to stick around at their casino until the odds start to run the other way.

A Guide to Tipping

Las Vegas, Reno, and Lake Tahoe are very much dependent on the tourist and conventioneer, and tipping is an essential element of the economy. In fact, it has its own name in the casino: toking. You will have an extraordinary opportunity to grease the palms of dozens of strangers on your visit, but it's not necessary to pay everyone you meet.

Here's a guided tour to outstretched hands.

Transportation. The standard tip for **taxi drivers** is in the range of 15 to 20 percent of the fare; you might want to give a little bit more for a driver who helps with the bags or one who puts out his or her cigarette at your request.

Valet parking. A tip of about $1 to $2 is standard.

Bartenders and cocktail waitresses. Most casinos offer free drinks to players at the tables and some extend the privilege to slot players; a tip of 50 cents per drink or $1 per round is standard.

Restaurant servers and room service. Again, a tip in the range of 15 to 20 percent is standard. A sore point among some waiters and waitresses are visitors to buffets who don't leave money for the people who clear away your dishes and bring you drinks.

If you have received a free meal, check to see if your comp includes a gratuity for the staff; if it does not, you should leave a tip equal to 15 to 20 percent of what the bill would have been.

Bell captains and bellmen. The usual rate is about $1 to $2 per bag; give $1 or $2 to a bellman who summons a cab for you.

Bingo and keno runners. A small tip every few cards, and a larger tip with a winning card.

Dealers. A small tip, in the form of cash or a chip a few times an hour is standard. Some dealers might prefer that you place a small bet for them every once in a while, especially if you are winning; ask them how they'd like to be toked. In theory, this will not give you any special advantage at the table, but it might earn you more friendly treatment.

Maids. About $1 per day is standard; more if you have created an unusual amount of work or if extra services have been provided.

Showroom maitre d'hotel. In the past, nearly every casino showroom had a maitre d' out front who determined where each guest was seated. Ignore him and you might end up in the back corner behind the coffee pot; make him happy and you would end up down front and center. The current trend, though, is toward reserved seats at most shows—especially the more expensive ones. Therefore, tipping the maitre d'—if there is one—is optional.

Shop Till You Drop in Las Vegas

Of course, once you are married, then comes the real excitement: shopping.

If you've got any money left in your wallet—or if you are traveling with a spouse who prefers to gamble on clothing or accessories instead of the roll of the dice—Las Vegas offers several major shopping areas.

Actually, the hottest shopping area for those with dough to blow, or dreams of the same, is connected to one of the most spectacular casinos in Las Vegas, at Caesars Palace. We'll start with the two largest conventional malls and a major factory outlet shopping center.

Fashion Show Mall

The **Fashion Show Mall**, located directly on the Las Vegas Strip at 3200 Las Vegas Boulevard South, at the head of Convention Center Drive and next to the Mirage, is a large mall with some 150 shops, including a wide range of clothing and specialty stores. It is within walking distance of most Center-Strip motels and the Las Vegas Convention Center. Valet parking is available. Hours are Monday to Friday 10 A.M. to 9 P.M.; Saturday 10 A.M. to 7 P.M., and Sunday noon to 6 P.M. For information, call 369-8382.

Restaurants within the mall are a cut above your basic mall food court. They include the gourmet Chinese restaurant **Chin's**. Three new toney eateries were added in 1995. **Dive** is a Los Angeles import with involvement by movie director Steven Spielberg. It puts diners within a re-creation of a submarine with simulated underwater scenes moving past the "windows"; the menu includes a range of subs, of course. **Sfuzzi** is a gourmet Italian restaurant. Another import is **Morton's**, a well-known steak house.

Women's Fashions: Abercrombie & Fitch; Ambiance; Benetton; Bullock's; Cache; Casual Corner; Chez Magnifique; Contempo Casuals; Deon's; Evening Classics; Judy's; Koala Blue; Kolonaki; La-dy Ferenc; Laise Adzer; Lane Bryant; Lauren & The Boys; Lillie Rubin; The Limited; Marshall-Rousso; Mondi; Next Door; Petite Sophisticates; Pizazz; Portofino; Private Collections; Size 5-7-9; Wet Seal.

Shoes: Bally of Switzerland; Bianca; Brass Boot; Cobbie Shop; Florsheim Shoes; Footlocker; Joyce-Selby; Kinney; Lady Foot Locker; Leeds; Norman Kaplan; Rocky Mountain; Rococo; San Remo.

Cards, Gifts, Toys, and Books: Animal Crackers; Carlan's Gifts; Crystal Palace; Expanding Wall; Fantasia; Gifts of the World; Serendipity Gallery; Waldenbooks; West of Dallas.

Art Galleries: Centaur Sculpture; Gallery of History; Minotaur Gallery.

Apparel, Specialty: American Sock; Banana Republic; Disney Store; Furs by Yolanda; I Love Hats; Koala Blue; Merle Harmon's Fan Fair; Midnight Lace; Miller Stockman Western Ware; North Beach Leather; St. Croix Shop; Units; Victoria's Secret.

Food: Bernie's Bagel; Cafe Capri; Chin's; Ethel M. Chocolates; Heidi's Frozen Yogurt; See's Candies; Sweets of Las Vegas; Food Court.

Men's and Family Apparel: Abercrombie & Fitch; Benetton; Brats; Custom Shop Shirtmakers; Camouflage; The Gap; Harris & Frank; JW; Lauren & The Boys; Melwan's; Miller's Outpost; Oak Tree; Schwartz Big & Tall; Shirt Shoppe; Steve Gordon's; Uomo Uomo Sport; Zeidler & Zeidler.

Jewelry: Bailey Banks & Biddle; Chainery; Fashion Shop Jewelry; Gold Factory; Lindstrom Jewelers; Weisfield's; Whitehall; Zales.

Specialty: Abercrombie & Fitch; Antique Emporium; Bag & Baggage; Collegetown USA; Electronics Boutique; El Portal Luggage; Futuretronics; Gallery of Collectibles; Gloria Jean's Coffee Bean; La Perfumerie; Lenscrafters; Louis Vuitton; Omni Chemists; Sam Goody's; San Francisco Music Box; Sharper Image; Suncoast Motion Picture; Sun Shade Optique; Tennis Lady Tennis Man; Vignettes.

Department Stores: Bullock's; Dillard's; May Company; Neiman-Marcus; Saks Fifth Avenue.

The Boulevard Mall

The **Boulevard Mall** is a typical suburban sprawl of shops decorated with real plants and palms under an attractive atrium. There's an open, bright feeling—sort of like being outdoors. It is located at 3528 S. Maryland Parkway, at the intersection with Desert Inn Road, about five minutes east of the Strip. It claims the mantle as the largest mall in Nevada. Hours are 10 A.M. to 9 P.M. weekdays, from 10 A.M. to 7 P.M. on Saturdays, and 11 A.M. to 6 P.M. on Sundays. Valet parking is available. For information, call 735-8949.

Accessories: Afterthoughts; Best of Times; Carimar; Claire's Boutique; Sporting Eyes; Sunglass Designs.

Men's Apparel: Coda; Harris & Frank; J. Riggings; JW; Oak Tree; Pacific Wave; Schwartz' Big & Tall; Structure; Zeidler & Zeidler.

Men's and Women's Apparel: Colorado; County Seat; The Gap; GapKids; Going to the Game; Gymboree; Hot Cats; Howard & Phil's Western; Merry-Go-Round; Sports Logo; Tshirt Plus; Wilson's Leather Experts.

Women's Apparel: Cacique; Casual Corner; Charlotte Russe; Contempo Casuals; Express; Fitting Image; Lane Bryant; Lerner; The Limited; Petite Sophisticate; Roland's of Las Vegas; Size 5-7-9; Victoria's Secret; Westport; Wet Seal.

Cards, Gifts, and Specialty: African & World Imports; Amy's Hallmark; Bath & Body Works; The Body Shop; Country Hutch; Disney Store; Hot Topic; Just a Buck; The Mole Hole; The Nature Co.; San Francisco Music Box Co.; Sanrio Surprises; Sesame Street General Store; Spencer; Things Remembered; Tinderbox; Trader's West.

Services: Glamour Shots; Great Expectations Hair Salon; iNatural Cosmetics; Kiddie Kandids; Lens Crafters Optique; Prestige Travel; Stark Express Shoe Repair; Styles Hair Salon; Trade Secret Beauty Salon.

Shoes: Bostonian; Dolci's; Famous Footwear; Foot Action; Foot Locker; Kids Foot Locker; Kinney Shoes; Lady Foot Locker; Leed's; Naturalizer; Nine West; Wild Pair.

Food: Calido Chile Traders; Cinnabon; China Star; Down Home Country Cookin'; Ethel M.'s Chocolates; Everything Yogurt; Fingrs; Flamers Hamburgers; General Nutrition Center; Gloria Jean's Gourmet Coffees; Great Steak and Potato Co.; Hot Dog on a Stick; Hibachi San; IHOP; La Salsa; McDonald's; Mrs. Field's Cookies; Orange Julius/Dairy Queen; Panda Express; Sbarro; Scully's Bread and Chowder; See's Candies; Sweet Factory; The Vineyard.

Pets, Hobbies, and Entertainment: B. Dalton Bookseller; Champs Sports; Energy Express; Frisky Pet Center; KayBee Toy & Hobby; Radio Shack; Ritz Camera; Sam Goody; Software Etc.; Suncoast Motion Picture Co.; Wherehouse Records.

Home Furnishings: The Bombay Co.

Jewelers: Bailey Banks & Biddle; The Chainery; J. Burton Jewelry; Lundstrom Jewelry; The Jewelers; Tiffin's Jewelers; Whitehall Jewelers; Zales.

Department Stores: Broadway Southwest; Dillard's; Marshall's; JC Penney; Sears; Woolworth's.

Factory Outlets

Las Vegas Factory Stores. Five miles south of Tropicana Avenue off the top of the Strip, this casual mall offers products from some of the best-known brand names. Located at 9155 Las Vegas Boulevard South. Open Monday to Saturday from 10 A.M. to 8 P.M., and on Sunday 10 A.M. to 6 P.M. For information, call 897-9090.

Stores include Adolfo II; American Tourister; Applause; Banister; Barbizon; Blue Wave; Book Warehouse; Cape Isle Knitters; Corning/Revere; Famous Brands Housewares; Famous Footwear; Florsheim Shoe; Geoffrey Beene; Gitano; IB Diffusion; Indian Traders; Leather Loft; Mikasa; Nine West; No Nonsense; Paper Factory; Perfumania; Prestige Fragrance & Cosmetics; Rocky Mountain Chocolate Factory; Toy Liquidators; Van Heusen; Welcome Home; Westpoint Pepperell; Westport Ltd.; and Whims.

Belz Factory Outlet World. 7400 Las Vegas Blvd. South, I-15 at the Blue Diamond exchange, south of Las Vegas. Open daily 10 A.M. to 9 P.M., and Sunday 10 A.M. to 6 P.M. Call 896-5599.

Stores include Adolfo II; Amity Leather; Afterthoughts; Aileen; Bass Apparel; Blue Wave; Bon Worth; Bruce Alan Bags; Bugle Boy; Burlington Brands; Buxton; Carter's Childrensware; Chez Magnifique; County Seat; Corning/Revere; Crown Jewels; Danskin; Designer Labels for Less; Ducks Unlimited; Ellen Ashley; Hushpuppies; Kitchen Collection; Kitchen Place; Leather Loft; L'egg's/Hanes/Bali; Levi's; Lucia; Music 4 Less; Naturalizer; Nike; Oneida; Osh Kosh b'Gosh; Perfumania; Pfaltzgraff; Prestige Fragrance; Publishers Warehouse; Ribbon Outlet; Ross Simons; Ruff Hewn; Springmaid Wamsutta; Stone Mountain Handbags; Stride Rite; Swank; Toy Liquidators; Trader Kids; Van Heusen; Village Hatter; Westport Ltd.; Whims/Sarah Coventry; and Young Generations.

Other Stores

Here are a few of our favorite stores located outside of shopping malls.

Bell, Book & Candle. 1725 East Charleston Blvd.; 384-6807. Crystal balls, magic potions and classes in witchcraft.

Bookstar. 3910 S. Maryland Parkway; 732-7882. One of the largest and best-stocked bookstores anywhere. And it's open late into the night; stop off on the way to the airport.

Cowtown Boots. 328 W. Sahara; 384-8622. A factory outlet for handmade leather boots from cowhide to snakeskin to Teju Lizard.

Desert Indian Shop. 108 N. Third St.; 384-4977. Art and artifacts of the west.

Flashback. 1460 East Charleston Blvd.; 598-0633. Remember all that stuff you threw out when you left college and got a real job? It's all here—out-of-date clothing, jewelry and other items for those who believe it's back in style.

Lance Burton Magic Shop. Hacienda Hotel, 3950 Las Vegas Blvd. South; 739-1920. Tricks, gags, books, and lessons for the amateur and professional.

The Magic Mansion. 4702 S. Maryland Parkway; 732-1714. A professional magic shop.

The Magic Shop. Riviera Hotel; 2901 Las Vegas Blvd. South; 733-1965.

Sunglass City. 506 Fremont St.; 388-0622. The eyes have it; watches, too.

Traveling Books & Maps. 4001 S. Dectaur #34; 871-8082. Just like it says, books on travel, maps, globes, and friendly assistance from this locally owned and operated shop.

Waldenbooks Superstore. 3783 S. Maryland Parkway; 369-1996. An over-sized version of your basic Waldenbooks store; if you can't find what you're looking for at Bookstar across the road, check here, or the other way around.

If you're determined to bring a bit of Las Vegas home with you (and if you've left a bit of money in your wallet or on your credit card) you may want to visit one of several stores that sell gambling equipment. Be sure you investigate state and local laws before you bring back machines. *You will find a discount in the coupon section of this book.*

Gamblers Book Club. 630 S. 11th; 382-7555; (800) 634-6243. They take their games seriously here, offering the biggest collection of gambling arcana we know of, as well as a fine collection of local history, travel, and fiction.

Gamblers General Store. 800 S. Main Street; 382-9903. Open to the public for slot machines, poker machines, personalized poker chips, and craps tables.

Paul-Son Dice and Card. 2121 Industrial Road; 384-2425. Gambling equipment, including used dice and cards from major casinos.

And for those with a very special predilection, you may want to visit the **Seventh Dimension** shop for your spiritual articles and metaphysical supplies. They apparently prefer ESP instead of telephone numbers; you may find the place on Las Vegas Blvd. North at Charleston Blvd. Then again, it may have disappeared.

Feeling Lucky?

Earlier in this chapter we mentioned the sad fact that some visitors to Las Vegas end up leaving more than merely their money behind; pawnshops are well stocked with rings, necklaces, musical instruments, cameras, and just about anything else that can be carried in for quick cash at a deep discount.

If you are a particularly adventurous shopper and you are able to tell the difference between a dud and a diamond, an Instamatic and a Nikon, and a Gibson and garbage you may want to go to a pawnshop to buy.

Be aware that most of these operations are not in the nicest parts of town, and few spend any money at all on decorations. There are more than a dozen pawnshops in Las Vegas and many more throughout the state; for some reason, they seem to be clustered wherever you find casino districts.

Hail Caesars!

And then there are the **Forum Shops at Caesars**, which has to qualify as among the most otherworldly, spectacular shopping venues anywhere in the world. In other words, perfectly appropriate for Las Vegas.

Healthy shopping. Though the Forum Shops may be dangerous to your bank account, the management has done its part for your health, making the entire shopping area a smoke-free environment.

The storefront facades and common areas are designed to appear like an ancient Roman streetscape, with huge columns and arches, central piazzas, ornate fountains, and classic statuary.

Overhead, on a barrel-vaulted ceiling, a painted dome emulates the Mediterranean sky. The sky turns from daylight to sunset to dawn to full daylight over the course of two hours. Check it out: the sun rises in the east and sets in the west.

The 240,000-square-foot-mall, built for a mere $100 million or so and opened in 1992 on a site that had been used by Caesars (mostly unsuccessfully) as a race track, has become one of the most successful shopping "streets" anywhere. According to the owners, on a typical day, the mall draws 40,000 visitors; on busy weekends as many as 90,000 show up. To put that into a bit of travel perspective, Walt Disney World on its busiest days of the year around Christmas will draw 75,000 to 80,000 people.

According to a *Forbes* magazine piece a few months after the mall opened, the stores and restaurants have been averaging nearly $3 million in sales per week, or $900 in annual sales per square foot. This compares with the average mall which draws about $158 per square foot. Nevertheless, there have been a few turnovers among stores from the opening; the big news for 1995 was the arrival of **Planet Hollywood**, a branch of the trendy eatery.

The Forum Shops were attached onto the north side of Caesars Palace, and the main entrance connects to the main casino. There is now an entrance and exit at the far end of the Forum Shops, allowing visitors to come into the shops without having to meander through the casino, or saving the need to double back at the end of a tour; the door may not be open in the evening, though.

Amazingly, there are no casinos within the Forum Shops area itself—although there are a few banks of slot machines right by the entranceway just to ease the transition. It has to be the only place in the world where an actor dressed as Bugs Bunny (at the Warner Brothers Studios Store) poses within 30 feet of slot machines.

The Forum area stays open until 11 P.M. most evenings, with some of the restaurants keeping later hours when necessary. When the shops are closed, you can still walk the simulated streets of ancient Rome in relative quiet and loneliness.

At the casino entrance to the mall is the **Quadriga** statue, four gold-leafed horses, a charioteer, and five heroic arches, an ancient symbol of great achievement. (*Quadriga* is a Latin word for a team of four, and is pronounced *kwod-reye-ja*.) As you look at the fountain, Jupiter is perched up top. Mars faces Gucci. Diana the Huntress checks out Louis Vuitton, and Venus and Pluto keep an eye on the casino.

At the far end of the U-shaped mall is the spectacular **Festival Fountain.** It may look like marble, but it is not; every hour on the hour, starting at 10 A.M., the statuary comes to life.

In the animated tableau, Bacchus, god of merriment and wine, hosts a party with Apollo, Plutus, and Venus. The seven-minute show stars Bacchus, who has already had more than a few sips from his goblet. He enlists the power of Apollo (god of music), Venus (goddess of love), and Plutus (god of wealth) in preparing a party for all of the guests gathered around his fountain.

Plutus will cast his jewels upon the waters of the fountain; Bacchus will summon a laser-drawn chariot to cross the sky above. From the sun, Apollo commands a beam of light that strikes Bacchus' wine goblet to explode it into light.

When the party is over, the statues return to marble-like silence. The statues are on a rotating platter and make a complete circle.

This high-tech fountain was brought to life by Ron Hays, who produced some of the animated statuary used in the spectacular Pirates of the Caribbean ride at Walt Disney World in Orlando, Florida. The effects include lasers, planetarium-like star displays, and music.

The best seats are probably on the floor, about 10 or 15 feet back from the statues. Young kids may become fidgety after a minute or two, and most adults will not want to see the show a second time. Like most free entertainment in Las Vegas, it's worth every penny you pay for it.

You may want to park the kids at the large **Cyber Station** video arcade on the lower level of the mall. Free parking is available in the Caesars Palace garage, with valet service offered.

By the way, the Forum Shops offer a service that will deliver any packages from Caesars Palace to your hotel—for a fee, of course.

New for 1995 is a branch of the **Disney Store** chain. This has to be among the most unusual locations for such a wholesome outlet: inside a gambling casino next to a Victoria's Secret and across from Planet Hollywood.

Women's Fashions: Ann Taylor; Bebe; Caché; Express Compagnie Internationale; Plaza Escade; St. John.

Specialty Apparel: A/X Armani Exchange; Beyond the Beach; Boogie's Diner of Aspen; The French Room; Gianni Versace; Gucci; Guess; North Beach Leather; Rose of Sharon—Size 14 and Up; Versus; Victoria's Secret.

Specialty Shops: Animal Crackers; Antiquities; Brookstone; Caesars World; Christian Dior; Crystal Galleria; Davante; Disney Store; El Portal Luggage; Endangered Species; Field of Dreams; Kids Kastle; Louis Vuitton; Magic Masters; Magnet Maximus; Museum Company; Porsche Design; Sports Logo; Stuff'd; Sunglass Hut; Warner Brothers Studios Store; West of Santa Fe.

Men's Apparel: Bernini; Cuzzens; Kerkorian; The Knot Shop; Structure; Vasari.

Jewelry: Bulgari; M.J. Christensen; N. Landau Hyman; Roman Times; Zero Gravity.

Shoes: Avventura; Just for Feet; Shoooz at the Forum; Stuart Weitzman; Via Veneto.

Art Galleries: Circle Gallery; Galerie Lassen; Minotaur's Forum Gallery; One World; Thomas Charles Gallery.

Food: Bertolini's; Boogie's Diner of Aspen; Chocolate Chariot; La Salsa; Palm Restaurant; Planet Hollywood; Spago; Stage Deli; Sweet Factory; Swensen's Ice Cream.

Warner Brothers Studios Store. Look up over the entrance for statues of

Sylvester the Cat, the Tazmanian Devil, and Daffy Duck—in togas! The inscription over the door reads "Warnerius Fraternus Studius Storius," which is a rough Latin approximation for Warner Brothers Studios Store.

Inside the shop, let your eyes drift upward to spot the Gremlins hiding at ceiling level. At the back of the store is a video wall showing snippets of clas-

The Econoguide to the Best of the Forum Shops at Caesars

Warner Brothers Studios Store
Just for Feet
Magic Masters
Palm Restaurant

Spago
Bertolini's
Porsche Design
Antiquities

sic and current WB movies and cartoons. A pair of computer paint programs allows kids to colorize their own cartoons. Nearby is Marv's Matomic Service, a crawl-through space for kiddies.

And then there are the things on sale: sweatshirts, T-shirts, stuffed animals, toys, and souvenirs with a Warner's theme, for children of all ages. Also on sale is a selection of original cels from WB cartoons with prices ranging from about $100 to $7,000 and more.

Just for Feet. An "interactive shoe store" with more than 100,000 pairs of sports shoes in a 12,000-square-foot space that includes a small basketball court and a treadmill so that customers can try out their footwear in real situations. They've even got tennis shoes for babies.

Magic Masters. A wood paneled room designed to look like Houdini's library. (Check out some of the framed photographs on the wall.) There's a secret door to the left of the counter that leads to a small room where secrets are unveiled to the buyer.

Palm Restaurant. An elegant extension of the famed New York eatery. Among its offerings is a $12 prix-fixe lunch menu that includes petite filet mignon, prime rib, or pasta. Dinner offerings include seafood crab cakes for $26, a New York strip steak for $27, and a 36-ounce double steak for two for $57; a variety of salads is also available.

Planet Hollywood. Don't count on meeting the Hollywood film star of your dreams; they're busy counting their money earned from this successful chain of fancified burger joints decorated with cinema stuff. You can contribute, though: hamburgers are $6.50, vegetable burgers $6.75, barbecued pizza goes for $9.95, and a Mexican shrimp salad for $10. Dinner platters include St. Louis Ribs for $12.95, and grilled ranch chicken for $10.95. There is also a merchandise counter out front where you can purchase Planet Hollywood merchandise.

Spago. Not your average pizzeria. Specialties at the open-air cafe, which sits under the beautiful artificial Roman sky, include spicy chicken pizza with caramelized red onions and chili pesto for $12; Mediterranean fish soup with lobster and couscous for $24, and grilled tuna with tomato-fennel salsa and crisp smoked salmon ravioli for $23.

Bertolini's. The most spectacular setting in the Forum, this "sidewalk cafe" Italian eatery faces the Fountain of the Gods. (It opened as Lombardi's, but changed its name and menu in 1994.) Specialties include unusual pizzas for about $9 and pasta dishes from about $10 to $14. It's the place to see and to be seen at, although the noise of the water in the fountain can become a bit overbearing.

Porsche Design. "Design is neither form nor function alone, but the synthesis of the two." So says F. A. Porsche, grandson of the legendary automaker Ferdinand Porsche; he began as a designer at the Porsche plant in Stuttgart where he was instrumental in the design of the famed 904 and 911 series of cars. He went on to set up his own design house in the Austrian town of Zell am See, working for clients including makers of motorcycles, large-screen televisions, cameras, computers, furniture, and lamps. In 1991, F. A. Porsche was named chairman of the family auto business.

His store showcases some of his company's elegantly functional forms including sunglasses, pipes, and shavers.

Antiquities. Not to be missed, this unusual store facing the Festival Fountain is proof of the theory that one man's garbage is another's collectible investment. Where else can you buy a beautifully restored Coke machine, a classic jukebox, or a fortune-telling machine?

The owners of the store include among their treasure mines the backyards of the deep South and the cellars of Brooklyn; recovered items are repaired, repainted, and in some cases improved. Everything works just as it did when the items were new.

On one visit we found a 1942 Wurlitzer Model 950 Gazelle jukebox, the one with colored liquid bubbles and neon. Only 3,400 were ever made, and the unit on display includes more than 300 hours of restoration. It was a bargain at $47,000.

Nearby was a 1940s coin-operated photo booth in working order for $9,800. Other unusual offerings included a restored 1937 Dodg'em bumper car and a Gypsy Grandma Fortune Teller from the 1940s. We saw a bleacher seat from the dear-departed Comiskey Park in Chicago; there are lots of autographed pictures and movie memorabilia, some more impressive than others.

If you're lucky, you'll be offered the chance to have your picture taken with a certified Las Vegas Elvis Impersonator.

It's always worth a trip to check out the constantly changing collection, since someone seems to be buying up all of this stuff.

Foto-Forum. Here's your chance to put your face on the body you've always dreamed of: a biker babe, a bikini beauty, or Southern belle for the ladies, or perhaps a hockey star, beefcake stud, or Hollywood leading man.

The shop uses computer and video wizardry to merge your face with images on file; the result can be a poster, a small portrait, a personalized coffee cup, or just about anything else.

According to the operators, the most popular image for men is (what else could it be in Las Vegas?) Elvis; for women, it's the chance to sit atop a pair of 50-D cups barely contained in a string bikini.

Cinema Ride. A new addition to the entertainment within Caesars Palace, the Cinema Ride is a four-capsule virtual reality simulator "ride" located downstairs next to the Cyber Station video arcade. As intense as these kinds of movies are, this one is made even more frightening with the addition of 3-D glasses.

Tickets for the five-minute movies are priced at about $4; look for discount coupons at the time of your visit. Films at the time of my visit included "Coaster Crazy," "Haunted Graveyard Run," and "Atlantis Submarine Race." You must be at least 42 inches tall to gain admission.

Chapter 12
An Index of Las Vegas and Area Hotels

Standard Rooms, Non-Peak Rates

$	$74 or less	LVBS	Las Vegas Boulevard South (the Strip)
$$	$75 to $124	LVBN	Las Vegas Boulevard North
$$$	$125 or more		

All phone numbers are in area code (702) unless otherwise indicated.

Las Vegas Strip

Aladdin Hotel & Casino. $$–$$$; 3667 LVBS; 736-0111; (800) 634-3424
Alexis Park. $$$; 375 E. Harmon Ave.; 796-3300; (800) 582-2228
Algiers Hotel. $; 2845 LVBS; 735-3311
Bally's Las Vegas. $$–$$$; 3645 LVBS; 739-4111; (800) 634-3434
Barbary Coast. $$; 3595 LVBS; 737-7111; (800) 634-6755
Boardwalk Hotel & Casino. $$; 3750 LVBS; 735-1167; (800) 635-4581
Bourbon St. Hotel & Casino. $$; 120 E. Flamingo Rd.; 737-7200; (800) 634-6956
Caesars Palace. $$–$$$; 3570 LVBS; 731-7110; (800) 634-6661
Carriage House. $$–$$$; 105 E. Harmon Ave.; 798-1020; (800) 777-1700
Center Strip Inn. $–$$; 3688 LVBS; 739-6066; (800) 777-7737
Circus Circus. $–$$; 2880 LVBS; 734-0410; (800) 634-3450
Days Inn Center Strip. $–$$; 3265 LVBS; 735-5102; (800) 828-8032
Desert Inn. $$–$$$; 3145 LVBS; 733-4444; (800) 634-6906
Diamond Inn Motel. $; 4605 LVBS; 736-2565
Econo Inn. $–$$; 3939 LVBS; 736-8031
Econo Lodge. $; 1150 LVBS; 382-6001
El Rancho. $; 2755 LVBS; 796-2222
Excalibur. $$–$$$; 3850 LVBS; 597-7777; (800) 937-7777
Flamingo Hilton. $$–$$$; 3555 LVBS; 733-3111; (800) 732-2111
Frontier Hotel & Gambling Hall. $$; 3120 LVBS; 794-8200; (800) 634-6966
Full Moon Hotel. $; 3769 LVBS; 736-0055
Fun City. $; 2233 LVBS; 731-3155
Glass Pool Inn. $; 4613 LVBS; 739-6636; (800) 527-7118
Hacienda. $–$$; 3950 LVBS; 739-8911; (800) 634-6713
Harrah's Las Vegas Casino Hotel. $$–$$$; 3475 LVBS; 369-5000; (800) 634-6765
Holiday House. $; 2211 LVBS; 732-2468
Holiday Inn Las Vegas. $$; 325 E. Flamingo Rd.; 732-9100; (800) 732-7889
Howard Johnson Hotel & Casino. $–$$; 3111 W. Tropicana Ave.; 798-1111; (800) 654-2000
Imperial Palace. $$–$$$; 3535 LVBS; 731-3311; (800) 634-6441

Klondike Motor Inn. $; 5191 LVBS; 739-9351
La Concha Motel. $; 2955 LVBS; 735-1255
La Quinta. $; 3782 LVBS; 739-7457; (800) 531-5900
Luxor. $$$; 3900 LVBS; (800) 288-1000; 262-4444
Maxim. $$–$$$; 160 E. Flamingo Rd.; 731-4300; (800) 634-6987
MGM Grand Hotel. $$–$$$; 3799 LVBS; (800) 929-1112
The Mirage. $$$; 3400 LVBS; 791-7111; (800) 627-6667
Monaco Motel. $; 3073 LVBS; 735-9222
Riviera Hotel & Casino. $$; 2901 LVBS; 734-5110; (800) 634-6753
Rodeway Inn. $; 3786 LVBS; 736-1434; (800) 228-2000
Sahara Hotel & Casino. $$; 2535 LVBS; 737-2111; (800) 634-6666
Sands Hotel Casino. $$–$$$; 3355 LVBS; 733-5000; (800) 634-6901
Stardust Resort & Casino. $–$$; 3000 LVBS; 732-6111; (800) 634-6757
Sun Harbor Budget Suites. $; 1500 Stardust Rd.; 732-1500
Sunrise Fountain Suites. $; 3801 LVBS; 434-0848
Tam O'Shanter. $; 3317 LVBS; 735-7331; (800) 727-3423
Travel Lodge Center Strip. $; 3419 LVBS; 734-6801; (800) 854-7666
Travel Lodge South Strip. $; 3735 LVBS; 736-3443; (800) 255-3050
Travel Lodge Strip. $; 2830 LVBS; 735-4222; (800) 422-3313
Treasure Island. $$–$$$; 3300 LVBS; 894-7111; (800) 944-7444
Tropicana Resort and Casino. $$–$$$; 3801 LVBS; 739-2222; (800) 634-4000
Vacation Village. $$–$$$; 6711 LVBS; 897-1700; (800) 338-0608
Westward Ho Hotel. $–$$; 2900 LVBS; 731-2900; (800) 634-6803

Near the Strip

Arizona Charlie's Hotel Casino & Bowling. $; 740 S. Decatur Blvd.; 258-5200; (800) 342-2695
Best Western Parkview Inn. $–$$; 905 LVBN; 385-1213; (800) 528-1234
Blair House Residence Suites. $–$$; 344 E. Desert Inn Rd.; 792-2222; (800) 553-9111
Bonanza Lodge Motel. $; 1808 E. Fremont St.; 382-9990
Budget Inn. $; 301 S. Main St.; 385-5560
Comfort Inn S. $–$$; 5075 Koval Ln.; 736-3600
Continental Hotel Casino and Resort. $–$$; 4100 Paradise Rd.; 737-5555; (800) 634-6641
Courtyard by Marriott. $$–$$$; 3275 Paradise Rd.; 791-3600; (800) 321-2211
Fairfield Inn (Marriott). $$–$$$; 3850 Paradise Rd.; 791-0899
Gold Coast Hotel & Casino. $$; 4000 W. Flamingo Rd.; 367-7111; (800) 331-5334
Grand Flamingo. $; 100 Winnick Ave.; 731-6100
Highlander Inn. $; 211 E. Flamingo Rd.; 733-7800; (800) 634-6774
Holiday Royale Apartment Suites. $$; 4505 Paradise Rd.; 733-7676
King Albert. $; 185 Albert Ave.; 732-1555; (800) 553-7753
King 8 Hotel & Gambling Hall. $$; 3330 W. Tropicana Ave.; 736-8988; (800) 634-3488
Meadows Inn. $; 525 E. Bonanza; 366-0456
Motel 6. $; 195 E. Tropicana Ave.; 798-0728
Moulin Rouge. $; 900 W. Bonanza Rd.; 648-5054
Nevada Palace Hotel and Casino. $–$$; 5255 Boulder Hwy.; 458-8810; (800) 634-6283
Palace Station Hotel & Casino. $$; 2411 W. Sahara Ave.; 367-2411; (800) 634-3101
Paradise Resort Inn. $$; 4350 Paradise Rd.; 733-3900
Plaza Suite Hotel & Casino (Howard Johnson's). $$; 4255 Paradise Rd.; 369-4400; (800) 654-2000
Quality Inn Hotel & Casino. $–$$; 377 E. Flamingo Rd.; 733-7777; (800) 634-6617
Quality Sunrise Suites. $$; 4575 Boulder Hwy.; 434-0848
Ramada Las Vegas Inn. $–$$; 1501 W. Sahara Ave.; 731-3222; (800) 228-2828
Residence Inn by Marriott. $$–$$$; 3225 Paradise Rd.; 796-9300; (800) 331-3131
Rio Suite Hotel & Casino. $$–$$$; 3700 W. Flamingo Rd.; 252-7777; (800) 888-1808
Sam's Town Hotel & Gambling Hall. $; 5111 Boulder Hwy.; 456-7777; (800) 634-6371

San Remo Casino & Resort. $$–$$$; 115 E. Tropicana Ave.; 739-9000; (800) 522-7366
Santa Fe Hotel & Casino. $–$$; 4949 N. Rancho Drive; 658-4900; (800) 872-6823
Sheffield Inn. $$; 3970 Paradise Rd.; 796-9000; (800) 632-4040
St. Tropez. $$–$$$; 455 E. Harmon Ave.; 369-5400; (800) 666-5400
Super 8 Motel. $; 4250 Koval Ln.; 794-0888
Town Hall Hotel & Casino. $; 4155 Koval Ln.; 731-2111; (800) 634-6541

Las Vegas Convention Center

Best Western Mardi Gras Inn. $$–$$$; 3500 Paradise Rd.; 731-2020; (800) 634-6501
Convention Center Lodge. $–$$; 79 E. Convention Center Dr.; 735-1315
Debbie Reynolds Hotel/Casino/Hollywood Movie Museum. $$; 305 Convention Center Dr; 734-0711; (800) 633-1777
Desert Paradise. $–$$; 465 E. Desert Inn Rd.; 735-5112; (800) 634-6635
D.I. 500 Motel. $$; 505 E. Desert Inn Rd.; 735-3160
Las Vegas Hilton. $$–$$$; 3000 Paradise Rd.; 732-5111; (800) 732-7117
Paddlewheel Hotel & Casino. $$; 305 Convention Center Dr.; 734-0711; (800) 782-2600
Royal Hotel & Casino. $; 99 Convention Center Dr.; 735-6117
Somerset House. $; 294 Convention Center Dr.; 735-4411
Villa Roma. $–$$; 220 Convention Center Dr.; 735-4151; (800) 634-6535

Airport Area

Airport Inn. $–$$; 5100 Paradise Rd.; 798-2777; (800) 634-6439
Best Western McCarran Inn. $$; 4970 Paradise Rd.; 798-5530; (800) 626-7575
E-Z 8 Motel. $–$$; 5201 S. Industrial Rd.; 739-9513

Downtown and Area

Ambassador East Motel. $; 916 E. Fremont St.; 384-8281
Apache Motel. $; 407 S. Main St.; 382-7606
Arrowhead Motel. $; 2403 LVBN; 399-9043
Aztec Inn. $; 2200 LVBS; 385-4566
Best Western Main St. Inn. $–$$; 1000 N. Main St.; 382-3455; (800) 851-1414
Best Western Marianna Inn. $–$$; 1322 E. Fremont St.; 385-1150; (800) 356-5329
Binion's Horseshoe. $$; 128 E. Fremont St.; 382-1600; (800) 622-6468
California Hotel Casino. $$; 12 Ogden Ave.; 385-1222; (800) 634-6255
City Center Motel. $; 700 E. Fremont St.; 382-4766
Convention Inn. $$; 735 E. Desert Inn Rd.; 737-1555; (800) 845-5564
Crest Budget Inn. $; 207 N. 6th St.; 382-5642; (800) 777-1817
Daisy Motel. $; 415 S. Main St.; 382-0707
Days Inn. $–$$; 3227 Civic Center Dr.; 399-3297
Days Inn Downtown. $–$$; 707 E. Fremont St.; 388-1400; (800) 325-2344
Downtowner. $; 129 N. 8th St.; 384-1441; (800) 777-2566
El Cid Motel. $; 233 S. 6th St.; 384-4696
El Cortez. $–$$; 600 E. Fremont St.; 385-5200; (800) 634-6703
El Morocco. $–$$; 2975 LVBS; 735-7145
Ferguson's. $; 1028 E. Fremont St.; 382-3500
Fitzgerald's. $–$$; 301 E. Fremont St.; 388-2400; (800) 274-5825
Four Queens Hotel & Casino. $$; 202 E. Fremont St.; 385-4011; (800) 634-6045
Gold Spike Hotel/Casino. $; 400 E. Ogden Ave.; 384-8444; (800) 634-6703
Golden Gate. $–$$; 111 S. Main St.; 382-3510; (800) 426-0521
Golden Inn. $; 120 LVBN; 384-8204
Golden Nugget. $$–$$$; 129 E. Fremont St.; 385-7111; (800) 634-3454
Hotel Nevada. $; 235 S. Main St.; 385-7311; (800) 637-5777
Jackie Gaughan's Plaza Hotel. $; 1 S. Main St.; 386-2110; (800) 634-6575
Lady Luck Casino Hotel. $$–$$$; 206 N. 3rd St.; 477-3000; (800) 523-9582
Las Vegas Club Hotel & Casino. $$; 18 E. Fremont St.; 385-1664; (800) 634-6532
Lee Motel. $; 200 S. 8th St.; 382-1297

Main St. Station. $; 300 N. Main St.; 387-5333
Nevada Hotel & Casino. $; 235 S. Main St.; 385-7311; (800) 637-5777
Ninth St. Motel. $; 117 N. 9th St.; 384-1908
Ogden House. $; 651 Ogden Ave.; 385-5200
Par-A-Dice Inn. $; 2217 E. Fremont St.; 382-6440
Queen of Hearts Hotel. $; 19 E. Lewis Ave.; 382-8878; (800) 835-6005
Rainbow Vegas Hotel. $–$$; 401 S. Casino Center Blvd.; 386-6166; (800) 634-6635
Sam Boyd's Fremont Hotel & Casino. $; 200 E. Fremont St.; 385-3232; (800) 634-6182
Shalimar Hotel & Casino. $; 1401 LVBS; 388-0301
Showboat Hotel, Casino & Bowling Center. $–$$; 2800 E. Fremont St.; 385-9123; (800) 826-2800
Town Palms. $; 321 S. Casino Center Blvd.; 382-1611
Travel Lodge Downtown. $; 2028 E. Fremont St.; 384-7540; (800) 255-3050
Union Plaza. $–$$; 1 Main St.; 386-2110; (800) 634-6575

RV Parks

Las Vegas

American Campgrounds. 3440 LVBN; 30 hookups; 643-1222
Bond Trailer Lodge. 284 E. Tropicana Ave.; 77 hookups; 736-1550
Boomtown Hotel Casino & RV Resort. I-15 and Blue Diamond; 263-7777; (800) 588-7711
Boulder Lakes RV Resort & Country Club. 6201 Boulder Hwy.; 417 hookups; 435-1157
Sam Boyd's California Hotel & Casino RV Park. 1st Street and Ogden Ave.; 220 hookups; 388-2602
Circusland RV Park. 500 Circus Circus Dr.; 421 hookups; 734-0410
Golden Mobil Manor. 252 E. Tropicana Ave.; 20 hookups; 736-4200
Good Sam's Hitchin Post Camper Park. 3640 LVBN; 195 hookups; 644-1043
Hacienda Camperland RV. 3950 LVBS; 451 hookups; 739-8214
Holiday Travel Trailer Park. 3890 Nellis Blvd. S.; 402 hookups; 451-8005
King's Row. 3660 Boulder Hwy.; 140 hookups; 457-3606
KOA Kampgrounds. 4315 Boulder Hwy.; 300 hookups; 451-5527
Mackie Trailer Park. 3375 Glen Ave.; 76 hookups; 457-3553
Maycliff. 4001 E. Sahara Ave.; 131 hookups; 457-9855
Nevada Palace VIP Travel Trailer Park. 5325 Boulder Hwy.; 168 hookups; 451-0232
Riviera Travel Trailer Park. 2200 Palm St.; 136 hookups; 457-8700
Road Runner RV Park. 4711 Boulder Hwy.; 200 hookups; 456-4711
Sam's Town RV Park Boulder. 5111 Boulder Hwy.; 291 hookups; 454-8055
Shady Acres. 1001 North Main St.; 384-4551
Silver Nugget Casino & RV Park. 2240 LVBN; 649-7439

Lake Mead Area Campgrounds

Boulder Camp Grounds. 293-8906
Callville Bay Resort. 565-8958
Cottonwood Cove Resort. 297-1125
Echo Bay Resort. 394-4000
Las Vegas Wash. 293-8906
Overton Beach. 394-4040

Boulder City RV Parks

Canyon Trail RV Park. 1200 Industrial Rd.; 156 hookups; 293-1200
Lakeshore Trailer Village. 2688 Lakeshore Rd.; 70 hookups; 293-2540

Laughlin

Riverside Resort Hotel and Casino RV Park. 1650 Casino Dr.; 640 hookups; 298-2535

Chapter 13
Eating Your Way Across Las Vegas

Las Vegas' Favorite Food: Buffets

Comedian Gary Shandling offered us the best reason we've ever heard for the popularity of buffets in Las Vegas. He told us of an unlucky visitor who had dropped $800 at the tables and found himself at an all-you-can-eat buffet at the casino. "By God, I am going to eat $800 worth of food if it kills me!"

The history of buffets in Las Vegas may go back to the town's origins as a provisioning center for miners and railroad workers. Bars would compete for business by offering the proverbial "free lunch" for customers who kept their glasses full.

Today's casinos, of course, view the buffet in somewhat the same way. They figure if they can lure you into their doors with the offer of an inexpensive meal you are quite likely to stop to play the tables or the slot machines on your way in or out. The casinos try to encourage this as much as they can by placing the buffets at the back of the casino. The casinos also try to find ways to encourage all-night gamblers to stick around for breakfast.

In case you were wondering, The Excalibur reports that each month it goes through 50,500 heads of lettuce; 27,000 pounds of bacon; 18,000 gallons of milk; 5,400 gallons of Pepsi; 330,000 bread rolls; 44,100 Cornish game hens; 24,000 watermelons; 15,000 pounds of hamburger meat; 9,600 pounds of ham; and 1,500 flats of tomatoes.

Whatever the reason for the buffets, it is true that *some* of the offerings represent the best values for food anywhere we know of. The best of the buffets offer top-quality meals in attractive settings for a mere fraction of the price of a sitdown restaurant. (The worst of the buffets are spectacularly ordinary and unattractive, but still represent better values than McDonald's or the neighborhood greasy spoon.)

In general, the best meals are the dinner buffets and the weekend brunches; a few casinos offer spectacular breakfasts. As you might expect, the more popular buffets can build lengthy lines; the best strategy is to eat a bit early—before 8 A.M. for breakfast and before 6 P.M. for dinner.

Prices are subject to change. Call to check hours. Most buffets offer lower rates for children. Soft drinks, coffee, and tea are included with most meals; alcoholic drinks are extra.

Buffets

Aladdin Hotel. Market Place Buffet. Breakfast 7:30 to 10:30 A.M., $4.95; lunch 10:30 A.M. to 3 P.M., $5.95; dinner 4 to 10 P.M., $6.95.

Arizona Charlie's. Wild West Buffet. Breakfast 7 to 10:30 A.M., $3; lunch 11 A.M. to 3:30 P.M., $3.50; dinner 4 to 10 P.M., $5.

Bally's. Big Kitchen Buffet. Brunch 7:30 A.M. to 2:30 P.M., $6.95; dinner 4:30 to 10 P.M., $11.95. Sterling Brunch Sunday, Bally's Steakhouse. Sundays, 9:30 A.M. to 2:30 P.M., $35.00.

Boomtown. Chuckwagon Buffet. Breakfast 7 to 11 A.M., $3.95; lunch 11:30 A.M. to 3:30 P.M., $4.95; dinner 4 to 10 P.M., $6.95.

Boulder Station. The Feast. Breakfast 7 to 11 A.M., $3.95; lunch 11 A.M. to 2 P.M., $4.95; dinner 4:30 to 10 P.M., $6.95.

Bourbon Street. Breakfast 8 to 10:30 A.M., $3.95; weekday lunch 10:30 A.M. to 2 P.M., $4.25; dinner nightly 5 to 9 P.M., $5.95.

Caesars Palace. Palatium Buffet. Breakfast Monday through Friday 7:30 to 11 A.M., $7.50; lunch 11:30 A.M. to 2:30 P.M., $9; dinner 4:30 to 10 P.M., $13.25. Palatium Brunch Saturday. 8:30 A.M. to 2:30 P.M., $13.25. Champagne brunch Sunday 8:30 A.M. to 2:30 P.M., $14.50.

Caesars Palace. Cafe Roma. Breakfast 7 to 11 A.M., $9.95; lunch noon to 2:30 P.M., $11.95; and dinner 6 to 10 P.M., $21.95.

Circus Circus. Plate of Plenty. Breakfast 6 to 11:30 A.M., $2.99; lunch noon to 4 P.M., $3.99; dinner 4:30 to 11 P.M., $4.99.

Continental. Florentine Room Buffet. Breakfast 7 to 10:45 A.M., $2.95; lunch 11 A.M. to 2:45 P.M., $3.95; dinner 4 to 10 P.M., $5.95. Crab leg buffet daily 4 to 10 P.M., $12.95.

Desert Inn. Weekend champagne brunch, Crystal Room. Sunday 9 A.M. to 2 P.M., $10.95.

Excalibur. Round Table Buffet. Breakfast 7 to 11 A.M., $3.99; lunch 11 A.M. to 4 P.M., $4.99; dinner, 4 to 10 P.M., $5.99. Weekends 9 A.M. to 1 P.M., $7.95.

Fiesta Casino-Hotel. Cactus Rose Buffet. Breakfast, $3.95; lunch, $4.95; dinner, $5.99.

Fitzgerald's. Molly's Country Kitchen & Buffet. Breakfast 7 to 11 A.M., $3.99;

lunch, 11:30 A.M. to 4 P.M., $4.49; dinner 5 to 9 P.M., $5.99. Champagne brunch weekends 8 A.M. to 4 P.M., $4.99.

Flamingo Hilton. Flamingo Room. Breakfast 6:30 A.M. to noon, $4.25; dinner 4:30 to 10 P.M., $5.95.

Fremont. Paradise Buffet. Weekday breakfast 7 to 10:30 A.M., $3.95; lunch 11 A.M. to 3 P.M., $4.95; dinner nightly except Tuesday, Friday, and Sunday, 4 to 10 P.M., $7.95. Champagne brunch Sundays 7 A.M. to 3 P.M., $6.95. Seafood Fantasy Tuesday, Friday, and Sunday 4 to 10 P.M., $11.95.

Gold Coast. Breakfast Monday through Saturday 7 to 10:30 A.M., $2.95; lunch 11 A.M. to 3 P.M., $3.95; dinner 4 to 10 P.M., $5.95. Sunday brunch 8 A.M. to 3 P.M., $4.95.

Golden Nugget. The Buffet. Breakfast Monday through Saturday 7 to 10:30 A.M., $4.95; lunch Monday through Saturday 10:30 A.M. to 3 P.M., $7.50; dinner 4 to 10 P.M., $9.50. Champagne brunch Sunday 8 A.M. to 4 P.M., $9.50.

Hacienda. El Grande Buffet. Monday through Saturday. Breakfast 7 to 11 A.M., $4.95; lunch 11:30 A.M. to 3 P.M., $5.95; dinner 5 to 10 P.M., $7.95. Sunday brunch 8 A.M. to 3 P.M., $6.95.

Harrah's Las Vegas. Galley Buffet. Breakfast 7 to 11 A.M., $3.99; lunch 11 A.M. to 4 P.M., $4.49; dinner 5 to 10 P.M., $5.99.

Imperial Palace. Buffet, Teahouse, Coffee Shop. Monday through Friday 7 a.m. to 3 P.M. brunch $5.95. Champagne dinner buffet nightly $7.95.
Imperial Palace. Emperor's Buffet. Breakfast 7 to 11:30 A.M., $3.99; lunch 11:30 A.M. to 4 P.M., $4.49; dinner 5 to 10 P.M., $4.99. Prime rib dinner buffet nightly 5 to 9:30 P.M., $7.95.

Lady Luck. Breakfast 6 to 10:30 A.M., $2.99; lunch 11 A.M. to 2 P.M., $3.99; dinner featuring prime rib, crab, and shrimp 4 to 11 P.M., $6.99.

Las Vegas Hilton. Buffet of Champions. Breakfast weekdays 7 to 9:30 A.M., $5.99; lunch 11 A.M. to 2 P.M., $7.99; dinner 5 to 10 P.M., $12.99. Champagne brunch Saturday, Sunday, and holidays 8 A.M. to 2:30 P.M.

Luxor. Manhattan Buffet. Breakfast, $4.49; lunch, $5.49; dinner, $7.49.

Maxim. Daily brunch buffet. 10 A.M. to 3 P.M., $4.95; evening buffet 4 to 10 P.M., $5.95. Weekend champagne brunch 9 A.M. to 3 P.M., $6.95.

MGM Grand. Oz Buffet. Breakfast 7 to 11 A.M., $6.29; lunch 11 A.M. to 4 P.M., $7.29; dinner 4 to 10 P.M., $9.39.

The Mirage. Breakfast 7 to 10:45 A.M., $6.75; lunch 11 A.M. to 2:45 P.M., $8.75; dinner 3 to 9:30 P.M., $10.75.

Palace Station. The Feast. Breakfast 7 to 11 A.M., $3.95; lunch 11 A.M. to 2 P.M., $5.95; dinner 4:30 to 10 P.M., $7.95.

Rio. Carnival World Buffet. Breakfast 7 to 10:30 A.M., $3.95; lunch 11 A.M. to 3:30 P.M., $5.95; dinner 3:30 to 10 P.M., $7.95. Weekend brunch 7 A.M. to 3:30 P.M., $6.95.

Riviera. World's Fare Buffet. Breakfast 7 to 10 A.M., $4.95; champagne brunch 10 A.M. to 3 P.M., $5.95; dinner 4:30 to 11 P.M., $6.95. Seafood Fair Friday 4:30 to 11 P.M., $11.95; prime rib Saturday 4:30 to 11 P.M., $6.95.

Sahara. Oasis Buffet. Breakfast Monday through Friday 7 to 11 A.M., $4.95; lunch 11 A.M. to 2:30 P.M., $5.95; dinner daily 4 to 10:30 P.M., $7.95.

Sam's Town. Uptown Buffet. Weekday brunch 8 A.M. to 2:30 P.M., $3.95; dinner Monday through Thursday 4 to 9 P.M., $6.49; dinner Friday through Sunday 4 to 9 P.M., $6.95.

San Remo. Ristorante del Fiori Buffet. Monday through Friday breakfast 7 to 10 A.M., $5.25; lunch 11 A.M. to 2 P.M., $6.25; dinner 5 to 9 P.M., $7.25. Champagne brunch weekends 7 A.M. to 2 P.M., $7.25.

Sands. Garden Terrace Buffet. Breakfast, $3.99; lunch, $4.99; dinner, $6.99.

Sands. Brunch 7 A.M. to 2 P.M., $5.99; Dinner Seafood Spectacular 4 to 10:30 P.M., $9.99.

Santa Fe. Lone Mountain Buffet. Breakfast 7:30 to 10:30 A.M., $3.50; lunch 11:30 A.M. to 2:30 P.M., $4.95; dinner 4 to 9 P.M., $6.95.

Showboat. Captain's Buffet. Lunch weekdays 10 A.M. to 3:30 P.M., $4.95; dinner Monday, Tuesday, and Thursday 4:30 to 10 P.M., $6.45; New York Strip Steak Buffet Wednesdays, $7.95; Seafood Extravaganza Fridays, $7.95; Prime Rib and Pasta Saturdays, $6.95.

Stardust. Warehouse Buffet. Breakfast Monday through Saturday 7 to 10:30 A.M., $4.95; lunch 10:30 A.M. to 3 P.M., $5.95; dinner every night 4 to 10 P.M., $7.95. Sunday champagne brunch 7 A.M. to 3 P.M., $6.95.

Treasure Island. Breakfast 7 to 10:45 A.M., $4.99; lunch 11 A.M. to 3:45 P.M., $6.99; dinner 4 to 11 P.M., $8.99.

Tropicana. Rhapsody Brunch. Sunday only 9:30 A.M. to 2 P.M., $20.95.

Vacation Village. Upstairs Buffet. Lunch, $4.95; prime rib dinner, $5.95.

Westward Ho. Breakfast 7 A.M. to noon, $4.95; lunch noon to 4 P.M., $5.95; dinner 4 to 10 P.M., $6.95.

Restaurants

Entree Prices Only

$	Inexpensive (Up to $10)	$$$$	Deluxe ($40 and over)
$$	Moderate ($10 to $20)	LVBS	Las Vegas Boulevard, South (the Strip)
$$$	Expensive ($20 to $40)	LVBN	Las Vegas Boulevard, North

You can get just about anything you want at a Las Vegas restaurant. We've already discussed the sometimes exceptional hotel/casino buffets. In this section, we'll give some details about many of the more interesting restaurants in town.

Most restaurants are open for lunch and dinner; weekend hours may vary. Be sure to call and confirm hours and check to see if a reservation is necessary.

All phone numbers are in the (702) area code.

American (the Strip or Nearby)

Alias Smith & Jones. 541 E. Twain Ave.; 732-7401. $$

All American Bar & Grille. Rio Hotel/Casino; 252-7767. Mesquite-grilled steaks and seafood. $$

All That Jazz. Harrah's Las Vegas Casino Hotel; 3475 LVBS; 369-5000. New Orleans atmosphere. Prime rib, crab legs, catfish, and steamed shrimp. Closed for dinner Wednesday and Thursday. $$

Bally's Steakhouse. Bally's Las Vegas; 3645 LVBS; 795-3990. Steaks, chops, and seafood served in a New York club atmosphere. $$

Barronshire. Las Vegas Hilton; 3000 Paradise Rd.; 732-5111. Closed Mondays. English style, featuring prime rib carved at your table; also fish and chicken entrees. **$$**

Big Dog's Cafe & Casino. 6390 W. Sahara Ave.; 876-3647. **$–$$**

Big Mama's. 3765 LVBS; 597-1616. Big Mama McWhorter's southern, Cajun, creole, and barbecue recipes. **$$**

Boogie's Diner. Forum Shops at Caesars. A '50s diner in all of its re-created glory. **$–$$**

Cafe Roma. Caesars Palace; 3570 LVBS; 731-7110. **$$**

California Pizza Kitchen. The Mirage; 3400 LVBS; 791-7111. **$–$$**

Caribe Cafe. The Mirage; 3400 LVBS; 791-7111. **$$**

Clay's Texas Pit BBQ. 414 N. Eastern Ave.; 399-7911. **$–$$**

The Coachman's Inn. 3240 S. Eastern Ave.; 731-4202. Prime ribs and sandwiches, all the time. **$$**

The Coffee Shop. Bally's Las Vegas; 3645 LVBS; 736-4111. **$–$$**

Country Inn. 2425 E. Desert Inn Rd.; 731-5035. **$**

Country Inn. 1401 S. Rainbow Blvd.; 354-0250. **$**

El Gaucho. Tropicana Hotel; 3801 LVBS; 739-2376. Steak, ribs, and lobster specials. **$–$$**

42nd Street Deli & Cafe. 3735 LVBS; 795-2010. **$$**

Gates Bar-B-Que. 2710 E. Desert Inn Rd.; 369-8010. A Kansas City–style barbecue joint; raucous and fun. **$–$$**

Iron Horse Cafe. Palace Station Hotel & Casino; 2411 W. Sahara; 367-2411. **$–$$**

Jeremiah's Steak House. 171 East Tropicana; 736-3044. **$$–$$$**

Jerome's. 4503 S. Paradise Rd.; 792-3772. San Francisco atmosphere, featuring pasta and seafood. Butcher paper tablecloths and crayons provided. **$$**

Kiefer's. 105 E. Harmon Ave.; 739-8000. Penthouse restaurant in Carriage House apartment complex with view of the Strip. Veal, steak, and seafood specialties. **$$**

La Promenade. Desert Inn Hotel & Country Club; 3145 LVBS; 733-4580. **$–$$**

Marie Callenders. 600 E. Sahara Ave.; 734-6572. American right down to the apple pies; just like the other couple hundred in the chain. **$–$$**

Marie Callenders. 4875 W. Flamingo Rd.; 365-6226. **$–$$**

MarketPlace Restaurant. Alexis Park Resort; 375 E. Harmon Ave.; 796-3300. **$–$$**

Oasis Coffee Shop. Aladdin Hotel & Casino; 3667 LVBS; 736-0111. **$–$$**

The Palm. Forum Shops at Caesars; 732-7256. The Vegas branch of the venerable New York steak and seafood house; casual and fun. **$$$**

Peppermill Lounge. 2985 LVBS; 735-4177. **$–$$**

The Pink Pony. Circus Circus Hotel Casino; 2880 LVBS; 734-0410. **$–$$**

Rafters. 1350 E. Tropicana Ave.; 739-9463. Fresh seafood, served in an intimate winery-like setting. **$–$$**

Ralph's Diner. Stardust Resort & Casino; 3000 LVBS; 732-6111. **$–$$**

Ristaurant dei Fiori. San Remo Casino Resort; 115 E. Tropicana Ave.; 739-9000. **$$**

Sadie's Southern. 505 E. Twain Ave.; 796-4177. Closed Monday. **$–$$**
Sherwood Forest Cafe. Excalibur Hotel/Casino; 3850 LVBS; 597-7777. **$–$$**
Skyrise Dining Room. Circus Circus Hotel/Casino; 2880 LVBS; 734-0410.
$–$$
Socorro Springs Cafe. Las Vegas Hilton; 3000 Paradise Rd.; 732-5111. **$–$$**
TGI Friday's. 1800 E. Flamingo Rd.; 732-9905. Closed Sundays. **$–$$**
Tony L's. 4801 S. Eastern Ave.; 736-7211. **$–$$**
Tony Roma's. 520 E. Sahara; 733-9914. Part of a chain of steak, seafood,
and pasta restaurants. **$$**
Tree House Coffee Shop. Maxim Hotel Casino; 150 E. Flamingo Rd.; 731-
4300. **$–$$**
Veranda Cafe. Harrah's Las Vegas Casino Hotel; 3475 LVBS; 369-5000. **$–$$**
William B's. Stardust Hotel/Casino; 732-6111. **$$**

American (Downtown and Out of Town)

California Pizza Kitchen. Golden Nugget Hotel and Casino; 129 E. Fremont
St.; 385-7111. **$–$$**
Carson Street Cafe. Golden Nugget Hotel and Casino; 129 E. Fremont St.;
385-7111. **$$**
The Dugout. Las Vegas Club Hotel & Casino, Downtown Casino Center;
Main and Fremont; 385-1664. **$–$$**
Green Shack. 2504 E. Fremont; 383-0007. The oldest continuously oper-
ating restaurant in Las Vegas, virtually unchanged since 1932 when it was
converted from a Union Pacific bunkhouse. Fried chicken, fish, and more. **$**
Hugo's Cellar. Four Queens Hotel/Casino; Fremont Street;
385-4011. A local institution; fine steaks, seafood, and fowl. **$$–$$$**
Marie Callenders. 4800 S. Eastern Ave.; 458-2127. **$–$$**
Mount Charleston Inn Hotel. 2 Kyle Canyon Rd.; Mt. Charleston, 872-
5500. Quail, rabbit, game, and other down-home specialties in a mountain
chalet. Check driving conditions in wintertime. **$$**
Mount Charleston Lodge. Mt. Charleston; 872-5408. Check for hours and
driving conditions. **$–$$**
Redwood Bar & Grill. California Hotel; 12 Ogden Ave.; 385-1222. Steaks,
ribs, and seafood in a comfortable English inn-like setting. **$$**
Skye Room. Binion's Horseshoe; 731-7731. **$$**

Asian/Middle Eastern (the Strip or Nearby)

Bamboo Garden. 4850 W. Flamingo Rd. at Decatur; 871-3262. No lunch Sun-
day. **$$**
Beijing. 3900 Paradise Road; 737-9618. No lunch Sunday. Vegetarian spe-
cialties and unusual seafood dishes complement standard fare. **$$**
Cathay House. 5300 W. Spring Mountain Rd.; 876-3838. A great panoramic
view of the Strip. Dim sum carts. **$$**
China Doll Restaurant. 2534 E. Desert Inn Rd.; 369-9511. **$–$$**
China First. 1801 E. Tropicana Ave.; 736-2828. Closed Monday. **$$**
China Star. 3582 S. Maryland Pkwy.; 732-1608. Luncheon buffet. **$–$$**
Chinese Garden. 5485 W. Sahara Ave.; 876-5432. **$–$$**

Chin's. Fashion Mall; 3200 LVBS; 733-8899. A decidedly modern and elegant Chinese restaurant. **$$**

Chung King. 3400 S. Jones Blvd.; 871-5551. A neighborhood Chinese eatery. **$–$$**

Emperor's Table. 4670 S. Decatur Blvd.; 876-9588. **$–$$**

Empress Court. Caesars Palace; 3570 LVBS; 731-7110. A most elegant Hong Kong–style Cantonese restaurant, including abalone, jellyfish, shark's fin, and bird's nest soups using rare spices from the Orient. Closed Tuesday and Wednesday. **$$$**

Garden of the Dragon. Las Vegas Hilton; 3000 Paradise Rd.; 732-5111. Szechwan, Peking, Northern, Mongolian, and Cantonese. Overlooking the Oriental gardens of Benihana. **$$–$$$**

Hakase. 3900 Paradise Road; 796-1234. Sushi, teppen yaki tableside Japanese cooking. Closed Monday. **$$–$$$**

Hamada of Japan. 598 E. Flamingo Road; 733-3005. Sushi, teppen yaki tableside Japanese cooking or menu items. **$$–$$$**

HoWan. Desert Inn Hotel & Country Club; 3145 LVBS; 733-4547. Authentic Mandarin, Szechwan, and Cantonese. Closed Monday and Tuesday. **$$$**

Iron Horse Cafe. Palace Station Hotel & Casino; 2411 W. Sahara; 367-2411. **$–$$**

Lotus of Siam. 953 E. Sahara Ave.; 735-4453. Lunch buffet Monday through Friday; dinner Saturday and Sunday. Thai specialties. **$–$$**

Ming Terrace. Imperial Palace Hotel & Casino; 3535 LVBS; 731-3311. **$$**

Moongate. The Mirage; 3400 LVBS; 791-7111. A lovely room with elegantly presented Oriental dishes. **$$–$$$**

Rik Shaw. Riviera Hotel and Casino; 2901 LVBS; 734-5110. **$$**

Saigon. 4251 W. Sahara Ave.; 362-9978. A very ordinary storefront restaurant with very extraordinary Vietnamese cooking. **$–$$**

Shalimar. 3900 Paradise Road; 796-0302. An authentic Indian menu, featuring Tandoori meat, curries, unusual rice, and vegetarian specialties. Closed Sunday. **$$**

Shalimar. 2605 S. Decatur Blvd.; 252-8320. A branch of the restaurant described above. Closed Sunday. **$$**

Silver Dragon Restaurant. 1510 E. Flamingo Rd.; 737-1234. **$–$$**

Sun Sun. Aladdin Hotel & Casino; 3667 LVBS; 734-0111. Chinese, Vietnamese, and Korean specialties. **$$**

Szechwan Restaurant. 3101 W. Sahara; 871-4291. Szechwan, Mandarin, Shanghai, and Cantonese cuisine. **$$**

Asian/Middle Eastern (Downtown and Out of Town)

Emperor's Room. Lady Luck Casino Hotel; 206 N. 3rd St.; 477-3000. Closed Sunday and Monday. **$–$$**

Fong's Garden. 2021 E. Charleston Blvd.; 382-1644. An old-line, old-style family Chinese restaurant. **$–$$**

Seoul B-B-Q. 953 E. Sahara Ave.; 369-4123. Ribs along with fish and kimchi (pickled cabbage) that will clear your sinuses for months to come. **$$**

Cajun

Joe's Bayou. Harrah's Las Vegas Casino Hotel; 3475 LVBS; 369-5000. Cajun and New Orleans–style seafood and other specialties. **$$**

Continental (the Strip and Nearby)

Alpine Village. 3003 Paradise Road; 734-6888. Country-style German and French specialties. **$$**

    Bacchanal. Caesars Palace; 3570 LVBS; 731-7110. An opulent seven-course Roman feast that will provide tales of near debauchery that will last for years. Closed Sunday and Monday. **$$$$**

    The Bistro. The Mirage; 3400 LVBS; 791-7111. **$$–$$$**

    Bootlegger Ristorante and Lounge. 5025 S. Eastern Ave.; 736-4939. An old family eatery with a lot of character. Closed Monday; no lunch Sunday. **$$–$$$**

    Cafe Michelle. 1350 E. Flamingo Rd.; 735-8686. A sidewalk cafe featuring Caesar salad, seafood, pasta, chicken, and veal dishes. **$$**

    Camelot. Excalibur Hotel; 3850 LVBS; 597-7777. Seafood, escargot, pasta dishes, rack of lamb, and beef Wellington in a Vegas version of a medieval castle. **$$–$$$**

    Da Vinci's. Maxim Hotel/Casino; 160 E. Flamingo Rd.; 731-4300. **$$**

    Embers. Imperial Palace Hotel & Casino; 3535 LVBS; 731-3311. **$$**

    Flamingo Room. Flamingo Hilton; 733-3131. **$–$$**

    GiGi. Bally's Las Vegas; 3645 LVBS; 739-4111. Closed Monday and Tuesday. **$$–$$$**

    House of Lords. Sahara Hotel; 737-2111. Closed Tuesday and Wednesday. **$$$**

    Kokomo's. The Mirage; 3400 LVBS; 791-7111. A Continental restaurant with seafood specialties, in a rain forest within a Las Vegas casino; we're not sure what it all has to do with a city in Indiana of the same name. **$$–$$$**

    Monte Carlo. Desert Inn Hotel & Country Club; 3145 LVBS; 733-4524. Very French. **$$$**

    Le Montrachet. Las Vegas Hilton; 3000 Paradise Rd.; 732-5111. Closed Tuesday. **$$$**

    Le Panache. San Remo Casino & Resort; 115 E. Tropicana Ave.; 739-9000. Closed Monday and Tuesday. **$$–$$$**

    Palace Court. Caesars Palace; 3570 LVBS; 731-7110. Among the best Continental fare on the Strip. **$$$**

    Pamplemousse. 400 E. Sahara Ave.; 733-2066. Closed Monday. A changing, fresh menu of French country specialties. **$$–$$$**

    Pegasus. Alexis Park Resort; 375 E. Harmon Ave.; 796-3300. Seafood, veal, beef. **$$$–$$$$**

    Regency Room. Sands Hotel; 733-5000. **$$**

    Rhapsody. Tropicana Hotel; 3801 LVBS; 739-2440. Closed Tuesday through Thursday. **$$–$$$**

    Seasons. Bally's Las Vegas; 3645 LVBS; 739-4561. **$$$**

    Second Story. 4485 S. Jones Blvd.; 368-2257. French and continental cuisine. Enclosed porch. **$$$**

Continental (Downtown and Out of Town)

Andre's French Restaurant. 401 S. Sixth St.; 385-5016. A re-created French country home, with great attention to detail in service and food. No lunch weekends. **$$–$$$**

Aristocrat Restaurant. 850 S. Rancho Rd.; 870-1977. No lunch on weekends. A quality, small Continental hideaway. **$$–$$$**

Burgundy Room. Lady Luck Casino Hotel; 206 N. 3rd St.; 477-3000. A comfortable, pleasant room and menu. **$$**

Elaine's. Golden Nugget Hotel and Casino; 129 E. Fremont St.; 385-7111. A beautiful setting and exceptional (and quirky) menu including seafood specialties. Closed Tuesday and Wednesday. **$$–$$$**

The Great Moments Room. Las Vegas Club Hotel & Casino; 18 E. Fremont St.; 385-1664. **$$–$$$**

Delicatessens (the Strip and Nearby)

Champions Deli. Desert Inn Hotel & Country Club; 3145 LVBS; 733-4513. **$–$$**

Derby Deli. Harrah's Las Vegas Casino Hotel; 3475 LVBS; 369-5000. **$–$$**

Jerusalem Kosher Restaurant & Deli. 1305 Vegas Valley Drive.; 735-2878. Closed Friday evening, all day Saturday. Open Sunday for lunch and dinner only. **$$**

Kady's Brasserie. Riviera Hotel & Casino; 2901 LVBS; 734-5110. **$–$$**

Luigi's Place. San Remo Casino & Resort; 115 E. Tropicana Ave.; 739-9000. Italian sandwiches featuring premium cold cuts, cheeses, and trimmings. **$–$$**

Park Deli. 3900 Paradise Rd.; 369-3354. No breakfast Saturday; closed Sunday. **$–$$**

Stage Deli. Forum Shops at Caesars; 893-4045. Imported lox, stock, and barrels from New York. **$$**

German (the Strip and Nearby)

Old Heidelberg. 604 E. Sahara Ave.; 731-5310. **$$**

Swiss Cafe. 1431 E. Charleston Blvd.; 382-6444. **$$**

Italian (the Strip and Nearby)

Amici Ristorante Italiano. 6120 W. Tropicana; 222-0384. Northern Italian cuisine. **$$**

Andiamo. Las Vegas Hilton; 3000 Paradise Rd.; 732-5111. Northern Italian cuisine. **$$**

Battista's Hole In The Wall. 4041 Audrie St.; 732-1424. A classic, comfortable family Italian restaurant. **$$–$$$**

Bertolini's. The Forum Shops at Caesars; 735-4663. **$$**

Cafe Picasso. 2605 S. Decatur, Suite 110 at W. Sahara; 367-3007. Outdoor patio in season. **$$–$$$**

Cangemi's. 4213 W. Sahara Ave.; 876-5698. **$$**

Carluccio's Tivoli Gardens. 1775 E. Tropicana Ave.; 795-3236. Closed Monday. Liberace's sequinned ghost is everywhere. **$$**

Caruso's. Bally's Las Vegas; 3645 LVBS; 739-4111. Northern and Southern Italian cuisine. **$$**

Cipriani Restaurant. 2790 East Flamingo; 369-6711. Closed Sunday. **$$–$$$**
DiMartino & Sons. 2797 S. Maryland Pkwy.; 732-1817. A friendly family spot. **$$**
Fisherman's Port. Aladdin Hotel & Casino; 3557 LVBS; 735-0111. Fresh seafood and special chicken, veal, pork, and pasta entrees. **$$**
Fratelli's Ristorante. 3311 E. Flamingo Rd.; 458-5555. A lively eatery with nightly entertainment. **$$**
Georgio's. 1020 E. Desert Inn Rd.; 735-1170. **$$**
La Strada Restaurant. 4640 Paradise Rd.; 735-0150. **$$**
Lance-a-Lotta Pizza. Excalibur Hotel; 3850 LVBS; 597-7777. **$–$$**
Manfredi's Limelight. Algier's Hotel; 739-1410. **$$**
Olive Garden. 1547 E. Flamingo Rd.; 735-0082. A national seafood and Italian chain that offers a bottomless salad bowl at your table. **$$**
Olive Garden. 1361 S. Decatur Blvd.; 258-3453. **$$**
Parma Ristorante. 1750 S. Rainbow Blvd.; 258-0680. **$$**
Pasta Palace. Palace Station Hotel & Casino; 2411 W. Sahara; 367-2411. **$–$$**
Pasta Remo. San Remo Casino & Resort; 115 E. Tropicana Ave.; 739-9000. Unlimited house salad. **$–$$**
Piero's. 355 Convention Center Drive; 369-2305. Quality Italian pasta, seafood, and meat specialties in an intimate room. Across the street from the Convention Center. **$$–$$$**
Pizza Palace. Imperial Palace Hotel & Casino; 3535 LVBS; 731-3311. **$–$$**
Portofino. Desert Inn Hotel & Country Club; 3145 LVBS; 733-4495. **$$–$$$**
Primavera. Caesars Palace; 3570 LVBS; 731-7110. Quality Northern and Southern Italian food in an attractive poolside setting. **$$–$$$**
Ristaurante Riva. The Mirage; 3400 LVBS; 791-7111. **$$–$$$**
Ristorante Italiano. Riviera Hotel & Casino; 2901 LVBS; 734-5110. **$$–$$$**
Romeo's Ristorante & Lounge. 2800 W. Sahara Ave.; 873-5400. Closed Sunday. Northern Italian. Attractive dining area and outdoor cafe. **$$–$$$**
The Shark Club. Cosmos Uptown Restaurant & Piano Bar; 75 E. Harmon Ave.; 795-7527 or 739-0330. Closed Monday. Nightclub open all night through breakfast. **$$–$$$**
The Sicilian Cafe. 3510 E. Tropicana Ave.; 456-1300. No lunch on weekends. **$$**
Spago. Forum Shops at Caesars; 369-6300. A truly eclectic, trendy, and generally satisfying eating experience under the electronically changing Roman sky. Very busy on weekends and when conventions are in town. **$$–$$$**
That's Amore. 3310 Sandhill Rd.; 435-5889. **$$**
That's Italian. 4601 W. Sahara Ave.; 873-8055. Closed Sunday. **$$**
Vincenzo Ristorante. 610 Naples Dr.; 737-5755. **$$**
Vineyard Restaurant. 3630 S. Maryland Pkwy.; 731-1606. **$–$$**

Italian (Downtown and Out of Town)

Cosmos Underground Italian. 32 E. Fremont St.; 382-0330. Closed on Monday. **$$**

Pasta Pirate. California Hotel Casino; 12 Ogden St.; 385-1222. **$–$$**

Stefano's. Golden Nugget Hotel and Casino; 129 E. Fremont St.; 385-7111. Singing waiters; the food and room are tuneful, too. **$$–$$$**

Japanese (the Strip and Nearby)

Ah'So. Caesars Palace; 3570 LVBS; 731-7110. Sushi and sashimi, sold either in the lounge or to dinner guests. The preselected, six-course dinner ($47.50) is prepared and served in teppen yaki style at your table. **$$$$**

Benihana Village. Las Vegas Hilton; 3000 Paradise Rd.; 732-5111. Two traditional Japanese restaurants (hibachi and robata), each with a different atmosphere. The food is classy; the entertainment, which includes a show starring animated stuffed birds and electronic fireworks, is straight out of Disney World. **$$–$$$**

Kabuto Japanese Restaurant. 324 W. Sahara Ave.; 388-1203. **$$–$$$**

Mikado. The Mirage; 3400 LVBS; 791-7111. **$$–$$$**

Mizuno Teppan. Tropicana Hotel; 3801 LVBS; 739-2713. Australian lobster, Gulf shrimp, gourmet steak served in teppen yaki style right at your table. **$$–$$$**

Nippon. 101 Convention Center Drive; 735-5555. No lunch Saturday. Closed Sunday. Sushi bar, sashimi. **$–$$**

Sakura Garden. 324 S. Sahara Ave.; 384-3524. Closed Sunday. **$$**

Sushi Bar San Remo. San Remo Casino & Resort; 115 E. Tropicana Ave.; 739-9000. **$$**

Teru-Sushi. 700 E. Sahara Ave.; 734-6655. Closed Sunday. **$$**

Mexican (the Strip and Nearby)

El Chollo Paradise. 4080 S. Paradise Rd.; 359-5334. **$$**

Garcia's Mexican Restaurant.1030 E. Flamingo Rd.; 731-0628. **$$**

Garcia's Mexican Restaurant. 2575 S. Decatur Blvd.; 876-6191. **$$**

Guadalajara Bar & Grille. Palace Station Hotel & Casino; 2411 W. Sahara; 367-2471. **$$**

Las Holas. Bally's Las Vegas; 3645 LVBS; 739-4111. **$$**

Macayo Vegas. 1375 E. Tropicana Ave.; 735-1898. A local chain. **$–$$**

Macayo Vegas. 1741 E. Charleston Blvd.; 382-5605. **$–$$**

Macayo Vegas. 4457 W. Charleston Blvd.; 878-7347. **$–$$**

Macayo Vegas. 3752 LVBN; 644-1020. **$–$$**

Paco's. Las Vegas Hilton; 3000 Paradise Rd.; 732-5111. Closed Wednesday and Thursday. **$–$$**

Ricardo's Mexican Restaurants. 2380 E. Tropicana Ave.; 798-4515. Another local chain. **$–$$**

Ricardo's Mexican Restaurants. 4300 Meadows Lane (Meadows Mall); 870-1088. **$–$$**

Ricardo's Mexican Restaurants. 4930 W. Flamingo Rd.; 871-7119. **$–$$**

Moroccan (the Strip and Nearby)

Marrakech. 3900 Paradise Rd.; 736-7655. Six-course French Moroccan meal, an array of domestic and imported wines, and full bar. With a belly dancer, of course. **$$–$$$**

Seafood (the Strip and Nearby)

Fisherman's Broiler. Palace Station Hotel & Casino; 2411 W. Sahara; 357-2411. Seafood specialties. Inexpensive luncheon seafood buffet. **$$**

    Fisherman's Port. Aladdin Hotel & Casino; 3667 LVBS; 736-0111. **$$–$$$**

    Nero's Steak and Seafood Restaurant. Caesars Palace; 3570 LVBS; 731-7110. **$$–$$$$**

    Seahouse. Imperial Palace Hotel & Casino; 3535 LVBS; 731-3311. Closed Wednesday and Thursday. **$$–$$$**

Steakhouses (the Strip and Nearby)

Beef Barron. Flamingo Hilton; 733-3502. **$$–$$$**

    Cattlemen's Steak House. 2645 S. Maryland Pkwy.; 732-7726. **$$–$$$**

    Cavalier Restaurant. 3850 E. Desert Inn Rd.; 451-6221. **$$–$$$**

    Charcoal Room. Hacienda; 739-8911. **$$$**

    Claudine's Steak House. Harrah's Las Vegas Casino Hotel; 3475 LVBS; 369-5000. Closed Monday and Tuesday. Onion soup to die for, steaks, chops, and more. **$$–$$$**

    Diamond Lil's. Sam's Town; 454-8009. **$$–$$$**

    Dickinson's Wharf. 953 E. Sahara Ave.; 732-3594. **$$–$$$**

    El Gaucho. Tropicana Hotel; 3801 LVBS; 739-2376. **$$–$$$**

    Embers. Imperial Palace; 794-3261. Closed Monday and Tuesday. **$$–$$$**

    Ferdinand's Steak House & Saloon. 5006 S. Maryland; 798-6962. Cajun blackened fish, sausage, and jalapeno hush puppies. **$$–$$$**

    Flame. 1 Desert Inn Rd.; 735-4431. Pick your own meat for breakfast, lunch, and dinner. Seafood and chicken specialties, too. **$$**

    Golden Steer. 308 W. Sahara Ave.; 384-4470. Pounds of steak and ribs; also game, fish, and poultry in a western atmosphere between the Strip and the Convention Center. **$$–$$$**

    Hilton Steakhouse. Las Vegas Hilton; 3000 Paradise Rd.; 732-5111. Prime steaks and fresh seafood prepared over mesquite wood. **$$–$$$**

    Kristofer's. Riviera Hotel & Casino; 2901 LVBS; 734-5110. **$$$**

    Philip's Supper House. 4545 W. Sahara Ave.; 873-5222. **$$–$$$**

    Play It Again, Sam. 4120 Spring Mountain Rd.; 876-1550. **$$–$$$**

    Port Tack. 3190 W. Sahara Ave.; 873-3345. **$$**

    Rib House. Imperial Palace Hotel & Casino; 3535 LVBS; 731-3311. **$$**

    Rosewood Grille. 3339 LVBS; 792-6719. **$$$**

    Ruth's Chris Steak House. 3900 Paradise Rd.; 791-7011. **$$–$$$**

    The Sandpiper Restaurant. 3311 E. Flamingo Rd.; 458-5555. **$$**

    Sir Galahad's. Excalibur Hotel; 3850 LVBS; 597-7777. **$$**

    Steakhouse. Bally's Las Vegas; 3645 LVBS; 739-4661. Closed Sunday and Monday. **$$–$$$**

    The Steak House. Circus Circus Hotel/Casino; 2880 LVBS; 734-0410. Award-winning steak house, offering prime rib, lamb chops, lobster, fish, chicken, and steaks broiled over mesquite. The celebrity portraits on the wall are not movie stars but dinner steers. **$$**

The Tillerman. 2245 E. Flamingo Rd.; 731-4036. **$$**

Tony Roma's. Stardust Hotel/Casino; 732-6500. **$$–$$$**

Yolie's Brazilian Steakhouse. 3900 Paradise Rd.; 794-0700. Unusual menu of marinated meats, sausage, and poultry cooked over wood-fired rotisserie that is part of the entertainment. **$$**

Steakhouses (Downtown and Out of Town)

Binion's Steak House. Binion's Horseshoe; 128 E. Fremont St.; 382-1600. Victorian-style decor, specializing in huge steaks and prime ribs. **$$**

Cassidy's Steak House. Fitzgerald's; 382-6111. **$$**

Nick's Supper Club. 15 Lake Mead Drive, Henderson; 565-0122. Summer closed Sunday and Monday; winter open 7 days. Lunch and dinner. **$$–$$$**

Tony Roma's. Fremont Hotel/Casino; 200 Fremont St.; 385-6257. **$$–$$$**

Chapter 14
Sports and Recreation

Spectator Sports

Las Vegas Stars Baseball

The Las Vegas Stars, the AAA farm club of the San Diego Padres in the Pacific Coast League, one step below the majors, play a 140-game season from April through September. Home games are played at Cashman Field, with 9,334 permanent seats and 3,000 bleachers in the outfield. Fans can also have dinner at the Club Level Restaurant and watch the game from there.

Games begin at 7:05 P.M. Monday through Saturday and at 6:05 P.M. on Sunday. Club level seats cost $7.50; field level, $6; plaza level, $5; reserved, $4.50; and general admission, $4. Seats in the air-conditioned Club Level Restaurant are $7.50. Children and seniors can purchase general admission tickets for $3. For ticket information, call 386-7200, or call Ticketmaster at 474-4000. We're not sure we want to test it out, but the Stars also have a special promotion for general admission tickets when the temperature is 100 degrees or more. The price drops 25 cents for each degree over the century mark, down to $1 when the thermometer hits 111.

The Stars are one of the most successful minor league franchises; they drew more than 430,000 fans in the 1993 season. In typical minor league fashion, there are many special promotions at games, including firework nights, "Catch or Splash" competitions, "Pitch for Cash" games, and "Dizzy-Dizzy" contests.

Other teams in the PCL and their major league affiliations are the Albuquerque Dukes (L.A. Dodgers), Calgary Cannons (Seattle Mariners), Colorado Springs Sky Sox (Colorado Rockies), Edmonton Trappers (Florida Marlins), Phoenix Firebirds (S.F. Giants), Salt Lake Buzz (Minnesota Twins), Tacoma Tigers (Oakland A's), Tucson Toros (Houston Astros), and Vancouver Canadians (California Angels).

At the start of the 1995 season, the Las Vegas Stars were coached by former major leaguer Tim Flannery; pitching coach was Jon Matlack. Among the present-day stars who played for the Stars in the past are Roberto and Sandy Alomar, Carlos Baerga, Joey Cora, Ozzie Guillen, John Kruk, Tony Gwynn, Benito Santiago, Kevin McReynolds, and Shane Mack.

Before the start of each season, the Stars hold the annual **Las Vegas Big League Weekend,** bringing in several major league teams for exhibition games in spring training.

To get there from the airport, take I-15 to I-93/95 South/Downtown exit, and then the Cashman Field/Las Vegas Blvd. exit. At the light on Las Vegas Blvd. turn left; at the third light you will see Cashman Field.

Las Vegas Thunder

Members of the International Hockey League, the Thunder play their games at the Thomas and Mack Center, which has 12,347 seats.

In the 1994–95 season, the Thunder had two talented and unusual backup goaltenders. Pokey Riddick is one of the few African-Americans in organized hockey; Manon Rheaume is the first (and only) woman to ever play a hockey

Las Vegas Thunder hockey team

game at the professional level. In 1992, she was in goal for Tampa Bay in an NHL preseason game.

Other teams in the IHL include the Atlanta Knights, Chicago Wolves, Cincinnati Cyclones, Cleveland Lumberjacks, Denver Grizzlies, Detroit Vipers, Fort Wayne Komets, Houston Aeros, Indianapolis Ice, Kalamazoo Wings, Kansas City Blades, Milwaukee Admirals, Minnesota Moose, Peoria Rivermen, Phoenix Roadrunners, and the San Diego Gulls. The IHL season runs from October through April. Call 798-7825 for tickets and information.

Las Vegas Dust Devils

Continental Indoor Soccer League. June through September. 739-8856.

Las Vegas Flash

Professional Roller Hockey. May through August. 262-9795.

Las Vegas Posse

Canadian Football League. June through November. 474-4000.

Las Vegas Sting

Indoor Arena Football League. May through August. 739-8856.

Las Vegas Motor Speedway

A new 1.5-mile speedway on 1,100 acres bordered by Las Vegas Boulevard North and I-15 is expected to open in mid-1996. An Indy car race is planned for September 1996, with possible NASCAR events also on the racing card.

UNLV Runnin' Rebels

The nationally ranked college basketball team plays home games at the Thomas and Mack Center. Tickets can be very hard to get for some matchups. Call 739-3761.

Rodeo

The National Finals Rodeo is held in December.

Las Vegas International Marathon

February. 876-3870.

World Firefighters Games

May. 434-1046.

Las Vegas Cutting Horse Annual

September. 385-5257

Recreation
Health Clubs

Many of the major hotels have health clubs for guests or can offer special arrangements for use of a commercial club. Following are some of the largest clubs that cater to short-term visitors; call to check on hours and availability of day or short-term passes.

Family Fitness Centers. West: 3055 S. Valley View; 368-1111. East: 2605 S. Eastern; 641-2222. North: 3141 N. Rainbow; 656-7777.

Gold's Gym. East: Flamingo and Sandhill; 451-4222. West: Sahara and Decatur; 877-6966.

Goodbody's Fitness Center. 6080 Burnham Avenue; 798-8111.

Harrah's Casino Hotel. 3475 Las Vegas Boulevard South; 369-5007.

Las Vegas Sporting House. Racquetball, squash, tennis, and volleyball courts; indoor and outdoor running tracks. Open 24 hours. 3025 Industrial Road (behind Stardust Hotel); 733-8999.

Racquetball

Caesars Palace. 731-7110.

Las Vegas Athletic Club East. 1070 East Sahara Avenue; 733-1919.

Las Vegas Sporting House. 10 racquetball and two squash courts. Open 24 hours. 3025 Industrial Road (behind Stardust Hotel); 733-8999.

Bowling

Gold Coast Hotel & Casino. 72 lanes. Open 24 hours. 4000 W. Flamingo Rd.; 367-4700.

Sam's Town Hotel Gambling Hall & Bowling Center. 56 lanes. Open 24 hours. 5111 Boulder Highway; 454-8022.

Santa Fe Hotel & Casino. 60 lanes. 4949 N. Rancho Drive; 658-4900.

Showboat Hotel, Casino & Bowling Center. 106 lanes. Open 24 hours. 2800 Fremont St.; 385-9153.

Horseback Riding

Bonnie Springs Old Nevada. Seven days a week through Red Canyon. Highway 159 West of Las Vegas; 875-4191.

Mt. Charleston Riding Stables. Seven days a week, on Mt. Charleston. Highway 157 North of Las Vegas; 872-7009

Ice Skating

Santa Fe Resort. The only public ice skating arena in southern Nevada, with an NHL regulation–size rink. Figure skating and hockey lessons and leagues. 4949 N. Rancho Drive; 658-4900.

Roller Skating

Crystal Palace. 4680 Boulder Highway; 458-0177.
   Crystal Palace. 3901 N. Rancho Drive; 645-4892.
   Crystal Palace. 4740 S. Decatur; 253-9832.
   Playland Skating Center. 1110 E. Lake Mead Drive, Henderson; 564-2790.

Skiing and Sledding

Lee Canyon Ski Area. Route 156, Mount Charleston.

Snow and road conditions: 593-9500
Ski school: 872-5462
Lee Canyon bus: 646-0008

Vertical	Elevation	Lifts
1,030	9,320	3

Base: 8,290 feet. Summit: 9,320 feet. A secret to many winter visitors to Las Vegas is that there is a ski hill less than an hour north of the Strip, 47 miles away.

Lee Canyon is not to be confused with one of the Sierra Nevada monsters in and around Lake Tahoe, but it does offer decent skiing from about December through April. Snow-making helps out where Mother Nature fails. The resort offers shuttle bus service from Las Vegas, and you can rent equipment from ski pants and jackets to skis, boots, and poles.

Lee Canyon is predominately an intermediate hill, with about 15 percent beginners' slopes and 5 percent expert terrain. Chairs 1 and 2 are each 3,000 feet long, rising 1,000 feet to intermediate and advanced runs; chair 3 serves Rabbit Peak for novice skiers.

The **Mount Charleston Hotel** is on Kyle Canyon Road; 872-5500.

Foxtail Snow Play Area. Lee Canyon Road, Mount Charleston. Bring your own sled, inner tube, or cafeteria tray. Check with Lee Canyon ski resort for local snow conditions first.

Cross-Country Skiing. The U.S. Forest Service, 2881 South Valley View Blvd., 873-8800, has maps of Mount Charleston available for sale.

Brian Head Ski Resort. Off Interstate 15 in Brian Head, Utah.
Information and lodging reservations: (800) 272-7426.

Vertical	Elevation	Lifts
1,161	11,307	7

It's a hike at 180 miles northeast (over three hours from Las Vegas) into Utah on Interstate 15, but the reward is a serious ski area. Brian Head has Utah's highest base elevation at 9,700 feet, drawing an average of more than 400 inches of snow per year. The resort typically opens in early November.

The ski resort is spread over two mountains and includes 53 trails. Brian Head Peak reaches to 11,307 feet; across the valley is the strictly beginner and intermediate Navajo Peak. Adult lift tickets, $32; children (6–12) and seniors (60–69), $20. Seniors 70 and over ski free. Afternoon half days, $24 for adults; $16 children. Brian Head includes special lodging packages at the site in the Brian Head Hotel or surrounding condominiums; there are also more than a dozen hotels and inns near the resort.

Miniature Golf

Funtazmic. 4975 Polaris Avenue, west of I-15; 795-4386.

Scandia Miniature Golf & Family Fun Center. 2900 Sirius Rd.; 364-0070.

Golf Courses

Angel Park Golf Club. Two courses. 100 S. Rampart Blvd.; 254-4653.

Black Mountain Golf and Country Club. 501 Country Club Dr., Henderson; 565-7933.

Boulder City Municipal Golf Course. 1 Clubhouse Drive, Boulder City; 293-9236.

Calvada Golf and Country Club. Red Butte, Pahrump; 727-4653.

Craig Ranch Golf Course. 628 W. Craig Rd.; 642-9700.

Desert Inn Country Club. 3145 Las Vegas Blvd. South; 733-4444.

Desert Rose Golf Course. 5843 Club House Dr.; 438-4653.

Las Vegas Golf Club. 4349 Vegas Dr.; 646-3003.

Las Vegas Hilton Country Club. 1911 E. Desert Inn Rd. Reservations available through the Las Vegas Hilton Box Office.

Legacy Golf Club. 130 Par Excellence Dr.; 897-2187.

Los Prados Golf and Country Club. 5150 Los Prados Circle; 645-5696.

Mirage Country Club. 3650 Las Vegas Blvd. South; 369-7111.

North Las Vegas Community Course. 324 E. Brooks Ave., North Las Vegas; 649-7171.

Painted Desert Country Club. 5555 Painted Mirage Way; 645-2568.

Peppermill Palms Golf Course. 1134 Mesquite Blvd., Mesquite; (800) 621-0187.

Royal Kenfield Country Club. 1 Showboat Country Club Dr.; 434-9009.

Sahara Country Club. 1911 E. Desert Inn Rd.; 796-0016.

Sun City Summerlin Golf Club. 9201-B Del Webb Blvd.; 363-4373.

Tennis

Aladdin. Three illuminated outdoor courts on the hotel's upper story pool deck. Dawn to 10 P.M. Priority to guests. 736-0111.

Alexis Park. Two lighted courts. Priority to hotel guests. 6 A.M. to 8 P.M. 796-3300.

Bally's. 10 outdoor courts, five illuminated. Reservations only. No fee to guests, minimal to others. Dusk to dawn. 739-4111.

Caesars Palace. Four outdoor courts. Guests and public welcome. Lessons available. Dawn to dark. 731-7786.

Desert Inn. Ten outdoor courts, five lighted. Open to the public. Lessons and rentals available. 733-4577.

Flamingo Hilton. A new tennis complex will be available after the completion of construction of a new entranceway at the hotel. 733-3344.

Frontier. Two illuminated outdoor courts. No fee for guests. 794-8200.

Hacienda. One illuminated court, 8 A.M. to 11 P.M. Reservations for hotel guests. 739-8911.

Hot Springs Tennis Club. Four illuminated outdoor courts. 361-5683.

Las Vegas Hilton. Six illuminated courts on pool deck. Hilton guests only. 732-5111.

Plaza. Four outdoor courts, all lighted. Rentals available. 386-2110.

Riviera. Two courts, both lighted. Guests first, others welcome. Reservations only. 734-5110.

Sports Club–Las Vegas. Two illuminated outdoor courts. Reservations required. 733-8999.

Studio 96. 10 indoor courts, four outdoor courts, all lighted. 735-8153.

Sunset Park. Eight illuminated courts. Court fee $2 per hour. 7 A.M. to 11 P.M. 455-8200.

Tropicana. Four outdoor courts, lighted. No fees for guests. Reservations recommended. 739-2381.

Twin Lakes Racquet Club. Eight outdoor courts, lighted. Open to the public. Reservations required. 647-3434.

Bicycle Rentals

Bikes USA. 1537 N. Eastern Avenue; 642-2453.

Blue Diamond Bicycles. 14 Cottonwood Dr., Blue Diamond; 875-4500.

City Streets Bike Tours. Bicycle rentals for Red Rock Park and Mt. Charleston, maps, and equipment. 596-2953.

Parks and Scenic Areas

Floyd Lamb State Park. 9200 Tule Springs Rd.; 486-5413.

Hoover Dam. 293-8367.

Lake Mead Recreation Area.
  Boulder Beach: 293-1891.
  Callville Bay: 565-8958.
  Cottonwood: 297-1464.
  Las Vegas Wash: 565-9111.
  National Park Service: 293-8096.

Lee Canyon. Mount Charleston in Toiyabe National Forest, northwest of Las Vegas on Highway 95 to Highway 156. 646-0008.

Spring Mt. Ranch. Blue Diamond. 875-4141.

Valley of Fire. Overton. 397-2088.

Chapter 15

Journeys North of Las Vegas: Mount Charleston, Lee Canyon, Red Rock Canyon, and Valley of Fire

As we've noted, Las Vegas is a lot more than just green felt, computer-controlled volcanic eruptions, and mock Egyptian pyramids. Few things make that point more clearly than a journey a few miles north of town along I-95.

Just past downtown the trappings of Las Vegas fall away quickly, yielding to the near-barren Mojave Desert. On the plateau to the right is the huge Nellis Air Force Base, and beyond that are two of the area's less well known attractions: the Nellis Air Force Range that runs for almost 125 miles from Las Vegas to near Tonopah, and the Nevada Test Site, a nuclear weapon testing area included within the range.

Nellis is generally off-limits to civilians, except for occasional open houses. Visitors can tour the home of the famed Thunderbirds aerial demonstration team on Tuesdays and Thursdays at 1:30 P.M. The 90-minute tour includes a film about the flyers, a museum, and a visit to a hangar to see an F-16. Call 652-4018 for information.

The top-secret status of the Nellis base and the vast size of the area have regularly spawned all sorts of interesting rumors about goings-on in the area, including reports ranging from testing of strange military aircraft (including the Stealth bomber) to detailed reports of military experiments on captured UFOs and their alien crews. We got that last tidbit, by the way, from Elvis, who has his hideaway on the range.

Going to Dreamland

And then things get really weird. About 120 miles northwest of Las Vegas is a huge government military installation that officially doesn't exist. There are several very long runways and dozens of hangars and buildings, but according to FAA pilot charts and U.S. Geological Survey topographic maps, it just ain't there.

The military installation, at Groom Lake, is known to some as Dreamland;

old government maps call it Area 51. When officialdom is pushed, they will acknowledge the existence of something called a "remote test facility."

According to *Popular Science,* which published an investigation of the air base in 1994, every weekday 10 to 12 Boeing 737 jets depart from special terminals operated by defense contractor EG&G Corp. at McCarran Airport, or in Palmdale, California. The planes, painted white with a broad red stripe down their lengths, make low-level 30-minute flights to Groom Lake with an estimated 1,500 to 2,000 employees per day.

What goes on there? According to unofficial observers, the base has been used for projects from testing of the ultrasecret SR-71 spy plane in the 1960s to flight tests of Soviet Sukhoi Su-22 and MiG-23 fighters somehow obtained by the military to training for the F-117A Stealth attack planes. And there are those who maintain that the U.S. government has captured UFOs and kept them at the base.

There is not much chance of taking a sightseeing trip to Dreamland, though. About as close as you can get is up in the hills near the tiny town of Rachel (population about 100). The Bureau of Land Management property outside the base is patrolled by sheriff's deputies; closer in is the boundary of the base itself, which is guarded with detection devices, video cameras, and signs warning, "Use of Deadly Force Authorized."

By the way, if you go to the trouble of driving to Rachel (I-15 north to Route 93 north, picking up Route 375 westbound near Ash Springs), you'll find the Little A'Le'Inn (pronounced "alien"), its walls covered with UFO memorabilia and a large photo of the base that doesn't exist.

Natural Wonders

On the left side of I-95 and the Strip, heading out of Las Vegas, are three expeditions worth taking. We suggest you fill up the gas tank in your car before heading out on a tour; gas stations are few and far between in this area.

Red Rock Canyon

Here is an extraordinary world of rusty red cliffs, Joshua trees, yucca plants, and sagebrush; just as otherworldly and much more real than the nearby manmade canyons of Las Vegas. It's heaven for hikers, perfect for picnickers, and a delightful drive even if you never leave your car.

Take I-15 to the West Charleston exit and drive west on Charleston Avenue toward the hills. About 10 miles out of town, Las Vegas is a garish memory and Red Rock Canyon is a garish reality. The sandstone cliffs, towering 2,000 feet above the desert floor, are an artist's palette of red, orange, yellow, pink, purple, and brown.

Check at the Bureau of Land Management Visitor Center on Red Rock Road to pick up hiking, bicycling, climbing, or general nature brochures. Marked hiking trails range from about two miles to a 14-mile tour to the top of the escarpment. There's also a 13-mile one-way driving loop with pull-offs at some of the more spectacular views, with even more "oohs" per mile than on the Las Vegas Strip.

The **Sandstone Quarry** area offers a climbing trail with access to some ancient Indian petroglyphs in Brownstone Canyon.

For much of the past 600 million years, the land that is now Red Rock Canyon was the bottom of a deep ocean basin; the western coast of North America was in present-day western Utah.

A rich variety of marine life in the waters left behind deposits of shells and skeletons more than 9,000 feet thick, which were eventually compressed into limestone and other carbonate rocks.

About 225 million years ago, movements in the earth's crust caused the seabed to slowly rise. Streams entering the shallower waters left behind mud and sand, which later became consolidated into shales and marine sandstones.

Large bodies of salt water became cut off from the sea and eventually evaporated, leaving behind salt and gypsum. The exposure of the sediments to the atmosphere caused some of the minerals to oxidize, changing their colors to red and orange.

Beep, beep! One of the most famous residents of Red Rock Canyon is the roadrunner. And yes, this chicken-size bird really does streak across the desert on foot. (And though there are coyotes, too, we are not aware of a local franchise for the Acme Dynamite Company.)

Another stage in the geologic history of Red Rock Canyon occurred about 180 million years ago when the area became an arid desert. A giant dune field stretched eastward to Colorado, with sand more than half a mile deep in some areas. The shifting sands left behind curved and angled lines known as "crossbeds" that were eventually cemented into sandstone in combination with calcium carbonate and iron oxide; this is the source of some of the red rock cliffs.

Most recently, some 65 million years ago, a thrust fracture in the earth's crust drove one crustal plate over another, placing the older gray carbonate rocks of the ancient ocean above the younger tan and red sandstone below. Red Rock Canyon is part of the Keystone Thrust Fault, a huge system that extends north into Canada.

Over thousands of years, at least four and possibly several other Native American cultures occupied the Red Rock area. They were drawn to the relative abundance of water in the canyon, which includes more than 40 springs and catchment basins. Archaeologists have found roasting pits and a historical sandstone quarry.

For information, call the Red Rock Canyon Visitors Center at 363-1921.

Rocking the treetops. More than 45 species are peculiar to Red Rock Canyon. Larger animals in the area include bighorn sheep, cougars, wild horses, and burros; other smaller creatures include kit foxes, coyotes, and bobcats.

The river areas are home to more than 30 species of reptiles and amphibians.

Beep-beep. The roadrunner rarely flies, but will make a short hop into the air when necessary to escape from danger or to pounce on a meal, including lizards, snakes, insects, and squirrels—these juicy foods are the primary source of moisture for the roadrunner.

Don't be a burro. Heed the warning signs against feeding the wild burros in the area; they bite. The state puts teeth into the warning with a $25 fine for unauthorized feedings.

Bonnie Springs Old Nevada. Long before there was a serious settlement at Las Vegas there were isolated ranches like this one, which originally dates back to about 1840. Today, though, the Bonnie Springs Ranch is a somewhat tired Western theme park in a very pretty setting at the southern edge of Red Rock Canyon. The park includes a petting zoo, a small railroad, a Western street with shops, demonstrations, and the occasional shootout.

Located on Highway 159, south of the exit from Red Rock Canyon in Blue Diamond. Open seven days a week, with tickets priced at about $6.50 for adults and $4 for children; 875-4191.

Spring Mountain Ranch State Park. An isolated ranch owned (along with hundreds of other Nevada properties) by Howard Hughes and used as a business retreat, it was originally the home of Lum of the "Lum 'n Abner" radio show of the 1930s, and then the home of Vera Krupp, widow of the German weapons maker. It is now operated by the State Park system; tours of the home are available. Call 875-4141 for information.

Mount Charleston

About 20 miles north of town, after a long jaunt along a flat desert floor, look for the Kyle Canyon exit (Nevada Route 157) branching off to the left. From here you will begin a long, steady climb. The road is one of the more dramatic ones we know of: for much of the early part of the climb you are able to look straight into the face of the mountain ahead of you.

Mount Charleston is a serious hill, reaching to 11,919 feet, the highest peak of the Spring Mountain Range and nearly two miles above the floor of the Las Vegas Valley. Much of the surrounding area is part of the Toiyabe National Forest.

The trip is an interesting exploration of the effect of elevation on climate and plant and animal life. The yucca, Joshua trees, and creosote bushes are able to survive the intense heat and lack of rain at the desert floor. At about the 5,000-foot level you'll find junipers, scrub pine, and sagebrush. Higher up the mountain the vegetation gives way to bristlecone pines that are adapted to the extremes of cold and wind on the mountain. Bristlecones are among the longest-living things on earth, with some plants believed to be nearly 5,000 years old.

About 10 miles up the road is the **Mt. Charleston Hotel**, an old-timey mountain lodge (okay, so it's about 10 years old; it still feels real) with beam ceilings and a large open fireplace. Rooms range from ordinary to extraordinary, including a few suites with fireplaces. The **Canyon Dining Room** is an attractive place to eat, especially on a moonlit night. Call 872-5500 for information.

At the very end of Kyle Canyon Road is a stunning resort area, first developed by the Civilian Conservation Corps during the Depression and now offering vacation homes, campgrounds, and picnic areas.

At the top of the road, the mountain continues to rise; there are a number of trails including a short walk to **Mary Jane Falls** or a more strenuous 15-mile hike to the **Charleston Peak** where on a clear day you can see into four states: Nevada, California, Utah, and distant Arizona. Forest Service Road 22, a branch road off of Route 157, leads to near **Robbers' Roost Caves**, a gathering of limestone caverns used as hideouts in the mid–19th century by Mexican bandits who preyed on settlers and travelers in the area.

Route 158 branches off to the right, just before the Mt. Charleston Hotel. This is a stunning, twisty mountain road that traverses a ridge over to Lee Canyon Road (Route 156). At the T, turn left into the mountain and climb for another four miles to reach the **Lee Canyon Ski Area.**

Lee Canyon benefits from its elevation—a lofty 8,290 feet at the base and 9,320 feet at the peak— and its meteorological conditions. As a mountain oasis in the desert, it gathers a fair amount of natural snow. Many of the trails are also covered with snow-making equipment. However, the season is extremely variable. In a good winter, skiers can "schuss" from as early as Thanksgiving to as late as early spring; in a dry or warm season, the slopes can turn to mud very quickly.

The ski hill itself has a respectable vertical drop of 1,030 feet served by three chairlifts. None of the 11 trails would qualify as a scary double-diamond expert slope; most of the trails are decidedly intermediate, with a separate, wide beginner's slope that has its own chairlift. A pleasant lodge with a sun deck sits at the bottom of the hill; rental equipment is available at the lodge or at one of several sporting goods stores in Las Vegas. Ski Lee runs its own charter bus service to the mountain from town. The area participates in the Ski Wee program for youngsters between 4 and 12 years of age.

For information, road, and ski conditions call 593-9500; 872-5462 for information about ski lessons; and 646-0008 for bus reservations.

An alternate route to Mount Charleston is to go past Route 157 and continue on I-95 for about 14 miles to Route 156. This road goes directly to the Lee Canyon Ski Area; from there you can also cross over the upper trail (Route 158) and descend on Route 157.

The **Mt. Charleston Riding Stables** on Highway 157 offer horseback riding, hay rides, and sleigh rides, depending on the season. The stables are just short of the Mt. Charleston Lodge on the left side of the road as you climb the hill. For information, call 872-7009.

Valley of Fire State Park. A bit farther away than Red Rock Canyon, but a bit wilder, this park includes spectacularly colored desert sandstone that has

Roll of the dice. In 1942, actress Carole Lombard was killed when her DC-3 airplane slammed into Mount Potosi southwest of Las Vegas in the Spring Mountains. She was returning from a war bonds rally in the midwest to Los Angeles and husband Clark Gable.

In remembrance of the popular Miss Lombard, an orange butterfly with black spots peculiar to the local hills was named the *Carole's fritillary.*

The name holds Las Vegas significance: *fritillary* comes from the Latin *fritillus,* meaning dice box.

Hot and cold. The climate of Nevada varies greatly, with tremendous extremes between the desert floors and mountaintops.

In the south, summers are generally long and hot and winters short and mild; at Las Vegas the average annual temperature is 66 degrees.

In the north, summers are short and hot and winters are long and cool; at Reno, the average annual temperature is 49 degrees.

Nevada is the driest state in the U.S., with average annual rain of just four inches in the southeast. The wettest parts of the state are the Carson Sink and the Sierra Nevada mountains of the northwest.

been sculpted by the wind and rain into fantastic shapes. The geology dates as far back as the Jurassic period.

You'll also find ancient petroglyphs (prehistoric rock drawings) on canyon walls; they are believed to date back more than two thousand years to the time of the Anasazi.

Trails lead to isolated parts of the park including **Mouse's Tank**, a shallow natural bowl that collects the scarce rainfall in the area. It was the hiding place of Mouse, a Paiute Indian who terrorized some of the area settlers almost a hundred years ago.

Stop at the Visitor Station for maps and information, or call 397-2088. The Valley of Fire is about 50 miles northeast of Las Vegas, off I-15 in Overton; you can make a loop that connects to the top of Lake Mead and down to Boulder and the Hoover Dam for a nice day trip.

Temperatures in the valley can become downright brutal in the summer; the best time to visit is from September through May. Bring water and supplies with you, even for a day trip.

Overton

The small town of **Overton**, on Route 169, was once the commercial center for the early Mormon settlements in the Moapa Valley in the 19th century. Before then, the area was populated by Anasazi tribes who developed farms, including irrigation canals branching off the Virgin and Muddy Rivers more than a thousand years ago. The largest of their buildings, the fabled Lost City at the confluence of the Virgin and Muddy rivers, included 94 rooms; that area is now below the waters of Lake Mead.

The **Lost City Museum** outside of Overton includes one of the most complete collections of ancient Pueblo Indian relics dating back thousands of years. It continues through the ancient Basketmaker cultures and through the Paiutes, who arrived about the year 1000 and whose descendants still live in southern Nevada. Outside of the museum is a replica of a Pueblo home; it was built as a Civilian Conservation Corps project during the Depression era. Also displayed are artifacts of the Mormon settlement of the region. The museum is open daily with a token admission fee. Call 397-2193 for information.

South of Overton, within the Valley of Fire State Park, is **Overton Beach**, a recreational area on upper Lake Mead. Beneath the waters east of the area is the former location of St. Thomas, a Mormon farming community; when the water level is low, parts of some of the buildings can be seen offshore.

Chapter 16

Journeys South of Las Vegas: Henderson, Hoover Dam, Boulder City, Lake Mead, and Lake Mohave

Henderson

Henderson, south of Las Vegas toward Boulder City, is Nevada's third most populous city (after Las Vegas and Reno) with more than 80,000 residents.

The town sprouted during World War II because of the Basic Magnesium plant, a huge facility that processed the mineral for use in munitions. The plant closed in 1944, but unlike the dozens of other ghost towns in Nevada, the residents of Henderson managed to find other industries. Henderson also serves as a bedroom community for workers in tourism and government installations. Downtown Henderson is (like Boulder City) somewhat frozen in time.

The Boulder Highway has been supplanted by superhighways that link Las Vegas to Boulder City and on to Los Angeles, but if you're looking for a glimpse of the past, this is still the best route to Henderson.

The **Southern Nevada Museum** on Boulder Highway includes Heritage Street, a collection of old buildings from throughout Southern Nevada, including houses built for the magnesium workers, early Las Vegas residences, and mining villages. An Indian Village celebrates the Native American culture of the area.

Also in Henderson is the **Ethel M. Chocolate Factory** and its nearby cactus garden. Both are open to the public daily.

Sweet tooths will want to continue to the nearby **Kidd & Co. Marshmallow Factory**, also open daily from 9:30 A.M. to 4:30 P.M. Call 564-5400 for information. Veterans of the self-guided tour are rewarded with a sample bag of marshmallows; there's also a gift shop with toys . . . and marshmallows.

Kidd's has been in business more than a hundred years, beginning in Chicago in the 1880s in the home of Albert Eugene Kidd where he and his family wrapped lemon drops on the kitchen table and roasted peanuts in the family oven. After World War II, the business was moved to Lionier, Indiana, and became a national brand. A second factory was built in 1987 to serve the west coast. The current factory was rebuilt after it was destroyed by the explosion of the

Henderson Chamber of Commerce. 100 E. Lake Mead Drive, Henderson, NV 89015; 565-8951. **Henderson Convention Center.** 200 Water Street, Henderson, NV 89015; 565-2171.

nearby Pepcon factory in 1989. Pepcon manufactured solid fuel used in the Space Shuttle until it was nearly launched from Henderson to the moon.

Also nearby in Henderson is the new **Cranberry World West** exhibit. You'll learn more than you ever imagined about the cranberry and see the juice processing plant. Open daily from 9 A.M. to 5 P.M., except holidays; free. Gibson Road, Henderson. 566-7160.

With an eye north to Las Vegas, Henderson has embarked on an ambitious series of developments in recent years, including the creation of **Lake Las Vegas**, one of the largest civil engineering projects in the country. The $100 million earthen dam has created a two-mile lake that is one day expected to be circled by 3,000 homes, several golf courses, and (of course) half a dozen hotel-casinos.

Hoover Dam

If they had a casino at Hoover Dam, it would be a building that would rival Luxor, Excalibur, Caesars Palace, and MGM Grand combined. They don't, of course, and though nearly 700,000 visitors a year come to visit this incredible monument to the attempts of our species to exercise control over our environment, this means that nearly 20 million other visitors to Las Vegas don't make the 40-mile trip south. There ought to be a law. . . .

The Colorado River, which flows 1,400 miles from the Rocky Mountains in Colorado to the Gulf of California is one of the great geological forces in the West, creating spectacular natural wonders including the Grand Canyon.

In the early days of settlement, the Colorado was the source of great respect and fear. Early settlers attempted to divert some of its waters for irrigation purposes. They were defeated by the tremendous seasonal changes from steady flow to summertime trickle to wild flooding in the spring as mountain snows melted.

Steam-powered riverboats navigated the Colorado River upstream from its mouth in the late 1800s, able to reach as far north as the Mormon settlement of Callville during certain parts of the year.

One of the most difficult parts of the 600-mile trip was passage through the Black Canyon rapids. Crews had to use a system of winches and cables strung through ring bolts anchored in the canyon walls.

It took a disastrous flood in California's Imperial Valley in 1905 to begin the move to finally tame the river. In that year, early spring flash floods washed away small earthen dams that had been created to divert water from the river to the Imperial Canal. The heavy water flow changed the course of the river and caused it to flow for the next two years into the Imperial Valley and the large Salton Sea east of San Diego, increasing the size of that body of water from 22 to 500 square miles; to this date the Salton Sea has not fully retreated to its turn-of-the-century size, covering about 300 square miles today.

The first step in harnessing the Colorado was agreement among the governments of the seven states through which it flows. In 1922 a commission, headed by Herbert Hoover, then Secretary of Commerce, produced the Colorado River Compact, dividing use of the water between Upper and Lower Colorado River Basins. In 1928, Congress passed the Boulder Canyon Project Act; construction of the dam was begun in 1931.

The first task for the construction crews when they began in April 1931 was to deal with the water already passing through the canyon. Four huge diversion tunnels, nearly 60 feet in diameter, were dug out of the walls of the canyon to the left and right of the eventual location of the dam. A year-and-a-half later they were ready to send the Colorado River through the tunnels and leave dry the dam's base.

More than 5,000 men worked day and night in a continuous pour of concrete that took two years—a total of 4.4 million cubic yards of concrete for the dam and supporting structures. Although there is a commonly held belief that some of the 94 workers who died in the course of the dangerous construction project are entombed within the concrete, dam tour guides will tell you otherwise.

The dam itself is described as an arch-gravity structure. Still the highest concrete dam in the western hemisphere, it rises 726 feet above the bedrock of Black Canyon. It is 660 feet thick at its base and 45 feet thick at the top, with a span of 1,244 feet across the canyon.

Nowheresville. The massive construction project of Hoover Dam takes on an even greater scope when you realize that at the start of the project Black Canyon was an isolated stretch of river with few roads and no support facilities. The nearest town of any significance was Las Vegas, which was still a small rest stop for the railroads. The huge influx of workers changed Las Vegas forever, setting it on its course as a gambling and entertainment mecca.

High way. The two-lane highway atop the dam connects Nevada and Arizona. By the way, Nevada is in the Pacific time zone, and Arizona is one hour later in the Mountain time zone.

The dam was completed in 1935, two years ahead of schedule, which has to be a record for a government project. The diversion tunnels were closed in February of 1935, and Lake Mead began to form behind the dam. The first power generator began operation in 1936; the 17th and final generator went on line in 1961.

The dam cost about $175 million to build at the time, and the cost has been repaid through revenues from the generation of power and the supply of water.

The energy distribution from the dam, as set by contracts among the states, sends about 19 percent of the power to the state of Arizona, about 25 percent to Nevada, 28 percent to the Metropolitan Water District of Southern California, and the remainder to various municipalities in California including Los Angeles.

The Lake Mead reservoir, which built up behind the dam, extends for 110

Power source. As important as the large hydro-electric plants of Hoover Dam and Davis Dam are, conventional thermal plants using fossil fuels produce more than 75 percent of the Nevada electrical power.

miles and usually stores about two years of average Colorado river flow, which is released as needed for irrigation and power generation. Water stored in the lake irrigates more than one million acres of land in the United States and half a million acres in Mexico.

The generators produce about four billion kilowatt-hours of energy per year, enough for 500,000 homes. The gravity-fed generators are non-polluting, and of course, water flow is a renewable resource.

Another effect of the dam is to clear the once-muddy waters of the Colorado for much of its downstream passage and within Lake Mead itself.

Tours of the dam are conducted by the Bureau of Reclamation daily except for Christmas. The tour passes down through the body of the dam to the generating stations and out onto the walkway near the diversion tunnels at the base of the dam. Call 293-8321 or 293-8367 for information on the tour.

An impressive new visitor's center, cantilevered out from the rock wall of the canyon on the Nevada side, is due for completion in 1995. Congressional critics have pointed out that the price tag for the visitor center will be higher than the cost of the dam itself.

Stop off at the **Alan Bible Visitor Center** on Lakeshore Drive (Route 166 just past the junction with U.S. 93) for information about Lake Mead and Hoover Dam.

Davis Dam, downstream of Hoover Dam, was completed in 1953. That rock and earth wall controls the flow of water from Lake Mohave. Self-guided tours are available at Davis.

Boulder City

Boulder City is a planned community created by the U.S. Bureau of Reclamation as housing for some of the construction workers for the dam and for administrative offices. The construction of the town coincided with a period of architectural design and government master planning; the result was a designed town with a great deal of un-Nevada-like greenery and parks. Think of it as a U.S. government–approved oasis in the desert.

Like a rock. The U.S. Bureau of Reclamation continued to own and operate the town, controlling almost every detail until 1960 when it gave up dominion and the town was incorporated. Only then was alcohol permitted to be sold; today, Boulder City continues as the only city in Nevada that bans public gambling.

The **Boulder City/Hoover Dam Museum** is worth a visit to ogle the impressive collection of construction photos. The museum is located at 441 Nevada Highway. Call 293-1823 for hours and information.

The **Boulder Dam Hotel**, built for government VIPs during the construction period, has been restored as a hotel.

Lake Mead

It seems odd to speak of a fabulous outdoor wonderland like Lake Mead as a creation of man, but so it is.

Before Lake Mead was formed when the diversion tunnels of Hoover Dam were closed in 1935, this area was almost untouched by humans. Indian tribes once inhabited some of the canyons. Explorers like John Wesley Powell went deep into the Grand Canyon and other areas and passed through the region; the first foreign settlers included fur trappers, Mormon settlers, and hardy prospectors.

Anson Call established a Mormon colony in 1864 with a trading post to service emigrants on their westward passage along the Colorado River. Callville was abandoned five years later, although the walls of part of the settlement were still in place when the entire region—including many ancient Indian sites—was flooded by the waters of the developing lake. It is a good question to ask whether Hoover Dam could have been built under today's historic preservation and environmental impact laws.

In any case, Lake Mead today is an incredible contrast of desert and water, mountain and canyon, magnificent wilderness and the triumph of man-made technology.

Lake Mead National Recreation Area includes the 110-mile-long Lake Mead, the 67-mile-long Lake Mohave, which backs up behind the smaller Davis Dam at Laughlin, the surrounding desert, and the isolated Shivwits Plateau in Arizona, which connects into the Grand Canyon National Park.

Down the drain. Nearly all of the state's streams and rivers drain internally into lakes or into dry lake beds called playas, or sinks. The major exception is the Colorado River.

The Humboldt rises in the northeast and flows west to disappear into the Humboldt Sink; and the Walker, Carson, and Truckee Rivers rise in the Sierra Nevada and flow east to the Walker, Carson, and Pyramid Lakes. Many other streams are dry for most of the year, filling their banks only in the spring with snow melt or after the rare summer rainfall.

You can't get there from here. The Shivwits Plateau can only be reached by unpaved roads from the north; check with park rangers for information on access.

Together, the two huge (274 square-mile) lakes sparkle in one of the driest, hottest places known to man.

In summer, daytime temperatures rise above 100 degrees regularly. From October to May, temperatures range from the 30s to the 50s.

Plan to include a stop at the Alan Bible Visitor Center, four miles northeast of Boulder City on U.S. 93. Travel south from Las Vegas on Route 93/95 and stay on Route 93 at the split. The visitor center offers maps and information on services in the park.

You can also go to the park headquarters at the intersection of Nevada Highway and Wyoming Street in Boulder City or visit one of the many park ranger stations.

Reservations may be necessary for most lodging and many services in the

summer. Campsites are available, for a fee, on a
first-come first-served basis; some have time limits for stays. Each camp area includes picnic tables,
grills, water, restrooms, and a trailer sewage dump;
no utility hookups are provided.

Backcountry camping is permitted along the
shore on both lakes and in designated sites along
unpaved backcountry roads.

Outside of the parks, you can find hotels, restau-
rants, and services in Las Vegas, Boulder City, Henderson, Laughlin, Searchlight, and Overton in Nevada; Bullhead City and Kingman in Arizona; and
Needles in California.

Lake Mead Cruises

Several companies offer cruises all year long on Lake Mead near Hoover
Dam.

The **Desert Princess** paddlewheel sails daily from the Lake Mead Resort
Marina on Lakeshore Road between Las Vegas and the Hoover Dam. The Desert
Princess, sister ship to the M.S. Dixie II on Lake Tahoe, has breakfast, sightseeing, and dinner/dance cruises priced from about $15 to $43. There are six
daily sailings from April 1 through October 31, with an abbreviated schedule for the rest of the year. For information and reservations, call 293-6180.

Park Facilities

	Distance from Visitor Center (miles)	Services
Lake Mead		
Boulder Beach	2	L T C M R F S
Las Vegas Wash	10	C M R F S
Callville Bay	27	C M R F S G H
Echo Bay	49	L T C M R F S G H
Temple Bar	50	L T C M R F S G H
Overton Beach	63	L T M R F S G
Lake Mohave		
Willow Beach	22	L T M R F S G H
Cottonwood Beach	54	L T C M R F S G H
Katherine	81	L T C M R F S G H

KEY:
L = Lodging   T = Trailer village (fee)   C = Campground
M = Marina   R = Restaurant   F = Food
S = Sewage dump G = Gasoline   H = Houseboat rentals

Animal Life in the Lake Mead Area

Living things have to be very hardy to survive in the temperature extremes
of the desert and with an annual rainfall of less than six inches.

The creation of Lake Mead dramatically changed the ecology of the region,
bringing waterbirds, fish, and aquatic plants. In the surrounding desert, more
than a thousand bighorn sheep live along the mountain ridges; they are among

the few desert animals active in the heat of the day. Other creatures include lizards, squirrels, rabbits, insects, and spiders.

The desert blooms year-round, but some of the flowers are so tiny that it is easy to miss them. A winter rain can cause a brief but glorious overnight bloom of wildflowers on the desert.

Fishing

The lake is a year-round bonanza for anglers. Check with park rangers or fishing guides.

In Lake Mead, the most sought-after fish is striped bass, which can reach 50 pounds and more. In Lake Mohave, especially in the upper reaches in Black Canyon, rainbow trout is the most popular. Other species include largemouth bass, channel catfish, black crappie, and bluegill.

Nevada and Arizona share jurisdiction over the two lakes. You must have a state fishing license to fish from shore. To fish from a boat, you must have a license from one state and a special use stamp from the other. Licenses and stamps are available at most marinas.

Swimming

Both lakes are clear and clean for swimming. Water temperatures across most of the two lakes average about 78 degrees in spring, summer, and fall. The coldest water is usually found in the northern portion of Lake Mohave.

Lifeguard beaches can be found in summer at Boulder Beach on Lake Mead and at Katherine Beach on Lake Mohave.

Boating

Boaters can get to some spots inaccessible to cars and can roam the entire 274 square miles of water of Lake Mead, including the narrow steep gorge of Iceberg Canyon.

Around the lake, many secluded coves are formed by fingers of the desert jutting out into the water; these are among the most popular campsites.

Sailboarding, a relatively new sport, is increasingly popular on the lake. Participants generally prefer near-shore areas with stronger breezes.

There are six privately operated marinas along Lake Mead and three on Lake Mohave, each offering services and supplies year-round. Free public launching ramps and parking areas (parking limited to seven days) are found at each site.

Several companies offer boat tours, including a paddlewheel boat depart-

Can you dig it? The original economic foundation of the state was mining, beginning with the gold and silver deposits of the Comstock Lode in 1859. Agriculture developed as the second most important segment of the economy.

Mining today represents about 33 percent of the annual value of goods produced in Nevada. Principal deposits are gold, barite, silver, and petroleum.

The largest current gold mine is west of Carlin, in northeast Nevada near Elko, although deposits are spread throughout the state. Nevada's mining industry also includes copper, lead, sand, gravel, mercury, gypsum, tungsten, salt, zinc, magnesium, and manganese.

Home grown. Agriculture represents about 14 percent of Nevada's economy. Livestock makes up about half of the industry. Farms are mostly located along snow-fed streams at the base of the Sierra Nevadas in the west and along the Humboldt River and its tributaries. Irrigation has expanded the growing areas in southern and southeastern areas.

Leading products are hay and potatoes. Other crops are wheat, barley, vegetables, fruits, nuts, and cotton.

Water proofing. Before going out on the water, call 736-3854 or monitor marine radio channel 162.55 for National Weather Service forecasts. High winds can arrive suddenly, building up waves as high as six feet; lightning storms pose particular hazards to boats on open water. If you are caught in a storm, seek shelter in a protected cove.

ing daily from the Lake Mead Marina. In summer, a boat tour through Boulder Canyon departs from Callville Bay every day.

On Lake Mohave, one-day raft trips are offered through the slow-moving waters of Black Canyon from Hoover Dam to Willow Beach.

Hiking

The best hiking months are October through May. Temperatures the rest of the year make for furnace-like conditions. You can explore on your own or join an escorted tour lead by naturalists. Always carry one gallon of water per person per day and let someone know where you are going and when you expect to return.

Health Considerations

The desert includes several species of dangerous animals, including rattlesnakes, scorpions, and Gila monster lizards. All of these will likely leave you alone if you do not disturb them. Wear sturdy boots to protect your feet.

A microscopic amoeba common to some hot springs can cause a rare infection that can become fatal; do not dive or submerse your head in springs and streams.

A toxic plant called oleander is common in non-wilderness areas, and hikers are advised not to eat unknown plants or drink water from ditches.

Lake Mead Resorts and Recreational Facilities

Boulder Beach Store. 290 Lakeshore Road, Boulder City; 293-1891. Public showers, grocery store, snack bar.

Callville Bay Resort. Callville Bay; 565-8958. Cafe/lounge, marina, houseboat rentals, small boat rentals, trailer village, RV sites, showers, laundry, auto/boat gas, dry boat storage, store.

Echo Bay Resort. Overton; (800) 752-9669, 394-4000. Restaurant/lounge, marina, boat rentals, houseboat rentals, trailer village, RV sites, hotel, showers/laundry, auto/boat gas, store, dry boat storage.

Lake Mead Cruises. Boulder City; 293-6180. Scheduled and charter sightseeing tours on the *Desert Princess* paddlewheel boat from Lake Mead Marina to Hoover Dam and back.

Lake Mead Resort. 322 Lakeshore Road, Boulder City; 293-3484. Call 293-

2074 for lodging reservations only, or (800) 752-9669 for other reservations. Restaurant/lounge, marina, boat rentals, store, dry boat storage, boat gas, and motel.

Lakeshore Trailer Village. 268 Lakeshore Road, Boulder; 293-2540. Trailer village with RV sites, dry boat storage, showers, and laundry.

Las Vegas Bay Marina/Las Vegas Boat Harbor. Henderson; 565-9111. Restaurant/lounge, marina, boat rentals, dry boat storage, store, boat gas.

Overton Beach Resort. Overton; 394-4040. Snack bar, boat rentals, moorings, fuel dock, auto/boat gas, store, showers, laundry, trailer village, RV sites, dry boat storage, summer jet-ski rental.

Temple Bar Resort. Temple Bar, Arizona; (602) 767-3211. Reservations (800) 752-9669. Restaurant/lounge, motel, trailer village, dry boat storage, store, marina, boat rentals, showers, laundry, auto/boat gas, RV sites.

> **Hot dogs.** Pets must always be leashed, and are prohibited from specified beaches and other public areas. Never leave a pet in a car; temperatures in a closed vehicle in the sun can reach 160 degrees.

> **Boulder City Chamber of Commerce.** 1497 Nevada Highway, Boulder City, NV 89005; 293-2034.
> **Boulder City Visitor Center.** 100 Nevada Highway, Boulder City, NV 89005; 294-1220.

Canoe/Raft Services

Down River Outfitters. Boulder City; 293-1190. Canoe/raft delivery and retrieval.

Jerkwater Canoe Co., Inc. Topock, Arizona; (602) 768-7753. Canoe delivery and retrieval.

Tincanebitt Taxi. Meadview, Arizona; (602) 564-2424. Boat/raft retrieval.

Hunting Guides

Aravaipa Outfitters. Globe, Arizona; (602) 425-1078.

Arizona Wildlife Outfitters. Kingman, Arizona; (602) 753-4867.

High Desert Outfitters. Las Vegas; 645-2817.

Nevada Desert Trophy Hunts. Smith; 465-2598.

Silver State Guide & Outfitting. Las Vegas; 645-8753.

Virgil's Nevada Desert Hunts. Sparks; 331-0900.

Wildlife West Taxidermy & Guide Service. Fallon; 423-5286.

Scuba Instruction

Lake Mead is a popular dive site because of its warm and clear waters. Special attractions include several wrecks as well as the remains of Callville and other submerged communities.

American Cactus Divers. Henderson; 564-3483.

Blue Seas Scuba Center, Inc. Las Vegas; 367-2882.

Colorado River Divers. Boulder City; 293-6648.

Desert Divers Supply, Inc. Las Vegas; 438-1000.

Dive West, Inc. Las Vegas; 459-3483.

Neptune Divers. Boulder City; 564-5253.

Water World Scuba Diving Center. Bullhead City, Arizona; (602) 763-5531.

Fishing Guides

A-1 Fishing Guide. Henderson; 564-5702.
  Howard E. Blum. Henderson; 565-7853.
  Capt. Don's Fishing Guide Service. Las Vegas; 647-7778.
  Patrick Donoho. Las Vegas; 451-4004.
  Fish, Incorporated. Henderson; 565-8396.
  Karen A. Jones. Las Vegas; 361-1972.
  William Spellman. Henderson; 564-1588.
  Zolan Tanner. Las Vegas; 452-7890.

Lake Mohave Resorts and Recreational Facilities

Black Canyon, Inc. Boulder City; 293-3776, (602) 767-3311. Raft tours from Hoover Dam to Willow Beach.

  Cottonwood Cove Resort. Cottonwood Cove; 297-1464. Cafe, marina, boat rentals, houseboat rentals, auto/boat gas, dry boat storage, store, showers, laundry, motel, trailer village, RV sites. **Forever Resorts** at Cottonwood Cove rents houseboats and deck cruisers. 297-1005, (800) 255-5561.

  Lake Mohave Resort. Bullhead City, Arizona; (602) 754-3245. Reservations (800) 752-9669. Restaurant/lounge, store, motel, auto/boat gas, marina, boat rentals, houseboat rentals, trailer village, RV sites, showers, laundry, dry boat storage.

  Willow Beach Resort. Willow Beach, Arizona. (702) 293-3776, (602) 767-3311. Reservations (800) 845-3833. Restaurant/lounge, marina, boat rentals, houseboat rentals, showers, laundry, auto/boat gas, store, motel, trailer village, RV sites, dry boat storage.

The Other Stateline

About 40 miles south of Las Vegas on I-15 at the California border is a new development of hotels and casinos at a wide spot in the road called Stateline. (Not to be confused with that other casino town on the California border at Lake Tahoe, also called Stateline.)

Three major developments, all owned by the Primadonna company, work hard to attract visitors and gamblers with some unusual attractions. Room rates are a notch or two below those at Las Vegas, starting at about $21.

Buffalo Bill's Resort and Casino

A new 614-room hotel with its very own roller coaster and log flume ride.

Actually, this is no ordinary coaster: the 225-foot-tall Desperado is claimed to be the world's tallest and fastest. Cars reach speeds of more than 80 miles per hour over more than a mile of track on a nearly three-minute ride. A flume ride circles the casino and enters within, past mining scenes. Other entertainment includes a motion simulator ride and a Western shopping mall. There is, of course, also a casino. Stateline; (800) 367-7383.

Also in Stateline

Primadonna Resort. 661 rooms; 382-1212.
  Whiskey Pete's. 777 rooms; 382-4388.

Chapter 17
Laughlin

Driving from Las Vegas to Laughlin

Driving from Las Vegas to Laughlin is a bit like taking a trip from Disneyland to Walt Disney World. What you leave and what you come to are pretty much the same; the interesting part is what you see along the way.

It's an interesting tour, though, and worth a day trip when you are ready to take a break from Las Vegas. Be sure to fill your gas tank and check your car's condition before heading out into the desert.

Take Interstate 93/95 south from Las Vegas through Henderson to the point where the roads split. I-93 heads to Boulder City and across the Hoover Dam and then south through Arizona; the direct route to Laughlin follows I-95, and we'll take that road.

Soon after the split, the barren desert is broken by electrical power lines that march across the landscape toward Las Vegas from Hoover Dam. You'll get a very real appreciation for the wildness of the desert that had to be crossed by the early settlers. On the broad, open desert between Nelson and Searchlight there are no houses or settlements at all. It is almost impossible to gauge the distance to the mountains that frame the desert because the land is so flat and there are no structures to give you a sense of perspective.

About four or five miles before Searchlight you'll come to some modern-day Wild West mining operations, made up mostly of ramshackle sheds and trailers. The signs say, "Guard on duty, don't trespass. You will be shot."

At **Searchlight**, you'll come to the first major crossroad since you left Boulder City some 36 miles back. Route 164 eastbound is a one-way path to Cottonwood Cove, a recreational area 14 miles away on Lake Mohave in the Lake Mead National Recreational Area. Cottonwood includes a campground, boat rentals and launching services, and cabins.

Westbound Route 164 connects to I-15, which eventually makes its way to Los Angeles. We'll stay on I-95.

Searchlight is a town of one gas station, a small general store, a liquor store, and (of course) a small gambling parlor, the **Searchlight Nugget Casino**. There is some additional development, including a museum, a mile east on Route 164 toward Cottonwood Cove.

Things were different in Searchlight at the turn of the century. The town was built up around a rich gold mine that was discovered in 1897. At its height in about 1907, Searchlight had a population of about 1,500 with more than 50 mines in production. There was a newspaper, a business district, and a rail line that connected with the Santa Fe at Needles, California. The mines petered out by about 1910, though, and there were only a few dozen residents remaining a few years later.

Searchlight received its name from a mining claim in the area, which was in turn named after a then-popular brand of matches. American composer Scott Joplin took note of the lively town with the "Searchlight Rag." Costume designer Edith Head grew up in Searchlight, and movie stars Rex Bell and Clara Bow had a ranch there in the 1930s before moving north and helping to launch the age of glamour in Las Vegas.

The next settlement is CalNevAri, named after the three state borders nearby. Even smaller than Searchlight, it nevertheless has a market, a part-time gas station . . . and a casino.

At this point we separate the men from the boys, the women from the girls, and the intrepid explorer from the white-knuckle driver. I'm talking about **Christmas Tree Pass**, an unpaved switchback road that cuts the corner from near CalNevAri to Grapevine Canyon just above Laughlin.

The road to Christmas Tree Pass branches off to the left about two miles past CalNevAri. In dry, clear weather the road should be passable in a passenger car; in wet conditions or snow, I'd recommend a four-wheel-drive vehicle or a resolution to come back another day.

The winding hard-packed dirt road gets narrower and narrower the further along you travel, becoming about a lane-and-a-half wide as you reach the top of the pass. Not that you are likely to meet any other cars on your expedition; I didn't pass another soul on my hour-long 17-mile trip. (No gas stations or emergency services, either.)

The road is marked by tiny white signs on the sides of the road that say designated route; resist the urge to follow the side roads off this side road unless you have a topographical map and an off-road vehicle.

At the very top of the pass—about nine miles along—the road suddenly turns into a one-lane switchback; go slowly, and honk your horn before you make the blind turn just in case there is another almost-lost soul ascending the pass.

Somewhere near the top you are likely to find a few forlorn desert bushes festooned with windblown Christmas ornaments; the pass has its name because of an old tradition apparently started by travelers through the pass.

On the down side of the pass you will enter into the Lake Mead Recreational Area, leading up to Lake Mohave. The roads in the park are even worse than the first half of the trip, although not quite as winding.

You'll pass some spectacular rock slide areas, including several mountains that seem to be made entirely of balanced boulders.

And then finally, you are in a valley and on a paved road. On your right is **Grapevine Canyon,** with its ancient petroglyphs. Just ahead is Route 163, at this point a four-lane highway zooming down to the Colorado River and Laughlin.

Then like a mirage in the desert you descend on Route 163 into a small version of Las Vegas with a dozen skyscraper hotels and neon lights.

A direct trip from Las Vegas to Laughlin on Interstate 95 to Highway 163 is about 101 miles, and just under two hours in time. If you take Christmas Tree Pass, figure on just under three hours in total.

A good place to stop as soon as you enter Laughlin is the **Laughlin Visitors Bureau** at 1555 Casino Drive, just before the Riverside Casino. The office has a healthy supply of brochures, newspapers, and magazines. Call 298-3321.

The Prehistory of Laughlin

The burgeoning community of Laughlin is unique in Nevada in at least two respects. First, it is among the few major settlements that has no real history of its own other than as a camp for the construction of the Davis Dam. There wasn't even a rest stop there! Second, the place was named by and for its founder, who still operates a major casino there.

Laughlin is the most important settlement of the tri-state area, where Clark County, Nevada, Mohave County, Arizona, and San Bernardino County, California, come together. If something seems even stranger than usual for a Nevada gambling town, consider that almost nothing in Laughlin dates back more than about 30 years; everything you see has grown up around the Riverside Casino. In fact, most of the construction only dates as far back as the mid-1980s.

In ancient times, the area was lush and wet. Climatic changes and volcanic uprisings some 100,000 years ago made the land very different. Today, the region is hot and dry in the summer, often reaching above 120 degrees, and cold and dry in the winter with lows below freezing. About three to five inches of precipitation fall each year, with what little rain there is falling in the winter or the heat of summer when occasional thunderstorms can sometimes bring flash floods.

Although some scientists believe that humans lived in the area as far back as 10,000 years ago, available evidence in the form of petroglyphs on the walls of canyons near Laughlin dates only some 4,000 or so years back. The first identified Indian tribe was the Patayans, who split into the Haulpai and Mojave tribes (Patayan is a Hualpai word meaning "ancient ones").

The National Park Service has identifed more than 100 Patayan campsites between Willow Beach near Hoover Dam, and Pyramid Canyon, the location of Davis Dam.

The Mojaves lived in the region for hundreds of years and were there when the Spanish claimed their land and when the Americans passed through and eventually came to settle. The first Europeans arrived in the 16th century when Spanish conquistadors led by Coronado came through on their quest for the mythical Seven Cities of Gold. Along the way, the Spanish found the Grand Canyon.

In the mid-19th century, sternwheel steamboats from California chugged upstream as far as the present site of Hoover Dam bringing supplies and taking away minerals and other booty. In 1857, Lt. Edward Beale surveyed a trail from Fort Smith, Arkansas, to the Colorado River and established a fort near the present site of Bullhead.

Beale's other significant accomplishment was the deployment of a caravan of camels operating out of Fort Mohave. The camels were used to carry freight and mail in the desert, and were taken as far north in Nevada as the foothills of the Sierras. Today the camels are commemorated in a lighthearted way in the annual camel races in Virginia City near Reno.

Although a number of small mines were explored in the area, boom times arrived in 1900 when gold was discovered at Katherine. At its height, the mine was producing 600 ounces of gold and silver a day. By 1910, though, most of the rich mines had petered out.

Everything's Up-to-Date in Laughlin

The possibility of a dam across the Colorado River at Pyramid Canyon had been considered as far back as 1902, but work was not begun until after the completion of Hoover Dam some 67 miles upstream. Work at Pyramid Canyon was begun in 1942 but was stopped soon afterward because of the war; construction was resumed in 1946, and the dam was completed in 1953.

Lake Mohave, created by the dam, extends 67 miles up the Colorado River to the base of Hoover Dam. At its widest, the lake is four miles across.

Bullhead City in Arizona began as a construction camp for the Davis Dam, just as Boulder City was created for Hoover Dam. It received its name from a local landmark called Bullhead Rock, now covered by the waters of the dam.

Laughlin was originally called South Pointe because of its location at the southernmost point of Nevada. It boasted a motel, bar, and a few other businesses to serve the construction workers. After the dam was completed, the motel was closed and most of the residents of Laughlin and Bullhead City left.

Don Laughlin, who had once owned the 101 Club casino in Las Vegas, came to the area in 1964. He purchased the shuttered motel along the river and rebuilt it as the **Riverside Resort**; he and his family lived in four of the motel rooms and rented out the other four. He added a small casino and restaurant.

According to local lore, the Postal Service gave Laughlin its name; others say the promoter volunteered it. Either way, from this very humble beginning, a new city was born.

At first, almost all of the workers in Laughlin lived in Bullhead City and were forced to take the circuitous route from Nevada to Arizona over the road at Davis Dam or to use one of dozens of little water taxis that sprang up across the Colorado River. Don Laughlin petitioned the states of Nevada and Arizona to build a bridge near Laughlin, but both governments pleaded poverty.

So, Laughlin built a $3.5 million bridge linking his casino town to Bullhead City in 1987 and then gave the bridge to the two states to maintain.

Today, Laughlin ranks third among Nevada resorts in gaming revenue, behind Las Vegas and Reno and ahead of Lake Tahoe. From 450 rooms in 1983, Laughlin now offers more than 10,000 rooms and boasts near-sellout conditions in the summer. In the winter off-season, the resort offers some of the best room rates anywhere; on one of our recent visits, two major hotels were offering rooms for $15 per night, and one gave the second night free.

The clientele at the Laughlin casinos is mostly drawn from Arizona, California, and nearby Nevada, and are older and more conservative than most of the visitors to Las Vegas. At several casinos I visited, I found $1 poker games; friendly dealers will invite you to join the games if you stroll nearby.

Laughlin is different from Reno and Las Vegas in another way, with a real connection to the natural surroundings of the area. Among other things, most of its casinos are designed with windows that let in sunlight and views of the Colorado River flowing in front of the buildings.

As you drive on Casino Drive (Laughlin's "Strip"), though, it is even possible to not realize that there is a river in the neighborhood. The Colorado is hidden by the wall of hotels and casinos.

As you descend into Laughlin from Highway 163, your first landmark is likely to be the steam plumes from the modern **Mohave Power Project** above town.

The Mohave Power Project has a total capacity of 1,580 megawatts from its two coal-fired steam turbine generators—about one-third the capacity of the massive Hoover Dam up the river. The generators receive their fuel from an underground river of its own: an 18-inch pipeline that brings a slurry of half coal and half water 275 miles from its source at a mine on the Navaho-Hopi Indian Reservation in Kayenta, Arizona.

The station is a joint operation of the Southern California Edison Company and smaller utilities that serve Nevada, Arizona, and California.

The Laughlin airport, located across the river in Bullhead City, opened in 1991 with a 7,500-foot runway, capable of handling 737s. Airlines serving the airport include America West Express, Reno Air, United Express, and Mesa Airlines, with connections to points in Arizona, California, and Nevada.

Just outside of Laughlin on the Nevada side, the development drops away to brown hills and scrub, although real estate signs saying things like "Hotel-Casino site" dot the desert. The Emerald River Golf Course past Laughlin toward the California border has some jarringly green greens, the result of massive irrigation and fertilization in the brown desert.

Casinos and Hotels in Laughlin
Don Laughlin's Riverside Resort Hotel & Casino
The start of it all, today offering 660 rooms, 830 RV spaces, a six-screen movie theater, five restaurants—and a casino. A 790-room expansion in a 28-story tower was due to open in 1995.

Restaurants include the **Gourmet Room**, featuring Continental and Amer-

Laughlin Chamber of Commerce. Box 2280, Laughlin, NV 89029; 298-2214, (800) 227-5245.
Laughlin Visitor Center. 1555 S. Casino Drive, Laughlin, NV 89029; 298-3321.

Uncommon Code. The area code for Arizona, except for the Phoenix area, was changed from (602) to (520) in 1995 as part of a national expansion of codes.

ican dishes from chateaubriand to rack of lamb to steak and lobster specials; open for dinner only. The **Prime Rib Room** offers beef carved at your table and an all-you-can-eat salad, potato, and dessert bar. The **Riverview Restaurant** is a 24-hour coffee shop. The **East Buffet** offers breakfast, lunch, and dinner; on Friday night, seafood is the special, and Saturday and Sunday feature champagne brunches. Finally, the **West Buffet** is open daily for dinner.

At the front entrance to the hotel is a showroom for part of Don Laughlin's classic car collection, augmented by cars on loan from the Imperial Palace collection in Las Vegas. Among the interesting vehicles is a 1935 Chrysler Imperial Airflow that was owned by Steve McQueen. It stands alongside a less impressive but even rarer 1908 Holsman Hi-wheeler Run-a-Bout.

As befits a place that has gone through many expansions and renovations, the place sprawls in all directions. Upstairs over the casino are a series of shops, a dance studio, a jewelry store, and a six-screen movie theater.

Across the river in Bullhead City, the Riverside runs the **River Queen Motel**, which includes a 600-space RV park; the two hotels are connected by 24-hour ferry service.

The Riverside even has its own "luxury" cruise ship, a spiffed-up houseboat that sails daily on 75-minute cruises along the Colorado River to the Davis Dam. Tickets are $10 for adults and $6 for children from 3 to 12. For information, call 298-2535, ext. 5770.

Rooms go for as low as $19, with weekends and holiday rates set as high as $105. Call 298-2535, (800) 227-3849, or (520) 763-7070.

Colorado Belle Hotel & Casino

Here's your basic 608-foot-long three-deck Mississippi River gambling boat, only it's on the Colorado, and it has never gone and never will go anywhere. The hotel includes four huge environmentally safe (they don't work) smokestacks; at night, strobe lights make the faux paddlewheels appear to be turning.

Within, the decorations are those of a turn-of-the-century New Orleans gambling (and probably more) house with excesses of red and bright brass. The high-ceilinged interior is made to look like the inside of a riverboat, with lots of red and gold furnishings.

There are 206 rooms in the "boat" and another 1,082 in a more conventional structure nearby.

Restaurants include the **Orleans Room**, specializing in seafood, steaks, and pasta. **Mark Twain's** features barbecued chicken and ribs, with a full rack priced at $11.50, and a half rack at $7.50. Also available are fried chicken and fish dishes. Open for dinner only 4 to 10 P.M.

Huckleberry's offers burgers, hot dogs, ice cream, and sodas. Nearby are **Mississippi**, a far-inland oyster bar, and the **Paddlewheel**, a 24-hour coffee shop.

Captain's Food Fair offers a breakfast buffet, lunch and dinner specials, and a Friday night seafood buffet. You can also order main dishes from a menu on the wall and augment them with selections from the buffet bar.

The **Colorado Belle** is owned by Circus Circus Enterprises, the most successful gaming company in the state. Room rates are generally in the range of about $40 to $65 but can be as low as $15 per night in the winter. Call 298-4000 or (800) 458-9500 for reservations.

The Edgewater Hotel/Casino

Next door to the Colorado Belle is a corporate cousin, a 1,475-room budget behemoth also run by Circus Circus.

Restaurants include the **Hickory Pit Steak House**, open for dinner and serving steaks, seafood, chops, barbecued ribs, and chicken; the **Garden Room**, a 24-hour coffee shop including a one-pound prime rib special; and the **Winner's Circle Deli.** The **Bountiful Buffet** is said to be Laughlin's largest buffet with a trio of 90-foot serving lines; meals are priced at $2.49 for breakfast, $3.19 for lunch, and $4.29 for dinner.

Room rates are generally in the range from about $27 to $49; in the winter, rates are as low as $15 per night. The hotel also runs a ferry to the Arizona side of the river. Call 298-2453 or (800) 677-4837.

Flamingo Hilton

A flashy Las Vegas–like resort with mirrors on the ceilings and lots of chrome in the casino, and 2,000 rooms in twin 18-story towers. As with other Hiltons in Nevada, there is a move toward accommodating young visitors with a video arcade and the Flamingo Funland carnival open during the summer season.

Restaurants include **Alta Villa**, open evenings for fine Italian dining from Friday to Tuesday. Chef's specialities include veal *saltimbocca* for $16.50, *tournedos* Bardolino (two sautéed tenderloins of beef with mushrooms in a red wine sauce) for $18.00, chicken *picatta* for $14, and scampi *livornese* for $17.

Beef Barron is a steak house open for dinner; fare includes prime rib from $10 to $14, baby back pork ribs for $9 and $12, and filet of blackened or deep-fried catfish for $9.

Casual eateries include the **Flamingo Diner,** a 24-hour '50s-style diner. And there's a Mexican-Chinese snack bar with the clever name of **Juan Ton's.**

The **Fruit Basket Buffet** is open for breakfast, lunch, and dinner, with an attractive window wall along the river. There's also a Burger King and ice cream parlor.

Rates start at about $29. At the time of our visit during the winter the sign outside the Flamingo said, "We will match any room rate." In theory, this means the classy Flamingo can go as low as $7.50 per night if they match lesser hotels with a $15, second night free deal. That's a great rate. For information call 298-5111 or (800) 352-6464.

Golden Nugget Laughlin

An opulent tropical-theme resort, including an indoor rain forest and more ferns than a Los Angeles singles bar.

The Golden Nugget is the successor to the second casino opened in Laughlin. The Bobcat Club was opened in 1967 as a bar and sold in 1970 to be renamed as the Nevada Club and run as a hotel and casino. It was eventually purchased by Golden Nugget Corp., now called Mirage Resorts. Mirage operates the Golden Nugget, the Mirage, and Treasure Island in Las Vegas, and other casinos elsewhere.

The hotel itself is somewhat hidden by a large parking garage on Casino Drive. Visitors enter through an arcade adorned with animatronic singing birds into a tropical atrium, a miniature tribute to the greenery of the Mirage in Las Vegas. The hotel has 300 rooms. Within the casino, the ceilings are surprisingly low, with the building stepped into the side of the hill.

Eateries include **Jane's Grill**, just off the casino floor and featuring a mesquite grill and wood-fired oven pizza. Offerings include pizza, burgers, and sandwiches priced from about $5 to $8.

The **River Cafe** is a 24-hour diner. Its late night special is steak and eggs for $1.98; breakfast specials include the "Four Deuces," $1.98 for two pancakes, two eggs, two strips of bacon, two sausages, and coffee.

The **Bountiful Buffet** is open for breakfast, lunch, and dinner with a special Friday night seafood buffet. Regular buffet prices are $2.79 for breakfast, $3.39 for lunch, and $4.79 for dinner. A prime rib dinner buffet is $3.99 on weekdays; also available is a New York steak buffet.

In the back corner of the casino is **The Deli**, a hideaway with reasonably priced sandwiches such as roast beef for $3 and pastrami or corned beef for $3.50. Pizza goes for $1 a slice. Dessert includes donuts, yogurt, and bear claws (the baked goods type).

Rates are as low as $25 in the winter, rising to as high as $55 for standard rooms. Call 298-7222 or (800) 950-7700.

Gold River Gambling Hall & Resort

A 1,003-room riverside box nearby the Emerald River Golf Course, designed to feel like being inside a mining camp. The main gambling hall on the lower level has an open atrium with large neon signs up top listing the names of famous mines in the area.

A small sleepy waiting area by the registration desk has a working fireplace and was filled with sleeping visitors on a recent visit.

Restaurants include **Sutter's Lodge**, a fine dining establishment featuring Continental and American cuisine in a Yosemite hunting lodge setting, complete with wooden beams, rough free stone pillars, and a glass wall with a view of the Colorado River below. The menu features beef and fish, as well as K-Paul's creole specialities including blackened redfish. The house specialty is barbecued ribs; we were also enticed by a petite filet and gulf prawns smothered in a peppered roux sauce. Entrees are priced from about $10 to $20.

The Lodge also offers a twilight dinner special, served Sunday to Thursday from 5 to 10 P.M. and Friday and Saturday from 9 to 11 P.M. for $9.95; the four-course dinner includes pâté, salad, entree, and desserts.

Pasta Cucina is a moderately priced Italian restaurant. **Cafe Victoria**, a garden cafe for breakfast, lunch, and dinner, offered at the time of a recent visit a prime rib dinner for $3.99 and a free shrimp cocktail with dinner entrees.

Aunt B's Snack Shoppe is a 24-hour coffee shop.

The **Opera House Buffet** is $3.49 for lunch and $5.99 for dinner; also offered is a two-for-one breakfast or lunch special on Wednesdays and Fridays.

The showroom at the Gold River offers adult-oriented shows such as "Bottoms Up" and "Pazazz." Tickets are priced at about $10.95, or $13.50 with a buffet.

Room rates are as low as $15 (with the second night free!) in the off-season. For information call 298-2242 or (800) 835-7904.

Harrah's Casino Hotel

A little bit of Mexico along the river, a 1,658-room outpost of the Harrah's chain set a bit apart from the rest of the casinos in a small canyon.

Restaurants include **William Fisk's** for steaks, seafood, and Continental cuisine in a Southwestern setting, open for dinner only. Steaks are priced from about $16 to $20; other offerings include venison, veal, seafood, and broiled ahi. A Sunday brunch is also served at Fisk's. The very attractive room is decorated in white and gold painted wood, with a window view of the river.

La Hacienda, just off the casino floor, offers fine Mexican and American dishes for dinner. Fajitas, tacos, and other such fare are priced from about $6 to $12.

The **Coronado Cafe** is your basic 24-hour coffee shop; there's also the **Del Rio Buffet**, as well as **Gringo's Grill** for hamburgers, french fries, and shakes. At the low end is a McDonald's, off the casino floor.

The Del Rio Beach Club rents one- and two-passenger jet-skis in season. Harrah's runs a free shuttle from Harrah's up to the Regency Casino, which is at the far end of the strip next to Laughlin's Riverside.

Winter room rates are ordinarily priced from $30 to $65, with mini suites $100. For information call 298-4600 or (800) 447-8700.

Pioneer Hotel and Gambling Hall

A Wild West–theme hotel with 414 rooms and riverfront suites and a swinging door entrance. The river facade features a huge neon cowboy called River Rick. Eateries include **Granny's Gourmet Room** for fine dining; **Granny's Old-Fashioned Champagne Brunch**; the **Boarding House Restaurant** offering menu items or buffet; and the **Fast Draw Snack Bar**.

The casino has a smoky, dark Western feel; the cocktail waitresses wear costumes that are out of *Li'l Abner*. The Pioneer opened a new addition in 1995, a motel with exterior entrances.

Room rates range from about $28 in off-season to about $50. Call 298-2442 or (800) 634-9469 for information.

Ramada Express Hotel Casino

A 1,500-room railroad-theme hotel, including a full-size train on a track circling the property on the hillside a block away from the river. The Ramada Express is run by the Aztar Corporation, which also runs the Tropicana in Las Vegas.

The main gambling hall is set up like an old train barn with an arched roof. Old replicas of railroad signs and some old railroading equipment decorate the walls, from lines as archaic as the Tonopah Goldfield Railroad and the Goldfield Bullfrog Railroad Company. The train that circles the hotel is an unrealistic replica.

Eateries include **The Steakhouse**; the **Dining Car Coffee Shop**; the **Whistle Stop** snack bar; and the **Round House Buffet** for breakfast, lunch, and dinner.

Room rates in off-season are as low as $15, with weekend rates as high as $57. For information call 298-4200 or (800) 272-6232.

Regency Casino

Just a casino, and a small one at that. The dining room specializes in prime rib and steaks. 298-2439.

Bay Shore Inn

A small motel with 105 rooms. Guests can rent wave runners and paddleboats. 299-9010.

Laughlin Buffets

Colorado Belle. Captain's Food Fare. 298-4000.

Flamingo Hilton. Fruit Basket Buffet. 298-5111.

Gold River. Opera House Buffet. 298-2242. Breakfast $2.99; lunch $3.49; dinner $5.99. Two-for-one breakfast or lunch on Wednesdays and Fridays.

Golden Nugget. The Buffet. 298-7111. Prime rib dinner, Monday through Thursday 4 to 9 P.M., Friday 4 to 10 P.M., $3.99.

Edgewater. Bountiful Buffet. 298-2453.

Harrah's. Del Rio Buffet. 298-4600.

Pioneer. Boarding House Buffet. 298-2442. That's Italian Buffet Thursdays, 4 P.M. to midnight, $3.99. Seafood Buffet Fridays, 4 P.M. to midnight, $5.95.

Riverside. Riverside Buffet. 298-2535.

Ramada Express. The Roundhouse Buffet. 298-4200. Prime rib dinner, 4 to 10 P.M., $4.95.

Laughlin Entertainment

Laughlin is not—at least not yet—ready to compete with Las Vegas for major entertainment; there are a lot of small lounges at casinos.

Don Laughlin's Riverside Resort. Don's Celebrity Theatre. The 800-seat showroom is used for concerts and appearances ranging from comedian Gallagher to the Coast Ballet Theatre.

Flamingo Hilton Laughlin. Club Flamingo. Home to production shows such as "American Superstars."

Gold River Resort & Casino. Palace Theatre. Production shows such as "Bottoms Up" and "Pazazz."

Laughlin Area Attractions

Davis Dam. The second leg in man's reworking of the Colorado River for water control and power generation, the Davis Dam stops the Colorado's water and fills out Lake Mohave, a narrow 67-mile-long waterway that reaches upstream to Hoover Dam. The third dam on this portion of the Colorado is the Parker Dam 80 miles downstream; Lake Havasu backs up behind it.

The earth-filled Davis Dam is 200 feet tall, 151 feet above the streambed and not as large, nor as visually impressive as the Hoover Dam up the river. But it does have its own peculiar appeal. You are on your own to explore the outside and interior of the dam daily from 7:30 A.M. to 3:30 P.M.

The Davis Dam and power plant are named in honor of Arthur Powell Davis, one of the pioneers in the creation of a national conservation policy and for many years the chief engineer and director of the Reclamation Service. Work on the dam was begun in 1942, but was suspended because of the war effort; it was completed in 1952.

Near the parking lot is an observation platform that gives a good view north up Lake Mohave, and south over the top of the dam and down into the valley with Laughlin and Bullhead City below. The gigantic 125-ton moving crane on the upper level is mounted on railroad tracks and is used to move equipment for the dam and generating plant. You can walk across the top of the dam and look down the sheer wall to the Colorado River below.

Lake Mohave serves as an after bay to regulate water releases from Hoover Dam. The main purpose of the Davis Dam is to regulate the water to be delivered to Mexico under the Mexican Water Treaty. The production of power is a secondary benefit.

Visitors enter the dam via an elevator that drops down 12 stories within the structure. The first stop on the tour is the pre-computer age control room; it is all gauges and dials rather than electronic readouts, looking like something out of a Frankenstein movie. The plant has an installed capacity of 240,000 kilowatts produced by five vertical shaft generators.

Perhaps the most impressive part of the whole tour is the turbine gallery where you see stretched out before you the five gigantic rotating shafts of the turbines. The floor of the room rumbles with the power of the spinning machines.

The interior of the dam is cool and sterile, unnaturally clean. On the day of my tour in January, I was the only visitor inside the dam—even the control room was empty. As much as I enjoyed my solo tour, I was very relieved when the elevator deposited me back at the top of the dam.

For information call (520) 754-3628.

Lake Mohave, built up behind the wall of Davis Dam, has 200 miles of shoreline reaching back upstream to the Hoover Dam at Boulder City. The waters are active with rainbow trout and bass.

Grapevine Canyon. To witness the petroglyphs at Grapevine Canyon, take Christmas Tree Pass road, off Highway 163 and about six miles west of Davis Dam. The gravel road runs into a flat valley dominated by sharp peaks, including Spirit Mountain, the most dominant hill. About two miles into the valley you will come to a spur road to the left, the entrance to the parking area for Grapevine Canyon. The walking trail leads several hundred feet to the mouth of the canyon.

Archaeologists believe there are three eras of art represented on the walls of the canyon, with the oldest about 600 to 800 years old and the most recent dating from about 150 to 200 years ago. Some of the oldest carvings may be below the present level of earth in the area, and others may have been eroded by water over the years. The drawings seem to have some religious significance.

Colorado River Museum. An interesting, eclectic small collection of historical and household objects. The museum is located on the Arizona side of the river, toward Davis Dam; cross the Laughlin Bridge and make a left turn onto Highway 68 and get into the left lane to cross the road a half mile east.

Outside the museum is a small model of Don Laughlin's first casino, which opened in 1966 and brought South Pointe and Bullhead City back to life. Inside you'll find photographs of some of the old mines, including Oatman and the Tom Reed Gold Mine, a fabulous find that produced $13 million worth of gold between 1906 and 1931. Another display shows barbed wire from the 1880s.

Nearby is a steamboat anchor found in the Colorado River near Hardyville. When a steamboat approached a sandbar it would turn stern-to and send a small boat ahead with the anchor; the anchor would be sunk in the sand and then as the paddlewheel dug its way through the sand, the anchor chain would be winched in to pull the boat over the sandbar.

Katherine's Landing. A rich gold and silver strike was made here in 1900, on the Arizona side of the river three miles north of the present site of Davis Dam. The mine produced $12 million worth of preinflation gold in the four decades until it was closed down in 1942.

Today, Katherine's Landing is a resort community and marina on Lake Mohave with boat slips, boat rentals, launch ramp, and sandy beaches with barbecues and picnic areas. (520) 754-3245.

Oatman. The town was born in 1906 as a gold mining tent camp; after tens of millions of dollars were extracted from the area, the town went bust in 1942 after Congress declared gold mining was no longer essential to the war effort.

At its height, the town had a population of more than 12,000 and featured its own local stock exchange.

The scenery around Oatman has been used for a number of movies including *How the West Was Won*.

The ghost town and historic gold mining area includes museums, shops, and eateries. Gunfighters stage weekend showdowns on the town's main street, on historic Route 66, approximately 30 miles southeast of Laughlin.

London Bridge, English Village, and Lake Havasu. London Bridge did not fall down; it was instead taken apart stone by stone and shipped to Arizona where it is the centerpiece of a small British theme park. For information, call (520) 855-4115. Depending on whether you take backcountry roads or seek out interstates, the distance is 67 or 97 miles, respectively; either way, it's about a two-hour drive to the southeast. (Highway route: east on State 68 to Kingman, Interstate 40 west 40 miles to Needles, south on State 95 to Lake Havasu City.)

Grand Canyon Caverns. About 100 miles east of Laughlin on Highway 66 between Kingman and Seligman, Arizona. For information call (520) 422-3223.

Historic Grand Canyon Railway. About 150 miles east of Laughlin, off Interstate 40. A turn-of-the-century steam train runs from Williams, Arizona, to the south rim of the Grand Canyon. For information call (800) 843-8724.

Colorado River Boat Tours

Blue River Safaris. Full day tours to Lake Havasu and Oatman by bus and boat. 298-0910, (800) 345-8990.

Fiesta Queen and Little Belle. Paddlewheel boats offer daily 90-minute tours of the Colorado River. 298-1047, (800) 228-9825.

London Bridge Watercraft Tours. Guided tours of the Colorado River from Needles, California. (800) 947-2345.

U.S.S. Riverside. Daily excursions on the Colorado River from the Riverside Casino. 298-2535, (800) 227-3849 ext. 5670.

Colorado River Boat Rentals

All Cities Boat Rentals. Rent cruising boats or jet-skis by the hour, day, or week. 4410 Highway 95, Bullhead City, Arizona. (520) 704-6100.

All Wet Sports. Float down the river on tubes, with pick-up service. 763-4938.

Del Rio Beach Club, Harrah's. Wave runners and jet boats. 298-6828.

New Horizons, Pioneer Hotel. Parasailing and wave runners. 298-2442.

Riverfront Water Sports. Bullhead City. Rentals and water skiing. (800) 342-3667.

Water Craft Beach. Bullhead City. Wave runners. (520) 763-8789.

Driving from Laughlin to Las Vegas Through Arizona

We'll return to Las Vegas with a slightly longer tour that will take us east toward Kingman, Arizona, and then northwest in the valley alongside the Cerbat Mountains and then across the Hoover Dam and back into Nevada.

The trip totals about 140 miles and should take just under three hours to complete.

Cross the Laughlin Bridge toward Bullhead City, and make an immediate left turn onto Highway 68 toward Kingman, Arizona. About 10 miles past the Colorado you will come to **Katherine Mine Road** on your left, which will take you down to the shores of Lake Mohave, the ruins of the once-fabulous gold mine there, and the town that grew up around it.

Gold and silver mining began in the Katherine and Union Pass areas in the mid-1860s, reaching a peak between 1900 and 1907. The mines were reopened in 1933 when the value of gold rose, but the mine structure was severely damaged by fire in 1934. Sporadic mining continued until 1943 when it was finally closed.

All that remains of the mine is a group of concrete pillars; deep below is a labyrinth of passages, now mostly flooded by Lake Mohave.

You'll cut through the first set of mountains on Union Pass at about 3,600 feet. The panorama of sharply peaked mountains on the Arizona side are much more spectacular than the ones you drove through coming down from Las Vegas.

Once you are over the mountain pass you are into a mostly flat high desert plateau within a ring of mountains called Golden Valley.

Kingman is where old Route 66, Route 93, and Route 68 all come together. Just short of Kingman, the road comes to a T at Interstate 93; head left to go north.

In the Cerbat Mountains to your right are dozens of small mining camps, some of which grew large enough to qualify as towns at their peak. The first you'll pass is **Cerbat**, which came into existence in the 1860s as a mining camp and had a mill, a smelter, a post office, school, stores, and saloons. Only a few sites remain now.

A few miles north on Interstate 93 brings you to a road to **Mineral Park**, located five miles northeast into the mountains. Now abandoned, it was the county seat from 1873 to 1887 and included a courthouse and jail, stores, hotel, saloons, assay offices, and two stagecoach stations.

I drove up Route 255 to Mineral Park. It had been raining in the valley, but as I climbed, it began to turn into snow and up above, the mountains were blanketed. The road ends in a box canyon and a mineral processing plant within barbed wire. On both sides of the road are capped pipes that sit over the top of former mine shafts. In the valleys are a few gigantic piles of tailings as tall as some of the mountains.

The next town of interest is **Chloride**, another mining boom town. There is a road that leads directly to Chloride from I-93, but I chose to explore a very rough dirt road that led from Route 255 near Mineral Park; I almost did not make it. The back road is made of soft earth and the rain had turned the path into mud. Just to make things worse, the rough road is marked at several points with warnings about the possibility of flash flood areas. As with Christmas Tree Pass, I'd recommend against taking the back road in less than perfect weather.

Chloride sits four miles east of Grasshopper Junction, off I-93. It began about 1863 with the discovery of the first silver mines in the area. By 1900 it had a population of 2,000, with more than 75 mines in operation including the

Tennessee Schuykill, a large producer of gold, silver, copper, lead, and zinc. The post office is the oldest continuously operated station in Arizona, dating from 1871. A coach line called the Butterfield Stage served Chloride from 1868 until 1919; the Santa Fe Railroad had a spur to Chloride from 1898 until 1935. The last of the mines were shuttered in 1944 when they were no longer profitable.

Chloride itself qualifies as one of those great mysteries of the West. You can understand why there was a town built there when the mines were running, but why are people still there?

Today, though, some 350 hardy souls live on the hill. Each summer they cater to tourists who want to come to see the somewhat-preserved boom town. There are a couple of lean-to shacks, and a couple of shops, three cafes, two saloons, and the old post office to visit. The town celebrates Old Miners Day on the last Saturday of June, with a parade (at high noon, of course), plus music, dancing, melodramas, and gunfights. Gay '90s melodramas are performed on the first and third Saturdays of the month in the summer. For information, contact the Chloride Chamber of Commerce at (520) 565-2204.

Back on Interstate 93, there's a small community and gas station near Willow Beach, and then the road climbs up into the mountains again and then drops down through a series of spectacular switchback turns that eventually lead to the Hoover Dam. The road passes right over the top of the dam and into Boulder City.

LAUGHLIN

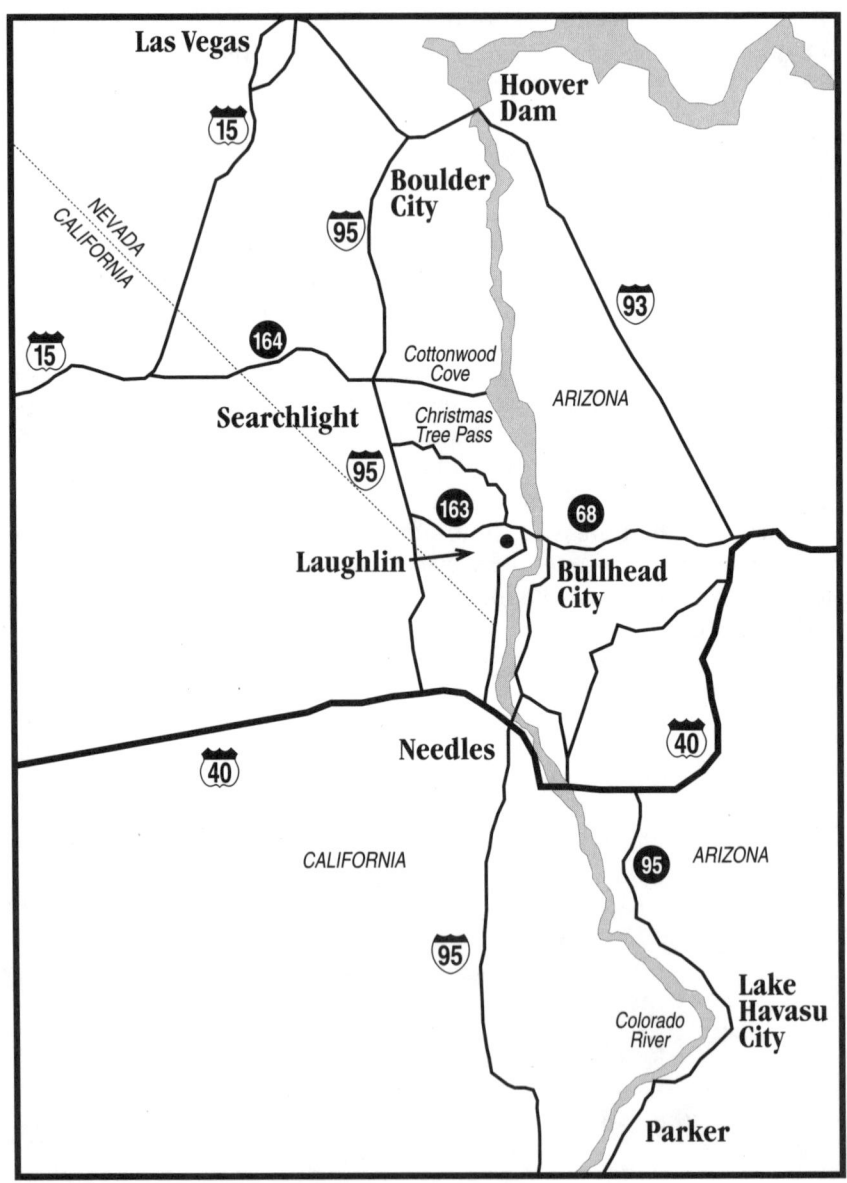

Part III
Reno, Virginia City, and Lake Tahoe

Chapter 18
The Biggest Little Chapter in this Book: Reno

We're not at all certain what it means, but welcome to a place that calls itself "The Biggest Little City in the World." That's the slogan on the famous arch that crosses Virginia Street in downtown; the original piece of street promotion went up in the 1920s and the most recent update was erected in 1987.

We do know that Reno is an unusual place, even by Nevada standards, because of the interesting mix of activities available to the visitor. There are, of course, the casinos in Reno and nearby Sparks; they range from ultra-modern corporate creations with all of the amenities to iconoclastic, small establishments with a great deal of individual character.

Winter is value season in Reno, which means rates at world-class hotel/casino and motel lodging are at their rock-bottom lowest except for the Christmas to New Year's period. And dining, whether it be a full-out breakfast buffet or a midnight snack, is more accessible and less expensive than at other winter resort destinations.

The Econoguide to
the Best Hotels/Casinos of Reno/Sparks

Eldorado	Reno Hilton
John Ascuaga's Nugget	Silver Legacy
Peppermill	

What is there to see within a few hours drive from Reno?

North:

    Spectacular **Pyramid Lake**, a high desert lake with unusual geological formations, is 33 miles northeast of Reno.

South:

    Virginia City, the living ghost of what was once the richest place on

Wheels and chains. If you are renting a car in Reno or Lake Tahoe, four-wheel drive vehicles and tire chains are usually available for an extra charge. If you are not familiar with how to use a 4WD car, or with the installation and use of chains, be sure to obtain instructions from the rental agency.

Earth, and one of the most fascinating places we know of for the amateur historian.

Carson City, the historic state capital.

Lake Tahoe, one of the most beautiful Alpine lakes in the world. At the southern tip of the lake are the new casinos of **Stateline**, which sit between spectacular snow-capped mountains and the lake. From there you can head north around the lake, pausing to admire **Emerald Bay** on the California side.

Some of the greatest ski mountains in the world, including **Heavenly** and **Kirkwood.**

World-class summer outdoor activities including boating, swimming, and horseback riding from sites around Lake Tahoe.

West:

Donner Pass and remote **Donner Lake**, the site of the tragic attempt to cross the Sierra Mountains in the winter of 1846.

More great ski mountains, including world-famous **Squaw Valley.**

East:

Sparks, a historic Nevada town.

Reno and Lake Tahoe Climate

The climate in the Reno-Tahoe area can vary greatly by elevation and location. The overall climate is very arid; the Reno area receives very little precipitation, with an average of about an inch per month. Snowfall can vary greatly, from about six inches per month from December to February to measurements by the yard in some mountainous areas.

Although the highways and major roads are plowed and sanded as necessary for safe driving conditions, many mountain passes are subject to closing because of poor visibility, ice, or blowing and drifting snow. Drivers must use snow tires in the winter and are generally advised to fasten tire chains to cross mountain passes.

For road and weather information, call:

California Department of Transportation Road Reporting Service at (916) 653-7623.

Nevada Department of Transportation Road Reporting Service at (702) 793-1313.

Nevada Weather Service at (702) 793-1300.

Reno-Sparks Convention & Visitors Authority at (800) 752-1177.

The area enjoys warm and dry days in spring, summer, and early fall, turning crisp though sunny for much of the winter. Nights turn cool year-round and sweaters or light jackets are usually appropriate even in summer. Sweaters and coats are needed in the winter. In ski season, ski clothing is acceptable in most casual restaurants and all casinos.

Reno/Sparks Average Temperatures

	Jan	Feb	Mar	Apr	May	Jun	Jul	Aug	Sep	Oct	Nov	Dec
High	45	50	54	63	70	79	89	87	81	70	56	48
Low	19	24	27	32	39	45	50	47	41	33	24	21

Mileage to Reno

Carson City	30	Pyramid Lake	33
Elko	289	Sacramento	125
Fallon	60	Salt Lake City	526
Genoa	40	San Francisco	229
Heavenly Ski Resort	55	South Lake Tahoe	59
Incline Village	35	Sparks	3
Jackpot	406	Squaw Valley USA	50
Las Vegas	440	Truckee	30
Los Angeles	469	Virginia City	24
New York City	2,711	Yosemite National Park	137

About Reno

The site of present-day Reno was settled about 1858 and was first known as Lake's Crossing. The town grew with the discovery of the Comstock Lode in nearby Virginia City. The railroad arrived in 1868, and the city was renamed for the American Civil War General Jesse Lee Reno (1823-1862).

The University of Nevada-Reno was established soon afterward in 1864. Now the seat of Washoe County, Reno was incorporated in 1879.

The city straddles the Truckee River, and civic leaders celebrate the revitalized downtown's Truckee River Walk with a festival in early June to begin the summer season and with a gala Christmas on the river in early December.

The early history of Reno, like Las Vegas, Carson City, and Genoa, was forged as a rest stop for travelers heading somewhere else. Many of the westward-bound settlers who chose a northern crossing of the Sierras followed the Humboldt-Carson trail; various branches of the trail crossed over at Carson Pass (north of Lake Tahoe) or a pathway through Truckee Meadows and over Donner Summit, named after the ill-fated expedition of the winter of 1846.

The wagon trains needed to find a place to cross the Truckee River, especially in the spring when the waters ran high, and several private entrepreneurs built toll bridges in the area. A young New Yorker named Myron Lake bought one of the bridges and opened an inn for the travelers; his bridge crossed the Truckee at the spot that is today the heart of Reno: First and Virginia Streets. Lake expanded his operations when he obtained the franchise to collect tolls on the Sierra Valley Road (now Virginia Street) and made his fortune with the boom that came with the discovery of the Comstock Lode in Virginia City.

Lakes Crossing, as the enterprise was known, came to control much of the land that would become Reno. In 1868, Lake made a business deal with the Central Pacific Railroad, which was pushing its tracks through the area. He gave the railroad 60 acres of land; the CP agreed to use the town site as a freight and passenger depot.

Point of reference. The Truckee River, which runs from Lake Tahoe to Pyramid Lake, travels from west to east as it passes through downtown Reno. The place where the river and Virginia Street intersect is the zero point for the street numbering of the city. Fourth Street, for example, is called West Fourth Street west of Virginia and (you figured this out, right?) East Fourth Street east of Virginia.

The north-south roads are similarly split: the main drag of Virginia Street is called North Virginia on the north side of the river and South Virginia on the south side. The higher the number, the farther away from the heart of downtown at the river and Virginia.

Namesake. Jesse Lee Reno, a native of Virginia, was a popular military leader in the U.S. Civil War and before that in the Mexican War. He was killed as he led the Union Army's 9th Corps at South Mountain in 1862.

Very much like what would take place 37 years later in Las Vegas, the railroad auctioned off 400 lots in May of 1868 and a town was born.

With its roots as a somewhat rough-and-tumble railroad city and trading post for the even-rougher mining men of Virginia City, Reno fulfilled the demand of many of its clients for sin. The red-light district was on Lake Street, and the gambling halls were semihidden on Douglas Alley.

Just as in Las Vegas, a power struggle over gambling, liquor, and prostitution took place just after World War I; the push to tone down what had become known as the "biggest little city in the world" eventually came to a vote in the 1923 election for mayor. E. E. Roberts, backed by some of the political and economic forces who had the most to gain, ran for office on a platform promising to do away with or ignore all laws that affected "personal choice." He won easily and kept his word to close his eyes.

Reno, with its proximity to California, began to pick up a large trade in quickie divorces and marriages because of the liberal laws in Nevada. And the fact that there were other diversions in the town helped make it a very popular place with residents of the Golden State.

Of course, the Wild West had always been a place where social mores were . . . looser. So it was with legalities like divorce. Nevada had a law allowing almost immediate divorce for any citizen for a variety of reasons. And because Nevada had such a history of massive influxes for its various mining and railroad booms, citizenship was available to anyone living within its boundaries for at least six months.

The wealthy industrial class at the turn of the century realized that this combination offered a relatively easy way out of marriages; the procedure became a national affair when former showgirl Laura Corey moved to Reno for a six-month stay in order to initiate a "quickie" divorce from her philandering husband William Corey, the multimillionaire president of U.S. Steel in Pittsburgh. The publicity from the Corey case launched an industry in Reno.

The conservative establishment tried to reel in Nevada's wild-wheeling reputation with a ban on gambling in 1909—widely ignored—and a 1913 change in citizenship rules to 12 months. But an obvious decline in Reno's economy led to a 1915 repeal of the citizenship rule. In 1931, faced with competition from other states including Arkansas and Arizona, Nevada dropped the citizenship requirement to six weeks and threw in legalized gambling for good measure. Reno's divorce industry was rejuvenated, with about 5,000 cases—about 20 a day—in 1931. (Some Reno hotels had "divorce specials" for the six-week stays.) The gambling helped Las Vegas thrive as thousands of workers arrived to build Boulder Dam.

Reno's casinos, though they were now legal, seemed stuck in the mold of the dark, hidden, illegal enterprise they had once been. This began to change with the arrival of Raymond "Pappi" Smith and his sons Raymond Jr. and Harold; their Harolds Club on Virginia Street was the first "carpet joint" in Reno, an attempt to swap sin for fun as an image. Smith dispatched bumper stickers, billboards, and other advertising devices all across the nation proclaiming "Harold's Club or Bust"; suffice it to say that Harold's Club did not go bust. He was followed by William Harrah, with a hotel/casino that bore his name.

New in 1995 is the **National Bowling Stadium**, expected to draw hundreds of thousands of keglers each year to downtown for tournaments. The building, one block in from Virginia Street, includes 80 championship Brunswick lanes; there are three levels of parking below the lanes.

Fallen arches. The famous Reno Arch across Virginia Street was first installed in 1926 in commemoration of the Victory and Lincoln highways that crossed the continent; the Victory Highway (Highway 40) climbed the Sierras to connect to Sacramento. The original slogan, "Reno Transcontinental Highway Exposition" gave way to the considerably more famous "The Biggest Little City in the World." That slogan had itself been coined for Reno as part of the hoopla over the Jim Jeffries-Jack Johnson prize fight that took place in Reno in 1910.

Updated arches were installed in 1934, in 1963, and once again in 1987.

Sponsors expect some 100,000 bowlers will participate in the American Bowling Congress championship tournament in 1995. The ABC will return to Reno in 1998, 2001, and 2004. The Women's International Bowling Congress will hold its championship tournament in Reno in 1997 and again in 2000 and 2003.

The stadium offers permanent seating capacity for 1,200. The video scoring system at the stadium includes the longest read-projection, high-definition video display in the world, at 450 feet in length. The Bowlervision II scoring system in the spectator section does more than keep score; visitors can order drinks and food from the monitor.

The Stadium Sports Shop includes a fully functioning bowling lane so that shoppers can try out equipment before they buy. An instant replay video system allows you to watch yourself in action with new equipment.

The focal point of the stadium is its giant silver ball, decorated on the outside with 15,000 feet of fiber optic lights that wash it with color at night. Within the ball is a 177-seat movie theater with an Iwerks 70-mm projection system and a 42-foot-wide by 31-foot-tall wraparound screen. Among the first films to be shown in the theater is a new film about the Reno-Tahoe area. You'll feel like you are on the back of a bucking bronco at the Reno Rodeo, or soaring like an eagle over the snow-covered Sierras.

The restaurant at the bowling stadium is Ruby's, a re-creation of a 1940s diner. Specialties include the Rubyburger, turkey pot pie, and meatloaf.

In early 1995, city officials reached agreement on a $300 million plan called **Reno Renaissance**, which is intended to redevelop a good part of downtown with a new convention and special events center, other facilities, and a new casino. Construction was scheduled to begin by the end of 1995, finishing some time in 1997.

About the Sierra Nevadas

The Sierra Nevada mountain range lies mostly in California, reaching into Nevada near Lake Tahoe.

Bounded on the north by a gap south of Lassen Peak and by the Cascade Range, and on the south by Tehachapi Pass, the range runs from northwest to southeast for about 400 miles in a 40- to 80-mile-wide swath.

The tallest peak in the Sierra Nevadas is Mount Whitney, which at 14,494 feet is the also tallest peak in the lower 48 states.

According to geologists, the Sierra Nevadas are made up of a single block of the earth's crust tilted upward toward the east. The predominant rocks of the range are granite, other igneous rocks, and metamorphic slate. Great quantities of gold have been found embedded in quartz, while silver has been mined on the eastern slope.

Reno's famous downtown arch
© *1995 Reno News Bureau*

The Best of Reno

★ MUST-SEE ★ Circus Circus Hotel/Casino

Yowzah, yowzah! It's Circus Circus, a smaller cousin of the Las Vegas original, but definitely a Reno must-see.

With 1,625 rooms, it is downtown Reno's largest resort, quite a way from its start in 1978 when it had just 104 rooms. It is therefore the World's Second Largest Hotel and Casino with a Circus and Midway and a Shuttle Tram.

The midway and circus area was spruced up in 1993, pulling it out of a bit of the doldrums. Circus acts—including high-wire bicyclists, aerialists, gymnasts, and clowns—start at about 11:15 A.M. and continue until nearly midnight. The circus acts are introduced by a ringmaster and sometimes accompanied by a somewhat bored and somewhat alive two-piece band. Each act is about 8 to 10 minutes long—the management doesn't want people to stay away from the tables too long.

> **Send in the clown.** The landmark "Topsy the Clown" sign in front is 148 feet tall to the top of his lollipop, weighing in at 44.8 tons (about 90,000 pounds).

The midway is a sure lure for children of all ages, offering coin toss, ring toss, shooting gallery, video arcade, face painting, and other such carnival entertainment. Concession stands offer food, drinks, and balloons.

Check out the shooting gallery that uses beams of light from the rifles; it's much better than your average mechanical ducks. We especially like the poor little canary atop the piano who will dance for you; hit the piano player in the behind and he'll provide the music.

And, of course, there is a casino, which is a pretty lively place at all hours. As you might expect, there do seem to be a few families with the youngsters dispatched upstairs to the circus and carnival and mom and dad downstairs gambling the dinner money.

The circus performers, according to the hotel, constitute a minor league for the major shows including Ringling Brothers and Barnum & Bailey Circus, the Moscow Circus, the Romanian State Circus, and other troupes.

The performers change regularly, but usually include trapeze artists, high-wire walkers, teeterboard acts, unicycle and trick bicycle performers, jugglers, and clown acts.

> **A dog's life.** Fantasia bills itself as a hotel so exclusive it doesn't accept humans. That is because it is a pet hotel, welcoming cats and dogs for stays at its heated kennels. The hotel even offers a "pet limo" service to pick up and deliver pets. Fantasia is located off North Virginia Street about equidistant between Reno and Sparks. Call 322-1199 for reservations.

The **Three Ring Restaurant** is open 24 hours, offering specials, priced from about $3 to $6, such as Belgian waffles, Reuben sandwiches, and vegetable stir-fry.

The **Big Top Buffet** is served beneath a red and white striped circus big top. Breakfast, offered from 7 to 11 A.M. for $2.79, includes fresh-squeezed orange juice, and ham carved to order. Lunch, available from 11 A.M. to 4 P.M. for $3.49, includes fried chicken, roast beef, and a build-your-own taco bar. Dinner is served from 4 to 10 P.M. for $4.79. A special Friday seafood buffet is $6.99.

The **Hickory Pit**, a dark brick wall room fairly well isolated from the casino floor, is open for dinner from 5 to 11 P.M. with entrees from about $10 to $20. Specialties include 12-ounce filet mignon with béarnaise sauce, broiled salmon, and king crab legs with drawn butter. The daily special is prime rib for $7.95.

Circus Circus Hotel/Casino. 500 N. Sierra Street; 1,625 rooms; 329-0711, (800) 648-5010.

▰MUST-SEE▰ Comstock Hotel/Casino

An eclectic casino worth a visit. The upper levels of the casino feature western scenes, including an animated piano-playing couple named Lulabelle & Slim.

The casino floor includes a few real one-arm bandits (slot machines that point a six-shooter at the player) as well as a sprinkling of life-like dummies on the floor—some of which seem livelier than some of the players at the tables.

At the center of the casino is a stairway to **Amigo's Mexican Restaurant**, an inexpensive eatery that sweetens the offer with two-for-one Margaritas and combination platters.

Or, you can take an escalator down through a simulated mining tunnel to the **Miner's Cafe**, a 24-hour coffee shop that in the past has offered entrees including a vegetarian burger for $2.59 and vegetarian platter with cheese and salsa for $5.29. For meat-eaters, there's a create-your-own hamburger for about $2 plus 10 cents a topping and chili for $3; other specialties are fried chicken for $5.39 and Pick and Shovel Pasta Primavera for $4.29.

Within the Miner's Cafe is **Hop Sing's Kitchen**, which offers Asian specials from 11 A.M. to 11 P.M. Representative entrees included Mongolian beef for $6.29, almond chicken for $5.59, and sweet and sour pork for $5.29. Dinner specials are about $4 for lunch and $5 for dinner.

Comstock Hotel/Casino. 200 W. 2nd Street; 310 rooms; 329-1880, (800) 648-4866.

▰MUST-SEE▰ Eldorado Hotel/Casino

The Eldorado is a very attractive, very classy modern casino worth a visit. It has a collection of some of the better hotel restaurants in town.

The lively casino includes what is billed as the world's largest roulette table, seating as many as 40 people.

A new 700-space parking lot was added in 1993. In true Las Vegas/Reno style, the 10-story structure is ringed with neon; it was lauded by civic officials as a new downtown gem. The Eldorado is a partner with its neighbor Circus Circus on

Visitor Centers in Reno/Sparks. For visitor information and room reservations, call 827-7366 or (800) 367-7366.

Visitor centers are located at: Reno Cannon International Airport; Reno Downtown Visitors Center, 275 N. Virginia St.; Reno-Sparks Convention Center, 4590 S. Virginia St.; Sparks Downtown Visitors Center, Pyramid Way and Victorian Ave., Sparks.

the new Silver Legacy Casino, which will sit between the two hotels. And finally, the Eldorado added a 12-story tower including an expansion to the casino, a 500-seat showroom, a health spa, a new buffet, a new restaurant including a microbrewery, and more rooms including 32 super-deluxe suites as large as 2,200 square feet.

Let's eat our way through the Eldorado.

First stop, near the entrance, is **Choices**, an all-in-one "express cafe" food court. Among the stands in the attractive open room decorated with glass brick and tile off the casino floor are **Chinatown**, which offers entrees for $4 to $5 including lobster Cantonese and roast duck, and appetizers including egg rolls and soup; **Little Italy**, offering pasta, pizza, and submarine sandwiches; **Virginia Deli**, with hot dogs, shrimp cocktail, and sandwich specialties; and the **American Kitchen**, featuring burgers, fried chicken, ham and eggs, and a steak and lobster special for about $10. The food court also offers a cheap shrimp cocktail with tiny, tiny shrimp.

Ristorante La Strada is a more formal room, serving dinner nightly from 5 P.M. Pizzas are prepared in a wood-fired brick oven. In addition to the basics, toppings include *pescatore* (fresh tomato, shrimp, scallops, clams, calamari with garlic and basil) for $9.95. Entrees range in price from about

> **A cuppa.** If you thought that wine tasting was complex, consider the process used at the Eldorado for testing new shipments of coffee beans. A small amount of green beans is roasted in a special sample roaster and then ground and prepared with a precisely measured amount of water for "cupping." The grounds and water are mixed in a special cup and the grounds are then allowed to rise to the surface. Cracking this surface cap releases the aroma and allows the taster to judge the quality. Then the mixture is drawn across the palate. Based on the aroma and taste, instructions on temperature, time, and blend are provided to the coffee roaster.

$11 to $20. Specials include *linguine del pescatore* (calamari, shrimp, scallops, and shellfish in tomato or white wine sauce); *tortellini alla panna* (veal-filled pasta in Parmesan cream sauce); *spiedini di gamberi al limone* (marinated skewered prawns grilled and served with a lemon-basil sauce), and *coniglo con polenta* (rabbit braised with rosemary and thyme in a mushroom wine demiglace).

The dark, copper pot and fern-filled La Strada shares its space with the attractively understated **Grill and Rotisserie**. This dinner place, closed Wednesday and Thursday, offered on a recent visit specialties including blackened rib steak for $12; barbecued baby back pork ribs for $11; grilled marinated scallops and prawn brochette for $14; spit roasted teriyaki chicken for $9.95; and roasted Sonoma duckling for $10.95.

And the attractions go on: be sure to stop at **Tivoli Gardens**, a high-scale food court decorated with overhead arbors and lots of brass with offerings from around the world. You'll know things are a bit different when you come to the elaborate coffee roaster at the entrance.

According to the Eldorado, it is the only hotel in the country with such an elaborate coffee setup. The selection of beans is made by the restaurant's executive chef, choosing premium arabica green coffee beans from

Mud in your eye. Coffees available at the Eldorado Coffee Company range in price from about $5 to $10 per pound and include products such as Ethiopian *Yergacheffe*, Mexican *Custepec*, Brazillian *Santos*, Guatemalan *Antigua* and Swiss water decaf. You can also order by calling (800) 348-5966.

the high altitudes of Central America, Africa, Indonesia, and Hawaii.

The high-temperature Probat roaster, made in Germany, triggers a complex chemical reaction in which sugars and starches in the green beans are transformed into the volatile oils that give coffee its rich flavor and aroma.

Most of the coffee sold at the Eldorado is roasted to the "full city" stage. The temperature profile and roasting time varies, but the process usually takes about 16 minutes for a batch of 16 kilograms (about 35 pounds). Visitors can buy the fresh beans to take home, or they can drink a brewed cup at the restaurant.

In addition to regular coffee, the Eldorado roasts beans for espresso, using a secret blend of six beans. The espresso roast results in a darker color, and the grind is made using pressure rather than gravity. The same amount of beans go into a cup of espresso as in a regular cup of coffee, but the amount of water is much less: one and half ounces versus six ounces.

Cappuccino, which is espresso with steamed milk, is also available, as is iced cappuccino, which is cold-water brewed using a coarse grind of the espresso blend.

Depending on your age, sex, and sweet tooth you may find the dessert carousel at Tivoli Gardens even more attractive than the cocktail waitresses who, just for the record, wear some of the skimpiest outfits in town. The fabulous cakes cost a reasonable $2.25 or so for a slice.

Tivoli Gardens serves breakfast 24 hours a day. International specials, priced from about $5 to $9 and served from 11 A.M. to 3 A.M. include Oriental pepper steak, Vietnamese sliced beef soup, Italian rosemary chicken breast with fettuccine Alfredo, Hawaiian pizza (bacon and pineapple), Thai chicken, and American liver and onions.

The Eldorado **Market Place Buffet** offers breakfast weekdays from 8 to 11 A.M. for $3.49 and lunch from 11 A.M. to 2 P.M. for $5.49. A prime rib dinner is offered Sunday to Friday from 4 P.M. to closing for $6.99.

And finally, there is **The Vintage**, a dark room with red velvet booths— your basic Nevada hotel hideaway. Specialties at the time of our visit included sole meunière, finished tableside for about $16. The restaurant is closed Monday and Tuesday.

Eldorado Hotel/Casino. 345 N. Virginia Street; 800 rooms; 786-5700, (800) 648-5966.

◄MUST-SEE► Flamingo Hilton Reno

An attractive, quality hotel, nice enough to almost forget for a while you are in a casino, the Flamingo Hilton offers 604 rooms, including 66 suites.

The hotel is actually located a block in from the Virginia Street strip but uses a street-level storefront (the former Paco's Casino) as a come-on to pedestrians. A series of escalators and a walkway connect you to the main hotel and casino.

The hotel draws its lineage back to Del Webb's Sahara; it then became the Reno Hilton and then the Flamingo Hilton.

The longtime attraction at the 1,200-seat showroom is American Superstars, a rotating series of celebrity impersonators. Acts include Elvis, Roy Orbison, Sammy Davis Jr., Bette Midler, The Blues Brothers, Charlie Daniels, the Temptations, and

> **Busy signal.** High-season at the Flamingo Hilton and much of Reno is generally from April to October, with the slowest period from December through February except for Christmas and New Year's Eve.

Madonna. There is one show Sunday through Thursday nights and two shows on Friday and Saturday nights; the theater is dark Tuesday. Tickets range from $12.95 to $14.95, and children are welcome; they may especially enjoy the confetti cannons at the conclusion of the show. Combination tickets with the Food Fantasy Buffet are also available, as is a package with the Top of the Hilton for $30.50. American Superstars returned in February 1995 to the Flamingo showroom along with all of the usual suspects.

The premier restaurant is the **Top of the Hilton**, which offers gorgeous views of the surrounding mountains. The eatery is paneled in dark wood like a private club, with gray carpet and chairs; an even more private dining area near the bar is available by reservation to large parties. High rollers and local regulars have their own locked liquor storage bins by the bar.

Open for dinner only, it is closed Monday. Offerings, priced from about $18 to $25, have included various steaks, swordfish, shrimp scampi, and roast rack of lamb. There's also a weekend champagne brunch with omelettes, eggs benedict, steak teriyaki, and ham for $15.95.

The **Flamingo Room** coffee shop has a 24-hour steak and lobster special for $11.95, or chicken and shrimp scampi for $5.95.

Standard rooms at the Flamingo Hilton are above average in quality; the suites on the top floor are quite impressive, but it is the Barron Suite, which includes two tubs and a large living room, that is most impressive. As in most Nevada casinos, the best rooms are generally reserved as comps for the high rollers.

Flamingo Hilton Reno. 255 N. Sierra Street; 604 rooms; 322-1111, (800) 648-4882.

Harolds Club

This lively place wins our vote as the friendliest place in town; the management seems to encourage its dealers to talk to the players and most of them have a spiel for each deal. Some even pretend to root for the players at their tables.

The famous mural on the exterior of the building celebrates the progress of the pioneers across the desert and mountains.

The sparkling casino has a small set of carousel horses in the center; a room-filling sound system plays instrumental music to pick up the pace. Near the front entrance is Bucky's Buckboard, one of a dozen contenders for the biggest

Home of the free.
Harolds Club is credited with introducing the concept of "comps" to casinos, rewarding regular customers with free meals and drinks. The club also organized the first junkets to bring in high rollers on all-expense-paid trips to Reno; all they had to do was risk their money at the tables.

slot machine in Nevada: this one has a bench that seats three players.

The fun continues at the **Roaring Camp Bar** at Harolds. Clients at the bar can play a special, oversized slot called "Bust the Barrels." If you can line up four beer mugs, everyone at the bar gets a free drink. (It also pays off in coins.)

By the way, this place is advertised as "The World's Most Famous Casino." Did you know that? We suspect that Harolds is no longer on the tips of most people's tongues, but there was a time when bumper stickers and signs across the nation proclaimed "Harolds Club or Bust."

The advertising campaign was just one element of the change that Raymond "Pappi" Smith, a former carnival owner, brought to Reno when he opened his club in 1935. (Harold, who ran the club, was Pappi's son.)

A new addition to Harolds is **Dick Clark's American Bandstand Club** on the second floor. The restaurant and dance club includes some of legendary broadcaster Clark's personal collection of rock 'n' roll memorabilia—from Chubby Checker's boots to Gloria Estefan's leather chaps. Video screens throughout the club feature classic footage from the American Bandstand television show and other performances.

American Bandstand features special events—the place was decked out for a celebration of Elvis' birthday at the time of one of our visits. The club is open daily; visitors must be 21 or older. Call 786-2222 for information.

Harolds Club. 250 N. Virginia Street; 329-0881.

Harrah's Casino/Hotel Reno

There's nothing particularly wrong with Harrah's Reno; in fact, it's not a bad place at all. It's just that there is not much that is memorable here, either.

Harrah's is a midsize hotel with your basic Nevada casino and a set of restaurants that range from a fine steak house to a McDonald's. It's history, though, reaches back to 1946 when it was the first major casino of William Harrah and one of the classiest joints in town; he had previously run several tiny operations around Reno.

Today Harrah's is part of the Promus Companies, which also operate Embassy Suites, Homewood Suites, Hampton Inns, and Bill's Casino.

New for 1995 is yet another outpost of **Planet Hollywood** on the corner; memorabilia includes Tom Arnold's senior year high school yearbook and the model of the submarine used in *Hunt for Red October*.

Across Center Street on Virginia and connected by a skywalk is the Harrah's Sports Casino, which is a very lively smaller casino more oriented toward the sports bettor and the slot machine crowd; dealers are dressed in referee stripes.

Entertainment is presented in **Sammy's Showroom**, named after Sammy Davis Jr., who made more than 400 appearances there over 22 years. The early show is "Stagestruck," a salute to the best of Broadway. Things heat up later with "High Voltage," an adult revue of singers and dancers. (The same singers and dancers from the earlier "Stagestruck" show, in fact).

Harrah's Skyway Buffet is an attractive, pleasant room with decent food and perhaps the only buffet room with a push-button cappuccino and espresso machine.

The **Garden Room** serves 24-hour breakfast in an unusually attractive coffee shop that features brass and wood with muted lighting. Specials, priced from about $5 to $15, at the time of a recent visit included corned beef hash and eggs, belgian waffles, burgers, chicken-fried New York steak, sirloin tips marsala, seafood kabobs, and shrimp scampi.

Seven-up. Founder Bill Harrah had a gambler's view of the world. According to lore, he drank exactly seven cups of coffee each day and opened his first casino in 1937; he even managed to marry seven times. The logo for Harrah's sports seven stars atop the seven letters of the company name.

A section of the Garden Room is devoted to the **Oriental Garden**, serving middle-of-the-road Chinese meals with entrees from $6 to $13, and prix-fixe meals under $10. Specialties include seafood in black bean sauce and Chinese pepper steak.

Harrah's Steak House is an award-winning restaurant, decorated in muted reds and hidden a floor below and a world away from the jingle-jangle of the casino. Lunch is served 11 A.M. to 2:30 P.M. weekdays, and dinner is from 5 P.M. every day. Luncheon offerings, from about $6 to $14, include Caesar salad, warm teriyaki chicken salad, and *fettuccine frutti di mare* with lobster, scallops, prawns, and fish.

The extensive dinner menu includes oyster, shrimp, and salmon appetizers and entrees priced from about $18 to $35 including veal chop, steak and lobster, broiled swordfish, chateaubriand, veal *osso bucco*, and veal Oscar.

Cafe Andreotti is open for dinner at 5 P.M. from Thursday through Monday nights. The kitchen is open to view and is worth a peek. For an appetizer, you can create your own pasta misto. Pastas include spaghetti, linguine, cheese tortellini, and cheese ravioli, and sauces include tomato basil, white wine, and red or white clam. Entrees, priced from about $8 to $15, have included red snapper with fresh basil sautéed with scallops, mushrooms, and sweet peppers and veal *saltimbocca*.

Hampton Inn at Harrah's Reno. New for 1996 is a 26-story, 408-room tower next to Harrah's Sports Casino in downtown Reno. The new building is intended as a moderately priced hotel with connections to the casino.

Hampton Inn is a corporate cousin to Harrah's, part of the Promus Companies.

Harrah's Casino/Hotel Reno. 206 N. Virginia Street; 566 rooms; 786-3232, (800) 648-3773.

Parking lots. The Reno Hilton welcomes RV vehicles to park in a special camperland area, with rates of about $15 per night. There are spaces for 286 RVs.

Goin' to the chapel. The Reno Hilton has an attractive wedding chapel for those who feel the urge or need for nuptials. Among the most unusual ceremonies performed there was the marriage of a pair of llamas who were in town for a rather sizeable convention of llama lovers. Emergency wedding cakes, gowns, and suits are available at stores in the shopping arcade; the llamas wore their own coats.

MUST-SEE **Reno Hilton**

It really is a city within a city, with 2,001 rooms and enough activities to entertain visitors for days at a time without venturing out the front door. The hotel includes a state-of-the-art 50-lane bowling alley with electronic scoring; the lanes were the site of a stop on the Ladies Pro Bowlers Tour in 1993.

The Reno Hilton was formerly a Bally's Hotel and before that the MGM Grand. At the time of our visit, it still bore some of the Hollywood markings of the MGM.

Downstairs is a pair of high-tech movie theaters showing first-run features. (The back section of the theaters includes love seats for those who are amorously inclined or who are generally more used to watching movies in the comfort of their living rooms or beds.)

The shopping arcade includes an electronic golf range where players drive their balls into projected images of famous courses around the world. Outside you can find **Hilton Bay Aqua Golf** on Lake Hilton, an artificial pond created during the excavation for the hotel. Using floating golf balls, players can test their swings on 100-, 150-, and 200-yard holes and hope to win prizes and free trips.

There is also one of the largest hotel health clubs we have seen, along with five indoor and three outdoor tennis courts.

The expanded **Sports and Race Book** includes state-of-the-art electronics in an attractive corner of the casino. There are small TV screens at each table as well as larger ones up on the wall. Hanging from the ceiling are some experimental and acrobatic airplanes and a Rutan canard-wing plane. A new casual eatery at the Sports Book, **Johnny Rockets,** offers burgers and munchies.

Most of the hotel's restaurants are located on Restaurant Row, a semiprivate alcove off the casino floor.

Marco Polo's offers Chinese and Mongolian fare. Offerings include Mongolian beef for $8.25, Singapore noodles for $7.95, and other interesting chicken, beef, and seafood dishes.

The premier Italian restaurant at the Hilton is **Caruso's,** an elegant place with lots of space between the tables and leather chairs. Appealing appetizers include *scampi alla livornese* (an appetizer of jumbo shrimp sautéed in olive oil with garlic, shallots, white wine butter sauce, and diced peppers) for $6.95. Entrees, priced from about $8 to $24, include *ravioli di gamberi* (raviolis filled with bay shrimps, fresh salmon mousse, and zucchini served in a light creamy tomato sauce), *tournedos al bardolino* (two petite filets mignons sautéed with mushrooms, rosemary, and garlic in bardolino red sauce), *aragosta al pomodoro e basilico* (lobster tails sautéed with plum tomatoes and sweet basil), and *trancia di salmone al burro di peperono* (filet of fresh salmon broiled and served with a light sweet bread pepper sauce) for $15.50, and veal medallions sautéed with prosciutto and Asiago cheese for $16.95.

Desserts include *tiramisu* (lady fingers flavored with espresso, chocolate, and marscarpone cream sauce), and *creazione Caruso* (a house specialty cappuccino mousse cake). You can finish off the meal with espresso or cappuccino, available plain or spiked with anisette or brandy.

The **Patio Room** serves breakfast anytime, with specialties including corned beef hash served with two poached eggs for $5.25 or steak and eggs for $8.95. Non-cholesterol egg substitutes are available; other healthwise selections include marinated turkey breast served with steamed rice, snow peas, and carrots for $6.95. Other Patio Room specialties include baked lasagna with meat sauce and garlic bread for $6.25. A children's menu includes French toast fingers with two bacon strips, peanut butter and jelly sandwich, or hamburger with french fries for $1.95.

The **Reno Hilton Steakhouse** features an English Tudor manor house setting. A salad bar is available. Light fare includes the Bagel Nosh (an open-faced smoked salmon and cream cheese bagel with potato salad or cole slaw) for $7.95, and croissant cordon bleu for $5.50. Dinner specialties include Pacific salmon for $16.95. Prime rib is available in $15.95 and $16.95 cuts; steaks range from about $16 to $25. Also offered was grilled double lamb chops with roasted shallots and pinot noir sauce for $24.50, and seared venison loin with lingonberries for $18.95. Desserts include black bottom ice cream pie. Homemade ice creams and sherbets are available with toppings including chocolate Kahlúa sauce, hot brandied fruits, vanilla hazelnut sauce, and butterscotch rum.

The **Grand Canyon Buffet** is a Southwestern-theme eatery set in a stone mountain lodge setting with attractive, subdued lighting; there is seating for 450 people for breakfast, lunch, and dinner.

Entertainment at the Reno Hilton centers on the **Hilton Theater**, the hotel's premier showroom, with 2,000 seats. Production shows including *Cats,* The Moscow Circus, and *Spellbound* and entertainers including Frank Sinatra, Liza Minelli, and Randy Travis have appeared here in addition to, would you believe, Dr. Ruth Westheimer? (We can only imagine the floor show.) The theater has one of the biggest showroom stages in the world. An interesting sidelight is the fact that when the showroom was constructed along with the hotel in 1978, the stage was built around a large mock-up of a jet plane that was used in the original long-running musical show at the hotel. The prop is so big— and the stage area so huge—that the plane was still there in 1993.

Nearby is the 250-seat **Just for Laughs Comedy Club**, a showcase for up-and-coming comics. There's music nightly at the **Confetti Cabaret** except Monday.

Whoopie! Many of the casino scenes of the film *Sister Act* with Whoopi Goldberg were shot in 1991 at the Nevada Club and at Fitzgerald's across the street.

Reno Hilton. 2500 E. 2nd Street; 2,001 rooms; 789-2000, (800) 648-5080.

Nevada Club

Readers of earlier editions of the Econoguide will recall that the Nevada Club had been a must-see casino in Reno. We favored it because of the essential weirdness of the place, a sense of time warp and the evidence of a company that was miles away from the slick gambling machines of Las Vegas.

It won our approval not because of the millions spent on lavish appointments: the casino was a barely improved storefront where you could all but smell the sawdust beneath the cheap carpet. The front of the building was an appropriately hideous purple, with signs and decorations that must have been all the rage in the 1950s. The old Nevada included a collection of strange and ugly one-of-a-kind slot machines.

And it got weirder and weirder: upstairs was a collection of pinball machines, a hand-cranked Mutoscope nickelodeon that displayed the slightly naughty antics of one Molly Malone, and a circa 1916 Seeburg KT Midget Orchestrion, a coin-operated orchestra that included a piano, mandolin, flute, tambourine, castanets, and triangle. There was also a famed gun collection that featured hundreds of priceless antiques from tiny pocket pistols to field pieces, from black powder wooden cannons to World War I machine guns.

Well, not all progress is good: the Nevada Club was sold to a new, corporate owner and nearly all of the weirdness is gone (we can only imagine where some of the strange stuff was dispersed). At the time of our visit, the Nevada Club had become a pretty unremarkable casino; we expect the new owner will pretty the place up a bit, but we doubt it will reclaim its place as the world of weird in downtown Reno.

Still in existence is **Kilroy's Diner** where you will find a collection of working, antique slot machines. They will eat your money as well as the new machines do, but there is a certain retro enjoyment to pulling the handle.

Kilroy's Diner is an authentic old diner with counters, pie racks, antique coke signs, and waitresses in polyester uniforms.

Nevada Club. 224 N. Virginia; 329-1721.

MUST-SEE Peppermill Hotel/Casino

The Peppermill is a thoroughly modern assault on the senses, including a riot of purple, green, and pink neon, and electronic signboards like those at a sports stadium.

The Peppermill is a bit isolated from downtown, a few miles south; it is one of the more lively casinos in town. In 1995, the hotel began construction of a 400-room addition and casino expansion; when it is completed, the Peppermill will have more than 1,200 rooms.

The **Peppermill Island Buffet** is one of the nicest buffet settings we have seen in Nevada. Private booths sit among lush (fake) greenery. The serving line sits beneath a chandelier of lights. The food is not quite as extraordinary as the room, but still better than average.

The **Food Court** includes several serving sections including the **Italian Deli, American Diner, Chinese Wok,** and a **Mexican Taco Bar,** with offerings ranging from 99-cent tacos to shrimp scampi for $5 and Chinese offerings for $4 to $5.

Le Moulin offers dinner specialties including lobster linguine a la Roma (lobster sautéed with garlic and white wine, combined with a creamy Romano cheese sauce) for $14.95, veal T-bone (a 14-ounce Provini T-bone, sautéed with button mushrooms and shallots) for $19.95, and an early bird special of prime rib and lobster for $9.95, served from 5 to 7 P.M.

Peppermill Hotel/Casino. 2707 S. Virginia Street; 1,200 rooms by 1996; 826-2121, (800) 648-6992.

Sands Regency Hotel/Casino

An older hotel-casino a few blocks off Virginia Street, the Sands is a strange jumble of slot machines, gaming tables, hotel desks, and donut counters. There's even a Baskin Robbins ice cream stand directly opposite the registration desk.

The matriarch of the founding Cladianos family is honored with **Antonia's**, open for dinner only, nightly except Tuesday. It is, though, at heart a rather ordinary coffee shop. Specialties include roasted chicken for $5.99, and seafood linguine (shrimp, scallops, clams, and crab in a garlic and cream sauce) for $12.99.

There's a branch of the **Tony Roma's** chain, offering ribs for $7.95 to $9.95 and boneless chicken for $7.95. Appetizers include potato skins for $3.95 and chicken wings for $2.95. Special offers include a $7.77 ribs and barbecued chicken combo, and an all-you-can-eat Cajun or Carolina honey ribs dinner served Monday through Wednesday from 4 to 10 P.M.

> **Family jewels.** At the entrance from the parking lot, check out the display of two old slot machines. The plaque identifies them as representing the original five machines bought in 1932 by Antonia and Pete Cladianos Sr., Greek immigrants who came to America penniless and unable to speak English. The hotel and casino they founded eventually became the Sands Regency in Reno, and the second and third generations of the family still operate the business.

Other franchise eateries at the Sands Regency include **Orange Julius, Winchell's Donuts,** and **Arby's.**

The **Palm Court** is a 24-hour coffee shop. Offerings include a veggie croissant (cucumbers, tomato, avocado, mushrooms, and alfalfa sprouts) for $4.79, a one-pound T-bone steak for $6.99; steak 'n lobster for $7.99, prime rib for $5.99, and chicken fingers for $3.99.

Sands Regency Hotel/Casino. 345 N. Arlington Avenue; 1,000 rooms; 348-2200, (800) 648-3553.

MUST-SEE Silver Legacy

The newest star of downtown Reno will undoubtedly be the Silver Legacy, a spectacular Las Vegas–like theme casino jointly developed by Virginia Street neighbors Circus Circus and the Eldorado Hotel/Casino that is scheduled to open in late 1995.

The "story" of the new resort is based on the fictional legend of "Sam Fairchild," a Nevada silver baron so rich that he shared his wealth with everyone. A 120-foot-tall mining derrick will rise from the casino floor with moving ore wagons, flumes of water and even silver ingots passing by; down below the slot machines and tables will pump cash from the visitors' pockets.

The $310 million project includes 1,720 rooms in three towers, including a 400-foot skyscraper.

There will be four themed restaurants and a special events and convention center.

Other Hotels and Casinos in Reno

Cal-Neva Club. Earplugs are optional at this adult playroom. Some of the slots are built into colorful but-not-all-that realistic mockups of trains and western buildings. There's a somewhat interesting collection of old railway signs scattered about.

Food is served from a dining car lunch cart or at the **Top Deck** coffee shop (featuring a 24-hour prime rib special at $4.95 or ham and eggs for 99 cents) or the **Copper Ledge** restaurant.

The club announced a 775-space "Parking Stadium" across the street on Center Street; the garage will be connected to the casino by a skywalk.

Cal-Neva Club, E. Second and N. Virginia; 323-1046.

Fitzgerald's Casino-Hotel. The wearing of the green can become a bit wearing in this little piece of Ireland in Reno. The mirrored ceilings add to the visual overload.

But for a touch of the blarney, if not the bizarre, be sure to visit the "Lucky Forest" on the second floor. There has got to be something here that will improve your luck at the tables: four-leaf clovers, rabbit's feet, horseshoe, a wishing well, Asian gods—if there's a good luck charm not represented here, we'd like to know about it.

Fitzgerald's, located in the heart of downtown in the shadow of the Virginia Street arch, is named after Lincoln Fitzgerald, another of the early casino developers of Reno.

Fitzgerald's Casino-Hotel, 255 N. Virginia; 351 rooms; 785-3300, (800) 648-5022.

Liberty Belle Saloon & Restaurant. The place features a private collection of antique slot machines, old wagons, and other unusual items of historical note.

Liberty Belle Saloon & Restaurant, 4250 S. Virginia; 825-1776.

Riverboat Hotel & Casino. Relatively quiet, small, and ordinary. Specials at the restaurant include a prime rib dinner for $5.99, served from 4 P.M. to midnight.

Riverboat Hotel & Casino, 34 W. Second; 120 rooms; 323-8877, (800) 888-5525.

Virginian Hotel-Casino. A low-roller haven, lively but ordinary. It is one of the few casinos with a 25-cent minimum craps table, which may be an attraction to those who want to try the game without risking serious money.

Virginian Hotel-Casino. 140 N. Virginia; 329-4664.

About Sparks

Sparks was Nevada's "Instant City," going from zero to 1,500 residents in 1904 when it was created out of swampland by the Southern Pacific Railroad.

The Golden Spike that united the westward and eastward tracks across the continent had been driven in 1870. Just 30 years later, railroad engineers decided to straighten out some of the railroad lines in Northern Nevada to eliminate treacherous curves and steep grades. As part of that effort, the Southern Pacific decided to abandon its former division point in Wadsworth near Pyramid Lake and move its operations south about 30 miles to a new site in the Truckee Meadows.

The previous owner of the railroad, the Central Pacific, had bypassed the area below Reno because of the swamplands. But the Southern Pacific decided to make its own dry land; it used its trains to haul in thousands of carloads of rock and dirt for four years to build a base for track and a huge round-house that could hold 41 engines.

The summer of 1904 saw the massive migration of workers, families, houses, and belongings from Wadsworth to the new town; all of the railroad equipment was also moved. By the fall, Wadsworth was all but empty and the new town—complete with a library, hotel, store, and boarding houses—was open for business.

In 1905, the settlement was officially named the city of Sparks in honor of Governor John Sparks. In 1907, Sparks became the home of the Mallet, the largest steam engine ever built; it was used to haul long trains over the Sierras into the Sacramento Valley of California.

Until deep into the 20th century, Sparks was a railroad company town. The old roundhouse and most of the other trappings of the railroad are gone, but the history of Sparks lives on in **Victorian Square** downtown, a restored turn-of-the-century center.

History and railroad buffs should make a stop at the **Sparks Heritage Foundation & Museum**, located at 820 B Street in Victorian Square. The unpretentious building includes a fascinating but helter-skelter collection of railroad and community memorabilia. How about a letter punch from about 1900 used to punch initials in hat bands for identification purposes?

You'll find a complete turn-of-the-century barber shop, railroad uniforms and equipment, and household furnishings. There is a collection of very old front pages—would you believe a New York paper's report of the death of George Washington on January 4, 1800?

A section of the museum features some of the fixtures from the Perry's Grocery Store as they appeared in 1918. In the back room is a collection of items from an old railroad station master's office including a telegraph key. One of the photos on the wall shows an incredible snow scene on Donner Summit with a Central Pacific Railroad locomotive up against a wall of snow in 1889.

Life goes on. Plant life at the lowest desert levels of Nevada includes creosote, mesquite, cactus, and yucca. In the higher northern areas, the predominant plant is sagebrush. On higher mountain slopes and higher elevations can be found juniper, pine, spruce, and fir.

Home on the range. Larger mammals native to Nevada include mule deer, pronghorn antelope, bobcat, and bighorn sheep; in some areas wild horses and donkeys can be found. Common smaller mammals are badgers, rabbits, porcupines, muskrats, and marmots.

Desert animal life features various lizards, tortoises, and snakes including the sidewinder rattlesnake. Birds include the thrush, horned lark, Nevada creeper, pheasant, partridge, and sage grouse.

The free museum is open from 1 to 4 P.M. Wednesdays through Sundays; call 355-1144 for information.

Across the square from the museum is the **Sparks Visitor Center** set within a replica of the original Southern Pacific Depot in Sparks. Pulled up at the station is a 1907 Southern Pacific 10-wheeler Baldwin Steam Locomotive, which had been used in and around Reno on branch lines. You can walk into the driver's compartment, an old-style affair where the engineer had to lean out the side of the cab to the left or the right in order to see around the big boiler.

Next in line is a Houston Club Car, constructed by the Pullman Company in 1911 and converted to an executive car in 1929 for the private use of a division superintendent of the Southern Pacific; it includes a parlor, several bedrooms, and a small kitchen. The end of the small train is a period caboose, complete with a cupola for observation and a stove for cooking and eating.

Also on the square is the relocated **Glendale School**, the oldest remaining school building in Nevada, used from 1864 to 1958. Glendale preceded Reno and was destined to be the population center on the Truckee River until the Central Pacific Railroad decided to bypass the community for a station at Lake's Crossing, which is now Reno.

The **Sparks Tourist Information Office** near the Railroad Museum is open Monday through Friday from 8 A.M. to 5 P.M.

If plans become reality, Victorian Square will be redone in a $235 million development that will include a shopping mall, a 5,000-seat arena, restaurants, high-tech games and rides, an IMAX movie theater, and bridges linking John Ascuaga's Nugget to the Silver Club. The project could be in place by the end of 1996.

The **Wild Island** family entertainment complex is open daily from May to October and includes a water park with water slides, a tide pool, and rafting. Next door is Adventure Golf, a 36-hole miniature golf course and ice-skating facility. Call 359-2927 for information.

Among other events, Sparks is home of the International Whistle-Off in August and the Sparks Indian Rodeo in September.

A new addition to Sparks, on Victorian Square, is a microbrewery and restaurant called the **Great Basin Brewing Co.** The pleasant little pub, home to jazz and other music from time to time, offers a range of beers including Nevada

Hold, Wild Horse Ale, Ichthyosaur Pale Ale, and Jackpot Porter. There are also seasonal special brews that in the past have included Kringle Cranberry, Outlaw Oatmeal Stout, McClary's Irish Red, Chilebeso Jalapeño Ale, and Ruby Mountain Red. Pints are priced at about $2.75, but we like the idea of ordering a row of 75-cent 4-ounce samplers and trying them all.

The pub also offers burgers, sausages, sandwiches, and other nibbling food. Great Basin Brewing Co., on Victorian Square; 355-7711.

Hotels and Casinos in Sparks

▰ MUST-SEE ▰ John Ascuaga's Nugget

By now you should have guessed that our favorite hotels and casinos are those with a bit of quirkiness and individuality. By those criteria, John Ascuaga's Nugget qualifies as a must-see in the Reno Valley.

The large hotel and casino complex is actually located in Sparks, a small town that is within sight of Reno, just east of downtown. The place definitely caters to large bus tours, but it is certainly a step up from most of the downtown houses.

You'll know something is a bit odd when you cross the huge parking lot and see signs marking an elephant crossing. Yes, that's right, and their names are **Bertha** and **Angel**, the official goodwill ambassadors of the Nugget.

It all began back in 1962 when Bertha was hired to perform in the Nugget's showroom, known then as the Circus Room. Bertha was born in India in 1951 (a full-size Asian elephant, she tips the scales at a bit over four tons). By comparison, Angel is a mere baby, born in 1988 in captivity at Busch Gardens in Tampa, Florida.

> **Double room.** Bertha and Angel live in the Elephant Palace at the hotel, which includes a swimming pool and exercise area. Visitors are welcome to stop by between 10 A.M. and 2 P.M. to watch them as they get ready for work. Every night, they walk to the Celebrity Showroom where they open the show twice nightly, six nights a week.

The dear departed Liberace used to make his stage entrance at the Nugget riding on Bertha's back. And Bertha has made her own stage debut, appearing on "The Steve Allen Show" in 1963 and "Hollywood Palace."

And then there is the **Golden Rooster**, which may be the only member of its species ever to serve time in a federal lockup. The story is this: in 1958, the Nugget was preparing to open a new restaurant called the Golden Rooster and it was decided to decorate the place with an unusual work of art: a solid gold statue of a rooster.

Seven months after it went on display inside a fortified glass case, officials of the U.S. Treasury Department charged the Nugget with violation of the Gold Reserve Act which made it unlawful for a private individual to possess more than 50 ounces of gold. Legal skirmishes continued until 1960 when the hotel was formally presented with a complaint entitled "United States of America vs. One Solid Gold Object in the Form of a Rooster." The statue was

One-man show. The Nugget has been owned and operated by John Ascuaga since 1960, an unusual one-man history in Nevada gaming.

Fishy business. Be sure to check out the large salt water aquarium that sits behind the bar at Trader Dick's. The tank is home to more than 100 exotic fish, including clown, grouper, damsel, yellow tang, and lion fish.

confiscated; the Nugget's offer to put up bail was denied.

Two years of captivity for the golden bird followed, until a jury trial was held in 1962; the government was unable to counter the arguments of the Nugget and art critics that the statue was a work of art, and the rooster was sprung and returned to its perch at the restaurant. In 1987, the Golden Rooster Room was closed, but the bird eventually received a new place of honor behind the registration desk of the hotel. The 18-karat solid gold statue, weighing 206.3 troy ounces (14.1 pounds), is insured for $140,000.

On the Victorian Avenue exterior of the Nugget is a 36-foot-tall statue called "Last Chance Joe." Built in 1952, it had to be routed from its assembly place in California through Oregon on a special flat car to make its way to Sparks.

The attractive, wide-open, U-shaped casino is a bit on the loud side. There's a bingo room for the low rollers.

The Rotisserie combines a buffet and a la carte menu. A glassed-in rotisserie cooks chickens near the entryway. Tuesday nights are chocolate nights.

Trader Dick's, a dark, lush tropical garden setting with palm fronds and grass thatching sits just off the main casino floor, serving South Sea and Polynesian lunch Monday through Friday and dinner every night. A prix-fixe dinner is available for $16.95; specialties include sesame chicken for $9.95; hoisin beef for $10.50; and a seafood luau with cold crab, shrimp, prawns, avocado, papaya, tomato, and asparagus for about $20. A soup and salad bar is offered for $4.95.

At the center of the room is a large Chinese smoke oven used to prepare spareribs, chicken, and pork menu items.

The **Steak House** serves steaks; lots of them. A sign outside its doors claims that its chefs have forked over three million of them since 1956.

At the far end of the casino are a few other casual eateries. The **Farm House** is a coffee shop–like establishment, offering omelettes and pancakes for breakfast, a range of sandwiches and salads for lunch, and dinner specials including fried deep sea scallops for $7.95, fried shrimp boat for $7.95, ranch-hand beef stew for $5.95, and liver and onions for $5.25.

Nearby is **John's Oyster Bar**, which carries a bit of a nautical theme including a ship's mast and yardarm overhead. Specialties include lobster surprise salad (topped with a remoulade sauce of mayonnaise, mustard, gherkins, chervil, tarragon, and capers with a touch of chablis) for $12.50, and a group of pan roasts in chablis, clam broth, cream, and butter: oyster or shrimp for $8.75 or both for $9. There's also a "lazy man's" cioppino without shells for $10.25.

The **General Store** is a dimly lit, open-space coffee shop with attractive ceiling fans. Specialties include deep fried catfish for $5.95 and nuggets of tenderloin (chunks of filet mignon breaded, seasoned, and fried) for $8.95. Other specialties include the steakhouse grill (20-ounce T-bone steak) for $17.95, and white sturgeon (8-ounce loin sautéed, topped with a fine wine and champagne sauce and served with wild rice and vegetables) for $16.95.

John Ascuaga's Nugget. 1100 Nugget Avenue, Sparks; 750 rooms; 356-3300, (800) 648-1177.

Smaller Casinos in Sparks

A smaller, unusual Sparks joint worth checking out is **Baldini's Sports Casino.** This is not a place for the claustrophobic; in fact, it feels as if you have descended directly into the innards of a slot machine. There's a country-western dance floor and nearly free food. The casino includes a 24-hour buffet ($3.99 for breakfast, $5.99 for lunch, $6.99 for dinner, and $2.99 for the graveyard shift from 11 P.M. to 5:30 A.M.).

Baldini's is located at 865 S. Rock Boulevard; 358-0116.

Across Victorian Road from the Nugget is the **Treasury Club,** a very unexceptional little slot club catering mostly to locals. And then there is the **Mint Casino,** a mint green box of slots.

The **Silver Club** on Victorian Avenue is an attractive, high-ceilinged place, quieter and smaller than the Nugget but with some amenities of its own. Restaurants include **Victoria's Steak House** where entrees run from about $10 to $15, including prime rib, scampi ala romano, and seafood fettucine. The sports bar on the second floor is called **Rails.** A new nine-story tower will add 260 rooms and an expanded casino in 1996.

Reno Area Hotel-Casino Listing

Reno

Adventure Inn. 3575 S. Virginia Street; 828-9000, (800) 937-1436.
Airport Plaza Hotel. 1981 Terminal Way; 348-6370, (800) 648-3525.
Americana Inn. 340 Lake Street, 786-4422.
Aspen Motel. 495 Lake Street; 329-6011.
Best Western-Continental Lodge. 1885 S. Virginia Street; 329-1001, (800) 626-1900.
Best Western-Daniel's Motor Lodge. 375 N. Sierra Street; 329-1351, (800) 528-1234.
Big 8 Motel. 795 W. 4th Street; 329-3420.
Bob Cashell's Horseshoe Lodge. 222 N. Sierra Street; 322-2178, (800) 843-7403.
Bonanza Casino. 4720 N. Virginia Street; 323-2724.
Bonanza Motor Inn. 215 W. 4th Street; 322-8632.
Cabana Motel. 370 West Street; 786-2977.
Capri Motel. 895 N. Virginia Street; 323-8398.
Carriage Inn. 690 W. 4th Street; 329-8848.
Cheers Hotel/Casino. 567 W. 4th Street; 322-8181.
Circus Circus Hotel/Casino. 500 N. Sierra Street; 329-0711, (800) 648-5010.
City Center Motel. 365 West Street; 323-8880.
Clarion Hotel/Casino. 3800 S. Virginia Street; 825-4700, (800) 723-6500.
Coach Inn. 500 N. Center Street; 323-3222.
Colonial Inn Hotel/Casino. 250 N. Arlington Avenue; 322-3838, (800) 336-7366.
Colonial Motor Inn. 232 West Street; 786-5038, (800) 255-7366.
Comstock Hotel/Casino. 200 W. 2nd Street; 329-1880.

Crest Inn. 525 W. 4th Street; 329-0808.
Days Inn. 701 E. 7th Street; 786-4070, (800) 942-3838.
Donner Inn Motel. 720 W. 4th Street; 323-1851.
Downtowner Motor Lodge. 150 Stevenson Street; 322-1188.
Easy 8 Motel. 255 W. 5th Street; 322-4588.
Eldorado Hotel/Casino. 345 N. Virginia Street; 786-5700, (800) 648-5966.
El Ray Motel. 350 N. Arlington Avenue; 329-6669.
Executive Inn. 205 S. Sierra Street; 786-4050, (800) 648-4545.
Fantasy Inn. 2905 S. Virginia Street; 826-1515, (800) 662-8812.
Fireside Inn. 205 E. 4th Street; 786-1666.
Fitzgerald's Casino-Hotel. 255 N. Virginia Street; 785-3300, (800) 648-5022.
Flamingo Hilton Reno. 255 N. Sierra Street; 322-1111, (800) 648-4882.
Flamingo Motel. 520 N. Center Street; 323-3202.
Gatekeeper Inn. 221 W. 5th Street; 786-3500, (800) 822-3504.
Gateway Inn. 1275 Stardust Street; 747-4220.
Gold Dust West. Vine Street; 323-2211, (800) 438-9378.
Gold Key Motel. 445 Lake Street; 323-0731.
Harrah's Casino/Hotel Reno. 206 N. Virginia Street; 786-3232, (800) 648-3773.
Heart o' Town/Chalet Motel. 520 N. Virginia Street; 322-4066, (800) 628-3395.
Holiday Hotel Casino. Mill and Center Streets; 329-0411, (800) 648-5431.
Holiday Inn Convention Center. 5851 S. Virginia Street; 825-2940, (800) 722-7366.
Holiday Inn Downtown. 1000 E. 6th Street; 786-5151, (800) 648-4877.
Horseshoe Motel. 490 Lake Street; 786-5968.
Hotel El Cortez. 239 W. 2nd Street; 322-9161.
In Town Motel. 260 W. 4th Street; 323-1421.
Juniper Court Motel. 320 Evans Avenue; 329-7002, (800) 648-7366.
Keno Motel. 322 N. Arlington Avenue; 322-6281.
Keno Motel #2. 331 West Street; 322-4146.
Lakemill Lodge. 200 Mill Street; 786-1500, (800) 531-5900.
La Quinta Inn. 4001 Market Street; 348-6100, (800) 531-5900.
Lido Inn. 280 W. 4th Street; 322-3822.
Longhorn Motel. 844 S. Virginia Street; 322-2633.
Majestic Inn. 400 N. Virginia Street; 322-2868.
Mardi Gras Motor Lodge. 200 W. 4th Street; 329-7470.
Mark Twain Motel. 2201 S. Virginia Street; 826-2101.
Miner's Inn. 1651 N. Virginia Street; 329-3464.
Monte Carlo Motel. 500 N. Virginia Street; 329-2010.
Motel 500. 500 S. Center Street; 786-2777.
Motel 6 Reno Central. 866 N. Wells Avenue; 786-9852.
Motel 6 Reno North. 666 N. Wells Avenue; 329-8681.
Motel 6 Reno South. 1901 S. Virginia Street; 827-0255.
Motel 6 Reno West. 1400 Stardust; 747-7390.
National 9 Inn. 645 S. Virginia Street; 323-5411.
Nevada Inn. 330 E. 2nd Street; 323-1005, (800) 999-9686.
Olympic Apartment Motel. 195 W. 2nd Street; 323-0726.
Oxford Motel. 111 Lake Street; 786-3170, (800) 648-3044.
Park-N-Walk/Reno Royal Motor Lodge. 350 West Street; 323-4477.
Peppermill Hotel/Casino. 2707 S. Virginia Street; 826-2121, (800) 648-6992.
Pioneer Inn Hotel/Casino. 221 S. Virginia Street; 324-7777, (800) 879-8879.
Plaza Resort Club. 121 West Street; 786-2200, (800) 648-5990.
Ponderosa Hotel. 515 S. Virginia Street; 786-6820, (800) 228-6820.
Ponderosa Motel. 595 N. Lake Street; 786-3070.
Reno Hilton. 2500 E. 2nd Street; 789-2000, (800) 648-5080.
Reno Ramada Hotel/Casino. 200 E. 6th Street; 788-2000, (800) 648-3600.
Reno Riviera. 395 W. 1st Street; 329-9348.
Reno Spa Resort Club. 140 Court Street; 329-4251, (800) 634-6981.

Reno Travelodge Downtown. 655 W. 4th Street; 329-3451, (800) 255-3050.
Riverboat Hotel/Casino. 34 W. 2nd Street; 323-8877, (800) 888-5525.
Riverhouse Motel. 2 Lake Street; 329-0036.
Rodeway Inn. 2050 Market Street; 786-2500, (800) 648-3800.
RR Lodge. 500 Lake Street; 788-2000, (800) 648-3600.
Sands Regency Hotel/Casino. 345 N. Arlington Avenue; 348-2200, (800) 648-3553.
Savoy Motor Lodge. 705 N. Virginia Street; 322-4477.
Season's Inn. 495 West Street; 322-6000.
Shamrock Inn. 505 N. Center Street; 786-5182.
Showboat Inn. 660 N. Virginia Street; 786-7486, (800) 648-3960.
Silver Dollar Motor Lodge Six Gun Motel. 817 N. Virginia Street; 323-6875.
Six Gun Motel. 1661 E. 6th Street; 329-3426, (800) 648-3074.
Spring Hill Inn. 1450 Mill Street; 788-8040.
Stardust Lodge. 455 N. Arlington Avenue; 322-5641.
Sundowner Hotel/Casino. 450 N. Arlington Avenue; 786-7050, (800) 648-5490.
Swan Motel. 501 Lake Street; 786-1751.
Time Zone Motel. 448 Lake Street; 322-4666.
Town House Motor Lodge. 303 W. 2nd Street; 323-1821, (800) 438-5660.
Townsite Motel. 250 W. Commercial Row; 322-0345.
Town View Motor Lodge. 131 W. 3rd Street; 329-1560.
Truckee River Lodge. 501 W. 1st Street; 786-8888, (800) 635-8950.
University Inn. 1001 N. Virginia Street; 323-0321.
Uptown Motel. 570 N. Virginia Street; 323-8906.
Vagabond Inn. 3131 S. Virginia Street; 825-7134, (800) 522-1555.
Virginian Hotel/Casino. 140 N. Virginia Street; 329-4664, (800) 874-5558.
Washoe Inn. 75 Pringle Way; 328-5080.
White Court Motel. 465 Evans Street; 329-1957.
Windsor Hotel. 214 West Street; 323-6171.
Wonder Lodge. 430 Lake Street; 786-6840.

Sparks

Blue Fountain Motel. 1590 Victorian Avenue; 359-0359.
Emerald Motel. 145 15th Street; 358-5930.
Inn Cal. 255 N. McCarran Boulevard; 358-2222, (800) 446-2257.
John Ascuaga's Nugget. 1100 Nugget Avenue; 356-3300, (800) 648-1177.
McCarran House Inn. 55 E. Nugget Avenue; 358-6900, (800) 548-5798.
Motel 6 Sparks. 2405 Victorian Avenue; 358-1080.
Nendels Inn. 60 East Victorian Avenue; 356-7770, (800) 547-0106.
Pony Express Lodge. 2406 Prater Way; 358-7110.
Silver Club Hotel/Casino. 1040 Victorian Avenue; 358-4771, (800) 648-1137.
Sunrise Motel. 210 Victorian Avenue; 358-7010.
Thunderbird Resort Club. 200 Nichols Boulevard; 355-4040, (800) 821-4912.
Victorian Inn. 1555 Victorian Avenue; 331-3203.
Wagon Train Motel. 1662 Victorian Avenue; 358-0468.
Western Village Inn/Casino. 815 E. Nichols Boulevard; 331-1069, (800) 648-1170.

Bed-and-Breakfasts

Bed & Breakfast South Reno. 136 Andrew Lane, Reno; 849-0772.
Deer Run Ranch. 5440 East Lake Boulevard, Washoe Valley; 882-3643.
Haus Bavaria. 593 North Dyer Circle, Incline Village; 831-6122, 800-468-2463.

Airlines Serving Reno

American Airlines/American Eagle. (800) 433-7300.
America West Airlines. (800) 247-5692.

Incline Village/Crystal Bay Visitor and Convention Bureau. 969 Tahoe Boulevard, Incline Village, NV 89451; 832-1606 or (800) 468-2463. **North Lake Tahoe Chamber of Commerce.** Box 884, Tahoe City, CA 95730; (916) 581-6900.

Lake Tahoe Visitors Authority. Box 16299, South Lake Tahoe, CA 96151; (916) 544-5050 or (800) 288-2463. **Sierra Ski Marketing Council.** Box 9137, Incline Village, NV 89450; (916) 581-1174.

Canadian Airlines International. (800) 426-7000.
Continental Airlines. (800) 525-0280.
Delta Air Lines. (800) 221-1212.
Northwest Airlines. (800) 225-2525.
Reno Air. 736-6247.
Southwest Airlines. (800) 435-9792.
United Airlines. (800) 241-6522.
USAir. (800) 428-4322.

Local Bus Service

RTC/Citifare. For information on bus service, call 348-7433. Fares are adult, 75 cents; youth 18 and under, 50 cents; senior 60 and older with Citifare ID, 30 cents; disabled, 30 cents. Children ages 5 and under ride free; transfers are free.

Long Distance Bus Service

Aero Trans. Airport and Tahoe destinations. 786-2376.
Airport Mini Bus. Airport, Reno, and Lake Tahoe. 323-3727, (800) 235-5466.
Bell Limo Service. Airport, Reno, and Tahoe. 786-3700, (800) 235-5466.
Greyhound Lines West. Reno. 322-4511.
Sierra Nevada Gray Line. Daily ski shuttle to Alpine Meadows, Squaw Valley, and Northstar-at-Tahoe. 329-1147, (800) 822-6009.
Tahoe Casino Express. Scheduled service from Reno Airport to South Lake Tahoe. 785-2424, (800) 446-6128.

Car Rentals in Reno

Action Auto Rental. 324-2885.
Advantage Rent-A-Car. 5301 Longley Lane; 825-9191, (800) 777-5500.
Agency Rent-A-Car. 1105 Terminal Way; 786-3381, (800) 321-1972.
Alamo Rent A Car. 1120 Terminal Way; 323-8306, (800) 327-9633.
All American Auto Rental. 225 Telegraph; 323-0420.
Apple Rent A Car. Airport; 329-2137, 329-2438.
Avis Rent A Car. Airport; 785-2727, (800) 331-1212.
Budget/Sears. Airport: 785-2545; downtown: 785-2880, (800) 527-0700.
Dollar Rent A Car. Airport; 348-2800, (800) 800-4000.
Enterprise Rent-A-Car. Airport; 329-3773, (800) 325-8007.
General Rent-A-Car. Airport; 785-2600, (800) 327-7607.
Hertz Rent A- Car. Airport: 785-2554; Flamingo Hilton downtown: 348-8860; Reno Hilton: 785-2605, (800) 654-3131.
Lloyd's International. 2515 Mill Street; 736-2663, (800) 654-7037.
Payless Car Rental. 225 Telegraph Street; 333-6543, (800) 729-5377.
Thrifty Car Rental. 2697 Mill Street; 329-0096, (800) 367-2277.

Chapter 19
Eating Your Way Across Reno and Sparks

Reno-Sparks Buffets

Baldini's. Triple Crown International Buffet. Breakfast 6 to 10:30 A.M., $3.99; lunch 11 A.M. to 3:30 P.M., $5.99; and dinner 4 to 10:30 P.M., $6.99. Graveyard from 11 P.M. to 5:30 A.M., $2.99. Weekend champagne brunch 7 A.M. to 3:30 P.M., $6.99.

    Circus Circus. Big Top Buffet. Breakfast 6 to 11:30 A.M., $2.29; lunch 11:30 A.M. to 4 P.M., $2.69; and dinner 4:30 to 11 P.M., $3.89. Friday seafood buffet is $5.99.

    Clarion. Toucan Charlie's. Breakfast, $4.99; lunch, $6.99; and dinner, $8.99.

    Eldorado. Marketplace Buffet. Breakfast 7:45 to 11 A.M., $3.49; lunch 11 A.M. to 2 P.M., $5.49; and dinner 4 to 10 P.M., $7.49. Saturday night Western buffet from 4 to 10 P.M., $9.99. Saturday brunch 8 A.M. to 2 P.M., $5.49; and Sunday champagne brunch from 8 A.M. to 2 P.M., $7.49. Special seafood buffet Friday and Saturday nights for $15.99 in the hotel's convention center.

    Fitzgerald's. Breakfast 7 to 11 A.M., $2.99; lunch noon to 4 P.M., $4.49; and dinner 4 to 10 P.M., $4.99.

    Flamingo Hilton. Breakfast 7 to 10:45 A.M., $3.49; lunch 11 A.M. to 3 P.M., $4 (weekdays) and $5 (weekends); and dinner 5 to 11 P.M., $5.99.

    Harrah's. Skyway Buffet. Breakfast 7 to 11 A.M., $4.74; lunch 11:30 A.M. to 3 P.M., $5.25; and dinner Monday to Thursday 5 to 9 P.M., $7.75. Friday seafood dinner buffet 5 to 10 P.M., $14.95. Saturday brunch 7 A.M. to 3 P.M., $6.50; Saturday grille from 4 to 10 P.M., $8.99. Sunday brunch 7 A.M. to 3 P.M., $6.50; Sunday dinner from 4 to 9 P.M., $7.75.

John Ascuaga's Nugget. Lunch Monday to Saturday 11 A.M. to 2 P.M., $6.95. Dinner 5 to 10 P.M.: Monday (fish), $11.95; Tuesday (chocaholic's dessert special), $10.95; Wednesday (ribs), $10.95; Thursday, $10.95; Friday (seafood), $13.95; Saturday, $13.95; and Sunday, $10.95. Sunday brunch 8:30 A.M. to 2 P.M., $8.95.

Peppermill. Island Buffet. Breakfast weekdays 7:30 to 11 A.M., $2.99; lunch weekdays 11:30 A.M. to 3 P.M., $4.99; and dinner Sunday through Thursday 4:30 to 10 P.M., $7.99. Friday seafood buffet dinner, 4:30 to 11 P.M., $14.99. Saturday breakfast 7:30 to 11 A.M., $5.99; lunch 11 A.M. to 3 P.M., $6.99; and prime rib dinner 4:30 to 11 P.M., $13.99. Sunday brunch, 9 A.M. to 3 P.M., $10.99.

Reno Hilton. Breakfast 7 to 10:30 A.M., $3.99; lunch 11:30 A.M. to 3 P.M., $4.99; and dinner 4:30 to 10 P.M., $7.95. Sunday brunch 10 A.M. to 2 P.M., $9.95.

Some of Greater Reno's Best Restaurants

(Be sure to also see restaurant descriptions in this section's hotel listings.)

American

Adele's Restaurant. Valley Bank Plaza, 425 South Virginia; 333-6503. Also, 1112 North Carson; 882-3353. Lunch and dinner. Reservations suggested.

Bagel Deli. 2600 South Virginia (across from Peppermill); 825-8866. Breakfast and lunch restaurant/bakery featuring 14 varieties of bagels, 18 choices of cream cheese, and Kosher-style deli meats. Open Tuesday through Saturday.

Bailey's Cafe. 4124 Kietzke Lane (across from the Convention Center); 825-6600. California cafe atmosphere and outdoor dining on garden terrace. Brunch-luncheon every day from 8 A.M. to 5 P.M.; dinner every evening from 5 P.M.

Casanova's. 1695 South Virginia; 786-6633. Private curtained booths for fantasies of all sorts, including abalone, lobster, scampi, salmon, quail, pheasant, partridge, elk, and antelope, plus pasta dishes.

Curt & Al's Family Dining. 9251 Lemmon Drive; 972-6144. Chicken-fried steak, chili, cornbread, pies.

Famous Murphy's Restaurant Grill and Oyster Bar. 3127 S. Virginia Street; 827-4111. The Grill serves sandwiches, burgers, salads, scampi, pan roasts, pasta, steamers, oysters, chowder, hot rocks, and more for lunch and dinner. The dining room serves steak, pasta, chicken, and seafood specialties. Lunch and dinner daily. Reservations suggested.

Hooters. 3655 S. Virginia Street; 829-9464. Chicken wings, burgers, sandwiches, seafood, salads, and franchised "Hooter Girls" with trays. Lunch and dinner daily; children under 12 eat free from kids menu.

Liberty Belle Saloon & Restaurant. 4250 S. Virginia Street; 825-1776. Prime rib, chicken, and salads in a venerable local favorite decorated with area antiques. Lunch weekdays, dinner daily.

Pyrenees Bar & Grill. 442 Flint Street; 329-3800. Located in one of the city's most beautiful and history-rich buildings built in 1910 as a residence. The menu combines Basque specialties with American favorites.

Tumbleweed Pizza Cafe. At the Boomtown Casino, seven miles west of Reno on I-80; 345-6000. Wood-burning oven pizza, burgers, and more.

Chinese

Asian Garden. Plumb & Virginia Streets; 825-5510.

Dynasty. 55 Mount Rose Street; north of Park Lane Mall; 786-3688. Szechwan, Hunan, Mandarin, and Cantonese fare.

Mandarin Restaurant. 5089 South McCarran Boulevard, Smithridge Plaza; 827-0222. Authentic Chinese cuisine.

Delicatessen

Chicago Express Deli and Restaurant. Days Inn Hotel, 7th and Wells; 333-0922. An informal luncheon delicatessen that transforms to a dinner house featuring pastas, lasagna, and other Italian specialties.

Paolo's. 921 W. Moana Lane; 827-3860. Italian specialties for lunch and dinner.

Espresso Cafes

Blue Star Espresso & Coffee Co. Town Center Mall, 100 N. Sierra; 333-2809. More than 40 flavors of coffee, espresso, latte, and cappuccino. A deli menu features sandwiches and soups.

Jacquic's Java. 1315 W. 7th Street; 747-6666.

Josef's Vienna Bakery. 933 W. Moana Lane; 825-0451. European pastries and cakes, French and German bread. Sandwiches, soups, and salads, plus espresso to wash it down.

The Cultured Bean. Mira Loma Plaza, Mira Loma and S. McCarran; 829-4547. Dozens of flavors of coffee and frozen yogurt.

Westside Cafe and Coffee Co. MaeAnne and McCarran; 746-3344. Coffee, espresso, cappuccino, mocha, along with breakfast, lunch, and dinner daily.

French

The Brasserie. 1695 S. Virginia Street; 785-7910.

Gold Hill Hotel. Main Street (Hwy. 342), Gold Hill; 847-0111. Built in 1859, this stone structure is Nevada's oldest hotel. Lavish accommodations decorated with period antiques and a fine French restaurant, the Crown Point.

La Table Francaise. 3065 W. Fourth Street; 323-3200. Chef Yves Pimparel's classic French restaurant, winner of the *Mobil Guide* Four-Star rating since 1979. Casual atmosphere and dress code for dinner. Closed Sundays and Mondays.

German

Bavarian World. 595 Valley Road at East 6th Street; 323-7646. Pork roast, sauerbraten, Alpine cuisine from schnitzel to schweinebraten, and famous rye bread. Open daily for breakfast, lunch, *und* dinner.

Galena Forest Inn. 17025 Mount Rose Highway; 849-2100. Six miles up Mount Rose Highway. Alpine cuisine combining Swiss, Austrian, northern Italian, French, and German specialties. Menu items include sweetbread fricassee with shallots, mushrooms, spices, and wine; sautéed frog's legs with tomato concasse and garlic butter; *escalope tessin* (veal scallops with prosciutto and

Emmentaler cheese); and rosette of beef with cognac morel sauce. Dinner is served Wednesday through Sunday from 5 P.M. Reservations suggested.

Indian

Sapna Indian Restaurant. 3374 Kietzke at Moana Road; 829-1537. Masala Dosa, vegetarian and meat curries, Mouglai, Biriyani, and Thalli specialties. Lunch and dinner daily; closed Sundays.

   Taj Mahal Indian Cuisine. 1030 S. Virginia Street; 322-5577. Tandoori, curries, sizzling platters. Luncheon buffets.

Italian

Bompi's. 300-A East Plumb Lane; 828-7300. Italian Tuscan food, plus pizza and pasta. Lunch and dinner daily. Reservations suggested.

   Coco Pazzo. 3446 Lakeside Drive; 829-9449. Traditional and specialty Italian cooking for lunch and dinner.

   Colombo's Restaurant. 145 W. Truckee River Lane; 323-7004. New York–style Italian food in an art deco eatery. Open for dinner every evening.

   Dante's Italian Ristorante. 1279 Baring Boulevard, Sparks; 355-9306. Seafood, veal, and pasta specialties for dinner daily.

   Davo's. McCarran and Kings Row; 746-4411. Local favorite. Dinner daily; lunch in summer.

   La Trattoria. 719 South Virginia; 323-1131. An Italian "little kitchen" cafe. Specialties include *ravioli de manzo* (steak ravioli in red wine sauce with carrots and onions) and *pasta 'n cacciata* (eggplant shell filled with penne pasta in marinara sauce). Open for dinner Monday through Saturday 5 to 10 P.M. and lunch Monday through Friday at 11 A.M.

   Pasta Maniacs. 927 West Moana Lane; 826-4446. Lunch weekdays; dinner nightly.

   Rivoli Italian Restaurant. 221 West 2nd Street; 784-9792. Northern Italian cuisine. Dinner nightly except Sundays and Mondays.

   Spaughi's. 1573 South Virginia Street; 323-5339. New York–style Italian cuisine. Lunch Tuesday through Friday; dinner nightly.

   Two Guys From Italy. 3501 S. Virginia; 826-3700. Menu items include fresh pasta and sauces, cioppino, vegetarian specialties, and pizza. Lunch weekdays; dinner nightly.

Japanese

Ichiban Japanese Steak House. 635 N. Sierra Street; 323-5550. Teppen yaki cooking in a garden setting; Chopstix Restaurant at same location offers Japanese, Chinese, and Korean fare. Lunch weekdays, dinner nightly.

   Kanpai Japanese Restaurant. 5085 S. McCarran Boulevard; 825-2552. A large selection of sushi plus other traditional dishes.

   Kyoto. 915 W. Moana Lane; 825-9686.

   Sushi & Terri. 5000 Smithridge; 827-9191. All you can eat sushi bar, teriyaki, tempura, and other specialties.

   Yoshi Japanese Restaurant. 4944 S. Virginia Street near Kietzke; 827-4445.

Lunch Tuesday through Friday. Dinner nightly. Sushi, sashimi, tempura, teriyaki. Closed Mondays.

Mongolian

Kubla Khan Restaurant. 3702 S. Virginia Street; 829-8787. Barbecue your own chicken, beef, pork, or seafood on skewers at your table.

Mexican

Eatos Burritos. 1420 S. Wells Avenue; 786-8500.

   Miguel's Fine Mexican Food. 1415 S. Virginia Street; 322-2722. Closed Mondays.

Natural Food

Blue Heron. 1091 S. Virginia; 786-4110. Vegetarian and macrobiotic cuisine, fresh breads, microbrewed and all-natural wines. Lunch daily, dinner weekends.

   Dandelion Deli & Marketplace. 1170 S. Wells Ave; 322-6100. Natural food, vegetarian, and gourmet specialties for lunch.

Southwestern

Chili's Grill & Bar. 5090 Smithridge Drive; 829-7775. Chili, fajitas, ribs, and margaritas.

   Porky's. Mira Loma Shopping Center, S. McCarran; 825-3777. Texas-style barbecue, chili, sandwiches. Open daily for lunch and dinner.

Steak Houses

Waddies Steak House. Seven miles west of Reno on I-80; 345-6000. Steak, ribs, prime rib, scampi, and more. Lunch Friday through Sunday, and dinner nightly.

Thai

Cafe de Thai. 3314 S. McCarran & Mira Loma; 829-8424.

The Basque Influence

The Basques, an adventuresome people with origins in the Pyrenees Mountains of France and Spain, came to Nevada in a circuitous route that began with migration to Argentina where they worked as shepherds. Many thousands moved north in the 1850s, lured by the California Gold Rush, and some then came over the Sierra Nevadas eastward to work in the mines of the Comstock and elsewhere in Nevada.

   There are still remnants of the once-thriving Basque culture in and around Reno, including festivals and restaurants. Most Basque eateries are decidedly informal, serving dishes family style. You will likely be served at a large table with strangers in a boisterous atmosphere; Basque restaurants are not the place for a romantic getaway, but they are a lot of fun and a lot of food for a reasonable price—usually in the range of $10 to $20 for a complete dinner.

A local favorite is the **Santa Fe Hotel**, at 235 Lake Street, next to Harrah's. Open every day for lunch and dinner. 323-1891.

The **Pyrenees Bar & Grill** at California and Flint, three blocks west of South Virginia Street, is by Basque standards a formal place. 329-3800.

The **Basque Restaurant** is at the Overland Hotel, 691 S. Main Street, Gardnerville, below Carson City on I-395, just below the exit to Route 207 on the southernmost route to South Lake Tahoe. Open for lunch and dinner; closed Monday. 782-2138.

Louis' Basque Corner, at 302 East Fourth Street, features Basque cuisine such as *tripas callos,* chicken, oxtails, shrimp, and *tonque a la basquaise, paella, lapin chasseur* (hunter's rabbit), and *veau panne* (breaded veal), served family style. Lunch Monday through Saturday from 11 A.M. to 2:30 P.M. Dinner Monday through Saturday from 5:30 to 10 P.M. and from 4:30 to 9:30 P.M. on Sunday. 323-7203.

Chapter 20
Reno/Sparks Area Attractions

Like Las Vegas, Reno is a lot more than casinos, showrooms, and restaurants. Here is a listing of the more interesting museums and entertainment areas, as well as sports and outdoor activities.

Be sure to also check listings in this book for Carson City, Virginia City, and Lake Tahoe. Information about ski areas at Mount Rose, Incline Village, South Lake Tahoe, and North Lake Tahoe, as well as other winter sports including sledding, skating, and snowmobiling can be found in the section about Lake Tahoe.

Call ahead of time to check on hours and fees, which are always subject to change.

Museums

Wilbur D. May Museum, Arboretum, and Botanical Garden. A fabulous assortment of animal trophies and other items from the personal collection of Wilbur May, the son of the founder of the department store chain that bears his name and a world traveler of great renown in the 1920s and 1930s.

The Living Room section of the museum includes some of May's own paintings, collections, and a recording of May's greatest hit, "Pass a Piece of Pizza Please," a song he wrote together with comic Jerry Colona. The collection of artifacts he collected includes a shrunken head, an elephant's ear, and other trophies. An indoor arboretum includes a three-story waterfall, and a hands-on science room called the Sensorium was added in 1993.

The museum is located in Washoe County's Rancho San Rafael Park, 1502 Washington Street in Reno. Admission is $2 for adults and $1 for seniors and children under 12. Hours vary through the year; call 785-5961 for information about the museum and 785-4153 for arboretum schedules.

Boomtown RV Park. I-80 at Garson Road, Verdi; 345-6000, (800) 648-3790. 230 sites. At Boomtown Hotel/Casino.

Chism Trailer Park. 1300 W. 2nd Street, Reno; 322-2281, (800) 638-2281. 50 sites.

Four Seasons RV Park. 13109 S. Virginia Street, Reno; 853-1423. 49 sites. 15 miles south of Reno.

Keystone RV Park. 1455 W. 4th Street, Reno; 324-5000. 104 sites. Free shuttle to downtown.

Reno Hilton Camper-land. 2500 E. Second Street; 789-2129, (800) 648-5080. 452 sites. Pool.

Reno RV Park. 735 Mill Street, Reno; 323-3381, (800) 445-3381. 46 sites.

River's Edge RV Park. 1405 S. Rock Boulevard, Sparks; 358-8533. 164 sites. On the Truckee River. Casino shuttle.

Next door to the May Museum is the **Great Basin Adventure** theme park. Included are mining exhibits, gold panning, petting zoo, a dinosaur park, and more. Open summer months. Closed Mondays. Call 785-4319 for information. *You will find a discount in the coupon section of this book.*

E. L. Wiegand Museum of Art. An eclectic collection of modern and fine art, located at 160 W. Liberty Street. The museum focuses on the art of the Great Basin region, and 19th and 20th century American art. Open Tuesday through Saturday from 10 A.M. to 4 P.M., and Sundays from noon to 4 P.M. except for major holidays. Admission is $3 for adults, and $1.50 for children from 6 to 12. Call 329-3333 for information.

Nevada State Historical Society Museum. A well-stocked and attractively presented collection of Indian artifacts, mining devices, and other elements of the Silver State's history, from prehistoric times to the Wild West to modern days. A research library includes many priceless manuscripts, records, maps, and other historical data. The gift shop is the answer to a history buff's prayer.

Located on the University of Nevada-Reno campus at 1650 N. Virginia Street near U.S. 395. Open Monday through Saturday from 10 A.M. to 5 P.M. Admission is $2 for adults; children under 18 are free. Call 688-1190 for information.

Fleischmann Planetarium. Next to the Historical Society Museum on the UNR campus. A stargazer's fantasy: a fascinating planetarium show, there are films, a display of meteorites, and scheduled use of telescopes.

The new SkyDome 8/70 uses extra-large film and special audio effects to present spectacular movies including *Ring of Fire* and *Yellowstone*. Planetarium shows include "The Light Hearted Astronomer" and "Star of Wonder." Call 784-4811 for hours. *You will find a discount in the coupon section of this book.*

Mackay School Museum of Mines. If a mining museum is what you're looking for, here is a fine example: an incredible collection of mineral wealth from Nevada, including gold and silver from the Comstock, as well as copper, lead, and other rocks that shaped the state. The collection was originally endowed by John Mackay, one of the men who made a fabulous fortune in the early days of Virginia City. On the UNR campus, within the Mackay Mining School. Call the school for hours and information at 784-6987.

National Automobile Museum. A spectacular collection of just some of the more than 1,000 vintage vehicles owned by casino developer William Harrah. Most of the cars were auctioned off after Harrah's death (some were bought for the equally spectacular and quirky collection at the Imperial Palace in Las Vegas); about 200 were given to a foundation set up by his heirs. The collection was moved into an attractive new building downtown in 1989; the architecture of the building is reminiscent of some of the chrome boats within.

Mill and Lake streets. Open every day but Christmas. Call 333-9300 for hours and admission fees. *You will find a discount in the coupon section of this book.*

Reno Art Galleries

Call for hours and special exhibits.

Addi's Gallery. Reno Hilton Casino Resort; 323-1920.

Artful Hen. 4065 Kietzke Lane; 826-0323.

Artist Co-op Gallery. 627 Mill Street; 322-8896.

Caughlin Club Gallery. 4100 Caughlin Parkway; 747-6010.

Cheese Board and Wine Seller-Bistro Gallery. 247 California Avenue; 323-3115.

Desert Moon Art Gallery and Tea House. 725 S. Center Street; 329-4959.

Gene Speck's Silver State Gallery. 719 Plumas Street; 324-2323.

Hermitage Gallery. 230 Evans Avenue; 786-6880.

Indian Outpost Gallery. 46 South C Street, Virginia City; 847-9025.

Limited Editions Gallery. 3366 Lakeside Drive; 825-1207.

Nevada Museum of Art's E.L. Wiegand Gallery. 165 W. Liberty; 329-3333.

Sheppard Galleries. Church Fine Arts complex on the University of Nevada-Reno campus; 784-6682.

Sierra Arts Center Gallery. 200 Flint Street; 329-1324.

Stremmel Gallery. 1400 S. Virginia Street; 786-0558.

TMCC Art Gallery (Red Mountain Gallery). Truckee Meadows Community College, 7000 Dandini Boulevard; 673-7084.

Verdi Art Gallery. 145 Bridge Street; on Highway. 40 in Verdi; 345-0501.

Amusement Parks

Amusement World offers go-carts, bumper boats, batting cages, a video arcade, and more. 12325 S. Virginia Street. Call 851-0961 for hours and fees.

Battle Born Splat World. The name just about sums it up, doesn't it? This is a paint-ball arcade for those who feel they can reduce stress by firing paint-filled balloons at each other in mock warfare. Go figure. 555 Dermody Way, Sparks. 356-1864.

Kiddie Playland at Idlewild Park is a small play area with trains, a merry-go-round, swimming pool, and rides. Call 329-6008 for hours and rates.

Wild Waters at Wild Island in Sparks offers a wave pool, water slides, and other wet entertainment in warm weather. Also at Wild Island is **Adventure Golf**, a 36-hole miniature golf course, open year-round weather permitting. Also at the park are three go-cart raceways and the **Tut's Tomb** video game arcade. 250 Wild Island Court (north from Sparks Boulevard exit of I-80). Call 331-9453 for operating days, hours, and rates. *You will find a discount in the coupon section of this book.*

Shamrock RV Park. 260 Parr Boulevard, Reno; 329-5222, (800) 322-8248. 121 sites.
Tiki Village Trailer Park. 4055 S. Virginia Street, Reno; 825-1507. 66 sites.

Performing Arts and Theater Groups

Nevada Festival Ballet. 329-2552.
Nevada Opera Association. 786-4046.
Reno Little Theater. 329-0661.
Reno Philharmonic Association. 825-5905.
Sierra Arts Foundation. 329-1324.
UNR Performing Arts Series. 826-0880.
Washoe County Community Concert Association. 359-7670.

Major Hotel Showrooms

Flamingo Hilton. 322-1111.
Harrah's Reno. 329-4422; (800) 648-3773.
John Ascuaga's Nugget. 356-3304; (800) 648-1177.
Reno Hilton. 789-2285; (800) 648-3568.

Nightclubs

Baldini's. 865 S. Rock Boulevard, Sparks; 358-0116.
Cantina Los Tres Hombres. 7111 S. Virginia Street; 852-0202.
Casanova's. 1695 S. Virginia Street; 786-6633.
Catch a Rising Star Comedy & Music Club. Reno Hilton, 2500 E. Second Street; 354-4544.
Clarion. 3800 S. Virginia Street; 825-4700.
Easy Street Cabaret. 505 Keystone Avenue; 323-8369.
Hacienda del Sol. 2935 S. Virginia Street; 825-7144.
Lime Lite. 50 E. Grove Street; 829-0448.
Noizemakers at Garfields. 1537 S. Virginia Street; 323-1600.
Pink Pussy Cat. 195 S. Wells Avenue; 322-0388. Non-stop topless shows.
Sierra Stix. 2130 Oddie Boulevard, Sparks; 331-4083.

Reno Area Annual Events

They love their festivals in Nevada, celebrating just about everything you can imagine. Of course, the fact that there are so many available hotel rooms and convention centers in the area, as well as the strong lures of the ski areas, golf courses, lakes, and mountains doesn't hurt.

If you're looking for an excuse to come to Reno, Sparks, or the surrounding area, here is a list of some of the major gatherings held annually. Call (800) 367-7366 for exact dates in 1996, or call the numbers where listed.

February

Reno Indoor Track & Field Games. (800) 367-7366. Reno Livestock Events Center.

USA Track & Field National Masters Indoor Championships. 747-0639 or (800) 531-3170. Reno Livestock Events Center. Nearly 1,000 athletes age 35 and over.

March

St. Patrick's Day Weekend. (800) 431-3134. Festivities in downtown Reno near Fitzgerald's Casino-Hotel.

California Gold Rush. (916) 426-3871. Soda Springs. Cross-country ski marathon.

Reno International Jazz Festival. 784-4046. University of Nevada-Reno.

Snowfest Winter Carnival. (916) 583-7625. North Lake Tahoe/Truckee.

April

Reno International Kite Festival. 827-7700. Rancho San Rafael Park.

May

Cinco de Mayo Fiesta Nevada Celebration. 353-2291 or 353-2284. Sparks Victorian Square filled with colorful dancers, live musical groups, arts and crafts, and Mexican food.

13th Annual Reno West Coast Wine Competition. 827-7711 or (800) 367-3766. Reno-Sparks Convention Center. More than 1,000 bottles of wine from across the West in competition.

Asian-Pacific Festival of Fortune. (800) 843-2427, ext. 3312. Victorian Square in downtown Sparks. Music, entertainment, and food.

Silver State Square Dance Festival. 359-2867. Reno-Sparks Convention Center.

Annual Sternwheeler Race. Lake Tahoe. Memorial Day weekend race between the *M.S. Dixie* and the *Tahoe Queen.*

Nugget All-American Suffolk Sheep Show and Sale. 323-3071. Reno Livestock Events Center.

June

Celebrate the River. 334-2414 or (800) 367-7366. Raymond I. Smith Truckee River Walk in downtown Reno. Music, arts and crafts, and food.

Night Curves: Beauties and Beasts, Music and Muscle Cars. 329-7469. Entertainment and exhibits of classic cars in downtown Reno.

Country Junction. (800) 367-7366. A parade, cattle drive, country music, and food kick off rodeo week in Reno.

West Fest. 345-6000. Boomtown Hotel Casino, seven miles west of Reno. Country music festival.

Reno Rodeo. 329-3877 or (800) 367-7366. Nine days of rodeo action at the Reno Livestock Events Center.

Logger Jamboree. 827-7705 or (800) 367-7366. Crosscut saws, chainsaws, and axes in action in downtown Reno.

Carson City Chamber of Commerce. 1900 S. Carson St., Suite 100, Carson City, NV 89701; 882-1565.

Carson City Convention and Visitors Bureau. 1900 S. Carson St., Suite 200, Carson City, NV 89701; 687-7410 or 800-638-2321.

Carson Valley Chamber of Commerce and Visitors Authority. 1524 Highway 395, No. 1, Gardnerville, NV 89410-7814; 782-8144 or 800-727-7677.

Greater Reno Chamber of Commerce. 133 N. Sierra St., Reno, NV 89503; 329-3558.

Tahoe-Truckee Air Show. (916) 587-4119. Truckee Airport.

Annual West Coast Wine Tasting. 827-7636. Culinary and oenological festival at the Reno-Sparks Convention Center, featuring menu items from northern Nevada's finest restaurants and great vineyards of the west.

Annual Windjammers Southern Crossing. A 27-mile race down the length of Lake Tahoe opens the sailing season.

Kit Carson Rendezvous. 687-7410. The Old West comes alive in Carson City each year with a series of contests and demonstrations of Indian and Western arts, crafts, and skills.

Handshake Day and Chili Cook-Off. 885-0411. A downtown Carson City street fair.

Stewart Indian Museum Pow Wow. 882-1808. An annual arts and crafts festival in Carson City.

July Fourth Celebrations

Skyfire. (800) 367-7366. Independence Day fireworks spectacular.

Carson City. 881-1565. Parade, picnic, fair, fireworks.

Incline Village. Fireworks and air show. Hyatt Lake Tahoe Beach.

Reno. (800) 367-7366. The Skyfire celebration at the University of Nevada-Reno.

South Lake Tahoe. 588-6611. Timber Cove Pier.

July

Sports Cars & All That Jazz. (800) 535-3045. Hundreds of the hottest cars and the coolest jazz musicians in downtown Reno.

Annual Sail Week. Lake Tahoe.

Capitol City Fair. 882-4460. County Fair in Carson City's Fuji Park.

Comstock Arabian Horse Show. 331-3300. At the Reno Livestock Events Center.

Nugget Jazz Festival. 358-2233. John Ascuaga's Nugget, Sparks.

Pacific Coast Cutting Horse Stakes. (916) 929-4144. Reno Livestock Events Center.

August

Hot August Nights. 829-1955 or (800) 367-7366. Great music and several thousand classic cars in Reno.

Reno 500 & National Truck Week. 826-6157. Downtown and way off the road in the desert near Reno.

Reno Renaissance Fair. 686-3047. Downtown Reno becomes a Renaissance village.

Basque Festival. 323-3000. Washoe County Fairgrounds.

Basque Festival. 785-3350. Food, crafts, and entertainment in Sparks' Victorian Square.

Nevada State Fair. 688-5767 or (800) 367-7366. Reno Livestock Events Center.

Carson Indian Colony Pow-Wow. 885-9759. Carson City, Fuji Park.

September

The Nugget Best-in-the-West Rib Cook-Off. 353-2284 or (800) 843-2427 ext. 3367. Competition for the "best ribs" and "best sauce" in the West. Sparks' Victorian Square.

The Great Reno Balloon Race. 829-2810. Rancho San Rafael Park, Reno. More than 100 of the nation's top balloonists.

Virginia City International Camel Races. 847-0311 or 847-7223.

National Championship Air Races. 972-6663 or (800) 367-7366. Reno/Stead Airport. The world's longest-running air race is the only event with all four race classes.

Street Vibrations. 329-7469 or (800) 367-7366. Hog Heaven in Reno for fanciers of Harley-Davidson and other custom tour bikes. Music, crafts, cruises, and parades.

World's Championship Chili Cook-Off and Americana Food Festival. 329-7469 or (800) 367-7366. More than 100 chili chefs, plus music, entertainment, arts and crafts.

Genoa Candy Dance. 782-8144. Local dance at the oldest permanent settlement in Nevada.

Pacific Coast Quarter Horse Association Spectacular. Reno Livestock Events Center.

Reno-Sparks Convention and Visitors Authority. 4590 S. Virginia St., Reno, NV 89502; 827-7600, 827-7366, or (800) 367-7366.
Reno-Sparks Indian Colony Tribal Council. 98 Colony Rd., Reno, NV 89502; 329-2936.
Sparks Chamber of Commerce. 831 Victorian Ave., Sparks, NV 89431; 358-1976.
Virginia City Chamber of Commerce. V&T Railroad Car, C St., Virginia City, NV 89440; 847-0311.
Nevada Department of Wildlife. Box 10678, Reno, NV 89520; 688-1500.
Pyramid Lake Fisheries. Star Route, Sutcliffe, NV 89510; 673-6335.
Bureau of Land Management. Box 12000, Reno, NV 89520; 785-6402.

October

Great Italian Festival. 786-5700. Eldorado Hotel Casino, Reno. Food, entertainment including a grape stomp and spaghetti-eating contest. Capped by the **Columbus Day Parade.**

Mainstreet Chili Cook-Off. 885-0411. Carson City.

Nevada Day Celebration (Oct. 31). Old-time festival and celebration of Nevada's admission to the United States, in Carson City.

November

Celtic New Year Celebration. (800) 535-3045. Reno. Pipe bands, dueling, dancing, entertainment, food, and crafts.

National Senior Pro Rodeo Finals. 746-0141, 323-3073, or (800) 225-2277. Reno Livestock Events Center.

Classic Country Dance Festival. 686-3047 or 829-5864. Dance exhibition and festival. Downtown Reno.

Christmas on the River. 334-2414. The Raymond I. Smith Truckee River Walk is the location for this holiday festival with all the trimmings.

December

Sparks Hometowne Christmas. 353-2284. Sparks Victorian Square. Parade, tree-lighting, caroling, crafts, entertainment, and food.

Buck'n Ball. (800) 444-2825. Reno Livestock Events Center. New Year's Eve. Rodeo, live music, and dancing till dawn.

Festival of Trees. 786-7765. Reno.

Western Nugget National Hereford Show and Sale. 356-3300. Heifers and bulls take over for the showgirls at the Nugget's showroom.

Zoos and Animal Preserves

Animal Ark. 969-3111. 1265 Deer Lodge Road, Red Rock.

Great Basin Wildlife Center. 3770 Butti Way, Carson City; 887-2172.

Sierra Safari Zoo. 10200 N. Virginia Street, Reno; 677-1101. A small private zoo, about 10 miles north of Reno on Highway 395 at Red Rock. More than 200 animals representing 40 species. Admission is $5 for adults, $3 for children 2 to 12. Closed December through March.

RENO

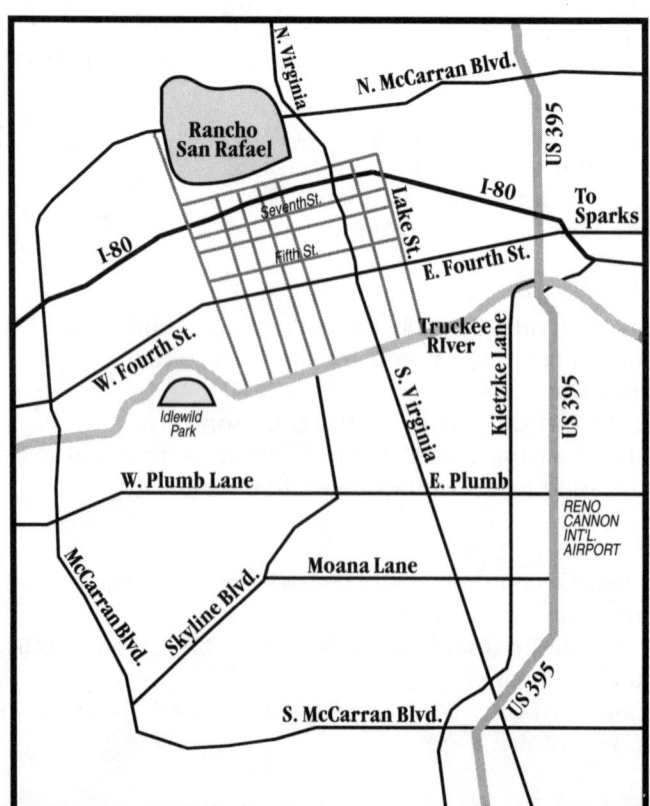

Chapter 21
The Great Outdoors in Reno/Sparks

Golf Courses

Most Reno-area courses are open year-round or close to it; courses north and south may be closed in the winter. Call for hours and fees. Listed yardage is for championship or men's course.

Brookside Municipal Golf Course. 700 South Rock Boulevard, Sparks; 322-6009. 9 holes. Par 36; 2,930 yards. Year-round. $5.

Lakeridge Golf Course. 1200 Razorback Drive, Reno; 825-2200. 18 holes. Par 71; 6,703 yards on championship course designed by Robert Trent Jones. Year-round. Summer rates April 1 through October 31, $49 with cart; off-season, $30 with cart.

Northgate Golf Club. 111 Clubhouse Drive, Reno; 747-7577. 18 holes. Par 72; 6,966 yards. Year-round except December 15 through January 31. Summer rates April 1 through October 31, $37 with cart; winter rates, $26 with cart; $13 without cart.

Rosewood Lakes. 6800 Pembroke Drive, Reno; 685-2893. 18 holes. Par 72; 6,661 yards. Year-round. $22 summer; $17 winter. Carts $16.

Sierra Sage Golf Course. 6355 Silver Lake Road, Reno; 972-1564. 18 holes. Par 71; 6,623 yards. Year-round. Weekdays $18; weekends $21. Carts $18.

Washoe County Golf Course. 2601 S. Arlington Avenue, Reno; 785-4286. 18 holes. Par 72; 6,695 yards. Year-round. Summer $21; winter $18. Carts $18. Built by the WPA in the 1930s.

Wildcreek Golf Course. 3500 Sullivan Lane, Sparks; 673-3100. 18 holes. Par 72; 7,105 yards. Year-round except December 15 through January 31. Summer rates April 1 through October 31, $37 with cart; winter rates, $26 with cart; $13 without cart.

Hunting Information

Contact the Department of Wildlife, P.O. Box 10678, Reno, NV 89520; or call 688-1500. Information is also available at most sporting goods stores.

Foreign language assistance. Northern Nevada Language Bank can offer assistance on a 24-hour-a-day basis for non-English-speaking visitors. Contact the answering service operator, who can connect the caller with a volunteer who speaks the necessary language. 323-0500.

Tennis Courts

Lakeridge Tennis Club. 827-3300.
   Reno Hilton. 789-2145.
   Reno Parks & Recreation Department. 334-2262.
   Reno YMCA. 329-1311.
   Sparks Recreation Department. 359-7930.
   Washoe County Parks Department. 785-6133.

Parks and Recreation

City of Sparks Parks and Recreation. 353-2376.
   Nevada State Parks Division. 687-4384.
   Reno City Parks and Recreation. 334-2662.
United States Forest Service/Toiyabe National Forest. 355-5302.
Washoe County Parks and Recreation. 785-6133.

Chapter 22
Shopping and Getting Married

Shopping Malls
Meadowood Mall

Located off South Virginia Street near the intersection with South McCarran Boulevard, past the Reno Cannon International Airport and the Reno-Sparks Convention Center. Open Monday through Friday 10 A.M. through 9 P.M.; Saturday 10 A.M. to 7 P.M.; Sunday 11 A.M. to 6 P.M. 827-8450.

Citifare bus service is available from the following points to Meadowood: Downtown (4th and Center Streets), Reno Hilton (tour bus entrance at south doors), the Peppermill (Virginia Street), and Victorian Square in Sparks (11th and B Streets).

Meadowood Mall has more than 75 stores in an attractive setting, including Macy's Reno, said to be the largest single department store in the state, JC Penney, The Gap, The Limited, and more.

Department Stores: JC Penney, Macy's.

Arts, Crafts, Hobbies, and Toys: Clown's Closet, Docktor Pet Center, Prints Plus, World of Toys.

Athletic Wear and Sporting Goods: Champs, Copeland's Sports, Eddie Bauer, Foot Locker, Lady Foot Locker, Track 'n Trail.

Books and Cards: Amy's Hallmark, Waldenbooks.

Children's Clothing and Shoes: Champs, Clown's Closet, Foot Locker, Kinney Shoes, Lady Foot Locker, Limited Too, Miller Stockman, Track 'n Trail.

Electronics, Music, and Video: AT&T Phone Center, Fun-N-Games, Musicland, Radio Shack, Sam Goody, Suncoast Motion Pictures Company, Waldenbooks, Waldensoftware.

Food and Restaurants: Alamo Restaurant, Cindy's Cinnamon Rolls, GNC, Honey Treat Yogurt, McDonald's, Manchu Wok, Marie Callender's, Mrs. Field's Cookies, Sbarro Italian Eatery, See's Candies, Spinnaker's.

Luggage: Eddie Bauer, Schillings.

Men's Fashions and Shoes: Champs, Copeland's Sports, County Seat, Dejaiz, Eddie Bauer, Florsheim Shoes, Foot Locker, The Gap, J. Riggings, Kinney Shoes, Miller Stockman, Miller's Outpost, Structure, Track 'n Trail, Victoria's Secret.

Women's Fashions and Shoes: 9 West, Accessory Place, Benetton, Brooks

Fashions, Caren Charles, Carimar, Casual Corner, Champs, Cobbie Shop, Connie Shoes, Contempo Casuals, Copeland's Sports, County Seat, Eddie Bauer, Express, Foot Locker, Gantos, The Gap, Jean Nicole, Kinney Shoes, Lady Foot Locker, Lane Bryant, Lerner, Miller Stockman, Miller's Outpost, Naturalizer, Petite Sophisticate, Switzer's, The Limited, Track 'n Trail, Units, Victoria's Secret.

Park Lane Mall

Across from the Peppermill Hotel, at Virginia Street and Plumb Lane. Open weekdays 10 A.M. to 9 P.M.; Saturday from 10 A.M. to 9 P.M.; and Sunday from 11 A.M. to 6 P.M. 825-7878. More than 90 stores.

Department Stores: Sears, Weinstock's, Woolworth's.

Women's Clothing: After Thoughts, Brooks Fashions, Career Image, Claire's Boutique, Clothestime, Five-Seven-Nine, Frederick's of Hollywood, Lizzie B, Modern Woman, Plenty Pretty, Touch of Pizazz.

Men's Clothing: Jeans West, KG Men's Store, Oak Tree.

Family Apparel: Hot Cats, Jay Jacobs, Kid's Mart, Miller's Outpost, Pro Sports Shope, Splatters Ink, T-Shirts Plus, Wilson's Suede and Leather.

Shoes: Athletic X-Press, Foot Locker, Huston's Shoes, Huston's Youngland, Kinney Shoes, Leeds Shoes, Lloyd Gotchy Shoes, Naturalizer Shoes, Payless Shoesource, Thom McAn, Wild Pair.

Toys, Hobbies, and Entertainment: Docktor Pet Center, Gordon's Photo Service, Jolly Time, Kay Bee Toy, Mirabelli's Music City, Radio Shack, Waldensoftware.

Food and Restaurants: Baskin Robbins, Bompi's, Carousel Snack Bar, Cinnamon Sams, Ethel M. Chocolates, Foxy Loxy, Great American Cookie Co., Great Earth Vitamins, Honey Treat Yogurt, Jia's Wok, Orange Julius, Pete & Jerry's, Pizza by Piece of the Pie, See's Candy, Swiss Colony, Taco Chips.

Gifts, Cards, and Books: Cartoon Junction, Crystal Island, Evans Art Company, Nicholson's Hallmark, Reno Gift & Souvenir, Rose Garden, Sierra Crystal Mines, Spencer Gifts, Things Remembered, Tinder Box, Waldenbooks.

Jewelry: Crescent Jewelers, Gordon's Jewelers, Helzberg Diamonds, J. Herbert Hall, JM Jewelers, Precision Diamonds, Time Square, Zales.

Factory Stores at the Parking Gallery

A new collection of stores near downtown Reno, at the corner of Sierra and 1st Streets. **Adolfo II, Anne Klein, Carole Little, Mikasa,** and others.

Shopping in Sparks

Factory Outlets of Nevada

Sparks Boulevard and I-80; 355-3200. An all-in-one factory outlet store with discounts on some 30 brands including Aileen, Banister Shoe, Bass, Book Warehouse, Brass Factory, Bugle Boy, Cape Isle Knitters, Corning/Revere, Designer Brands, Earthly Creations, Fieldcrest Cannon, Gitano, Hawaiian Cotton, Home Again, Leather Loft, London Fog, Prestige Fragrances, Sierra Trading Post, Socks Galore, Toy Liquidators, and Van Heusen.

Greenbrae Shopping Center

Greenbrae Drive and Pyramid Way; 329-2233. 35 stores.

Silver State Plaza.

McCarran Boulevard and E. Prater Way. 825-4000. 42 stores.

Shopping in South Lake Tahoe and Stateline

A few miles over the border into California is a stretch of factory outlet stores offering clothing, accessories, and household items.

Factory Stores at the Y

Intersection of Highways 50 and 89, South Lake Tahoe. (At the point where Highway 50 continues on toward the California Coast and Highway 89 heads up along the western shore of Lake Tahoe.) The California number is (916) 541-8314; in Nevada call 265-2436. There are 12 stores, including Bass Shoes, Capezio Shoes, Cape Isle Knitters, Geoffrey Beene, Great Outdoor Clothing Outlet, Home Again, Oneida Silver Company, Pfaltzgraff, Sierra Shirts, and Van Heusen.

Tahoe Factory Stores

2501 S. Lake Tahoe Boulevard; (916) 544-8784. Book Warehouse, L'egg's/Hanes/Bali, Leather Loft, and Prestige Fragrance & Cosmetics.

London Fog Factory Store

2019 Lake Tahoe Boulevard, South Lake Tahoe; 541-8869.

Mikasa Factory Store

2011 Lake Tahoe Boulevard, South Lake Tahoe; 541-7412.

Oneida Factory Store

2014 Lake Tahoe Boulevard, South Lake Tahoe; 541-0826.

Van Heusen Factory Store

960 Emerald Bay Road, South Lake Tahoe; 541-3820.

Harvey's Shopping Arcade

Within Harvey's Resort Hotel, Stateline, Nevada. Includes David Grace Collections, clothing for men and women; The Sport Shop, clothing for winter and summer sports; and Jewelry Factory Gallery.

Shopping in Truckee
Tahoe-Truckee Factory Stores

I-80 to 12047 Donner Pass Road; (916) 587-5726. Bass Shoes, Dansk, Fragrance Outlet, Gorham, Home Again, Izod, L'egg's/Hanes/Bali, Swank, Van Heusen, and Villeroy & Boch.

Getting Hitched

Marriage licenses are issued to males and females 18 or over. Both must appear before the County Clerk. The marriage license fee is $35 and may be obtained at the Marriage Bureau in the courthouse. Legal identification with proof of birth date is required, such as a certified copy of the birth certificate, a valid driver's license, identification from Department of Motor Vehicles, or a passport. No witness is necessary to obtain a license.

Courthouse Locations: Washoe County Recorder's Office, corner South Virginia and Court streets, P.O. Box 11130, Reno, NV 89520; 328-3275. Hours: 8 A.M. to 12 midnight, daily.

Parental Consent: Males & females between the ages of 16 and 18 may obtain marriage licenses if they have their parents' or legal guardians' consent. This consent may be given in person or in writing (notarized) to the County Clerk. Identification with proof of birth date is required such as a certified copy of the birth certificate from the county where the birth was recorded (hospital certificate not accepted), identification from Department of Motor Vehicles, or a passport.

Civil Marriages: Civil marriages in Reno and Sparks are performed by the Commissioner of Civil Marriages, 195 South Sierra Street, Reno, NV 89501; 328-3275. Fee: $35. No appointment is necessary.

In Incline Village/Crystal Bay, civil marriages are performed by the Incline Village Justice of the Peace, 865 Tahoe Boulevard. Open 8:30 P.M. to 5 P.M. Monday through Friday. Fee: $35. An appointment is necessary.

Marriage Records: A temporary certificate is issued until the original is mailed. If you need a certified copy of the recorded certificate, contact Washoe County Recorders Office, P.O. Box 11130, Reno, NV 89510; 328-3275.

Wedding Chapels in Reno, Sparks, and Nearby

Adventure Inn. 825-1087, (800) 937-1436.
    Candlelight Wedding Chapel. 786-5355.
    Chapel of the Bells. 323-1375, (800) 872-2933.
    Church of the Ponderosa. 831-0691.
    Cupid's Chapel of Love. 323-2930, (800) 582-4737.
    The Dream Maker. 831-6419, (800) 252-3732.
    Heart of Reno Chapel. 786-6882.
    Incline Village/Crystal Bay Cal-Neva Lodge. 832-4000.
    Lady of the Lake. 832-0505.
    Nugget Hotel Wedding Chapel. 356-3300 ext. 3480, (800) 648-1177.
    Park Wedding Chapel. 323-1770.
    Reno Hilton Wedding Chapel. 322-5353, (800) 255-1771.
    Reno Wedding Chapel. 323-5818, (800) 248-6933.
    Riverside Wedding Chapel/Little Church of the Sierras. 322-3474.
    Silver Bells Wedding Chapel. 322-0420, (800) 221-9336.
    Starlite Wedding Chapel. 786-4949.
    Unity Church of Reno. 747-2207.
    Wedding Bells Chapel. 329-0909.

Chapter 23

Drive, He Said: Eight Trips from Reno and Lake Tahoe

The Econoguide to the Best Driving Trips from Reno and Lake Tahoe

Lake Tahoe	Pyramid Lake
Emerald Bay	Virginia City
Heavenly	
Incline Village	
Squaw Valley	

I. A Mirage in the Desert: North to Pyramid Lake

Trip 1: Pyramid Lake

Reno

Pyramid Lake

A spectacular sea in the desert, **Pyramid Lake** is unlike any body of water in the world. Named for the distinctive rock formation that rises from its waters, Pyramid Lake is the largest remnant of a giant inland sea that once covered more than 8,000 square miles. Ancient petroglyphs depicting Paiute Indian life line the hills surrounding the lake, and its Anahoe Island (closed to the public) is a sanctuary for beautiful pelicans.

The west shore of the lake is a straight shot up Route 445 from Reno, about 25 miles. Highway 445 from Sparks starts out as a city street, and for a while becomes a four-lane highway called Pyramid Way. The road passes through mile after mile of horse and cattle ranches; about 8 miles outside of Sparks the road drops back to a two-lane road that takes you along a high mountain plateau winding your way through mountain tops with few signs of development.

As you cross the mostly barren desert toward the lake, the area to the east includes the former Rocketdyne test sites where the rocket engines for the lunar lander were built and tested in the 1960s.

About 26 miles outside of Sparks you enter into the **Pyramid Lake Indian**

Reservation, past the ruins of Pyramid City, a silver mining boom camp of the 1870s. The Pyramid Lake Indian Reservation was created in 1859 in an effort to contain the Paiute. You can pick up fishing permits at the Pyramid Lake Store just after you enter the reservation; just past the store the road makes a sharp turn and you will have your first glimpse of the lake below. Eventually you will come to a pull-off with the view most visitors come for: Frémont's Pyramid.

There is no paved road that circles the lake, so you'll have to decide whether to continue up the western shore through Sutcliffe, or go southeast to Nixon on Route 446.

The Paiute tribe operates a fish hatchery for Pyramid Lake cutthroat trout and cui-ui at **Sutcliffe,** and informal tours are usually available. Call 476-0500 for information.

The road to Nixon meets up with Route 447 north, which follows the eastern shore of the lake from a distance. You will be rewarded with some starkly beautiful scenery, but you'll have to double back, unless you want to go the very, very long way around; there's hardly a settlement for hours in any direction.

Pyramid Lake is a remnant of ancient Lake Lahontan, which covered some 8,450 square miles in western Nevada at the time of the Ice Age. In caves and rock shelters along the shores of the lake, explorers have found evidence of a prehistoric people with a well-developed community life.

John C. Frémont came upon the lake on January 10, 1844, and named it for the pyramid-shaped island just off the east shore. Just south of the pyramid is Anahoe Island, which was established as a national wildlife refuge in 1913; today it is one of the largest white pelican nesting grounds in North America.

The road comes to a T near the shoreline of the lake, with Highway 445 continuing north a short distance to Sutcliffe, and 446 turning south along the shoreline of the lake toward Nixon. You might want to go north for a short distance to get a good view of the pyramid across the lake before turning back and descending to the lake on 446.

The shoreline features all kinds of strange rock formations; the first big one you come to as you head toward Nixon is called Indian Head. It looks more like a stone castle as you approach it, but look back over your shoulder to see a small outcropping of rock near the top to see where the rock gets its name.

If you take Route 447 south from Nixon toward Wadsworth along the Truckee River you can pick up Interstate 80 west back to Sparks and Reno. As you drop down on Route 447 you will be driving through the area of the **Pyramid Lake War of 1860.**

Although early relations between explorer John Frémont and the Paiutes at Pyramid Lake were peaceful, the increasing influx of whites created by the Comstock Bonanza brought problems. In May of 1860, several whites were found killed near Williams Station on the Carson River east of Carson City; the circumstances of their deaths was never fully explained, and historians say that the attack may have been retribution for the kidnapping and rape of several Indian women just before. Nevertheless, an "army" of more than 100 volunteers was gathered for retribution.

The men arrived at Wadsworth, about 15 miles south of Pyramid Lake on May 12, 1860, and marched into a trap set by the Paiutes; more than half of the men were killed. The battle began with a skillful ambush north of Nixon and continued along the plateau almost to the present site of Wadsworth. More white men died than in any prior white-Indian engagement in the far west.

A second, larger army of nearly 1,000 came back to the lake on June 2 and

RENO, VIRGINIA CITY, AND LAKE TAHOE

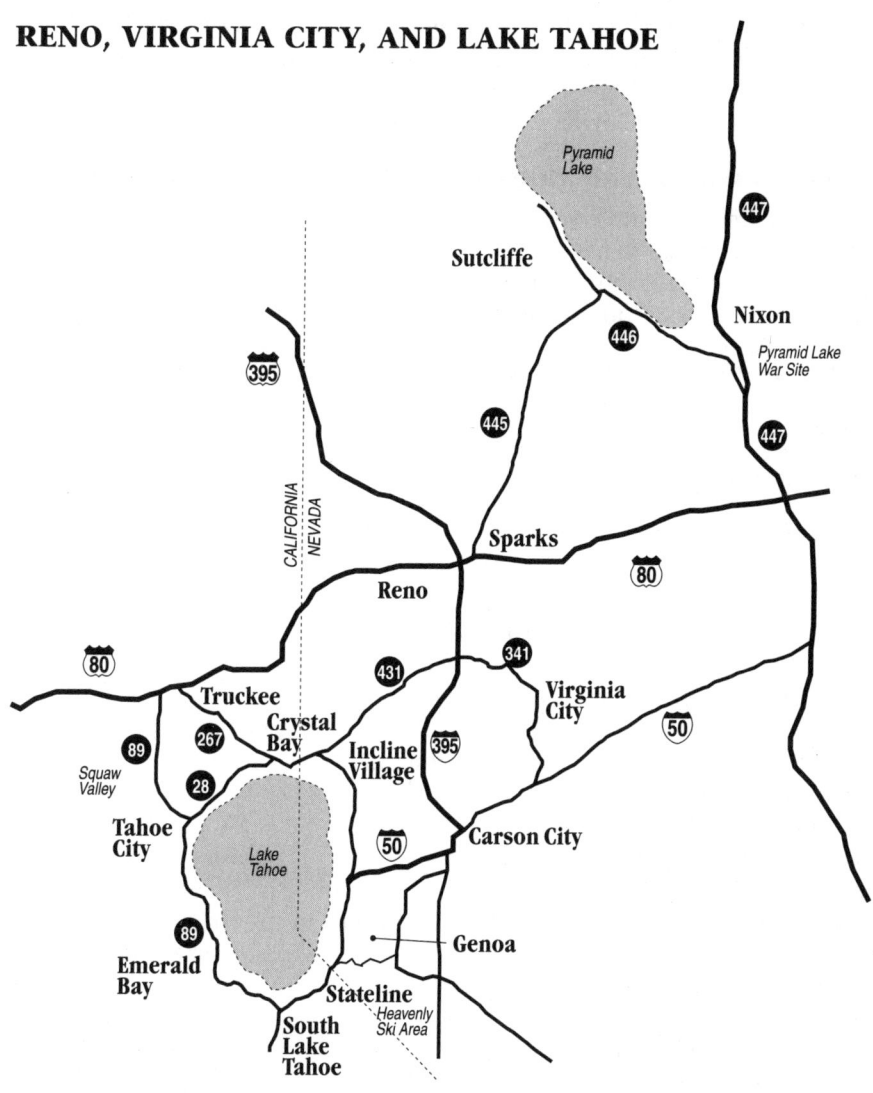

this time prevailed over the natives, killing 160 of them. Several hundred braves fought long enough to allow their women, children, and elders to escape. A forced peace treaty was negotiated ending the "war."

About a half mile further down past the historic marker for the Pyramid Lake War, you will come to the Numana Hatchery Visitors Center, which is operated by the Pyramid Lake Fisheries and the Pyramid Lake Paiute Tribe in cooperation with the Bureau of Indian Affairs. It is open daily from 9 to 11 A.M. and 1 to 3 P.M.

If you're up for a full day of exploring, you can continue on Route 447 past Interstate 80 to Silver Springs and pick up Route 50 west, which enters into the south end of the Comstock silver mining area and into Carson City. At Carson City you can head back north to Reno on Interstate 395 or cross the front range of the Sierra Nevadas on Route 50 to Lake Tahoe.

The trip to Pyramid Lake gives a fascinating glimpse of a portion of the Old West that has changed very little from the way it appeared at the time when Nevada and California were being settled.

II. The Jewel in the Mountains: South to Lake Tahoe

From Reno and Carson City there are three passages through the front range of the Sierra Nevadas to Lake Tahoe. All are spectacular, and each has its own appeal. Any road will be fine in summer and early fall; winter conditions can make driving treacherous as can spring melts and refreezes.

Trip 2: The Easy Way to South Lake Tahoe

Reno	*Zephyr Cove*
Glenbrook	*Edgewood*
Spooner Summit	*Stateline*
Cave Rock	

The easiest, and *almost* weatherproof route from Reno to Lake Tahoe is across Spooner Summit at midlake. Take Interstate 395 south out of Reno past Carson City for 35 miles and then turn right onto Route 50 toward the face of the mountains. From there it's 10 miles up and over Spooner Summit at 7,146 feet and down to the lake; continue 25 miles farther south through the Cave Rock Tunnel, Zephyr Cove, and Edgewood to Stateline.

Except in the worst of weather, these roads are kept clear of snow and ice and are well patrolled. The trip is about 62 miles, and about an hour and 15 minutes in good weather.

The first climb from Carson City on Highway 50 is a 6 percent grade for five or six miles, one of the most sustained climbs on a major road in this country.

On a stormy January day, each twist and turn in the road revealed a new winter sight. There was a blizzard underway at the top of distant peaks, light snow on the pass, huge snowbanks in the canyons, and even a few blue holes in the clouds overhead.

There's not much of a descent after Spooner Summit before you come to the Alpine level of Lake Tahoe. On my stormy-day visit, there were wind-whipped waves on the lake.

At the bottom of the grade where Route 50 meets the lake and turns south toward Stateline is **Glenbrook**, once the center of the logging industry that all but denuded the hills for miles around to serve the needs of the Comstock Mines and Virginia City. It was also the location of the first large, fancy hotel on the lake, the Glenbrook House.

Lumbering operations in Glenbrook began in 1861. By 1872, consolidation of flume systems in and around Clear Creek Canyon made it possible to float lumber and logs from **Spooner Summit** to Carson City and to eliminate wagon hauling over the narrow and treacherous mountain roads. A small rail line ran from Glenbrook to Spooner Summit and the top of the flume.

Logging began first on the east shore of the lake and moved across the west shore later where the trees were logged and dropped by flumes into the lake and then towed across by a tugboat to the mill at Glenbrook.

Depletion of the timber at Lake Tahoe and the slowdown of mining in the Comstock ended lumbering in the area in 1898, after the Glenbrook operation had taken 750 million board feet of lumber and 500,000 cords of wood from the Tahoe Basin forest.

The highway takes a short detour at **Cave Rock** and passes through a pair of tunnels through a gigantic volcanic rock. Cave Rock had been a place of religious significance to the native Washoes, who believed that the cave at the site was the home of an avenging Giant of the Sierras. Much of the cave was destroyed with the construction of the road at the turn of the century.

Tahoe Tessie, the supposed mysterious monster of the deep, is said to live in an underwater cavern beneath the cave—that is, when she is not on vacation at Loch Ness.

By the way, there have been enough reported sightings of an unusual creature in the waters of Lake Tahoe to have drawn some scientific interest; some scientists believe the "monster" may be a large lake sturgeon, a particularly ugly fish known to have existed in area waters. In 1888, a seven-foot sturgeon was caught at Pyramid Lake above Reno; Pyramid Lake is connected to Lake Tahoe by the Truckee River.

Zephyr Cove draws its name from the winds that often sweep across the lake. In summertime, the beach, marina, and stables are popular attractions; the glass-bottom *M.S. Dixie* paddlewheel is based there. In the winter, it is a takeoff point for snowmobile tours, sleigh rides, and cross-country ski trails.

Pull in at the **Visitors Center** and the **Tahoe Douglas Chamber of Commerce**, which is just past Zephyr Cove on the mountain side of the road, to mine a treasure load of brochures, coupons, and maps.

Things have changed greatly in **Edgewood**, a residential community just outside of Stateline. In the 1860s, it was the site of **Friday's Station**, a waystation on the Pony Express route established by Friday Burke and Big Jim Small; it was the home station of "Pony Bob" Haslam, one of the most famous of the Express riders. The toll booth in front of Friday's Station was one of the most profitable such franchises at the height of the reverse migration from California to the Comstock, bringing in as much as $1,500 per day.

The Pony Express was a privately owned and operated courier service, sort of the Federal Express of its day. The service, which charged $5 per ounce for letters, stretched from St. Joseph, Missouri, to Sacramento, California. There were about 75 way stations where horses were swapped. As famous as is the Pony Service, it is interesting to note that it lasted less than two years, put out of business by the coming of the transcontinental railroad and the telegraph.

The restored Friday's Station Inn—now a private residence—still stands across the highway from today's watering hole, the Edgewood Golf Course. The golf resort is considered one of the top public courses in the country.

Next stop is **Stateline**.

Trip 3: To the Top of the Lake and Down the Eastern Shore

Reno	*Ponderosa Ranch*
Mount Rose	*Sand Harbor Beach*
Incline Village	*Stateline*
Crystal Bay	

The views keep getting better and better as you follow the switchbacks on Mount Rose Highway. This is the most direct route to the north end of Lake Tahoe, and the slower, scenic route to the eastern shore and the south end of the lake.

Take Interstate 395 south from Reno about 11 miles to the intersection with Highway 431 and 341. (If you turn left onto Route 341, you will climb Geiger Grade into Virginia City; see Trip 6 for details on that must-see tour.) Instead, turn right onto Highway 431 toward the imposing face of the mountains.

At the intersection of Interstate 395 and the Mount Rose Highway and a bit further up the approach road to the mountains, you will find several places where you can buy snow chains for your car if necessary. You can also rent ski equipment, tubes, and snowboards before you get to the ski areas. Ski reports can be heard on several radio stations in the area, including 590 AM.

The Mount Rose Highway presents a 25-mile, twist-and-turn climb up Mount Rose. The road reaches an altitude of 8,911 feet; **Mount Rose** itself continues to a summit elevation of 10,338 feet.

The road includes several switchbacks hanging out into space and very few guardrails. If you have a little bit of nerve and a decent car with a good set of tires, and most important, dry pavement, the Mount Rose Highway is a quite exciting approach to the north end of the lake.

Near the top of the highway, just before you get to the Mount Rose ski area, sneak a peak back to your left for a view that extends all the way north to Reno and south toward Carson City.

Try to put yourself back in the days before there were cars and a paved road. Imagine what it was like to lay out this trail through the tall trees and along the mountain ridges. And then think about what it was like to go up the trail by foot, by horse, or by wagon.

Galena Creek Park, on the slopes of the mountain, includes picnic areas, hiking trails, and other facilities for summer and winter recreation. The park is run by the Washoe County Department of Parks & Recreation; call 849-2511 for information.

Mount Rose is named after Jacob Rose, who exploited diggings in Gold Canyon and brought a large crew of Chinese workers to the area in 1856 to build a water ditch.

A bit further on is the **Mount Rose/Slide Mountain** ski area. The two facilities, which combined into a single resort several years ago, has the region's highest base elevation at 8,250 feet, which is a pretty good guarantor of dependable snow. There is a 1,450 foot vertical drop with 27 trails served by a half dozen lifts. Call 849-0704 for information.

Still further into the mountain pass is the proposed location for a large new ski complex, the Galena Resort, which may open in coming years if it can get past challenges from environmentalists. At the highest point on the road is a turnoff to the left to **Mount Rose Campground.** The road begins a gradual descent and about six miles later you will enter **Incline Village** at the northeast corner of Lake Tahoe.

At Incline Village, bear left onto State 28 south for 14 miles to where it joins with Route 50 south into Stateline.

Incline Village was wilderness until the mid-1800s when loggers began using its timber to shore up the rich silver mines of Virginia City some 20 miles away on the other side of the easternmost mountain range. The mountain-sides were stripped of nearly all hardwood, and the sawdust and debris from sawmills choked many of the creeks, all but destroying the trout population of Lake Tahoe for decades.

On the mountain at Incline Village, behind the Ponderosa Ranch, lie the remnants of the **Great Incline of the Sierra Nevada,** a gigantic machine that now exists only in memory. Completed in 1880, this 4,000-foot-long lift was constructed by the Sierra Nevada Wood and Lumber Company. A steam-powered cable railway pulled cordwood and lumber 1,800 feet up the double tracks to the top on canted cars.

At the top of the mountain, the wood was automatically dumped into a V-flume and tumbled down to the Washoe Valley where it was loaded onto wagons for use in the mines of the Comstock. At the height of the enterprise, 300 cords of wood a day were moved from the mill at what is now **Mill Creek.**

A small settlement was established in 1884, but the area did not gain much attention until 1927 when the first casino was built in **Crystal Bay.**

The **Cal-Neva Lodge** at Crystal Bay is famous for its swimming pool, which sits atop the state border, allowing swimmers to start in California and end up in Nevada where there is, of course, a casino.

Nearby, off Reservoir Drive, is the **Crystal Bay Fire Lookout,** which offers a spectacular view of the lake from the north shore.

The development of the area for condominiums and homes also began in the 1960s and included a spectacular 18-hole championship golf course designed

Incline Village/Crystal Bay Visitors and Convention Bureau Lodging Information. (800) 468-2463.
Reno/Sparks Visitor's Authority (800) 752-1177.

Reruns. The original *Bonanza* series ran for 13 years on network television in the United States and has been seen in 85 other countries. It was the first major series to be regularly broadcast in color, making use of the area country for many of its settings.

by Robert Trent Jones Sr. and the development of a skiing area called Ski Incline. The ski area, greatly expanded, is now called Diamond Peak.

Other major construction included what is now the **Hyatt Regency Lake Tahoe Resort and Casino**, a second golf course, beach facilities, and the Lakeside Tennis Resort.

By the way, Crystal Bay was not named after the clear waters of Lake Tahoe, but rather after lumberman George Iweis Crystal who owned much of the area in the 1860s.

In the summer, special events at Incline Village include the **Shakespeare at Sand Harbor** festival, with plays presented from the end of July through August. Call (800) 468-2463 for information.

The **Ponderosa Ranch**, the mythical setting of the Cartwright family made famous in the *Bonanza* television series, has been brought to life in Incline Village in a mix of original artifacts from the show and re-creations in a historic setting along the shores of Lake Tahoe at an elevation of 6,350 feet.

The main attraction is the Cartwright home, the actual set used to film interior scenes with Ben Cartwright and his three sons, Hoss, Little Joe, and Adam. Visitors are taken on a guided tour, which includes antique furnishings and Hop Sing's kitchen, where the table is all set for Ben and his boys.

Just outside the home is a western theme park, including a general store, gambling hall, old-time photo parlor, and numerous shops. Other attractions include a shooting gallery, antique autos, one of the country's largest collections of farm and ranch equipment, a western memorabilia museum, and an 1870 church where old-fashioned weddings are celebrated. Children can visit a petting farm, gold panning slough, and Hoss' Mystery Mine.

Each morning from Memorial Day to Labor Day, visitors are invited to take the Haywagon Breakfast Ride, a tour that climbs through a rich pine forest to a scenic point high above Lake Tahoe. There an all-you-can-eat breakfast of scrambled eggs, sausage, pancakes, juice, and coffee is provided.

More than 300,000 people annually visit the Ponderosa Ranch. In 1994, the admission rate for adults was $8.50, and the rate was $5.50 for children ages 5 to 11. The Haywagon Breakfast Ride is an additional $2 per person. Hours are 9:30 A.M. until 5 P.M. daily from May to October.

Sand Harbor Beach State Recreational Area, about five miles south of Incline Village, offers a small but pretty sand beach on an inlet of Lake Tahoe. Rocks are piled on top of each other reaching out into the lake like little jetties. The beach sits at the base of an almost sheer cliff mountainside. In summer, there is an entrance fee of $2; the charge to launch a boat is $5.

Follow the outlines of the lake toward **Spooner Lake** where you will meet up with Route 50. Swimming is not recommended in Spooner Lake because of harmless but annoying leeches. Continue on Route 50 south through the Cave Rock Tunnel to Zephyr Cove and into Stateline.

The regular traffic to and from the Mount Rose ski area and the top of the lake and other points in California to Reno will keep the roads clear except in the worst weather but the mountain crossing here is twice as long as the one at Spooner Summit in midlake. The trip is about 66 miles, and about an hour-and-a-half in good weather.

Trip 4: Driving the Route of the Pony Express

Reno   *Kingsbury Grade*
Genoa   *Stateline*

My favorite approach to South Lake Tahoe is a piece of cake in good weather, a white knuckle trip in ordinary winter weather, and impossible in a storm. But what a ride!

Take Interstate 395 out of Reno past Carson City for 46 miles (11 miles past the point where Route 50 branches off). Just past the tiny Douglas County Airport, look for the signs to the historic settlement of **Genoa**; turn right toward the wall of mountains.

Genoa was the first permanent settlement in Nevada, established by one of Brigham Young's traders in 1849 and originally called **Mormon Station**. It was located at the base of the front range of the Sierra Nevadas in a meadow fed by a small creek that came down from the mountains. At the station, they sold supplies—brought all the way from Salt Lake City—to travelers preparing to go up and over the mountains westward to California.

For a short time, the little outpost was the most important point between Salt Lake City and Placerville, on the road to San Francisco. In 1854, Mormon Station was renamed as Genoa (pronounced jin-no'-ah) and became the seat of government of Carson County of the Utah Territory. In 1857, most of the Mormons were recalled to Salt Lake City to bolster Brigham Young in a confrontation against federal troops over local government; they mostly abandoned their settlement in place.

In 1857, the history of the area changed dramatically with the discovery of gold in a placer deposit—in the runout of a stream—on what was to become known as Gold Creek, a tributary of the Carson River near the village now called Gold Hill. Significant amounts of gold in rock outcroppings were found in January of 1859 a bit to the north on Sun Mountain, sparking a gold rush; the boom took off when miners realized that the "blue mud" that stood in the way of the gold and was treated as a nuisance actually contained significant amounts of silver.

The result was a reverse migration, with many miners returning across the Sierra Nevadas from California, through Genoa, and on to the Gold Creek area. For a while, the **Johnson Cutoff Trail** (now known as the Pioneer Trail above the present location of Stateline, at the southern end of Lake Tahoe) became the most heavily traveled highway in the West.

That same year the first territorial legislature met in Genoa in 1859 and drafted a demand to separate the region from the Utah Territory.

Most of the town, including the original Mormon Fort, was destroyed by fire in 1910.

There's a small display in the **Genoa Courthouse Museum** on Main Street. The building served as the justice center from 1865 through 1916, and as a school from 1916 through 1956. It is open daily from mid-May to mid-October; call 782-4325 for information.

Displays at the Courthouse include the Buckaroo Room with ranching and farming items from the early 19th century, including snowshoes for a horse. A blacksmith shop, located in the former jail, includes tools and a bellows that once belonged to Colonel John Reese, the founder of Genoa. A period classroom includes old maps, textbooks, and furniture.

For general information on events, call the Genoa Town Board at 782-8696.

There are nearly 30 buildings on the National Register of Historic Places in the tiny settlement, including the **Genoa Saloon**, claimed as Nevada's oldest bar.

On nearby State 206 (Foothill Road) is **Mormon Station Historic State Park**, with a museum and restored trading post open from about May 1 to October 15. Call 782-2590 for information.

At Genoa, turn left and follow the base of the mountains on Foothill Road until you come to Route 207 (Kingsbury Grade). **Kingsbury Grade** was built about 1860 as the route of the Pony Express; it was also the principal path for the Bonanza traffic from the west to Virginia City.

Head west up and over Daggett Pass (elevation 7,334 feet) and then descend into Stateline through Haines Canyon, dropping about 3,000 feet over six miles. This path should take a bit less than two hours.

The Kingsbury Grade is a shorter but somewhat more treacherous pass over the front range than Route 50 over the Spooner Summit. You'll proceed up an incredible set of switchbacks on a two-lane highway with what looks like a dangerously frail guardrail between you and the abyss.

At some points, you can see three or four stepped levels of the road above or below.

Trip 5: Into the Olympic Valley and Donner Lake

Reno	*Squaw Valley*
Kings Beach	*Truckee*
Tahoe Vista	*Donner Lake*
Carnelian Bay	*Verdi*
Tahoe City	*Boomtown*
Alpine Meadows	

Take Interstate 395 south from Reno about 11 miles to the intersection with Highway 431 and 341. Turn right onto Highway 431 toward the imposing face of the mountains and go up and over the summit.

Kings Beach, across the border into California, sits at the absolute "top" of the lake and affords a spectacular view down its length. On a clear day—

and there are many—you will be able to see the Heavenly ski resort 22 miles away, towering over the casinos of Stateline. Kings Beach, which includes some lovely beaches and marinas for boating and other water sports, was self-named by Joe King, a gambler who supposedly won the property in a poker game in 1925.

Just past Kings Beach, Route 267 branches off toward Truckee. At that intersection is a popular snowmobiling course on the nine-hole Old Brockway Golf Course.

Skiers and tourists can take a six-mile sidetrip on Route 267 to explore **Northstar-at-Tahoe**, a resort complex that includes a ski area, golf course, stables, and more. Northstar is a legitimate ski hill with a 2,200-foot vertical drop.

The next settlement westward around the lake is **Tahoe Vista**, which overlooks Agate Bay. It was named after a spectacular hotel of the early 1900s, which sat up on a hill overlooking the lake. Tahoe Vista was also one of the first subdivisions on the lake in 1911, a period when speculators almost succeeded in ruining the pristine wilderness forever. In a strange turn of fate, Tahoe Vista's subdivision may have failed because of the notoriety attached to one of its first land buyers, Miss Cherry de St. Maurice, an infamous Sacramento madam.

Although much land was sold in small lots, the region's wilderness was preserved in part by the stock market crash and the Great Depression, which caused many of the purchase contracts to go unpaid in the 1930s.

Carnelian Bay takes its name from the reddish semiprecious stones called carnelian, which were found on its beach by the Whitney Survey party in 1860s. An early establishment there was Dr. Bourne's Hygenic Establishment, a health resort later renamed as the Carnelian Springs Sanatoria. Dr. Bourne also tried to rename Lake Tahoe as Lake Sanatoria, an attempt which thankfully failed.

Tahoe City was established as a lumbering camp and as a port for freight traffic on the lake. Today it sits at the northern end of man's intrusion on the beauty of the lake.

A small city at about 5,000 year-round population, Tahoe City is built at the site of a dam first built across the mouth of the Truckee River, the only outlet from Lake Tahoe. The passage over the river is called the **Fanny Bridge**; it supposedly draws its name from the outstretched posteriors of those fishing for cutthroat trout along its railings. Alongside the bridge is the **Gatekeeper's Cabin and Museum**, which includes artifacts of the early days of Lake Tahoe development, items from ancient Indian history, and items from the 1960 Winter Olympics held at nearby Squaw Valley. The cabin was used from about 1909 until it was destroyed by fire in 1978; the museum occupies an exact replica built by the North Lake Tahoe Historical Society. Call (916) 583-1762 for information.

The dam was first built in 1870 as part of a plan to drain some of the lake's waters to San Francisco through a tunnel to be bored through the Sierras. This was before environmental concerns, of course, but the tunnel was never built. One result of the damming of the outlet, though, was to raise the level of

Someone has to do it.
Yes, that really is a U.S. Coast Guard station just north of Tahoe City at Lake Forest Park. Because of its size and the fact that it is an interstate navigable waterway, the whole of the lake falls under the supervision of the federal Coast Guard in what must be one of the most desirable assignments in the service.

the lake by several feet, changing its outlines in many places.

There were actually several efforts to drain the lake for the use of San Francisco, including a proposal in 1900 to construct a system that would divert from 30 to 100 million gallons of Tahoe water per day. A second plan in 1903 called for a tunnel under the Sierras to send the water into the Rubicon branch of the American River, which leads into San Francisco. The final—and almost successful effort—was supported by the U.S. Reclamation Service and would have sent the water into the dry Nevada desert for irrigation and power needs. Luckily, bureaucracy stalled the plan when the chief forester for the Department of Agriculture held up the project for years on something close to environmental objections.

In 1871, the Grand Central Hotel was opened at Tahoe City, setting a new level of luxury at the lake. The completion of a narrow-gauge spur railroad in 1900 from Tahoe City to Truckee, where the transcontinental main line passed, established the area as an important gateway to Lake Tahoe.

The Big Tree in the center of town is a big tree, celebrated as a landmark and town Christmas Tree for more than a century. The **Watson Cabin Living Museum** is within a small, authentic Lake Tahoe cabin. Nearby are several small shopping areas, the Boatworks Mall, the Roundhouse Mall, and the Lighthouse Shopping Center.

To go to Alpine Meadows and Squaw Valley turn left onto Highway 89 at Tahoe City and enter the Olympic Valley.

On your left about six miles up the road you will come to the **Alpine Meadows** ski area. Though not as well known or anywhere near as large as Heavenly Valley to the south or Squaw Valley just north over the mountain range, Alpine Meadows is still one big hill full of snow with about 100 runs.

A few miles farther along on Route 89 is the approach road to **Squaw Valley** with its Tower of Nations and the Olympic rings, a remnant of the VIII Winter Olympic Games held here in 1960.

The ski resort, with 33 lifts including a 150-passenger gondola and more than 100 runs, is set in a bowl of mountains including KT-22 at 8,200 feet, Emigrant Peak at 8,700 feet, Squaw Peak at 8,900 feet, and Granite Chief at 9,050 feet.

Summer activities include arts and writers conferences and a world class golf course.

After it leaves Squaw Valley, Route 89 will meet up with Interstate 80 just west of Truckee.

Truckee presents an interesting freeze-frame of the Wild Old West in its historic downtown. More than 100 of the structures in and around Commercial Row date from the 19th century, and at least one—the Truckee Hotel—date from Truckee's boom lumber and railroading time in 1871. Another important industry was ice harvesting. Cakes of ice were cut from rivers and lakes and stored in warehouses; Truckee ice was shipped east and west for hundreds of miles by railroad until the 1920s. Truckee Ice was considered a delicacy in San Francisco.

Canopied wooden walkways are maintained in some of the sections. Jibboom Street, one street in from Commercial, was the active red-light district of Truckee and also houses the Truckee Jail, in use from 1875 until 1964. The streets are not quite as redolent of history as Virginia City, but worth a visit if you're on the north end of the lake.

The town received its name in honor of a Paiute Indian guide who helped a party migrating west across the Sierras; Truckee was a chief and father of Winnemucca. The westward party named the lake they found Mountain Lake; it was called Truckee's Lake in 1846 when the ill-fated Donner Party was stranded there for the winter.

Sites to see in downtown Truckee include the famed **Rocking Stone**, a 17-ton boulder that was balanced atop a larger rock and was used by ancient Indians as much as 15,000 years ago as a place to grind meal and by later generations as a ceremonial location. Though first thought to be a natural occurrence, more recent studies have concluded that the upper stone may have been chiseled to serve the purpose of a grinding place thousands of years ago. The stone was enclosed within a tower in 1893, and again in the 1950s; it has been cemented into a fixed position for safety's sake.

A plaque on Front Street records the actions of the **601**, a vigilante group from the Wild West days. Across Commercial Row is the **Southern Pacific Depot**, which dates to 1896.

From Truckee, you can head east back to Reno or take a short jog about four miles west on Donner Pass Road to **Donner Lake** and the Donner Memorial State Park.

The story of the Donner Party is one of the most famous tragedies of the American cultural consciousness.

Two families, the Donners and the Reeds, made up the largest portion of a group of 87 emigrants who left Sangamon County, Illinois, in 1846 for California.

Under the leadership of George Donner, they made a series of bad decisions and mistakes in choosing trails across the Great Salt Lake in Utah and then the Sierra Nevadas. They were trapped by unusually heavy snows in the mountains above Reno in October and were forced to camp for the winter at a small lake about 13 miles northwest of Lake Tahoe. They ran out of food and other supplies, and some of the members of the group resorted to cannibalism in order to survive—those few who would talk about their experience afterward claimed they ate only those who had died naturally from the harsh conditions.

Come spring, 47 of the 87 emigrants were eventually brought to California by rescue parties, traveling over what is now known as Donner Pass.

A memorial and museum about the ill-fated Donner Party expedition is located at **Donner Memorial State Park.** The park includes the Emigrant Monument with a statue representing the Donner party atop a 22-foot-high pedestal; the pedestal represents the depth of snow recorded in and around the lake that terrible winter of 1846–'47.

The park is a strange mix of pleasant surroundings and awful memories, a sense of history and a connection to the present in the form of Interstate 80, which passes by a few hundred feet away with a steady stream of trucks thundering by.

But if you walk down the little trail that leads from the museum, you enter into a much quieter place, an area that hints at the terrifying loneliness of this place in 1846. You'll come to a large house-size rock with a plaque that reads, "The face of this rock formed the north end and the fireplace of the Murphy cabin. General Stephen W. Kearny on June 22, 1847, buried under the middle of the cabin the bodies found in the vicinity." There is a listing of several dozen names including seven "Donners."

Kearny, by the way, went on to become commander of the Army of the West in the Mexican War and served as military commander of California.

The small **Emigrant Museum** at the park is open year-round and includes a selection of books about the Donner Party and the area; the campgrounds are open from Memorial Day into October. Admission to the museum is $2 for adults and $1 for children ages 6 to 17. Call (916) 587-3841 for information.

As you head east back into Nevada toward Reno, you will pass through the former logging boomtown of **Verdi.** The town grew in the early 1860s around a logging mill cutting wood for railroad ties for the Central Pacific Railroad and a bridge across the Truckee. The settlement was named in honor of Italian opera composer Giuseppe Verdi, who was at his peak of fame at the time. Verdi is claimed by some to be the site of the first train robbery in the West. Bandits held up a CP train in 1870, making off with some $40,000 in payroll money for the Yellow Jacket mine. The robbers were eventually collared in mine shafts on nearby Peavine Peak above the town; all but $3,000 of the cash was recovered.

The town was kept alive as a rest stop on U.S. 40, and later the town center moved a bit east to serve Interstate '80; that new area is called **Boomtown.** The Boomtown Hotel Casino, just off the interstate, has an indoor miniature carousel and an arcade with 100 games.

A round trip from Reno over Mount Rose to Crystal Bay and through the Olympic Valley should take about three hours.

III. The Mines of the Bonanza

Trip 6: Frozen in Time

Reno	*Silver City*
Virginia City	*Carson City*
Gold Hill	

Follow I-395 south out of Reno and drive to the intersection with Highway 431 and 341, about 10 miles from downtown Reno. Turn left onto Route 341 and begin the slow but steady climb up Geiger Grade into Virginia City.

When you finally make it up the hill you will find yourself in **Virginia City** itself; there is no mistaking where you are, either. Every western movie ever made included a Hollywood version of this place. *See Chapter 24 for more details about Virginia City.*

After you've visited the wonders of Virginia City, continue on Route 341 to the point where it splits: take the right fork, marked as Route 342, to see the ruins of **Gold Hill** and **Silver City**, two of the mining outposts of the time. The road will soon join up with Route 341 again, which will eventually come to a T at Route 50. Make a right turn, west.

Route 50 will come to another T, at Interstate 395. Head south for a short jog to explore **Carson City**, or head north for the rapid return to Reno.

On your way back to Reno, you may want to branch off of the interstate at Route 429 to visit the historic **Bowers Mansion**, constructed by one of the original discoverers of the Comstock Lode, Lemuel Sanford Bowers. Bowers' new wife Eilley Orrum spent what was at the time a fortune— at least $200,000—on building and furnishing the house in 1864. Her husband, though, did not live to enjoy the house much, dying of miner's lung disease in 1868; by that time, too, the Gold Hill mine had gone bust and there was not much money left for Mrs. Bowers; she tried running the mansion as a hotel and resort, but eventually saw the mansion sold at public auction. For information on the mansion, call 849-0201.

Weather or not. On a January trip to Virginia City, I learned firsthand the variations in weather in and around the Sierra Nevadas.

A sudden, severe storm had passed through the Lake Tahoe region overnight, dumping 27 inches of snow at Squaw Valley and blanketing most of the other mountains in the area. Interstate 80 was closed at Donner Summit, and Route 50 was limited to vehicles with snow chains. As I set out from Reno there was a cold rain in the valley, but I could see snow falling in the hills.

As I began to drive up Geiger Grade, the rain turned to ice pellets and then to snow near the summit. Virginia City wore a light coat of white; across the broad valley I could see a blizzard in progress somewhere around Incline Village.

The trip from Reno to Virginia City is about 45 minutes. To make the full tour from Reno to Virginia City, continuing on to Gold Hill and to I-395 at Carson City before returning to Reno, allow about two hours. Add extra time to visit Virginia City, Carson City, and the Bowers Mansion.

IV. North from Lake Tahoe

The western side of the lake offers some of the most spectacular waterside views and the older, more historic communities. Much of the development of the west shore came from California money, with San Francisco's high society setting up camp along the lake.

Trip 7: North Along the Western Shore

Stateline	*Meeks Bay*
Bijou	*Rubicon Bay*
Camp Richardson	*Sugar Pine Point State Park*
Tallac Historic Site	*Homewood*
Fallen Leaf Lake	*Idlewild*
Emerald Bay	*Tahoe City*

West of Stateline on the California side is the little community of **Bijou.** It draws its name from a lovely little beach along the lake; don't look for the strand, though: it's gone. In 1910, the lake's level was raised by the construction of a dam at its outlet near Tahoe City, and the beach was drowned.

Bijou now includes two marinas, including the home of the *Tahoe Queen* paddlewheel, which makes cruises year-round.

The **Osgood Toll House** near Rufus Allen Boulevard is the oldest building in Lake Tahoe. Dating to 1859, it once served as a tollhouse on the Bonanza Route near Meyers; it was moved to the city for preservation.

Along the mountain side of Route 50 is a city park that includes the **Lake Tahoe Arts Center** and the **Lake Tahoe Historical Society Museum.** The museum includes old photographs of the valley; for information, call (916) 541-5458.

Back on Route 50 at the very base of the lake is **Al Tahoe,** a turn-of-the-century subdivision of cottages and campgrounds. It draws its unusual name from developer Al Sprague who named his hotel and the land around it after himself and the lake. A small beach meets the water.

Continue on Route 50 to the Y where Route 50 continues westward toward Sacramento and Route 89 heads in a northerly direction around the lake as far as Tahoe City and from there to Truckee and Donner Pass. Bear right onto 89, and the trappings of the tourist zone fall away quickly.

Camp Richardson, the first settlement you'll come across as you head north on Emerald Bay Road, was established in the 1880s as a logging camp; a narrow-gauge steam railroad line ran from the site. It later became an early resort along the shores of Lake Tahoe. Today it offers a large campground, marina, and horse stables.

Just past the camp is the **Tallac Historic Site,** a U.S. Forest Service Preserve that includes the sites of nearly a dozen former grand residences and the location of the fabled Tallac Hotel. The Tallac, opulent for its turn-of-the-century time, was known as the "Saratoga of the Pacific." The **Tallac Point House** was built in the 1870s; in 1880, it was taken over by Elias "Lucky" Baldwin, who expanded it into a luxurious resort that included a ballroom with a spring-mounted dance floor and croquet and tennis courts; guests could also take steamer excursions from the hotel. The hotel was torn down in 1916.

Among the estates open to the public at Tallac are the **Baldwin, Pope** and **Valhalla** estates. The Pope estate dates to 1894. It was expanded in 1899 to become one of the most spectacular in the area; it now serves as the visitors center for Tallac. The Baldwin home was built in 1921 by Dextra Baldwin, granddaughter of Lucky Baldwin. The Valhalla estate dates from 1924; it is used for community events. Special events held at the site include a Renaissance Festival each June and a Native American Festival in August. For information, call the Tallac Historic Site at (916) 541-5227.

The **Kiva Beach Recreation Area** offers one of the nicest beaches on the lake, set in a nearly untouched pine grove. The U.S. Forest Service Visitors Center on Kiva Beach Road offers trail guides and an interesting display about the geology and

> **Park Information.** For information on California State Parks and advance reservations at some facilities, call (800) 444-7275.

wildlife of the region. Nearby is an outdoor amphitheater where slide shows and other presentations are made in summer.

Several short interpretive trails branch off from the visitors center at Kiva. They include the **Rainbow Trail** that leads through a mountain meadow to the **Stream Profile Chamber** where you can look through an underwater window into a salmon spawning pool. The **Lake of the Sky Trail** descends to the lakeshore, while the **Trail of the Washoe** climbs a small section of the hill across the road from the visitors center.

Across the road is **Mount Tallac**, at 9,735 feet, the tallest mountain directly on the lake itself. On the northeastern face of the mountain is a cross-shaped indentation that is called the "Snowcross" when filled with the snows of winter.

If it weren't for the overshadowing glories of Lake Tahoe, **Fallen Leaf Lake** might be world famous as a spectacular alpine lake in the Sierra Nevadas. As it is, this is a side trip well worth taking on a tour of the California side.

Fallen Leaf Lake is three miles long and a mile wide, with depths up to 418 feet. The Fallen Leaf Lodge and surrounding cabins, dating back to the 1910s, are now privately owned. A boathouse and marina are opposite the lodge, and the lake is a prime fishing area. Hiking trails—some of them quite isolated—lead into some even more remote and smaller lakes including Azure and Heather.

There are two resorts and marinas and several campgrounds at the lake, as well as the trailheads of a number of hiking trails that lead into the Desolation Wilderness.

The lake, at 6,377 feet, is about 100 feet higher than Lake Tahoe. The waters are fairly cold for swimming most of the year, warming up to a tolerable level by the end of summer. The lake is open to fishing year-round.

To reach the lake, turn left onto Fallen Leaf Lake Road. The lake lies at the end of the road, about five miles in; it may not be accessible in winter.

There's an even more remote set of lakes on the mountainside above: **Upper Angora Lake** and **Lower Angora Lake**. They draw their names from a flock of Angora sheep tended by an early resident near the turn of the century. Today you will find the **Angora Lake Resort**. There are a few cabins for rent; call (916) 541-2092 for information.

To reach Angora Lakes, start on Fallen Leaf Lake Road and take the first left and then the first right. You will come to the Angora Fire Lookout at 7,290 feet; continue on the dirt road until you come to a parking lot. A half-mile trail continues to the resort.

Heaven's Gate. The state has a gate across the road just short of Emerald Bay that closes off Route 89 from time to time when the danger of snow avalanches or rockslides is high, or when the road is actually blocked. If the road is closed, there is no real alternative other than to backtrack and take Route 50 around the eastern side of the lake.

Information about trails in the Fallen Leaf Lake area can be found at the visitors center on Highway 89 near Fallen Leaf Lake Road. Call (916) 573-2674.

North of Tallac, the road begins to twist and climb, finally revealing the spectacular **Cascade Lake** and even-more spectacular **Emerald Bay**.

Cascade Lake, on the mountain side of the road, was the setting for several well-loved motion pictures, including *Rose Marie* with Nelson Eddy and Jeanette McDonald. The lake is named for White Cloud Falls at its southwest corner; mountain streams plunge 100 feet into the lake. The falls are usually at their fullest in the spring as the snow melts; in winter, the stream and the lake itself are often frozen. Visitors to the lake have included writers Mark Twain, John Muir, and John Steinbeck.

You'll know you've reached Emerald Bay when you hear a collective "Wow" from everyone in your car; it's an automatic reaction to one of the most spectacular sights in the West. The road approaches the southern edge of the bay and then circles 180 degrees around it; there are several spots to stop and take a picture.

In the mouth of the bay is a tiny island that holds a tiny one-room "tea house" built in the 1930s during another of the periodic tourist booms around the lake.

If you can take your eyes away from the view of the bay to the right, look to the left to see the foothills of Desolation Wilderness, some 60,000 acres of, well, desolate wilderness. Several rough roads and hiking trails lead off into the hills. They are not for amateurs and often inaccessible in winter; check with park rangers for conditions.

At the north end of the bay is a parking lot at the head of a steep mile-long trail that descends to the shoreline of the lake and **Vikingsholm**, another treasure of the Tahoe Valley. The 38-room stone structure, built in 1929 by Lora Josephine Moore Knight, a wealthy socialite, is a replica of a 1,200-year-old Viking castle. Actually, Mrs. Knight had planned to bring back fabulous antiquities themselves from Norway and Sweden, but the Scandinavian governments declined to allow them to be removed and instead expensive replicas were made.

Some 200 workmen were brought to Lake Tahoe in the spring of 1929, and the house was completed by the end of that summer. The estimated cost of Vikingsholm, in 1929 dollars, was $500,000.

There are two towers with turrets; part of the building is covered, in Viking style, with sod roofs that bloom with wildflowers in the spring. Inside, the castle is filled with antique and reproduction furnishings from Norway and other Scandinavian countries. The beams in the ceiling of the living room are intricately carved with dragon heads.

Vikingsholm is now managed by the state, and tours are conducted in summer months, generally from July 1 to Labor Day. There is a $2 admission fee for adults and $1 for children. For information, call (916) 525-7277 or 541-3030.

The Rubicon Trail, a four-mile hiking path, connects to the **D. L. Bliss State Park** at the north end of the lake in **Meeks Bay**. Some tour boats pull up at a dock near the castle, and private boats can also approach Vikingsholm from the lake.

The state park includes 1,237 acres of forests and a sand beach at **Rubicon Bay**. Naturalist programs are offered in the summer, and the park is open from mid-June through mid-September. There is a daily use fee. In the summer, parking is extremely limited at Bliss Park, with only 25 $5 day passes sold per day; the lot is usually filled by 10 A.M. For information, call (916) 525-7277.

The 2,000-acre **Sugar Pine Point State Park** runs from Sugar Pine Point on the lake across the highway and up General Creek into Desolation Wilderness and the Tahoe National Forest. The park includes many majestic sugar pines, some as tall as 200 feet. Down near the lake is the Ehrman Mansion, a 1903 estate that was one of the social centers of the West Shore in the Roaring '20s.

Summer hiking trails, including the Dolder Nature Trail, become nordic ski trails in the winter.

The **Homewood Ski Area** extends to within feet of the highway at Homewood, with a marina on the lake side of the road. North of the ski area is a seaplane base for tourist flights and charters.

Idlewild, just below Tahoe City, was developed in the 1890s as a colony of the well-to-do from San Francisco.

Just south of the Idlewild, you'll pass the imposing stone walls of **Fleur du Lac** (Flower of the Lake), built in 1939 for wealthy industrialist Henry Kaiser. There was a fabulous stone mansion surrounded by six cottages intended for the heads of Kaiser's six companies. Kaiser got his start with a road paving business and went on to participate in the construction of the Boulder (now Hoover) Dam, the Grand Coulee Dam, and the San Francisco–Oakland Bridge. His Kaiser Industries included steelmaking, construction, and auto making.

Fleur du Lac was used as the site of much of the location filming for the film *Godfather II* in the 1970s. Many of the original buildings are now gone, replaced by privately owned condominiums.

We're now at **Tahoe City**. From here you can continue across the top of the lake and back to Reno on the Mount Rose Highway, or go northwest to Truckee and Donner Lake and then east to Reno.

Trip 8: Eastward Ho! The Great Bonanza road from California

Meyers   *Stateline*
Pioneer Trail
Although our modern movie-shaped perceptions put the emphasis on the great westward rush of settlers, personified by the Donner Party tragedy of 1846–47,

Forewarned. Pay attention to weather forecasts in the winter and spring, especially if you must cross one of the mountain passes. Rain at the "lower" elevations of Lake Tahoe or Reno may well be heavy snow in the passes. Highway 431 and Route 207 are regularly shut down in the winter because of storms. And Route 89 on the west shore of the lake is closed so often that there are permanent barriers that can be swung across the road to stop traffic at Emerald Bay.

Much of Route 89 on the California side and Routes 207 and 431 in Nevada have no guardrails to block the spectacular view—and the tremendous drop to the rocks below.

the process reversed for a while in the 1860s with the discovery of silver in and around Virginia City.

The present Route 50 brought back thousands of miners and merchants from Sacramento and Placerville, California. The road follows the south fork of the American River for part of its route and then descends from the mountains into Meyers. From there it heads north to near the present site of South Lake Tahoe and adjoining Stateline, Nevada. Also from Meyers, though, is the Pioneer Trail, also called the Placerville-Carson Road, which stays above the shoreline of the lake and heads for the front range of the Sierra Nevadas.

We'll start our short tour from Meyers and head toward South Lake Tahoe and Stateline. If you're coming from Stateline, we'd suggest you follow Route 50 along the lake west to Meyers and then double back.

Meyers was settled in 1851 and included a trading post called **Yank's Station**, named for owner Ephraim "Yank" Clement. About ten years later, Yank's Station became an important remount point for Pony Express riders.

Today Meyers is a popular winter sports area with cross-country ski trails in and around Echo Lake; several companies run snowmobile tours to the mountain meadows.

Coming from California, the **Pioneer Trail** bears off to the right at Yank's Station, about six miles before the Y where Route 89 heads north around the lake and Route 50 turns toward Stateline. At the peak of the eastward return from California to Virginia City about 1864, this section of the trail was said to be the busiest road in the West. Thousands of would-be miners and workers crossed above Lake Tahoe on foot, by stagecoach, or by horse. Each day some 300 tons of cargo was pulled along the narrow dirt or corduroy wood roads. There were many inns and other way stations; the location of many of them are marked with wooden pegs or signs.

Among the inns along the road, near where Cold Creek crosses the road, was the Sierra House. This inn was supposedly frequented by the infamous highway robbers Black Bart and Jack Bell among others.

The completion in 1869 of the transcontinental railroad farther to the north through Truckee and across Donner Summit ended most of the slow traffic on the Pioneer Trail.

Chapter 24
Virginia City: A Side Trip Back in Time

A century ago, Virginia City went from desolation to the richest place on earth and then back to desolation in the course of a few decades.

Today it is a living ghost town, a museum in place, and one of our favorite places to visit and dream. There are few places on Earth that, by their mere existence, speak so eloquently of their history.

As you stand on C Street in Virginia City and feel the mass of Mount Davidson over your shoulder, you may think that you are on solid ground, but in fact you are perched atop a near-hollow shell. Millions of tons of rock have been removed from beneath your feet and the hills around you are honeycombed with 750 miles of tunnel.

The Carson Valley Rest Stop

Like many of the settlements described in this book, the Carson Valley began as a rest stop. Thousands of emigrants seeking their riches in the 1840s Gold Rush of California passed through northern Nevada, and many of them stopped for provisions or spent the winter in the valley before making the treacherous crossing of the Sierras.

While they were in the area, some of the would-be California gold-seekers explored a bit on the eastern side of the mountains. In July of 1849, Abner Blackburn and the members of a Mormon wagon train spent some time on the banks of the Carson River; Blackburn found a few specks of gold in his pan near the present-day town of Dayton, but it was not enough to make the travelers stay.

In the coming few years there were small discoveries among wagon trains waiting for the snows to melt in the mountain passes. One group panned its way up a small stream that flowed into the Carson River; they optimistically named the waterway Gold Creek. On June 1, 1850, one of the men discovered a gold nugget at an isolated rock formation now known as Devil's Gate.

Over the coming decade, many small finds were made, including, according to the legend, a major discovery in Gold Canyon by brothers Allen and Hosea Grosh. Unfortunately, both brothers died—one from blood poisoning

Traffic report. In winter and especially the uncertain spring, pay attention to the altitudes listed in weather forecasts. It may be raining in Reno but sleeting or snowing in Virginia City.

We strongly recommend you come in from the Reno side of Highway 341, climbing the Geiger Grade; it is much more exciting and interesting than the approach from Carson City.

In the Reno area, tune your AM radio to 530 or 1610 to monitor road condition reports.

because of an accident and the other as the result of severe frostbite suffered on a crossing of the Sierras on a trip to California to raise money for a new mine.

This brings us, then, to scrappy miners Pat McLaughlin, Peter O'Reilly, and their grabby neighbor Henry Comstock. They began to mine the area at the head of Six Mile Canyon in 1859, grinding the rock in search of gold and casting aside the black rock that got in the way.

Early gold miners had complained about the sticky blue-gray mud that fouled their picks, clothing, and shovels. It wasn't gold; some thought it was low-value lead.

McLaughlin, O'Reilly, and the other miners, who had been earning about $876 per ton for gold-bearing ore stopped complaining when the mud was assayed and discovered to be silver ore, worth $2,000 to $3,000 per ton. The Comstock Lode had been found.

Getting to Virginia City

I-395 South ends about 10 miles south of Reno and becomes a two-lane highway; continue until you come to a traffic light at the intersection of two of the most interesting roads most drivers will ever experience: Highway 341 and 431. Head left to Virginia City on 341 or right to Lake Tahoe.

Virginia City sits at 6,200 feet; Route 341 follows the Geiger Grade, which twists back and forth for 13 miles to its highest point of 6,799 feet before descending slightly as you reach the town. The trip is a total of 23 miles from Reno.

As you drive up the twisting and turning Geiger Grade to Virginia City, think about how the miners and the suppliers brought their equipment and logs up the grade, and how they brought their silver and gold ore back down. Take advantage of some of the turnoffs on the drive up; from some of the higher points you can see the remains of the original Geiger Trail, which was even steeper and more twisty than the road you are negotiating in the relative comfort of your car.

The Old Geiger Grade was constructed by Davison M. Geiger and John H. Tilton in 1862, and served as the most direct connection between the Comstock Lode and the Truckee Meadows until it was replaced by the present paved highway in 1936. Concord stages, mud wagons, and ten-mule "freighters" carried thousands of passengers and millions of dollars in precious cargo across this section of the Virginia Range.

In addition to the unpredictable winds, snow, and landslides, this area was also popular with highwaymen. A marker near the top of the grade points out the location of the descriptively named **Dead Man's Point** and **Robbers Roost**.

Just after you cross the summit of Geiger Peak, you will find a marker on your left for **Louse Town.** Near its location was a station established in 1860 on Geiger and Tilton's new toll road from Truckee Meadows.

Around Louse Town—what a picture that name paints—was a large population of teamsters, stock, and sheep men. The steep hillside area included the first Virginia City railroad surveys, a race track, a trap shooting range, and other amenities.

As you drive up the Geiger Grade, you will be assaulted by sign after sign proclaiming your approach to something called the "Suicide Table" at the **Delta Saloon.** It sounds a lot more sinister than it really is: the Suicide Table is an 1860 faro table that apparently was the source of lost fortunes for three of its owners, each of whom killed himself.

When you reach the town itself, find a parking space—a lot easier in the winter than the summer, when you may have to use an outlying lot— and walk to C Street. One good place to start is the privately run **Visitor Center,** which in addition to selling knickknacks continuously shows an interesting video about Virginia City made a few years back as a promotional effort.

A City Above and a World Below

Mark Twain, under his real name of Samuel Clemens, worked for a while as a reporter for the *Territorial Enterprise.* Years later he wrote about the town: "Virginia was a busy city of streets and houses above ground. Under it was another busy city, down in the bowels of the earth, where a great population of men thronged in and out among an intricate maze of tunnels and drifts, flitting hither and thither under a winking sparkle of lights, and over their heads towered a vast web of interlocking timbers that held the wails of the gutted Comstock apart."

The money-making engine for Virginia City was the fabled Comstock Lode, a two-and-a-half-mile deposit that paid out some $500 million in silver and $700 million in gold. About 20 million tons of ore were brought out of the 750 miles of workings.

Dying to get in. Just below town is the Virginia City Cemetery. According to legend there were 88 violent deaths before someone spoiled it all by dying of natural causes.

Insert peg A into slot B. Several years into the boom, a German engineer named Philip Deidesheimer invented the square-set method of timbering that supported the crumbling rock and enabled shafts to be dug to depths of more than 3,000 feet.

The timbering of the mine had another effect: the near denuding of the forests for miles around. In fact, the search for more wood to timber the mines of Virginia City and Gold Hill extended over the Sierra Nevada. One of the more ambitious engineering schemes of the day took place in what is now called Incline Village, at the north end of Lake Tahoe. There, a lumber company built a primitive tramway that lifted logs up the side of a mountain to a flume where they were tumbled back down to waiting wagons that transported them to Virginia City.

Bright lights, big city. When Ben Cartwright sent "the boys" to town for supplies or adventure in the television series *Bonanza,* he was sending them over the mountain ranges into Virginia City. A re-creation of the Ponderosa Ranch can be found in Incline Village at the north end of Lake Tahoe.

Namesake. Virginia City got its name from one of the first miners, James Finney, nicknamed "Old Virginny" after the state of his birth. Returning from a revelry, he supposedly dropped and broke a bottle of booze. Instead of crying over spilt whiskey, he christened the tent city on the slopes of Mt. Davidson "Old Virginny Town" in his own honor.

Discovered in 1859, the Comstock Lode began a wild 20-year boom that helped bring Nevada into the Union in 1864 and continued to build San Francisco. There were seven major mines, several of which can be seen from C Street.

At boom time, Virginia City was home to 40,000 people, 100 saloons, six breweries, 50 dry goods stores, four banks, and five newspapers. The local payroll reached $500,000 a month. Restaurants imported lobsters, raw oysters, champagne, caviar, and other fineries from San Francisco; the wives of the mine owners furnished their homes with European crystal and wore Parisian gowns.

According to one of the many versions of the discovery of the riches in the hills and valleys south of Reno, miners Pat McLaughlin and Peter O'Reilly discovered a small quantity of gold-bearing rock at the head of Six-Mile Canyon in 1859. Henry Comstock, another prospector, made a loud but dubious claim that the men were trespassing on his property, and the lucky-then-unlucky miners settled the dispute by giving Comstock a neighboring piece of land. It was there that the gigantic Lode was first found, and its riches were named after him and not its unfortunate discoverers.

By the 1880s, though, most of the riches had been extracted, with the profits taken to San Francisco, New York, or overseas. In fact, between 1880 and 1890, the population of all of Nevada declined by 25 percent, and between 1890 and 1900 still further. Nevada's mining boom reignited about 1900 with the discovery of gold and silver in the center of the state at Tonopah and Goldfield; those fields led in great part to the development of Las Vegas as a railroad town.

The decline of the boom towns on the western and northwestern side of the state continued, though. Virginia City probably would have completely disappeared were it not for the birth of the tourist industry in the second half of the 20th century.

Almost Everything You Wanted to Know About Mining

Dan DeQuille, whose real name was William Wright, headed west from Ohio with the news of the silver discoveries in the Comstock Lode. Failing as a miner, he became a journalist and in 1862 joined the staff of the *Territorial Enterprise* in Virginia City. In that same year, the newspaper also hired Sam Clemens (later to gain fame as Mark Twain) for a brief stint. In 1875, Clemens persuaded Wright to publish his remembrances of the wild times in Virginia City. Wright's book was called *The Big Bonanza,* and it paints a vivid picture of the difficulties and rewards of the time.

Ink in his veins. William Wright joined the *Territorial Enterprise* in 1862 and was its leading writer until it shut down in 1893. His friend Mark Twain brought him back east in 1875 to write *The Big Bonanza,* but he returned after the manuscript was completed.

As rich as the Comstock Lode was, the Hollywood myth of miners carving out huge chunks of gold or silver rarely happened. Instead, there were tiny flakes of precious metal embedded in quartz or other rocks. There was much hard work involved in extracting the wealth. The first test of the worth of a piece of ore was usually done on the spot. Wright described the process:

> In gold-bearing quartz small specks of gold were often to be seen with the naked eye or aided by a small magnifying glass. . . . If gold could be seen at all, with either naked eye or the glass, it was considered a good sign. In order to test the specimen further, it was then either beaten to a powder in a mortar or ground as fine as flour on a large flat stone, using a smaller stone for a muller. This pulverized ore was then placed in a "horn," a little canoe-shaped vessel made of the split horn of an ox, when it was carefully washed out, much as auriferous gravel is washed in a pan. The gold, in case the ore experimented upon contained that metal, was found lying in a yellow streak in the bottom of the horn, generally small particles of gold dust, almost as fine as flour.

The results of the test in the horn were generally enough to tell the miner whether to load up a larger sample and bring it into town to an assayer's office. There, a determination would be made of the value of the ore by the ton.

> If a specimen of ore was supposed to contain silver, it was pulverized in the same way as gold-bearing quartz, then was placed in the horn, and the lighter matter it contained washed out. . . . The heavy residuum was then washed from the horn into a matrass (a flask of annealed glass, with a narrow neck and a broad bottom). Nitric acid was then poured into the matrass until the matter to be tested was covered, when the flask was suspended over the flame of a candle or lamp and boiled until the fumes escaping (which are for a time red) came off white.
>
> When the contents of the matrass had been allowed to cool and settle, the liquid portion was poured off into a vial of clear, thin glass, called a test-tube. A few drops of a strong solution of common salt was now poured into the test-tube. If the ore . . . contained silver, the contents of the test-tube would at once assume a milky hue.

Anyone who has worked in a darkroom has worked with the same basic set of chemicals, by the way. What the test produced was a silver salt, which is the basis of photographic film and paper. In fact, some miners would take the test tube out into the desert sun for a few minutes and observe the effect

Pool's gold. The Brunswick Ledge, a rich ore body about a mile east of the Comstock Lode, probably received its name in honor of the billiard tables in the back rooms of several of the bars in Virginia City.

of strong light on the solution: if there was silver in the salt solution, the liquid would turn purplish-black.

Virginia City: History Underfoot

Stop for a moment in Virginia City and absorb the history that surrounds you. The old buildings with their wooden walkways on C Street mostly date from about 1875, the year when fire nearly wiped out the town, destroying more than 2,000 structures. After the Great Fire, the entire town was rebuilt within six months, so strong was the faith that the underground riches would continue forever. Of course, this did not happen, but there was just enough activity in the mines to keep the town alive.

In 1875, 30,000 people lived in town. The Fourth Ward School, built in 1876 and still standing, was one of the first commercial buildings with indoor plumbing west of the Mississippi. The six-story International Hotel had the West's first elevator, which they called a "rising room."

As befits a wild place with a lot of money, Virginia City quickly became home to celebrities, Shakespearean plays, opium dens, newspapers, competing fire companies, police precincts, and a red-light district.

The Combination Mine was the deepest mine in the region, going down 3,262 feet—half the way to sea level. These deep mines did suffer from a significant problem, that of flooding from underground springs. To make things even more difficult, the water was often hot and sulphurous. Mine owners were forced to install huge pumps like the Cornish pump at the Union Mine, which had a 45-foot flywheel and a pump rod that extended 2,500 feet down the shaft and could lift more than 1 million gallons of water to the surface each day.

The grandest scheme for removing the water from the mines, though, was that of businessman Adolph Sutro who came from Prussia in 1850 in search of wealth in California. He amassed his first fortune in retail and real estate ventures in San Francisco, but he was drawn to Virginia City in 1860. He ran a successful reduction mill at Dayton.

Sutro saw the problems of ventilation and removal of water from the deep mines and came up with the idea of a deep tunnel that would run from three miles east of Dayton near the Carson River under the base of the mountains to link up with the mines of Virginia City. Mine operators would only have to drain their operations to the Sutro Tunnel and not to the surface. He expanded his concept to include the use of the tunnel as an emergency evacuation route for miners and as an underground transportation system that would bring the ore from the various mines to mills at the mouth of the tunnel.

It took more than eight years to secure all of the various permits and permissions, as well as financing, for the project. He even had to obtain a special act of Congress, the Sutro Tunnel Act of 1866, which granted him the land and the right to charge royalties to companies using the tunnel. Investors came from as far away as England and Germany.

Construction of the 3.8-mile tunnel began on October 19, 1869; it was July 8, 1878 when the tunnel connected with the Savage Mine at the 1,640 foot level. However, by the time the tunnel was completed, most of the major mines had gone far deeper than that. The tunnel did serve its original purpose as a means of getting some of the water out of the tunnels, but little more. Sutro eventually returned to California where he made more money in real estate and even served a term as mayor, from 1895 to 1897.

The **Ponderosa Saloon**, established in 1873, has some of its walls lined with old flume boards from the Virginia and Gold Hill Water Company. Iron pipes brought water from the High Sierras down across the Washoe Valley and up to a reservoir five miles from town. From there, wooden flumes brought water to Virginia City. The original system was used until 1957.

The Ponderosa Saloon is located in the former site of the Bank of California, established in 1864. Within the saloon you can walk into the old bank vault; the Bank of California provided much of the capital for the early growth of the Comstock mines. Much of the billion dollars in earnings passed through the doors to be stored in the vault, which is lined from ceiling to floor with half-inch steel plate; the outside walls are two feet thick.

On October 25, 1927, the Bank of California was robbed of $32,000. The robbers were eventually caught, but much of the loot was never recovered and is supposedly hidden in the hills around Six Mile Canyon.

At the back of the Ponderosa is a hoisting cage salvaged from one of the many mines in the area. There are some rather unique safety features in the upper frame. The weight of the cage hanging on the flat woven steel cable would turn the safety to the flat side; if the cable should break, the theory was that the safety would roll outward, sinking the gear teeth into the wooden guide beams on the side of the shaft and stopping the cage from plunging to the bottom.

One of the greatest dangers of the mines was the extremely fast ascent and descent of the cages. The waist-high fencing on the cage was installed to protect miners from being injured or killed by banging into the sharp rock on the sides of the shaft.

You can visit a portion of the **Ponderosa Mine** by descending an antique elevator from the back of the Ponderosa Saloon on C Street. The mine tour at the Ponderosa descends into a portion of the 1869 Best and Belcher Mine and goes about 300 feet deep into the underground works. Admission to the 25-minute tour is $3 for adults, $1.50 for children, or $7.50 for a family of two adults and children under 12. Tours are available year-round but are more frequent in the summer.

In the summer, the **Chollar Mine** on D Street is also open for tours.

The front window of the **Red Garter** saloon celebrates the famous gift made by "Barbara," one of the most sought-after ladies of the night, to her new husband.

The inscription on the window reads, "To Judge Orville Hardison from his

Hands off. Children can enter the casinos and saloons of Virginia City, but as in other parts of Nevada they must stay away from the gaming devices.

Low finance. In 1869, John Mackay and James Fair bought an interest in the failing Hale and Norcross mines. Joined by James Flood and William O'Brien, a pair of San Francisco saloonkeepers turned stockbrokers, they bought the barren Consolidated Virginia Mine in 1872 for about $50,000.

They sunk an even deeper shaft and eventually struck the "Big Bonanza" 1,167 feet down. That one lode brought out $135 million in ore; in today's money that is worth more than $2 billion.

Mackay went on to lay the first Trans-Atlantic and Pacific telegraphic cable for a company competing against Western Union. Fair became a U.S. Senator from the new state of Nevada. O'Brien and Flood spent their money.

loving wife Barbara on the occasion of her retirement and our marriage, July 23, 1893." The gift came from Barbara's personal collection of business tools: a .41-caliber ivory-handle Colt Derringer, a bone-handled dagger, and her red garter.

We suspect you will be unable to resist the insistent come-ons for the Suicide Table at the **Delta Saloon.** While you are there, check out the old nickelodeon at the back of the saloon, which features "Grandpa's Pin-Up Girls in 3D." The Delta also includes a great collection of old coin-operated devices including a gypsy fortune teller and an Electric Traveling Crane that can scoop up candy and trinkets.

The Delta was the first saloon rebuilt after the disastrous fire of 1875. Of the 100 saloons—that's no mistake, 100—in Virginia City, the Delta was the most famous because of its gaming room where a significant portion of the riches of the Bonanza was gambled away in games of Rocky Mountain (a variation of blackjack) or another card game called faro.

Directly opposite the Delta Saloon on C Street is a small monument constructed out of pieces of ore from every Nevada county. It was erected in 1958 commemorating the 100th anniversary of the discovery of silver.

The Delta was opened in 1862 by Colonel James Orndorff. The current carved wooden bar dates from 1876. Period decorations include a handmade world globe from 1880, valued at more than $100,000.

The *Territorial Enterprise* **Museum** on C Street commemorates the famous newspaper of the same name, as well as some of its most famous employees including Sam Clemens (Mark Twain) and Dan DeQuille. The *Enterprise* was Nevada's first newspaper and most celebrated in the Old West. Founded at Genoa in 1858, it was moved to Virginia City in 1859. The paper suspended publication in 1916 but was revived in 1952.

The **Crystal Bar** on C Street first opened in 1871; it has remained in one family since 1909. The original crystal chandeliers and mirrors arrived at San Francisco by ship from France and were sent by railroad to Virginia City. During Prohibition, the Crystal Bar was officially converted to an ice cream parlor; unofficially, it continued as a speakeasy.

At the top end of C Street is the **Fourth Ward School**, built in 1875. The cut stone foundation is anchored in solid granite from Mt. Davidson. The four-story structure was built to accommodate 1,025 students in 14 classrooms and two study halls. The last grammar and high school students to use the school were members of the Class of 1936. After sitting dormant for many years, it was restored by the Nevada State Museum and includes a fascinating exhibit about the history of the Comstock, including models of the mines and their works. The museum, at the end of C Street on the way out of town toward Gold Hill, is open from May to November.

The modern-day Virginia City High School, home of the "Muckers" football team, is down in the valley below the town.

For a decidedly offbeat view of old Virginia City, you might want to check out the **Red Light Museum** on C Street. (The sign out front warns that the exhibit is not for the "faint of heart.") We didn't see anyone being carried out on stretchers, but we did see an exhibit not often seen in museums: opium pipes and other drug paraphernalia, slightly risqué (by today's standards) French postcards, and leftovers from the local brothels were among the items on display.

The **Virginia and Truckee Railroad** was built to serve the needs of the mines in 1869. The first track linked Virginia City to Carson City; in 1872, the line was connected to Reno, 30 miles north, directly linking Virginia City to the transcontinental line from the East to San Francisco on the West Coast.

At its height, as many as 45 trains a day arrived and departed from Virginia City. Think about that number: that's several an hour, day and night.

Work began in April of 1868, with more than 1,000 mostly Chinese workmen working on parts of the line spread from Virginia City to Carson City; the rails were tied together and the first train ran on November 12 of that year. The line had an almost immediate effect, dropping the cost of supplies brought into the mining area and reducing the freight for the ore moving out; the lowered cost made some of the marginal mines more profitable and extended the boom.

The distance to Carson City was only 21 miles, but it was a very difficult distance to traverse. The tracks dropped about 1,600 feet over 13 miles, making 20 complete circles and crossing a huge wooden trestle at Crown Point.

By 1938, traffic had diminished so much that the link to the state capital was discontinued, and in 1950 the last train was run to Reno. Parts of the line were rebuilt and restored in 1976 for the tourist trade, and the railroad takes visitors on an interesting circuit through the mining areas in the summer months, pulled by a real steam engine.

The 35-minute trips go from the V & T depot on F Street past the Chollar Mine and through Tunnel Number 4 to Gold Hill and back; passengers can get off the train at Gold Hill and catch a later trip back to Virginia City. Fares are about $4 for adults and $2 for children; an all-day pass is $8. For information, call 847-0380.

In 1952, the celebrated *Territorial Enterprise* newspaper was purchased by former New York society columnist Lucius Beebe and his associate Charles Clegg. They came to town in great Eastern style, running the paper until 1961.

Citizen Hearst. George Hearst, the father of newspaper magnate William Randolph Hearst, started the family fortune as a stockbroker in Virginia City. He claimed that his fortune was built entirely on commissions from sale of stock and that he never had any direct involvement in Comstock shares.

Among the changes they brought to Virginia City were their ornately decorated railroad cars.

The **Nevada Gambling Museum** is a small display of slot machines—some of them playable for free, and one of the few chances for children to lay hands on a slot machine, even though they can't win any money—as well as guns, knives, and weapons, cheating devices, and rare photos and gambling artifacts. The museum is within the Palace Emporium Mall, 20 C Street, across from the Delta Parking Lot in the center of town.

And now we come to one of the stranger elements of today's Virginia City: the **International Camel Races.**

It all began with the little-known fact that camels were used in some parts of the Wild West as pack animals; there was even a U.S. Army Camel Corps. They were brought to the Comstock to carry salt and general supplies in the early, disorganized days of mining. Once the major mines were functioning and the Virginia & Truckee Railroad was the main freight carrier, the camels—not known as particularly affectionate pets—were turned loose in the hills and eventually disappeared.

In the 1950s, though, in the tradition of Mark Twain, Dan DeQuille, and other tongue-in-cheek writers for the paper, the *Territorial Enterprise* published a totally fabricated account of the result of a great camel race. In 1960, a race was held for real in a challenge that reached to San Francisco, with movie director John Huston winning the first race on a camel borrowed from the San Francisco Zoo. Quite logically, ostrich races were added in 1962.

Traditionally, the camel races are held on the weekend after Labor Day in Virginia City in an arena east of F Street, and in mid-May in Alice Springs, Australia, sister city to Virginia City.

Other unusual events in Virginia City include the **Ferrari Club of America Hill Climb** and apparently unrelated World Championship **Outhouse Races** and **Privy Parade,** all held in October of each year. In November and December, Virginia City celebrates **Christmas on the Comstock.** And in March there is the **World Championship Mountain Oyster Fry.** (If you don't know what a mountain oyster is, be sure to ask before you take a bite.)

The **Virginia & Truckee Railroad** train ticket window and the **Virginia City Chamber of Commerce** are located within a bright yellow rail car on C Street. V & T Car No. 13 is said to be the only railroad car ever designed expressly for transportation of precious metals, built in 1874 for the Virginia & Truckee and used until 1939 to transport millions of dollars in silver and gold from Virginia City to the mint at Carson City and to the Southern Pacific Railroad at Reno. For information on events, contact the chamber at 847-0311.

Off the Beaten Track in Virginia City

Virginia City is laid out in an above-ground mirror of the squareset timbering that holds up the mines below ground. The main streets run north and south and are labeled from "A" (highest up on Mount Davidson) to "F" Street down in the valley. Cross streets run east and west and carry names, many drawn from those of the founders or wealthy landowners of early days.

The main commercial district, described above, runs along C Street; many of the once-grand mansions were built on "Millionaire's Row" on B Street up the mountain while some of the workers lived down below. Some of the upper homes managed to escape the 1875 fire.

Start your tour at the south end of town on B Street at **The Castle.** This local must-see is a snapshot of how the world came to Virginia City when it was at its peak. Built from 1863 to 1868 for Robert Graves, the superintendent of the Empire Mine, the 16-room mansion was designed to look like a castle in Normandy and was furnished with the best money could buy. Furnishings include a 600-year-old Heidelberg sideboard, crystal chandeliers from Czechoslovakia, and elegant wallpaper from France. It is even more amazing when you consider that virtually everything in The Castle was sent by boat from Europe around the Horn to San Francisco and then overland through the Sierra Nevadas and into Virginia City.

The Castle was above the fire, and most of the original furnishings are still intact; it is open for tours from May to November.

At 158 South B is the **A. M. Cole Mansion**, a classic Victorian built in 1887 for a successful pharmacist. Nearby at 130 South B is the **Water Company Building**, constructed in 1875 for the offices of the Virginia City and Gold Hill Water Company.

Providing drinking water to the burgeoning city at the top of the mountain was a difficult matter; what little ground water there was available quickly became fouled by runoff from the mines and in any case there was nowhere near enough for 40,000 residents.

The solution was yet another gargantuan project for Virginia City, a system that imported water nearly 20 miles from Hobart Creek near Lake Tahoe, eight miles across Washoe Valley and back up a 1,500-foot climb over the mountains to Virginia City. Almost immediately the water supply was insufficient, and so the wooden pipes and sluiceways were extended another eight miles to Marlette Lake high up in the Sierra Nevadas.

Our tour continues on to the **Storey County Courthouse**, built in 1877 to replace an earlier building destroyed by the fire. The Victorian-style courthouse is still open and used for government offices. Take a close look at the statue of Justice. What's wrong with the picture? Justice is not blindfolded, and the scales are in balance. It could be sloppy work; then again, it may be a message from the past.

The next building of note is **Piper's Opera House.** Every decent Western boom town had to have an opera house; in fact the miners and upper class of Virginia City probably received a richer diet of culture than do modern Americans. John Piper's wooden structure—the third in a succession of theaters he built on the Comstock—was completed in 1885 and featured carpeted floors, hanging balconies, and a spring-mounted dance floor. Perfor-

mances ranged from Shakespearean plays to Italian operas to dog fights. Great
actors and performers seen at Piper's included Edwin Booth, Harry Houdini,
Lillie Langtry, John Philip Sousa, and Buffalo Bill Cody. Inside are the raked
stage and elegant proscenium boxes, along with some of the original scenery.

Three different **International Hotels** once stood on a single spot just below
Piper's Opera House. The first hotel, a 14-room wood structure, was built in
1860 and dismantled in 1863. The second, a 100-room four-story brick building was destroyed by the Great Fire of 1875. The third and grandest International Hotel opened its doors in March of 1877 with 160 rooms on six floors,
complete with hot and cold running water, steam heat, gas lighting, and the
first hydraulic elevator in Nevada. The hotel was destroyed by fire in 1914
and was not rebuilt because of the Comstock's decline.

Past the courthouse is the **Knights of Pythias Hall**, built in 1876. Next
door is the **Miners Union Hall**, organized in 1863 as the first such protec-
tive association for miners; among its accomplishments was the negotiation
of a munificent minimum daily wage of $4; the Union Hall offered the rough
and tough miners a ballroom, library, and chess room.

As you face the Union Hall, look up the mountain and to the right to see
the **Orphir Pit**, the site of the original gold strike.

Climb up to A Street; from here we will head back to the south. At 6 South
A Street is the Victorian home built for George Hanning, a prosperous Virginia City merchant.

Here you'll find a marker near where the Great Fire began early in the morning of October 26, 1875, when a coal oil lamp was knocked over in Crazy
Kate's boarding house. Strong winds spread the flames and supplies of blasting powder in and around the mines made the blaze much worse. In all, 33
blocks of structures were leveled. Losses included St. Mary's in the Mountains
Catholic Church, the Storey County Court House, Piper's Opera House, the
International Hotel, and city offices of most of Virginia City's business district. The offices and hoisting works of nearby mines were also destroyed.

The marker is near a small hose house that was part of a new hydrant system put into place after the fire. The system is still in use today.

There are two short streets above A Street with a commanding view of the
valley. At 66 Howard Street is the **King Mansion**, a castle-like structure built
in 1861 for George King, secretary of the Virginia & Truckee Railroad.

Now we drop down below the C Street commercial district.

The former red-light district was located on D Street, just below the Silver
Dollar Hotel on D Street between Union and Sutton Streets.

According to legend, the queen of lower Virginia City was surely Julia Bulette.
Some of the grand stories about her—which may or may not be true—said
that she was at the center of Virginia City's cultural establishment with her
own box at the opera and drove around town in a formal horse-drawn
brougham with her own crest on the door. The tourist guides will tell you
she also sold her charms for as much as $1,000 per night. They'll say she was
a favorite of the miners and had a mine named after her; the railroaders put

her name on a V & T car, and she was named an honorary member of Fire Engine Company No. 1.

An undisputed fact is that on the morning of January 20, 1867, Bulette was found brutally murdered in her bed; a chest full of valuable jewelry and other possessions *may* have been missing. Many of the men of the town—including the firemen—showed up for her funeral, and again for the trial and eventual hanging of the accused murderer, a Frenchman named Jean Millain.

Bulette's house was located on D Street at Union directly above the V & T depot and freight yards. Look up over the slot machines in the Ponderosa Saloon for a rosey painting of Ms. Bulette. Moving southward you will come to the **Mackay Mansion** at 129 D St., originally built as the office for the Gould & Curry Mine, which had its shaft across the street; after the Great Fire of 1875, mining millionaire John Mackay took over the building as his home.

Continue south to the **Savage Mansion** at 146 D Street; this building had a similar history, with the offices of the Savage Mine on the ground floor and the residence of the mine manager on the upper two levels.

Near the south end of D Street, below the Fourth Ward School, is the **Chollar Mansion**, built in 1883 as an office and residence for the Chollar-Potosi Mining Company.

Drop down one more row to E Street to the famed **St. Mary's in the Mountains** church. The Victorian Gothic structure was rebuilt after the Great Fire; according to legend, Silver King John Mackay paid for the reconstruction after he had convinced the priest to send his parishioners to help save the mine buildings and let the church burn. Within the church is a display of history. A railroad tunnel for the V & T once ran in front of the church to the depot at the end of the line.

On F Street at Union at the bottom of town is **St. Mary's Hospital**, built in 1875 with much of the funding from Mackay; the former Chinatown, a community of almost 2,000 people, was located in front of the hospital. St. Mary's is now an arts center.

A Guided Tour

For those who want an escorted tour of town, **Virginia City Tours** offers 20-minute narrated tours in a replica of a San Francisco Trolley or an open-air trailer pulled by a farm tractor. The vehicles leave from the Delta Saloon parking lot. Rates are $3 for adults and $2 for children from 6 to 12. For information, call 786-0866.

A&M Horse Drawn Carriage Rides takes small parties on slower-paced tours of Virginia City; it loads near the V & T train station. For information, call 246-0322.

Surrounding Towns

As you drive out of Virginia City toward Carson City, you will come to Gold Hill, site of other major discoveries. There are remains of former mines on the left and right as you traverse the switchbacks, including one of the sharpest

S-turns you will experience, alongside a mountain side that has been completely dug away in modern-day pit mining.

Gold Hill, just outside of Virginia City, was the actual location where the Comstock Lode was first found. By 1865, just six years after the first strike, Gold Hill had three foundries, two banks, two newspapers, and several thousand residents; the population peaked at 9,000. The mines, though, petered out in the 1870s, and Gold Hill became a ghost town in the first half of the 20th century. Since then there have been sporadic attempts to bring out ore using modern methods, the most recent ending in 1983.

You'll see some old workings and hoisting wheels in and around the **Gold Hills Hotel and Saloon.** The 1859 stone and brick building was the first hotel in the Comstock and the oldest hostelry in the state. Restored to something approaching its boom town finest, it is once again open for guests.

A nearby marker is on the site of the first recorded claim in the Comstock Lode. Across from the saloon is the site of the Gold Hill Brewery.

A somewhat notable eatery in the area is the **Cabin in the Sky,** off Highway 342 between Gold Hill and Silver City. For information and hours, call 847-0733. The restaurant offers steaks, ribs, seafood, and Italian specialties in a location with a panoramic view of the mountains and mining country. The Cabin was opened by Joe Conforte, better known for his pioneering houses of prostitution in the area including the Mustang Ranch.

Silver City

Silver City was another mining town on the Comstock, and the location of the toll booth for the locally famed **Devil's Gate Toll Road** that led up the winding canyon from Dayton and Carson City to Virginia City.

But for an accident of history, the story of the Comstock Lode might have centered on Silver City instead of Virginia City up the road. The brothers Allen and Hosea Grosh discovered silver here in 1856, but both died in 1857 before their ore was assayed.

Below Silver City is the former location of McCone's Foundries, first established in 1862 at John Town two miles southeast in Gold Canyon. After two years, the operation was moved to Silver City. A fire on May 15, 1872, left nothing standing but the walls. McCone then bought the Fulton Foundry in Virginia City and made it the largest in the state employing 110 men at its peak. All the early castings of the Virginia & Truckee Railway were manufactured at Fulton's.

Henry Comstock, who horned his way into history with a cut of the fabulous lode that now bears his name, operated a store in Silver City for a short while after he sold his claim (for a paltry $10,000); he went broke when the mines petered out and left for new boomtowns in Montana, eventually committing suicide in 1870.

Dayton

Dayton, at the location where the Gold Canyon empties into the Carson River, was a rest stop for travelers on their way to California and a Pony Express

Station. A permanent settlement and a tent trading post were established about 1851, just after Genoa was founded; the area was at first called Chinatown because of the Chinese railroad workers who populated the area. After the gold discoveries on the other side of the range, the community was renamed as Dayton and, with a population of about 2,500, was considered as a site for the state capital before it ended up a few miles west in Carson City.

Adolph Sutro lived in Dayton and operated a stamp mill there to serve mining interests. It was in Dayton where Sutro located the exit for his fantastic tunnel into the Comstock Lode to drain water and remove the ore; there were great hopes when the Sutro Tunnel was being planned and constructed, but the boom never came.

Dayton has the oldest cemetery in the state, with tombstones recording the names of many of the pioneers mentioned in this book, including James "Old Virginny" Finney, who gave Virginia City its name.

After a hundred years of decline, Dayton was once again a glittering boom town for a short time in 1960 when Hollywood came to town to film *The Misfits*, with stars including Marilyn Monroe and Clark Gable.

Accommodations in the Virginia City Area

Remember: you're looking for historical ambiance and realism, right? You are not going to find the opulence of a Caesars Palace or the big-city hotel amenities of a Reno Hilton here in the hills. You will, though, find old-time bed-and-breakfasts, inns, and an antique hotel or two. (If you must have more modern facilities, continue on down the hill to Carson City.)

For general information about Virginia City, call 847-0311.

Chollar Mansion. A bed-and-breakfast within the former mansion and office built in 1861 for a mine superintendent. The hotel includes rooms decorated with Victorian-era furnishings, an arched vault that once stored millions of dollars worth of silver and gold bullion, and the paymaster's booth. The guest library includes a large collection of books on Virginia City and the surrounding area. Rooms range from about $75 to $125 for a double; there is also a guest cottage available. 565 South D Street, Virginia City; 847-9777.

Edith Palmer's Country Inn. A country home, built in 1862 by a prosperous wine merchant, now operating as a bed-and-breakfast. Five guest rooms are available, with double room rates from about $60 to $75. South B Street, Virginia City; 847-0707.

Gold Hill Hotel and Crown Point Restaurant. Nevada's oldest operating hotel, this Victorian country inn was built in 1859, less than a mile down the canyon from Virginia City in Gold Hill. There are 14 refurbished guest rooms, four with private fireplaces; a separate building offers three kitchen suites. The hotel's Great Room features a massive open hearth stone fireplace. Room rates range from about $40 to $150. Main Street, Gold Hill; 847-0111.

House on the Hill. A bed-and-breakfast overlooking the Comstock Mine and Gold Canyon. Three suites are available. Room rates range from about $45 to $95. Sky Lane, Gold Hill; 847-0193.

Silver Dollar Hotel. A Victorian relic with 14-foot ceilings. A honeymoon suite is available. Downstairs is the Silver Dollar Pub with a deck overlooking Silver Dollar Mountain. 11 North C Street, Virginia City; 847-9051.

Comstock Lodge. A motel-like lodge just outside of downtown, with room rates of about $50 to $80 for a double. South C Street, Virginia City; 847-0233.

Virginia City Motel. Open year-round. Room rates range from about $33 to $50. 675 C Street, Virginia City; 847-0277.

The RV Park. A 50-spot park designed to look like an old mining camp. Open year-round. Carson and F Streets, Virginia City; 847-0999.

Chapter 25

Carson City: A Capital Before There Was a State

Like the state for which it serves as capital, Carson City is a bit unusual. To begin with, it is one of the smallest capitals in the nation, with just 40,000 or so residents.

The site of Carson City lay in the Eagle Valley on the Overland Trail, over which stages and the Pony Express crossed the Sierras on the south side of Lake Tahoe en route to Sacramento, California. Once again, here is the story of a city—a state capital, even—that grew from a rest stop.

The commercial founder of Carson City was Abraham Curry, a business-man from Ithaca, New York, who arrived in Eagle Valley in 1858, just a year before the discovery of the Comstock Lode. Curry sought his riches as a merchant, buying an existing ranch and trading post to serve both the emigrants heading to California and, as it turned out, gold-seekers coming the other direction to the Comstock.

Though the idea of Nevada as a state was still a rather remote dream, Curry immediately began to develop the site as a future capital, even calling the "downtown" of his hardscrabble sand empire Capitol Square. He named the developing town Carson City after the famed guide Kit Carson, who was still alive at the time.

In addition to his skill as a merchant, Curry proved to be an able politi-cian. He promoted his town site at every opportunity and also struck an alliance with the territorial governor, James Nye, another refugee from New York. The first territorial government was centered in Carson City, and in 1864 when statehood was granted, it became the capital.

Among his other activities, Curry served as the warden of the first terri-torial prison—inmates constructed many of the early sandstone buildings that make up the core of the city today. In 1865, the federal government ordered the construction of a branch of the U.S. Mint in Carson City to convert some of the gold and silver into the coinage of the realm, and Curry built the struc-ture to house it and served as its first superintendent.

Carson City, along with much of the western part of the state, went into decline about 1880 as the Comstock Lode petered out. The population of Reno

Little big man. The famed mountain guide and trapper Kit Carson was born in 1809 in Missouri. He was a little guy, never topping five-foot, six-inches in height. Carson's father was killed by a falling tree limb when the boy was just 9, and when he was 15 his mother apprenticed him to a saddler and harness maker. There he met some of the early adventurers heading west; he talked his way into one of the lowliest jobs on the wagon train—that of cavy boy, the driver of the spare mules and oxen.

He went on to demonstrate his prowess as a frontiersman, and he was hired by John C. Frémont as a guide for expeditions in 1842 and 1843, including a midwinter crossing of the high Sierra Nevadas. He went on to great fame during the Mexican War.

Map your course. Stop at the cartographic mother lode in the State Department of Transportation at 1263 S. Stewart (Room 206) where you can purchase a full range of official maps of almost every description. Call 885-3449 for hours and information.

did not recover to its 1880 level of about 7,500 until about 1960.

Touring Carson City

The **Nevada State Museum** is a small but rich collection of artifacts and displays that tell the story of Nevada from prehistoric times to the current day. The museum is housed in the old Carson City Mint Building, where the mint operated from 1870 to 1893 and produced nearly 60 million coins, including the famous Carson City silver dollar. All told, the Carson City mint struck $49,274,434.30 in coinage.

The sandstone blocks for the building were quarried at a nearby prison. Out front is a time capsule that was put in place on October 31, 1964, for the centennial of Nevada, and to remain sealed until the year 2064.

As you enter the museum, one of the first major exhibits is the original coin press, a six-ton apparatus manufactured by Morgan and Orr of Philadelphia. On February 11, 1870, the big press struck its first coin, an 1870 silver dollar.

Up to 175 tons of pressure was required to strike a gold double eagle. The intense strain soon caused a crack to develop in the arch of the press; the foundry at the shops of the Virginia & Truckee Railroad in Carson City cast a new three-ton iron arch in 1878 to repair the press. In 1899 the press was dismantled and shipped to the Philadelphia mint. It was rebuilt in 1930 to work with an electric motor and was transferred to the San Francisco mint in 1945 where it operated for 10 more years. When that mint closed, the press was saved from the scrap heap and returned to its first home as part of the Nevada State Museum. In 1964, the coin press was loaned to the Denver mint for three years to help alleviate a national shortage of coins.

The press is still used occasionally to stamp out commemorative bronze and silver coins sold at the museum's gift shop.

Another fascinating exhibit displays the exquisite silver service of the U.S. *Nevada*, commissioned in 1916. The plates and serving pieces were a gift from the State of Nevada to its battleship namesake, fashioned from 5,000 ounces of silver. In World War II, the *Nevada* served off the Aleutians and then stood off the coast of France during the Normandy landing of D-day, its 14-inch guns pounding the shore. The *Nevada* ended its life a bit ignominiously, serving as a target ship for an atomic bomb test at the Bikini Atoll; the silver service had been removed first. According to Naval records, though, even the atomic bomb could not sink her and the Navy scuttled the ship.

An exhibit on the geology of Nevada includes the skeleton of an *imperial mammuthus* (a North American woolly mammoth) that died about 17,000 years ago in Nevada's Black Rock Desert; it is the largest such skeleton on exhibit in America. Nearby is the skeleton of an early horse, *equus pacificus*, a large Ice Age horse about 25,500 years old and recovered from near Pyramid Lake.

The well-stocked book section in the gift shop is worth some serious browsing. At the time of a recent visit, the nearby rotating exhibit was devoted to the Chinese influence on Nevada including some beautiful clothing and artifacts brought to America by Asian railroad and mine workers.

The Environmental Gallery teaches about the animal and plant life of the state, from dinosaurs to today; the Earth Science Gallery explains the complex geology that formed not only the gold and silver deposits of Nevada but also the dramatic mountain ranges and deserts. Also on display is an impressive collection of artifacts of ancient Native American cultures.

The last exhibit is a recreation of one of the mines of the Comstock, so well done that some visitors may suffer from claustrophobia. Along the low-ceiling path you will step into a "Dillon Box," a mine cage used to lower men into the deep shafts. The floors of the "mine" include pieces of old rails, which were actually wood covered with metal straps; displays include mine faces made up of actual ore.

The museum is located at 600 N. Carson Street and is open every day from 8:30 A.M. to 4:30 P.M. Admission is $3 for adults; children under 18 are admitted free. Call 687-4810 for information.

Another essential stop on the tour of Carson City is the **State Capitol** on Carson Street between Second and Musser streets. The stone building, first erected in 1871 and expanded in 1915, is distinctive for its huge log rafters within. It is set in a four-block, elm-shaded park—Abraham Curry's Capitol Square. The governor maintains his office in the building, but the original legislative and Supreme Court chambers are used for exhibits including an amazing museum of official and unofficial state items on the second floor.

There is a strange mix of buildings as you move on to the **Legislative Building**, which is open to the public interested in seeing the Assembly and Senate. For information, call 687-6800.

The legislative mall includes statues of Kit Carson, Adolph Sutro, and Abraham Curry.

The **Nevada Supreme Court** is located at 201 S. Carson Street and is jarringly modern in this old city. Completed in 1992, the building is sometimes used to house exhibits on state history. Oral arguments are open to the public during the session from September to June; call 687-8675 to check on the

Safer that way. In Nevada, the legislature is very much a part-time job, in session (except for emergencies) only for a few months at the beginning of odd-numbered years. There are only 63 legislators—21 senators and 42 members of assembly, the fourth-smallest state legislature in the nation. (Representatives are paid just $130 per day for a 60-day session, too.) We might all be better off if the U.S. Congress was to adopt such semi-retirement.

schedule and special events. The Supreme Court also meets in Las Vegas, on the other side of the state, for part of its schedule.

Just outside Carson City and before the point where Highway 50 and Interstate 395 split is the office of the **Carson Ranger District of the U.S. Forest Service.** You can stop in for a wilderness permit or obtain information on hiking trails in the area. It is also a good place to check on road conditions and weather forecasts. The ranger station is open weekdays from 8 A.M. to 4:30 P.M.

Railroad buffs and children of all ages are not going to want to miss the **Nevada State Railroad Museum,** which mostly commemorates the Virginia & Truckee Railroad. The V & T rail line running from Virginia City to Carson City was completed in 1869 and the tracks were extended north to Reno in 1872 where they met the transcontinental lines.

At the museum, there are engines, passenger cars, railroad construction equipment, and a display of model railroad cars that is definitely a cut above the old Lionel set you had as a kid.

In the summer season, you can take a short ride around the museum property on an old engine. The museum is located south of Carson City on I-395 at Fairview Drive and is open weekends and a few days during the week. Call 687-6953 for hours and rates.

Next door to the railroad museum is the **Carson City Visitor Center** and the **Chamber of Commerce.** An old Prairie Schooner wagon sits outside.

The **Stewart Indian Museum** is located at 5366 Snyder Avenue on the campus of the former Stewart Indian School. Exhibits include displays on tribes of the Great Basin, including the Washoe, Paiute, and Shoshone, and irreplaceable photographs taken by E. S. Curtis, who lived with more than 80 Western tribes from 1898 to 1928. A trading post offers arts and crafts. The museum is open daily from 9 A.M. to 4 P.M. and is free. For information, call 882-1808.

A new attraction in an old place is the **Amuseum** children's museum, located in the Carson City Civic Auditorium at 813 N. Carson Street. The museum is open daily except Tuesday; admission is $4 for adults and $2 for children from 2 to 12.

The **Great Basin Wildlife Center** is an educational experience for children and adults, located at 3770 Butti Way in Carson City. Admission is $2 for adults and $1 for children under 13. For information, call 887-2171.

The **Brewery Arts Center** celebrates the arts, not beer, although it is located within the former site of the Carson Brewing Company at King and Division streets. The building was built in 1864 and was operated as a brewery more or less continually until 1948; it then became the printing plant for the Nevada *Appeal*, the state's older continuously published daily newspaper. It became the center of Carson City's cultural arts in 1975, offering art exhibits and sponsoring performances in the area. For information on events, call 883-1976.

The **Carson City Visitors Information Center** and the **Carson City Convention and Visitors Bureau** are located in a building at the entrance to the Nevada State Railroad Museum, at 1900 S. Carson Street; these resources contain a wealth of brochures, maps, and local information. Open daily. Call 882-7474 for information.

Yes, There Are Casinos

You cannot compare the gambling establishments of Carson City with those of Las Vegas or Reno, or even with the historically interesting slot palaces of Virginia City. But you can make a bet of almost any description.

The **Nugget** is definitely a casino for the hardcore. How else to describe a place that was nearly packed with locals at noon on a drizzly Friday? At the time of our visit, the Nugget offered an eminently forgettable buffet with several varieties of indeterminate meat, poultry, and fish-like substances, tired salads, and scary Jell-O. 507 N. Carson Street.

The historical award goes to the **Ormsby House** at 600 S. Carson Street, which had its birth in 1859, the same year as the discovery of the Comstock Lode. It was established by Major William Ormsby, a buddy of Abraham Curry (and in whose name the county was named). A major renovation was undertaken in recent years, but hard financial times brought it down. In 1995, though, plans were set for a grand re-opening of the hotel-casino.

A considerably newer casino is **Carson Station** farther south at 900 S. Carson Street. 883-0900.

LAKE TAHOE

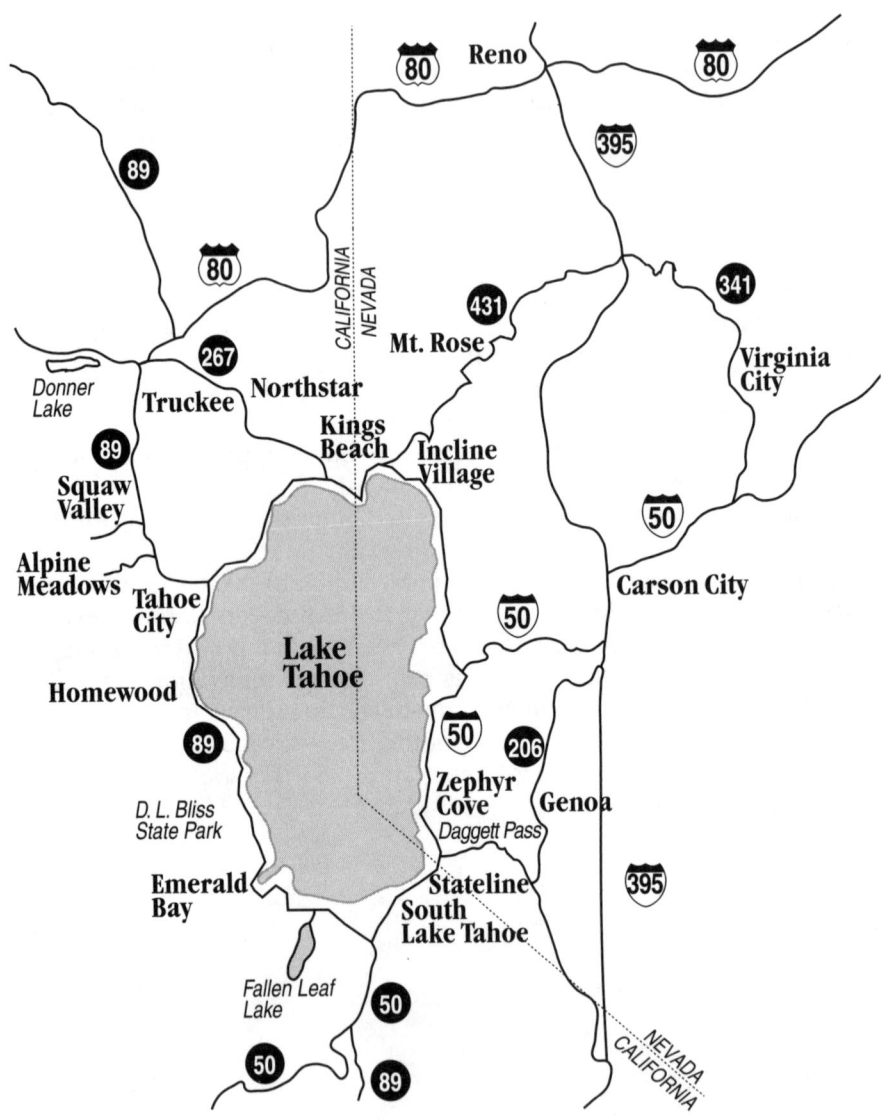

Chapter 26
Lake Tahoe: Mountain Shangri-La

A Heavenly Emerald

As a travel writer and journalist, I have been to many spectacular places around the world, but on a stressful day at the keyboard, my mind regularly drifts back to a view of Lake Tahoe from Emerald Bay, with the Heavenly Ski Area towering over the casinos of Stateline.

Lake Tahoe is, without argument, one of the most breathtaking places on earth, and its natural beauty is complemented—for the most part—by resorts and developments to suit most tastes.

The lake was formed by the rise and fall of faults about 5 to 10 million years ago, which created a deep valley; then about 2 million years ago, lava flowing from the Mt. Pluto volcano on the north shore blocked the north-eastern outlet of the basin. Geologists say that the initial height of Lake Tahoe was 600 feet higher than its present level.

Today the lake itself covers the Nevada-California border, 59 miles southwest of Reno and 100 miles northeast of Sacramento. Lake Tahoe has a surface area of about 192 square miles, containing some 39 trillion gallons of water, with a circumference of 72 miles.

At 12 miles wide and 22 miles long, it is the largest alpine lake, the third deepest lake in North America, and the tenth deepest in the world with an average depth of 989 feet and 1,645 feet at its lowest point; at its bottom, the lake is 92 feet below the level of Carson City on the other side of the Sierra range in Nevada.

The lake is fed by 63 streams, but only one waterway—the Truckee River—flows out; it goes through Reno and on to Pyramid Lake. As such, Lake Tahoe is one of the few major bodies of water in North America that does not eventually empty into the ocean.

The surface of Lake Tahoe is more than a mile above sea level, at 6,227 feet. During times of drought, the surface of the lake can drop below the outlet to the Truckee and become a self-contained lake.

In the summer, the top 12 feet of the lake warms to as much as 68 degrees. In winter months, and in the lower depths of the lake, the temperature remains

Over and under. The U.S. Bureau of Reclamation controls the top 6.1 feet of the lake as a reservoir. The water is claimed to be 99.9 percent pure. The lake contains an estimated 39.75 trillion gallons of water, enough to cover the entire state of California to a depth of 14 inches.

at a constant—and life-threatening—39 degrees. However, the lake is not known to have ever frozen over because of the constant turnover of water from the bottom to the surface; Emerald Bay has frozen, though, in especially cold winters, most recently in 1989.

The highest peak rising directly from the shoreline is Mt. Tallac at 9,735 feet. The highest point in the basin is Freel Peak at 10,881 feet.

The exact source of the name "Tahoe" is a bit obscure. In any case, the spectacular body of water has held many names over the years. When explorer John C. Fremont, accompanied by famed guide Kit Carson, came to the lake on February 14, 1844, he named it Lake Bonpland, after a French botanist who had been with him on earlier explorations. But mapmaker Charles Preuss wrote it down as Mountain Lake.

Despite all of this, it was commonly referred to as Frémont Lake until 1852 when California Governor John Bigler led a party to the area to rescue some snowbound travelers; the lake was renamed as Lake Bigler at the time.

But again, other names were applied to the still-remote area, including Truckee Lake and Maheon Lake. When the Civil War broke out, the politically correct on the Union side sought to strike Bigler's name from the lake because of his supposed Southern sympathies. It was at this time that the word "Tahoe" was proposed, supposedly meaning "high water." There was little historical support for the meaning of the word, but it nevertheless stuck; some suggest the word is actually a corruption of the Spanish word "tajo," pronounced taho and meaning a "cut."

Just to make things difficult, the State of California went ahead and entered into its laws an official designation of the waterway as Lake Bigler, a name that was not officially withdrawn until 1945.

The Econoguide to the Best Lake Tahoe Hotel/Casinos

Bill's Casino	Harrah's
Caesars Palace	Harvey's

The Econoguide to the Best Lake Tahoe Buffets

Harrah's	Caesars Palace

> **The Econoguide to the Best Lake Tahoe Places to Visit**
>
> | | |
> |---|---|
> | Emerald Bay | Lake Tahoe |
> | Heavenly Tram | Virginia City |

Mileage to South Lake Tahoe

Las Vegas	468
Reno	59
Sacramento	100
San Francisco	198
Virginia City	50

Lake Tahoe Average Temperatures

	Jan	Feb	Mar	Apr	May	Jun	Jul	Aug	Sep	Oct	Nov	Dec
High	36	39	44	50	60	69	79	80	70	51	47	40
Low	16	18	21	26	32	37	43	42	37	31	24	20

Like No Other Nevada Casinos

If you are going to Nevada to gamble, there is not a lot of difference between the major resorts of Stateline, Reno, or Las Vegas. They all have slot machines and blackjack tables and myriad other ways to lose your money. The major resorts all offer lavish stage shows and headliner acts—admittedly, the headlines are larger in Las Vegas, but that doesn't necessarily mean the shows have more to offer you. The best of the restaurants in Stateline, Reno, and Las Vegas are all satisfying.

But what you do get in Lake Tahoe that you get nowhere else is the combination of the excitement of the casinos and all they offer, with the tremendous range of outdoor activities available in the Tahoe Basin. Here are just a few: downhill skiing, cross-country skiing, ice skating, sleigh rides, sledding, dogsled rides, snowmobiling, horseback riding, and indoor and heated outdoor pool swimming in the winter; waterskiing, lake and pool swimming, hiking, camping, horseback riding, hot-air-ballooning, boating, and cruises in the summer, spring, and fall.

Getting to Lake Tahoe from Reno

Lake Tahoe is an easy drive from Reno, less than an hour to Crystal Bay and about 90 minutes

White stuff. Snowfall at alpine skiing elevations averages 300 to 500 inches per year. At the lake level, the average is about 125 inches. At high elevations, it has been known to snow in any month of the year. On December 28, 1992, snow began to fall at South Lake Tahoe, eventually reaching rates of up to six inches per hour. Over the next 48 hours, the ski resort received more than nine feet of snow, one of the largest recorded snowfalls ever.

They made them a deal. Among the films made in and around Lake Tahoe are *Indian Love Call*, starring Jeannette McDonald, *The Godfather*, and *The Bodyguard*.

Econoguide alert. You'll find most of the major fast-food chains on the California side, along with a large assortment of factory outlets and discount stores. You will also find cheaper ski rental and equipment stores past the entrance to the Heavenly resort toward California.

to South Lake Tahoe. *See the section on Driving Trips from Reno for guided tours from Reno to North and South Tahoe.*

If you have the time, make the great circle tour around the lake, using Routes 50 and 28 on the east shore and Route 89 on the west shore, for a round trip of about two hours.

Several bus and shuttle companies offer scheduled and on-demand service from Reno to South Lake Tahoe. One such company is **Tahoe Casino Express**, which has 14 departures in each direction, charging $15 per person.

Air Travel

More than two million passengers pass through the Reno Cannon International Airport each year, and in winter months about 25 percent of all travelers are destined for Lake Tahoe.

Reno Air offers nonstop jet service from the West Coast to Reno. Alpha Air serves the small Lake Tahoe Airport, seven miles from Heavenly with flights from California. Plans called for expansion of Southern California service from John Wayne Airport in Orange County. American Eagle offers service from San Francisco and other connections.

Hotels and Casinos in South Lake Tahoe

The state border runs more or less down the middle of Lake Tahoe, dividing Nevada from California and demarking the line between two rather different cultures.

The Nevada villages of Crystal Bay, Incline Village, and Stateline each feature small-scale versions of Reno or Las Vegas casino resorts, with all that entails: gambling, glitzy shows, buffets, and fine dining. The largest collection of casinos can be found in Stateline, along both sides of a half-mile stretch of Highway 50. The very last casinos sit directly on the border between California and Nevada.

On the other side of the border, the hotels in California must find different lures. They generally go for high luxury or low price; either way, they do not have casinos to subsidize the room rates.

Three miles into California on Route 50, you'll find a tiny amusement park called the Magic Carpet Golf and Arcade on the lake side of the road. Rides include bumper cars, a small ferris wheel, and a slide. The park is closed during the winter.

Tahoe resorts are generally more expensive than their equivalents in Reno and some Las Vegas resorts, partly because of the additional appeal of winter and summer recreation.

High-season in Lake Tahoe is generally mid-June to Labor Day and into September. Low-season is April and May, and November into early December. New Year's and Christmas are busy times. The "shoulder" or middle season is February and March, when ski and winter sports enthusiasts sell out the hotel on weekends.

Harvey's Resort Hotel/Casino

It pretty much all started here. Harvey Gross moved to isolated South Lake Tahoe about 1940 to operate a meat company. In 1944, he opened Harvey's Wagon Wheel Saloon & Gambling Hall in Stateline on Highway 50. It was a one-room log cabin with a six-stool lunch counter and the only 24-hour gas pump between Placerville, California, and Carson City on the other side of the Sierra Nevadas. Oh, and it also included three slot machines and a pair of blackjack tables.

From that humble beginning, Harvey and his wife Llewellyn helped build Stateline into a year-round resort; one early winter they joined with Tahoe residents in shoveling out Echo Summit before the state of California committed heavy equipment to the task.

Harvey's has undergone several stages of expansion, with its two main towers rising in the 1960s and 1980. (In 1980 an extortionist's bomb blew a five-story hole in the hotel tower.)

Today, Harvey's occupies the catbird seat in Stateline with some of the best views of the lake from its towers and restaurants. The attractive lobby is a floor away from the casino, and nicely insulated; it is possible to forget that there is a world of blinking lights, bouncing coins, and shuffling cards.

Rest assured, though, that there is a full-featured casino at Harvey's including the Land of the Giants, five seven-foot-tall slot machines against the wall between the California Bar and Sage Room. Harvey's has a Vegas-sized casino, at 88,000 square feet, offering 2,300 slot machines, 121 table games including blackjack, red dog, fast action hold 'em, poker, pai gow, baccarat, craps, and roulette plus a race and sports book. The cocktail waitresses glide by in (skimpy) black velvet.

The 740 rooms and suites are among the nicest in Lake Tahoe. The prime Lake Suites include a Jacuzzi, private lakeview balcony, two color TVs, and a marble bath and dressing area. Hotel facilities include a heated outdoor swimming pool, health club, wedding chapel, and four tennis courts. Room rates range from about $95 to $170, with suites from $179 per night.

Downstairs in an arcade is the Orbitron, an Ultra Gravity Simulator that propels riders through a fighter jet ride, re-creating all of the G-force sensations of flight without ever leaving the ground.

Orbitron advice. Professional thrill-riders recommend you keep your eyes straight ahead on the screen and avoid looking from side to side; there is also an emergency stop button at each seat.

Tickets for the four-minute trip are about $3.50 and are restricted to those taller than 42 inches and over the age of seven. Pregnant women and those with health problems are advised not to take the journey.

Just slightly less adventuresome are arcade challenges like the four-seat Namco Endurance Championship Race, which permits head-to-head motorcycle racing. Nearby is a Galaxy Force machine, a moving fighter-pilot simulator.

At the rear of the arcade is a shooting gallery with a room full of animated Smurf-like creatures; the targets may be a bit too realistic for the tastes of some parents. More traditional amusements include a wide variety of video games and a skee-ball bowling alley.

Restaurants at Harvey's include the **Seafood Grotto**, a somewhat ordinary room with windows opened toward the slot machines. Lunch sandwiches and salads range from $7 to $11 and include the Clipper Salad (greens with shrimp, crabmeat, avocado, asparagus, cucumber, tomato, and onion).

> **Buyer beware.** Lake Tahoe seems especially prone to misleading come-ons from time-share resorts. Several casinos, including Harvey's, have desks that seem to be offering $50 in free chips or other such freebies. Once they've got your attention, you'll learn that the price of such largesse is a few hours of your time at a real estate promotion.

Dinner entrees range from about $10 to $25 and include spinach fettuccine *pescatore, cioppino,* a Pacific clambake for two (lobster, prawns, chicken, corn on the cob, and potatoes steamed with wine and herbs), broiled New York steak teriyaki, and bouillabaisse Marseilles.

At **Llewellyn's**, a stunning rooftop restaurant with wraparound windows, you'll find dishes priced from about $16 to $25 such as mesquite-broiled quails with creamy polenta and wild rice; salmon *involtini,* stuffed with asparagus, leeks, and carrots wrapped in phyllo dough with sun-dried tomato butter; and lamb Gilroy, in caramelized garlic with couscous and ratatouille.

Llewellyn's is open for lunch Wednesday through Saturday from 11:30 A.M. to 2:30 P.M., and for dinner daily. A champagne brunch is offered Sundays from 10 A.M. to 2 P.M. for about $17.

El Vaquero is a pleasant den-like setting decorated in Santa Fe reds and blacks; don't back into the cacti in the dark. Specialties include enchiladas Acapulco (flour tortillas filled with your choice of shrimp or crabmeat or both, covered with ranchera sauce and covered with melted cheeses and sour cream) for about $12. For lunch, offerings include sautéed red snapper topped with a tomatillo sauce and served with black beans for about $8. Open for dinner every night, and for lunch from Wednesday to Sunday, El Vaquero also offers karaoke parties in the lounge Friday and Saturday at 10 P.M.

The Carriage House is an attractive 24-hour coffee shop that offers a variety of standard offerings, plus a special breakfast and lunch on-the-run deal for skiers and travelers: for about $8, you get an egg or pancake breakfast and leave the restaurant with a box lunch of fried chicken or ham and cheese sandwich along with fresh fruit, cookie, and granola bar.

The **Garden Buffet** offers themed dinner buffets: Monday Mexican, Tuesday Barbecue, Wednesday Pasta, and Thursday German for $7.95. There's a Friday night seafood dinner, served from 4 to 10 P.M. for about $17. Included are two broiled lobster tails, cracked crab, shrimp, and champagne. The Saturday Brunch, offered from 7 A.M. to 2 P.M., includes scrambled eggs, top round, and baked ham. On Saturday nights, it's prime rib for $12.95, and Sunday is

New York Steak Night for $11.95. Brunch is also served daily for $6.25 during the week and $7.25 on weekends.

The **Sage Room** steak house, open for dinner from 6 P.M., features entrees from about $16 to $22, including peppercorn steak filet mignon with sauce béarnaise; roast duckling "bigarrade" (Long Island duckling topped with an orange sauce and flambéed with Grand Marnier). Other unusual offerings include honey rabbit sausage lasagne and venison grand *veneur* with melted Brie cheese.

Harvey's **Peak Lounge**, a small room alongside Llewellyn's, offers light fare including chilled prawns or crab, minted split pea soup with lobster, vanilla soufflé, and hot spiced wine.

Harvey's Resort/Hotel Casino. Highway 50, at Stateline; 588-2411, (800) 427-8397.

Bill's Lake Tahoe Casino

This is a high-fun, low-roller joint, the self-proclaimed "Quarter Capital of Nevada." Bill's, which is part of the same company that owns the next-door Harrah's Casino, has gone out of its way to encourage its young staff of dealers and attendants to be friendly to its crowd of skiers, summer vacationers, and party-goers. The serious gamblers are elsewhere.

They even encourage the taking of photographs on the casino floor.

Bill's includes a McDonald's and a Bennigan's within its walls. Along the streetfront, it includes a large collection of older mechanical slot machines. And there is "Billie Jean," described as the World's Largest Free Pull Slot Machine.

Bill's Lake Tahoe Casino. Highway 50, Stateline; 588-2455.

Harrah's Casino Hotel Lake Tahoe

Harrah's is one of the class acts of South Lake Tahoe. The 18-story, 534-room hotel begins with some of the most beautiful views of the mountains and the lake and also includes a domed swimming pool and an indoor family fun center. By Nevada standards, Harrah's is one of the more understated and elegant hotels in town.

The lobby has been remade to look like an alpine lodge, with slate tile floors and Persian rugs, wood and brass, a natural stone fireplace, and a waterfall.

Payment due. Some casinos will advertise their "overdue" jackpots on progressive machines, giving the implication that your chances of winning are higher if you play on one of them. Actually—assuming as you must that the machines are honest—the chances of winning on an overdue machine are the same if it has been 10 years since it has paid off or if the machine just paid off five minutes ago.

Think of it this way: if you flip an honest quarter 49 times and it comes up heads every time, the odds of it coming up tails on the 50th toss are still 50-50.

Old money. While you're in the registration area, look for the display of antique slot machines, including a circa 1902 Mills Duplex Ten-Way and a Caille's Centaur double, fitted out in oak and chrome.

A small **Warner Brothers Studio Store** has been installed right off the registration lobby of Harrah's.

A large L-shaped casino, it is relatively muted compared to some of the other casinos in town. Harrah's draws a lively mix of skiers, lake visitors, and gamblers. It offers a set of nice restaurants tucked away from the casino floor.

Guests staying at the nicely appointed rooms have access to a dome-covered swimming pool and spa and health clubs.

Room rates at Harrah's start at about $69 per night in the off-season; the hotel runs a number of special promotions throughout the year, including midweek and weekend packages. Also available are ski packages in conjunction with Heavenly, Kirkwood, Sierra-at-Tahoe, or Northstar ski resorts and golfing packages with the Dayton Valley Golf Course.

The hotel's Value Season runs from January 1 to mid-June and from mid-September through mid-December with room rates starting at $119 ($20 higher on weekends). The Summer Season occupies the middle of the year, with rooms starting at $139 in midweek.

One Harrah's service we haven't seen duplicated elsewhere was an offer from "The Ski Renter" for fittings of boots and equipment in your room.

The hotel's South Shore Room debuted "Playboy's High Voltage" in 1995, a music and dance show that includes giant projection screens and three cameras producing live video of the show. Tickets were priced at $17.50 for all seats.

Harrah's new **Family Fun Center,** located on the lower level of the hotel, is a smoke- and alcohol-free indoor playground including two levels of slides, ball pools, climbing areas, and games of skill including video games, skee-

Harrah's, Lake Tahoe

ball, and air hockey. The play area is open 9 A.M. to midnight or later.

The **PlayPal** indoor playground for young children includes a two-story plastic obstacle course with tunnels, ball bins, ladders, slides, and moonwalks. Admission to PlayPal is $3 for the first hour, and $1 each additional quarter hour; adults are admitted free and must supervise the very young.

Nearby is the **Zone Hunter** virtual reality game, in which contestants wear a headset with video and audio simulation of a futuristic hunting adventure. Players can enter the zone alone, or compete against a second contestant. Each round costs $3.

The exquisite **Summit Room** is on the 16th and 17th floors, not quite the summit of the High Sierras, but still a highly recommended gourmet experience for dinner; reservations are necessary. The two-story windows offer spectacular views. The restaurant is located in the former site of the Star Suite, one of Harrah's private luxury suites for high rollers.

Family tree. Harrah's is part of the Promus Companies, which also operate Embassy Suites, Homewood Suites, Hampton Inns, and Bill's Casino; in fact the hotel is sandwiched between a new Embassy Suites on the California side and Bill's on the Nevada side. Guests at Embassy Suites can use some of the health club facilities at Harrah's, and when Harrah's is oversold, some of its guests are put up next door in California.

The menu changes, but on various visits we have seen offerings such as an appetizer selection that included ragout of wild mushrooms in puff pastry, Chesapeake blue crab timbale, marinated grilled quail with apple fritters, a "mosaic" of domestic caviar served with blue corn blinis and flavored vodka

Harrah's, Lake Tahoe

**Indian Councils
Battle Mountain Band
Council**
35 Mountainview Drive,
#138–13
Battle Mountain, NV
89820
635-2004
**Carson Indian Commu-
nity Council**
2900 South Curry Street
Carson City, NV 89701
883-6431

**Indian Tribes
Duck Valley Shoshone-
Paiute Tribes**
P.O. Box 219
Owyhee, NV 89832
757-3211
**Duckwater Shoshone
Tribe**
P.O. Box 68
Duckwater, NV 89314
863-0227

for $15. Soups included spicy black bean soup and lobster bisque laced with Armagnac and crème fraîche.

Entrees, priced from about $26 to $45, have included Jamaican thresher shark steak with plantains, slow-smoked game hens with wild rice pancakes and lingonberry relish, grilled venison with kiln-dried cherries and melted Brie, and filet of Black Angus beef Gilroy for $29.

Other main courses include grilled veal chop with white bean cassoulet for $29, roasted rack of lamb with an anise crust and truffled mashed potatoes for $32, and free-range chicken stuffed with roast garlic and tomato coulise for $26.

The chef's selection in the winter of 1995 consisted of cider marinated quail with apple fritters, Caesar salad, cranberry sorbet, roast rack of lamb with an anise crust, live Maine lobster thermador, and Grand Marnier soufflé, priced at $55.

And, of course, there are some fabulous desserts including the aforementioned Grand Marnier soufflé, mango mousse, and crème brûlée.

Another fine restaurant is **Friday's Station Steak & Seafood Grill** on the 18th floor. Named after a famous stop on the Pony Express near Stateline, Nevada, it offers views of Lake Tahoe and the Sierras matched only by the food.

Offerings, which range from about $20 to $30, include Black Angus beef; pan-fried sea scallops and prawns in brown butter and lemon thyme; cheese-battered Alaskan halibut in pesto cream with bay shrimps and asparagus; and a mixed grill of lamb chops, filet of beef, smoked quail, Andouille sausage, and peppered filet mignon in green peppercorn sauce with brandy.

Or perhaps you'd like to sample smoked medallions of beef Gilroy, topped with roasted garlic and blue cheese served with a cabernet wine sauce for $21.95, or a seafood mixed grill of shrimp, scallops, lobster, swordfish, and salmon with red pepper remoulade and a creamy lemon wine sauce for $26.95.

We were especially impressed with the offer on the menu to broil, poach, sauté, steam, or blacken most seafood entrees to taste.

An attractive, reasonably priced Italian restaurant is **Cafe Andreotti**, with entrees priced from about $10 to $20. Specialties include an antipasto plate of Italian meats, cheese, marinated vegetables, olives, and bread sticks; and *pollo picatta* (chicken breasts dipped in Parmesan egg batter, sautéed with mushrooms and capers in lemon butter). We saw a San Francisco *cioppino* of scallops, shrimp, crab claws, and clams for $14.50, *paella* with shrimp, sausage, chicken, and clams in a Spanish saffron sauce over pasta for $10.95. Various pizzas range from the Gridiron Special (pepperoni, sausage, tomato sauce, and cheese) to the Hawaiian (Canadian bacon, pineapple, pizza sauce, and cheese), and the Mexicali (ground beef, olives, green onions, tomato sauce, and cheddar cheese).

The 24-hour **Sierra Restaurant** features sandwiches from $4 to $10 and burgers, fish, and chips. Breakfast omelettes range from $5 to $9. A Cobb salad is priced at $8.25 and Reuben sandwich at $6.25.

Asia offers a variety of Oriental specialties for dinner in a corner of the Sierra Restaurant. On one visit, appetizers included Vietnamese calamari with spicy dipping sauce, *kim chee* (Korean pickled cabbage), Chinese pot stickers, and Thai chicken wings braised with chilies.

Indian Councils and Tribes
Elko Band Council
P.O. Box 748
Elko, NV 89801
738-8889
Ely Shoshone Tribe
16 Shoshone Circle
Ely, NV 89301
289-3013

Entrees, which range from about $7 to $15, included Szechwan scallops, Thai coconut shrimp, Mongolian beef, Thai ginger beef, and Chinese *kung pao* chicken. We sampled Hunan chicken, stir-fried with chili peppers, green peppers, and mushrooms for $7.95.

The **North Beach Deli** offers San Francisco decor and specialties, including pasta, submarine sandwiches, espresso, and desserts 24 hours a day. Entrees start at about $7. One of the specialties is San Francisco Bay dilled bay shrimp with lettuce and tomato on sourdough baguette. Skiers and travelers can order sandwiches to go.

The **Skyway Buffet** offers eggs cooked to order for breakfast and prime rib every dinner. On Friday night, there's a special seafood buffet, and brunch is served on Saturday and Sunday.

The **Forest Restaurant** offers a breakfast buffet Monday through Saturday and a Sunday brunch including French toast, Canadian bacon, and cheese blintzes. Lunch and dinner buffets are offered Saturday through Thursday; the Saturday seafood buffet includes caviar, smoked salmon, and scallops.

The 800-seat **South Shore Room** has been the home of regular headline entertainment including Hollywood and Broadway-theme productions. It also features late-night "Nevada adult entertainment"; in other words, near-naked women and men in dance, music, and comedy routines with titles like "Beyond Bare Essence" and "E*ROCK*TICA."

A new lounge, the **Center Stage**, was opened late in 1994.

Harrah's Casino Hotel Lake Tahoe. Highway 50, Stateline; 588-6606, (800) 648-3773.

Caesars Tahoe

Smaller than the Las Vegas landmark and considerably less opulent, Caesars Tahoe nevertheless carries through its Roman theme pretty well. Among the touches of Vegas transported to the lake is the legion of cocktail waitresses in off-the-shoulder togas. Unlike the Vegas floor, though, the skimpy costume does not include cone-headdresses.

He'll be back. According to publicists for Caesars Tahoe, Arnold Schwarzenegger hit a $500 jackpot at a $1 slot machine while posing for photographers at the grand opening of Planet Hollywood. They claim it was strictly a matter of luck.

Fallon Paiute Shoshone Tribe
8955 Mission Road
P.O. Box 1650
Fallon, NV 89406
423-6075
Fort McDermitt Indian Reservation
P.O. Box 457
McDermitt, NV 89421
532-8259

Many of the 440 suites and rooms offer circular bathtubs for those who like to bathe in the round. Other facilities include an indoor pool, health spa, racquetball, and tennis courts. Room rates range from about $89 to $175; suites go from about $300 to $650 per night.

The casino is attractive but a bit cramped. Top headliners perform in the 1,600-seat Circus Maximus Showroom. Music, magic, and comedy are presented in the 300-seat Caesars Cabaret, and there is live music and dancing at Nero's 2000 Nightclub.

The newest magnet at Caesars, part of a growing trend to attract "Generation X" to the casinos, is the new **Planet Hollywood** restaurant, open every day from 11 A.M. to 2 A.M. The restaurant's grand opening included some of the restaurant chain's celebrity owners such as Bruce Willis and Arnold Schwarzenegger.

The exterior of the restaurant is adorned with a huge set of Hollywood-style sunglasses. Memorabilia on display at the restaurant include Mel Gibson's motorcycle from *Lethal Weapon III*, Arnie's cyborg from *Terminator II*, the gambling dice from *Indecent Proposal*, Don Johnson's pants from "Miami Vice," and Freddy's shirt, as worn by *Nightmare on Elm Street* actor Robert Englund.

The toniest Chinese restaurant in town is the **Empress Court**, a small, dimly lit elegant room decorated in Oriental blues and reds with gold accents. Prix-fixe meals are available in the range of $12.95 to $19.95. Specialties include sautéed scallops and shrimp in black bean sauce for $18.50, crispy sesame chicken with lemon sauce for $11.75, ginger beef with pineapple for $13.50, crystal prawns with glazed walnuts for $18.50, and slowly roasted imperial Peking duck for $38.

The **Broiler Room** is an unusual cubbyhole with dark brick walls and dim candelabras and sconces. Menu items includes New York steak for $18.95, veal piccata for $22.95, and T-bone steak for $26.95. Seafood specialties include Spanish gambas (jumbo prawns marinated in olive oil and herbs, broiled, and served with garlic croutons and sauce Catalan) for $19.95.

Also on the menu is a selection of spicy creole foods using recipes from the famed K-Paul's Louisiana Kitchen in New Orleans. Offerings include Louisiana seafood gumbo for $5.95, K-Paul's favorite blackened prawns for $19.95, and jambalaya with plump shrimp and spicy Andouille sausage for $16.75.

The **Pisces Bar** lives up to its name with offerings including clams on the halfshell for $1.65 each, and sea scallops "Pisces" for $18.00. Other specialties include angel hair pasta pomodoro in basil-tomato sauce for $11.

Casey's Seafood Restaurant is a very attractive light blue and coral room.

Entrees include *caciuco*, a hearty seafood and tomato stew for $24.50, grilled ahi tuna with cabbage and soy for $20, seafood linguine for $16.50, and grilled lamb chops $21.

The **Cafe Roma** features the Cafe Roma burger (ground beef with melted cheese and a strip of bacon on a freshly baked bun) for $5.25, two eggs any style with pancakes for $2.95, and *huevos con chorizo* (Mexican pork sausage scrambled with eggs and garnished with fresh tomatoes and green onion, served with breakfast potatoes) for $5.95. The Cafe is a large, open space with wall murals and Roman columns.

Caesars Tahoe. Highway 50, Stateline; 588-3515, (800) 648-3353.

Moapa Tribal Store
P.O. Box 340
Moapa, NV 89025
865-2787

Pyramid Lake Paiute Tribe
P.O. Box 256
Nixon, NV 89424
786-5626

Reno-Sparks Indian Colony
98 Colony Road
Reno, NV 89502
329-2972

Stewart Indian Museum
5366 Snyder Avenue
Carson City, NV 89701
882-1808

Horizon Casino Resort

A very lively and busy casino with a big collection of nickel slots; we'd recommend dark glasses. The mirrored ceiling makes you feel like you're inside a huge powder room turned sideways.

There are 520 rooms and suites, many with lakeview balconies. Facilities include a large outdoor pool and hot tubs. Winter room rates start at $69 during the week and $89 on weekends.

Entertainment, featuring headline acts, is presented in the 1,200-seat **Grande Lake Theatre.** Shows and revues are offered in the 200-seat **Golden Cabaret**, and there is live music nightly in the **Aspen Lounge.**

Josh's restaurant, a rather ordinary setting, offers a special lobster dinner for $10.95 every night but Saturday. Other entrees include shrimp scampi for $15.50, fillet of petrale sole sauté Veronique (a grape and almond butter sauce) for $13.75, blackened red snapper for $13.95, and Kansas City rib eye steak for $14.95. Two cuts of prime rib—big and bigger—are offered for $13.95 or $15.50.

The 24-hour **Four Seasons** coffee shop includes burgers for $5 to $6, chicken fajita salad for $7.75; shrimp Louie for $8.95, and cold deli sandwiches for $4.25 to $6. A New York steak special is priced at $7.99.

The **LeGrande Buffet** offers a weekday brunch buffet for $2.99; Saturday and Sunday brunches are priced at $4.99; the dinner buffet is $4.99 every night but Saturday, when it is priced at $6.99.

Horizon Casino Resort. Highway 50, Stateline; 588-6211, (800) 648-3322.

Embassy Suites Resort

An all-suites hotel with 400 rooms, just across the state line into California and sharing some of its facilities with its corporate and physical neighbor, Harrah's. Offers an indoor pool, whirlpool spa, and workout room.

Entertainment is presented at the **Turtles Sports Bar** & **Dance Emporium,** where you can also get a bite to eat. Other restaurants include **Zackary's**, **Pasquale's**, and **Julie's Deli**.

And guess what? No casino. That is, unless you want to walk a few feet into Nevada.

Embassy Suites Resort. Highway 50, South Lake Tahoe, CA; (916) 544-5400, (800) 362-2779.

Ridge Tahoe Resort

Tucked away on the Kingsbury Grade and just above the Stagecoach Lodge of Heavenly Ski Resort, the Ridge offers guests their own private 10-passenger gondolas to take them to the lodge for a day of skiing. Other amenities include an indoor/outdoor pool, tennis and racquetball courts, and a health club.

The Ridge Tahoe Resort. Stateline; 588-3553, (800) 334-1600.

Restaurants in South Lake Tahoe and Stateline

As befits a year-round vacation playground, the south end of Lake Tahoe is well supplied with a wide variety of restaurants. Following are some of the more interesting eateries outside of the casinos.

The Beacon. 1900 Jamison Beach Rd., Camp Richardson; (916) 541-0630. Lunch and dinner. Burgers and sandwiches for lunch on the beach. Dinner entrees include Fresh Lake Trout, Chicken Tallac (chicken breast rolled and stuffed with fresh spinach, Swiss cheese, pine nuts, sage, and wild mushrooms), and Macadamia nut prawns priced from about $10 to $25.

The Brewery. 3542 Highway 50; (916) 544-2739. Lunch and dinner. A microbrewery and pub. Brews include local specialties like Needle Peak Ale, Alpine Amber, and Bad Ass Ale; munchies include beer-steamed shrimp.

Cafe Fiore. 1169 Ski Run Boulevard; (916) 541-2908. Breakfast, lunch, and dinner.

Cantina Los Tres Hombres. 765 Emerald Bay Road; (916) 544-1233. Lunch and dinner. An ambitious menu of Mexican and Southwestern specialties from steak, chicken, and shrimp *fajitas* to *chile colorado* in mild red chile sauce and *chile verde* in green chiles. Entrees range from about $7 to $20. The bar serves at least seven unusual Margarita concoctions.

The Eagles' Nest. 472 Needle Peak Road; 588-3245. Lunch and dinner. Restaurant and jazz club with live performances most weekends. A lively eatery with entrees from New York! New York! (a New York steak with green peppercorn sauce for $12.95) to Hep Catfish (Louisiana-style blackened catfish for $9.95), and A Real Jazz burger for $5.95. Fun appetizers include roasted garlic, hot wings, onion rings, and nachos.

Emerald Palace. 871 Emerald Bay Road; (916) 544-2421. Lunch and dinner. An ambitious Chinese menu, from unusual soups such as Spinach Bean Cake, Chicken Corn, and Shrimp Sizzling Rice, to a full range of standard and exotic beef, seafood, chicken, pork, and vegetable dishes, priced from about $7 to $12.

Fresh Ketch. 2433 Venice, Tahoe Keys Marina; (916) 541-5683. Lunch and dinner. Oysters to smoked salmon, sashimi to burgers, chowder to filet mignon. Entrees priced from about $6 to $24.

Grand Central Pizza. 2229 Highway 50; (916) 544-1308. Lunch and dinner. Basic to fancy pizza, from spaghetti to lasagna.

The Greenhouse. 4140 Cedar Avenue; (916) 541-5800. Dinner. Salads, escargots, veal piccata, chicken cordon bleu, tournedos of lamb, and roast duckling a l'orange, with entrees priced from about $12 to $22.

Marie Callender's. 3601 Highway; (916) 544-5535. Breakfast, lunch, and dinner. An outpost of the California-based burger, pie, sandwich, pie, pasta, pie, and chicken cafe. Did we mention the pies? Entrees from about $7 to $15.

Nepheles. 1169 Ski Run Boulevard; (916) 544-8130. Lunch and dinner. "Creative California Cuisine." Appetizers include seafood cheesecake, fresh swordfish egg rolls, and stuffed mushrooms Milano. Entrees, priced from about $14 to $20, include baked fresh ahi in Asian peanut sauce, wild boar in prunes and cabbage and topped with orange apricot brandy sauce, and chicken teriyaki.

Rojo's. Highway 50 and San Francisco Avenue; (916) 541-4960. In an atmosphere described as "rustic old Tahoe." Lunch and dinner. Steaks, burgers, ribs, and Italian offerings, priced from about $7 to $16.

Samurai. 2588 Highway 50; (916) 542-0300. Dinner. Sushi, teriyaki, tempura, and *nabemono* grilled beef or seafood, priced from about $10 to $16.

Sato. 3436 Highway 50; (916) 541-3769. Dinner. Japanese fare from a full range of Sushi dishes to tempura and teriyaki entrees, priced from about $8 to $14. Sato's Love Boat is a special sampler dinner including California roll, sushi, tempura, teriyaki, and soup, priced at about $15 per person.

Scusa! 1142 Ski Run Boulevard; (916) 542-0100. Dinner. From unusual pizzas such as a pie with smoked chicken, Andouille sausage, cilantro, and mozzarella to stuffed eggplant, seared sea scallops Mediterranean, and chicken piccata, priced from about $10 to $15.

Swiss House. 787 Emerald Bay Road; (916) 542-1717. Lunch and dinner. Sandwiches and schnitzels, priced from about $10 to $17, and cheese fondue for two for $26.

Tep's Villa Roma. 3450 Highway 50; (916) 541-8227. Dinner. Serious Italian fare, including all of the usual suspects such as all sorts of pasta dishes, a full range of shrimp, veal, steak, and chicken offerings, and more. Entrees, priced from about $10 to $18, include a salad bar.

Water Wheel South. Crescent V Shopping Center; (916) 544-4158. Dinner. Chinese fare, from about $6 to $10. Chef's specialties include beggar's chicken and Peking duck at about $24.

Hotels and Casinos in North Lake Tahoe

Cal-Neva Lodge, Crystal Bay

Famous for its swimming pool, which sits atop the state border. Swimmers can start in California and end up in Nevada where there is, of course, a casino.

There are 200 rooms, most with lake views, with a few private chalets. Rates in the winter started at about $59 per weekday night for a package that included a ski lift ticket.

Early guests included mobster Pretty Boy Floyd. During Prohibition, the Cal-Neva was one of the most famous speakeasies in the country. Later on, the hotel was owned by singer Frank Sinatra and was one of the gathering places for the "Rat Pack" Hollywood crowd during the 1960s.

The hotel's main room is the impressive Indian Room, with vaulted ceiling and huge beams and a rock fireplace split by the state line. The room includes a display on the Washoe tribe as well as antique hunting trophies from the lake region. As befits a casino, the room is open 24 hours a day.

Cal-Neva Lodge. Crystal Bay; 832-4000, (800) 225-6382.

Hyatt Regency Lake Tahoe Resort & Casino, Incline Village

A 458-room, four-star resort with mountain- and lake-view rooms and suites, as well as 24 lakeside cottages on the hotel's private beach. Other amenities include a health club, outdoor heated pool and jet spa. Camp Hyatt is for kids from 3 to 12.

Restaurants include **Stetson's** for fine dining; **Ciao Mein**, which combines Italian and Chinese specialties; and the **Sierra Cafe** with breakfast, lunch, and dinner buffets as well as coffee shop service.

Winter packages, including a day of skiing at Alpine Meadows, Diamond Peak, or Northstar, start at $69 during the week and $99 on weekends.

Hyatt Regency Lake Tahoe Resort & Casino. Country Club Drive and Lakeshore Drive, Incline Village; 832-1234, (800) 553-3288.

Tahoe Biltmore Lodge & Casino, Incline Village

A big old-style hotel, with a group of small wooden motel units along the lake. 5 Highway 28, Incline Village; 831-0660.

Resort at Squaw Creek, Squaw Valley

A spectacular resort set in and among the trails at Squaw Creek with ski-in/out access, cross-country trails, golf course, three swimming pools, four spas, tennis center, horseback riding, and more. There are 405 rooms, including 204 suites.

Restaurants at the resort include **Glissandi** for elegant French cuisine; **Cascades**, an all-day eatery with buffet and a la carte offerings; **Ristorante Montagna**, with Italian pasta and other specialties; the **Bullwhackers** pub and steak house; the **Sun Plaza Deck** barbecue wagon for lunch; and the **Sweet Potatoes Deli.**

Resort at Squaw Creek. Olympic Valley, CA; (916) 583-6300, (800) 327-3353.

North Lake Tahoe Restaurants

Bacchi's Inn. Italian and seafood specialties, including fettuccine a la Romana for $11.75, spaghetti Caruso with chicken livers and mushrooms for $11.75, veal piccante tenderloin for $17.25, Italian barbecue spare ribs for $14.50, and beef a la Stroganoff for $18.50. Dinners include hors d'oeuvres, minestrone soup, salad, and pasta. Lake Forest, northeast of Tahoe City; (916) 583-3324.

Bluewater Brewing Company. Beer made in the brewery on premises, and all sorts of food to eat with beer including Woody's Wild Wings (in hot, atomic, or insane sauce) for $4.95, hummus plate for $4.95, salads, Bluewater burgers for $5.95, black beans and rice cooked in beer and spices for $4.50, and beer chili for $5.95. Beers include Misty Mountain Oatmeal Stout, Arrowhead Red Ale, and the brew of the month. 850 North Lake Boulevard, Tahoe City; (916) 581-2583.

Boulevard Cafe & Trattoria. Classic northern Italian fare, including *osso bucco di vitello con Gremolada* (braised veal shanks with vegetables, garlic and herbs) for $20, *anatra al Forno all Ciliege* (roast duck with balsamic vinegar and sun-dried cherry glaze) for $16, and *conchiglie con spinaci e salsicce* (pasta shells stuffed with spinach, sausage, and ricotta cheese) for $10. 6731 North Lake Boulevard, Tahoe Vista; (916) 546-7213.

Captain Jon's Seafood. Entrees include oysters Florentine (baked Malpeque oysters on a bed of spinach topped with Brie cheese) for $19, scampi for $18, filet mignon Roquefort broiled and served in a cognac, demiglace, and Roquefort sauce for $25, and angel hair pasta in white cream sauce with scallops and prawns for $18. Open for lunch and dinner in summer, and dinner only in winter. 7220 North Lake Boulevard, Tahoe Vista; (916) 546-4819.

Jason's Saloon & Grille. An interesting mix of seafood, chicken, steak, and burgers including Bayou shrimp for $17, Louisiana chicken for $14, baby back ribs for $15, and a Russian burger (with horseradish cream sauce and bacon) for $6.25. 8338 North Lake Boulevard, Kings Beach; (916) 546-3315.

Lakehouse Pizza. Not just pizza, they say: Polish pirushki stuffed with peppers, mushrooms, olives, tomatoes, onions, and sauce for $7.25; Italian calzone for $7.50; American Salad . . . and pizza. 120 Grove Street, Tahoe City; (916) 583-2222.

Las Panchitas. A full range of Mexican specialties including tacos, enchiladas, burritos, chili, and tostadas. Dinners, priced from about $11 to $12, include steak Ranchero (top sirloin in a special sauce, refried beans, and Spanish rice, and *achiote* halibut served on black beans). North Lake Boulevard, Kings Beach; (916) 546-4539.

Mofo's Pizza. New York–style pizza from basic to unusual such as clam and garlic, spinach, and vegetarian. Also offered are sandwiches, calzones, lasagna, and a salad bar. Christmas Tree Village, Incline Village; 831-4999.

Old European Restaurant. From sauerbraten to kassler rippchen (smoked pork loin) to Vienna *schnitzel* garnie, priced from about $11 to $16. Specialties include chateaubriand for two for $45. Highway 89 north of Tahoe City; (916) 583-3102.

Soule Domain Restaurant. Gourmet dining in a log cabin, across from the Tahoe Biltmore Casino. Appetizers include garlic raviolis, wild shiitake mushrooms, and soft-shell crabs. Entrees, priced from about $13 to $20, include sea scallops poached in champagne with kiwi and papaya cream sauce for $17, fresh pasta with lobster, prawns, and scallops in lemon garlic butter for $22, and curried cashew chicken with snow peas and teriyaki sauce, for $13. Stateline Road, Crystal Bay; (916) 546-7529.

Willii B's. A "taste of the South" at the north end of the lake in the far west. Entrees include seafood jambalaya for $14.95, Delta *bouillabaisse* for $17.95, and seafood or duck gumbo for $15.95. Tahoe City; (916) 583-0346.

Yama Sushi & Robata Grill. A wide range of the real thing: from more than two dozen types of sushi to *gyoza* dumplings to *robatayaki* skewers of asparagus, eggplant, quail eggs, beef tongue, salmon, and a dozen more. Entrees, priced from about $9 to $18 include tempura, sashimi, and *udon* soups. 950 North Lake Boulevard, Tahoe City; (916) 583-9262.

Lake Tahoe Region Hotels and Accommodations

Moderate: $100 or less during nonholiday periods.

Expensive: More than $100 during nonholiday periods.

Lake Tahoe Visitors Authority. (800) 288-2463. Lodging referral service.

Heavenly Central Reservation. P.O. Box 2180, Stateline, NV 89449; (800) 243-2836.

Lake Tahoe Accommodations. (800) 544-3234. Offering vacation homes, resort condominiums, cabins, and ski chalets all around the lake with offices in North and South Lake Tahoe.

South Lake Tahoe Motels and Condominiums

Best Western Station House Inn. (916) 542-1101, (800) 822-5953. 100 rooms. Breakfast, ski shuttle. Moderate.

Fantasy Inn. (916) 544-6767, (800) 367-7736. 53 themed rooms and suites. Spas, ski shuttle. Expensive.

Forest Inn Suites. (916) 541-6655, (800) 822-5950. 107 suites, 17 hotel rooms. In the woods partway up the mountain. Pools, spas, ski shuttle. Moderate.

Holiday Inn Express. (916) 544-5900, (800) 465-4329. 89 rooms with refrigerators. Indoor spa. Continental breakfast. Moderate.

Inn by the Lake. (916) 542-0330, (800) 877-1466. 100 suites and rooms. Heated outdoor pool, spa. Continental breakfast, ski and casino shuttles. Moderate.

Lakeland Village Beach & Ski Resort. (916) 544-1685, (800) 822-5969. Pool, spa; fireplaces in all rooms. Moderate.

Pinewild Condominiums, Zephyr Cove. 588-2790, (800) 822-2790. 135 condominiums on 27 acres of lakefront property. Fireplaces in lakeside units. Expensive.

Sierra-Cal Lodge. (916) 541-5400, (800) 541-0202. 124 rooms in the pines. Casino and ski shuttles. Moderate.

Tahoe West. (916) 544-6455, (800) 522-1021. 60-room hotel. Spa, casino and ski shuttles. Moderate.

Travelodge. Casino Area, (916) 541-5000; South Tahoe, (916) 544-5266; Stateline, (916) 544-6000. Toll-free for all three: (800) 255-3050. Three properties with a total of 175 rooms. Casino and ski shuttles. Inexpensive to moderate.

Other South Lake Tahoe Motels

Cedar Lodge. (916) 544-6453.

Elm Inn. (916) 541-7900.
Heavenly Valley Motel & Spa. (916) 544-4244, (800) 422-2467.
LaBaer Motor Lodge. (916) 544-5232.
LeGeraniums Bed & Breakfast. (916) 544-6450.
Nendel's Blue Jay Motel. (916) 544-5232.
Richardson's Resort. (916) 541-1801, (800) 544-1801.
Riviera Inn. (916) 544-3448.
Royal Valhalla Motel. (916) 544-2233.
Sorensen's Resort. (916) 694-2203, (800) 423-9949.
Tahoe Chalet Inn. (916) 544-3311, (800) 821-2656.
Tahoe Marina Inn. (916) 541-2180, (800) 448-4577.
Tahoe Tropicana Motel. (916) 541-3911.
Tahoe Valley Motel/Condominium. (916) 541-0353, (800) 669-7544.
Tahoe Villa. (916) 544-3041.
Thunderbird Motel. (916) 544-5741.
Viking Motor Lodge. (916) 541-5155, (800) 288-4083.
Walley's Hot Springs Resort. 782-8155.
Zephyr Cove Lodge. 588-6644.

North Lake Tahoe Motels and Condominiums

Club Tahoe. Incline Village; 831-5750, (800) 527-5154. Condominium resort. Spas, sauna, racquetball. Expensive.

Donner Lake Village Resort. (916) 587-6081, (800) 621-6664. 64 hotel rooms, plus lakeside townhouses. Marina with boat rentals; ski packages available. Moderate.

Squaw Valley Inn. (916) 583-1576, (800) 323-7666. 60-room inn originally built to house participants in the 1960 Winter Olympics. Spas. Expensive.

Squaw Valley Lodge. (916) 583-5500, (800) 922-9970. 154 ski-in, ski-out suites. Spas, kitchenettes. Moderate to expensive.

Tahoe Sands Resort. (916) 546-2592, (800) 438-9139. Beach front condominiums at Tahoe Vista. Spa, marina. Moderate.

Cabins and Campgrounds

Cabins to Castles. (916) 544-5397, (800) 422-2467.
Carney's Cabins. (916) 542-3361.
Carson Valley Inn RV Park. 782-9711.
Echo Creek Ranch. (916) 544-5397, (800) 462-5397.
KOA Campground. (916) 577-3693.
Lakeside RV Park. 588-4220.
Michelsen Vacation Rentals. 588-4811, (800) 568-2463.
Pine Cone Resort. 588-6561.
Reservation Bureau. (916) 544-4244, (800) 422-2467.

All phone numbers are in the (702) area code unless otherwise specified.

Richardson's Resort. (916) 541-1801, (800) 544-1801.
Sorensen's Resort. (916) 694-2203, (800) 462-5397.
Tahoe Pines Campground. (916) 577-1653.
Tahoe Valley Campground. (916) 541-2222.
Walley's Hot Springs Resort. 782-8155.
Zephyr Cove Lodge and Campground. 588-6644.

Cruises Around the Lake

M.S. Dixie II. A new version of a Lake Tahoe classic, making $1\frac{1}{2}$- to $3\frac{1}{2}$-hour cruises to Emerald Bay (about $14 for adults and $5 for children) and sunset dinner and dance cruises (about $34, including dinner). Based at the Zephyr Cove Marina, four miles north of Stateline on Route 50. The glass-bottom sternwheeler can accommodate 350 passengers.

> **Tahoe North Visitors and Convention Bureau.** Box 5578, Tahoe City, CA 95730; (916) 583-3494, (800) 824-6348.

Passengers on the Dixie can also watch "The Sunken Treasures of Lake Tahoe," a video presented on board each cruise; cameras show underwater canyons, ancient petrified forests hidden by the lake, the sheer vertical cliffs of Rubicon Bay and the scuttled Steamer Tahoe, 500 feet below the surface of Glenbrook Bay.

The boat runs from May 1 through Christmas, weather permitting. Free shuttle service is offered from South Lake Tahoe, Carson City, Reno, or the North Shore of the lake. Call 588-3508 or 882-0786. *You will find a discount in the coupon section of this book.*

Tahoe Queen. A 500-passenger glass-bottom paddlewheeler, based at Ski Run Marina, South Lake Tahoe. In warm weather, the Queen cruises to Emerald Bay or Glenbrook (about $14 to $16.50 for adults and $5 to $8 for children) and sunset dinner dance cruises (about $38, including dinner). In winter, Lake Tahoe Cruises runs a water shuttle to and from the top of the lake, connecting to buses to the Squaw Valley ski resort. Call (916) 541-3364 or 541-4652 for information.

Woodwind. A large trimaran sailing vessel, it makes day cruises (for about $14 for adults and $7 for children) and sunset champagne cruises (about $20 for adults) from May to October. Call 588-3000 for information.

Getting Around in Lake Tahoe

Airports

Tahoe Valley Airport. South Lake Tahoe, CA; (916) 541-4080.
Truckee-Tahoe Airport. Truckee, CA; (916) 587-4119. Private and corporate service.
Carson Airport. Carson City, NV; 882-1551. Private and corporate.
Douglas County Airport. Minden, NV; 782-8277. Charter service.

Car Rentals

Action Auto Rental. 885-2885.

Adventure Sport Vehicle Rentals. South Lake Tahoe; (916) 541-7155, (800) 223-2999.

Avis Rent A Car. Tahoe Valley Airport; (916) 542-5638. Embassy Suites hotel, South Lake Tahoe; (916) 542-5710. Nationwide; (800) 331-1212.

Budget/Sears. Caesars Tahoe, Stateline; 588-5145. South Lake Tahoe Airport; (916) 541-5777, (800) 527-0700.

Dollar Rent A Car. Horizon Casino Resort, South Lake Tahoe; 588-4849, (800) 800-4000.

Enterprise Rent-A-Car. South Lake Tahoe; (916) 544-7788, (800) 325-8007.

Hertz Rent A Car. Harrah's Stateline; 588-4911. South Lake Tahoe Airport; (916) 544-2327. Incline Village; 831-4371. Nationwide; (800) 654-3131.

Tahoe Rent-A-Car. Tahoe Valley Motel, South Lake Tahoe; (916) 544-4500.

Road and Weather Information

California Highway Conditions. (916) 581-1400.

California Highway Patrol. (916) 587-3510.

Caltrans Road Information. South Lake Tahoe; (916) 577-3550. Truckee; (916) 587-3806. Reno; 793-1313.

Nevada Highway Patrol. 793-1313.

Bus Service

Dial-A-Ride/Lake Tahoe Transportation System. South Lake Tahoe area; (916) 577-7000.

Five Star Enterprises Limo Service. Airport to Reno and North Lake Tahoe; (916) 587-7651, (800) 782-4707.

Greyhound Lines West. South Lake Tahoe; (916) 544-2351. Truckee; (916) 587-3822.

STAGE (South Lake Tahoe Area Ground Express). South Lake Tahoe area; (916) 573-2080.

Ski Area Shuttle Buses

The following ski areas provide shuttle services; call for schedules and pickup locations:

Alpine Meadows. (916) 583-4232.
Diamond Peak. 832-1177.
Northstar. (916) 562-1010.
Squaw Valley. (916) 583-6985.
Sugar Bowl. (916) 426-3651.
Mount Rose. 849-0704.

More State and National Parks.
Death Valley National Monument. Death Valley, CA 92328; (916) 786-2331.
Great Basin National Park. Baker, NV 89311; 234-7331.
Humboldt National Forest. 976 Mountain City Highway, Elko, NV 89801; 738-5171.

Breathe deeply. Altitude sickness is caused by the fact that there is less oxygen in the air at the slightly lower pressures of the mountains; this causes chemical changes in your bloodstream.

Lake Tahoe Health

Altitude Sickness. Feeling a bit faint, tired, nauseated, headachy, or short of breath? Having trouble sleeping, or does the fabulous spread of a casino buffet hold no particular appeal?

You may be suffering from a mild case of altitude sickness. Lake Tahoe sits at about 6,235 feet above sea level; if you have come from an east or west coast city, you are living more than a mile higher than you are used to.

The cure is to avoid overexertion, get plenty of rest, and drink plenty of fluids. You also should eat lightly and cut down on alcohol consumption. The ultimate cure is time: your body should adjust within two or three days.

If your symptoms are especially severe, or if they don't seem to pass, you should see a doctor. Persons with heart conditions or high blood pressure should check with their doctor at home before heading for the mountains.

Frostbite. It gets very cold up in the hills. Cover all exposed parts of the body, and go indoors frequently during cold weather.

Frostbite occurs when the water in your body cells literally freezes. Superficial frostbite usually involves the fingertips, ears, nose, toes, and cheeks; symptoms include a burning sensation, tingling, or numbness and a whitish discoloration of the skin. Deep frostbite is more serious and can result in the death of the cells and even open wounds that are susceptible to infection.

If you develop frostbite, find warm shelter immediately. *Do not* rub frostbitten skin; instead, immerse the affected parts of the body in *lukewarm* (not hot) water. If the skin does not return to its normal color, or if blistering, swelling, pain, or numbness develops, seek medical attention.

Hypothermia. This serious condition results when the body's core (internal) temperature drops below the normal range of about 98.6 degrees and the body is unable to restore the proper temperature. Left untreated, hypothermia can lead to organ malfunction, damage, and eventual death.

Symptoms include fatigue, mood changes, and impaired motor skills. Wear warm, layered, dry clothing including hats and gloves; avoid alcohol and take indoor breaks.

Sunburn. The higher elevation of mountainous areas increases your risk of sunburn; ultraviolet rays are about five times as strong as at sea level.

Doctors generally recommend use of a sunscreen with a rating of 15 or 20, including PABA; lip balms with PABA or zinc oxide are also suggested. Sunglasses are also recommended to protect your eyes.

If you receive a sunburn without blisters, apply cool compresses to the affected area and take aspirin for pain and Benadryl to relieve itching. Blisters are a sign of a second-degree burn. Do not pop blisters, and stay out of the sun to avoid further damage. You should see a doctor for any facial blisters or blisters with cloudy liquid, or for severe pain.

Chapter 27
Winter Sports in the Lake Tahoe Region

We don't know of many places more breathtaking than Lake Tahoe, especially when seen from the top of a spectacular snow-packed plunge. And there aren't many groups of more than a dozen world-class ski resorts that lie within a one- to two-hour drive from a full-feature city like Reno. (The only other candidate we would propose is Salt Lake City.) Add in the attraction of gambling casinos, restaurants, and showrooms of Reno and Lake Tahoe and you've got a wintertime bet worth making.

If you're in Reno for a casino visit or a business stop, it is a very simple matter to rent a car or take a shuttle bus down to Lake Tahoe and take in a day's skiing; if you are staying at Lake Tahoe, it is equally easy to take a break from the slopes to drive north to Reno to see the big city and sample all it has to offer.

The Queen of South Lake Tahoe ski areas is Heavenly, a massive resort whose lower slopes can be seen from Stateline/South Lake Tahoe, and from much of the lake itself.

Ruling over the north end of the lake area is Squaw Valley USA, site of the 1960 Winter Olympics.

The Lake Tahoe ski season typically runs from about November through mid-April. Many of the major areas now have snowmaking capability which can start the season off right, patch up mid-season bare spots, or even save the day when nature doesn't cooperate. In the 1994–95 season, a snow drought came to a halt when storm after storm passed through the area over the winter. At the time of one of my visits in February, there was 12 to 16 feet of snow at the top of several of the resorts, including Heavenly, Kirkwood, and Squaw Valley.

Lake Tahoe Ski Areas
Heavenly Lake Tahoe

Skiers get to see sights that many of the rest of the flatlanders miss. Though I have been to many of the most spectacular ski areas of the world, Heavenly Lake Tahoe took my breath away. The highest ski trails on this massive hill seem to hang suspended above the blue of the lake below; at one point, I found myself skiing down through a white cloud to a panorama of the lake.

Heavenly opened in 1955 with one chair lift and a small hut on U.S. Forest Service land on the south shore of Lake Tahoe. Today it includes 25 lifts, six day lodges, 4,800 acres of terrain, 700 acres of snowmaking, and parts of two states. In 1995, the Dipper triple chair was replaced with the Dipper Express quad lift on the Nevada side, and snowmaking was added on several more trails.

There's an exciting expansion of the hill on the drawing boards. If local authorities and environmental groups approve, Heavenly plans to add a new gondola system that would run from the Stateline casino area itself behind the Embassy Suites hotel to a new restaurant and lodge about two-thirds of the way up the mountain. This would allow casino visitors to sample the mountain, and allow skiers to walk directly from the casinos to the gondola. Other plans include development of additional ski runs on the mountain.

What you see from the road in South Lake Tahoe or Stateline is perhaps one-third of just one face of the mountain. Sixteen of its lifts lie in California, and nine are in Nevada, including the resort's famous aerial tramway, two detachable quads, eight triple chairs, eight double chairs, and six surface lifts. The tram runs from the base lodge on the California side 1,700 feet up the mountain at an average angle of more than 45 degrees; a restaurant awaits at the upper tram base.

The hill, impressive as it is, is a decidely intermediate area. There are 68 runs—20 percent beginner, 45 percent intermediate, and 35 percent advanced/

Heavenly ski area, Lake Tahoe

expert. Among the skiable areas is the Mott Canyon Trail, one of the steepest in America.

The vertical drop is 3,500 feet, with the top elevation at 10,040 feet. The base elevation in California is at 6,540 feet, and in Nevada it is at 7,200 feet. The longest mountain descent is five and a half miles.

Heavenly receives an average annual snowfall of 300 inches, and in recent years has put down an additional 120 inches of machine-made snow. The season usually runs from mid-November through April. Area hotels usually offer packages based on three seasons, running from least crowded to busiest.

Cold Science. Machine-made snow is just like natural snow, only more so. Water and air are pumped through a network of more than 100,000 feet of pipe to the snowmaking guns. The water is atomized by the air and then shot out into the cold atmosphere where the droplets crystallize and form snowflakes. Water and air settings can be adjusted to achieve a particular type of snow—early in the season, snowmakers make heavier snow to build the base; after the base is in place or after natural snowfall, snowmakers use less water to make a light, dry snow for best skiing.

Value Season: Just after Thanksgiving to just before Christmas, or approximately November 29 to December 17.

Regular Season: Thanksgiving and January through the end of March, except for the President's Week holiday, or approximately November 25 to 28, January 3 to February 11, and February 15 to March 31.

Holiday Season: Christmas through New Year's and President's Week, or about December 18 to January 2 and February 12 to 14.

The **Monument Peak Restaurant** is located at the top of the Heavenly Aerial Tram, 2,000 feet above Lake Tahoe. It's an unusually sophisticated (tablecloths and silverware!) restaurant for a ski resort, especially for one where many of the visitors are wearing boots. The restaurant serves an interesting mix of Italian and Oriental cuisine, salads and sandwiches, as well as spectacular vistas.

Non-skiers who ride the tramway up the hill are also welcome. Lunch is available daily, and dinner is available during the summer.

Facts and Figures on Lake Tahoe Skiing

*(N-I-A is Novice-Intermediate-Advanced)

Heavenly

P.O. Box 2180, Stateline, NV 89449; (916) 541-1330, (800) 243-2836.

Vertical	Summit	Lifts	Rating (N-I-A)*
3,500	10,040	24	20-45-35

Longest trail: 5.5 miles. Lifts: 1 tram, 2 detachable quads, 8 triples, 8 doubles, and 6 surface lifts. Complimentary shuttle throughout South Lake Tahoe. Location: South Lake Tahoe, on the California/Nevada border, 55 miles southwest of Reno and 180 miles east of San Francisco.

1995 rates: Adult $42 (half day $29); youth (13 to 15) $30; child (6 to 12) $18; seniors $18; (child/senior half day $12).

Alpine Meadows

Tahoe City, CA; (916) 583-4232.

Vertical	Summit	Lifts	Rating (N-I-A)*
1,800	8,637	12	25-40-35

Longest trail: 2.5 miles. Base: 6,840 feet. Lifts: 2 high-speed quads, 2 triples, 7 double chairs, and 1 surface lift. Call for information on daily and multiple-day tickets and interchangeable multiple-day tickets for other North and South Lake Tahoe areas. Complimentary shuttle bus from South Lake Tahoe/Stateline and from North Shore of Lake Tahoe. Location: 6 miles northwest of Tahoe City on State Route 89.

Right outside the base lodge are two high-speed quad lifts, accessing two mountain peaks and six open bowls.

Alpine Meadows claims the longest season in the Tahoe region, usually from mid-November through the end of May and even later.

1995 rates: Adult $43 (half-day afternoon $29); child $18 (half-day afternoon $12).

Boreal Ski Area

P.O. Box 39, Truckee, CA 96160; (916) 426-3666.

Vertical	Summit	Lifts	Rating (N-I-A)*
600	7,800	10	30-55-15

Longest trail: 1 mile. Base: 7,200 feet. Lifts: 1 quad, 2 triples, and 7 doubles. Location: 10 miles west of Truckee, 90 miles east of Sacramento.

1995 rates: Adult $33 (half-day afternoon $25, night $16); child/senior $10.

Diamond Peak

1210 Ski Way, Incline Village, NV 89451; 831-3211, (800) GO-TAHOE.

Vertical	Summit	Lifts	Rating (N-I-A)*
1,840	8,540	7	18-49-33

Longest trail: 2.5 miles. Base: 6,700 feet. Lifts: 1 quad, 6 doubles. Complimentary shuttle service within Incline Village. Pickup by reservation for groups of 10 or more from Reno or South Lake Tahoe. Location: Northeast shore of Lake Tahoe in Incline Village.

Diamond Peak is directly above Incline Village.

1995 rates: Adult $35 (half day $27); child $14 (half day $11); seniors $14. Call for rates for first time beginner packages.

Donner Ski Ranch

(916) 426-3635.

Vertical	Summit	Lifts	Rating (N-I-A)*
720	7,751	5	25-50-25

Base: 7,031 feet.

Granlibakken

(916) 583-4242.

Vertical	Summit	Lifts	Rating (N-I-A)*
280	6,480	2	50-50-0

Base: 6,200 feet.

Kirkwood Ski Resort

Kirkwood, CA; (209) 258-6000, (209) 258-7000, (800) 545-2034.

Vertical	Summit	Lifts	Rating (N-I-A)*
2,000	9,800	11	15-50-35

Longest trail: 2.5 miles. Lifts: 7 triples, 3 doubles, and 1 surface lift. Ski shuttle from major South Lake Tahoe resorts. Location: 35 miles south of South Lake Tahoe, Highway 88 at Carson Pass. Take Highway 89 south to 88 west.

Kirkwood sits in a spectacular alpine meadow valley. The views from the summit extend into the central valley of California. The resort has its own small village at the base, including some condominiums where guests can ski up to their door.

The 2,000 acres of skiable terrain includes 65 runs; wide, rolling trails; steep chutes; and open bowls. The base elevation of 7,800 feet is the highest in northern California, and the natural snow magnet attracts an average of 425 inches each year, allowing Kirkwood to sometimes stay open as late as July 4.

1995 rates: Adult $39 ($28 half day); young adult (13 to 23) $29; child (12 and under) $5.

Skiing Museum. Way back when, cross-country skiing and snowshoeing were not sports but means of transportation. The **Western American SkiSport Museum** is located at the Boreal Ski Area and includes displays on Pioneer days, the mining era, and the 1960 Winter Olympics. The museum is open year-round. For information, call (916) 426-3313.

Mount Rose

22222 Mount Rose Highway, Reno; 849-0704.

Vertical	Summit	Lifts	Rating (N-I-A)*
1,440	9,700	5	30-35-35

Longest trail: 2.5 miles. Base: 8,260 feet. Lifts: 2 quads, 3 triples. Location: 22 miles southwest of Reno, on State Route 431, 11 miles from Incline Village.

The nearest of the Lake Tahoe ski areas to Reno, the high base elevation makes good conditions likely even into the spring. The area offers a morning half-day ticket, which might allow a bit of skiing on your departure day.

1995 rates: Adult $32 ($23 half day afternoon); children (6 to 12) $14 ($8 half-day afternoon). Seniors ski for half price. Non-holiday period specials include free two-hour group workshops on Tuesdays, and free rentals on Wednesdays. There is also a "Runs 'N Roses Family Fun Pack" available anytime, offering passes for two adults and two children for $70.

Northstar-at-Tahoe

(916) 562-1010, (800) 533-6787.

Vertical	Summit	Lifts	Rating (N-I-A)*
2,200	8,600	11	25-50-25

Longest trail: 2.9 miles. Base: 6,400 feet. Lifts: 1 gondola, 4 express quads, 2 triples, 2 doubles, and 2 surface lifts. Interchangeable tickets with other Lake Tahoe resorts available. Complimentary shuttle bus between Incline Village/Kings Beach and Northstar. Reno airport pickup for groups. Shuttle to South Lake Tahoe runs twice weekly. Location: 40 miles southwest of Reno on California Highway 267 and 196 miles northeast of San Francisco.

New development on the "backside" of Mt. Pluto opened up 200 more acres including tree skiing.

1995 rates: Adults $42 (half-day afternoon $28); child $18 (half-day afternoon $12).

Sierra at Tahoe

(Formerly Sierra Ski Ranch.) 9921 Sierra Ski Ranch Road, Twin Bridges, CA; (916) 659-7535.

Vertical	Summit	Lifts	Rating (N-I-A)*
2,212	8,852	9	25-50-25

Longest trail: 3 miles. Base: 6,640 feet. Lifts: 3 detachable quads, 1 triple, and 5 doubles. Complimentary shuttle bus from South Lake Tahoe/Stateline casino area. Location: 12 miles west of South Lake Tahoe on Highway 50, 72 miles west of Reno.

The 2,000 acres of terrain feature 44 trails including heart-stopping fall line plunges on the West Bowl.

1995 rates: Adult $35 all day; Teen Advantage $27; child (12 and under) $17.

Ski Homewood

Homewood, CA; (916) 525-7526.

Vertical	Summit	Lifts	Rating (N-I-A)*
1,650	7,880	10	15-50-35

Longest run: 2 miles. Base: 6,230 feet. Lifts: 1 quad, 2 triples, 2 double chairs, 5 surface lifts. Location: on Highway 89 along the west shore of Lake Tahoe, 6 miles south of Tahoe City and 19 miles north of South Lake Tahoe.

The base of Homewood is just above the western shore of Lake Tahoe, and the mountain offers 1,200 acres of skiable terrain.

1995 rates: $32 ($24 half day afternoon); youths (9 to 13) $11 (half-day $9); seniors $12 (half-day $10). Two-through seven-day packages available.

Soda Springs

(916) 426-3666.

Vertical	Summit	Lifts	Rating (N-I-A)*
650	7,352	2	30-55-15

Base: 6,702 feet.

Squaw Valley USA

Squaw Valley, CA; (916) 583-6985.

Vertical	Summit	Lifts	Rating (N-I-A)*
2,850	9,050	33	25-45-30

Longest trail: 3 miles. Base: 6,200 feet. Lifts: 1 heated 120-passenger cable car, 1 six-passenger gondola, 3 detachable quad chairs, 9 triple chairs, 14 double chairs, 5 surface lifts.

Site of the VIII Olympic Winter Games in 1960, this is a ski world almost beyond imagination. The 4,000 skiable acres are served by 33 lifts including a cable car. At the top of the cable car is the High Camp Bath & Tennis Club, which includes an Olympic-sized outdoor skating rink, swimming lagoon and spa, tennis courts, a museum with memorabilia about the Olympic games, an 80-foot bungee jumping tower, and more.

New for 1995 is night skiing on a 3.5-mile run from the top of the cable car. A new intermediate run, Olympic High, was added to the front side of the mountains, and the Children's World day care facility was opened.

Shuttle services from various North Lake Tahoe and South Lake Tahoe locations. Location: 50 miles west of Reno, 200 miles east of San Francisco.

1995 rates: $43 ($28 half-day afternoon); kids under 13 and seniors over 65, $5.

Sugar Bowl

Norden, CA; (916) 426-3651.

Vertical	Summit	Lifts	Rating (N-I-A)*
1,500	8,383	9	20-30-50

Longest trail: 2 miles. Base: 6,883 feet. Lifts: 1 gondola, 1 quad, and 7 doubles. Location: Donner Summit near Soda Springs, 44 miles from Reno.

1995 rates: Adult $37 (half day $24); child $10.

Tahoe Donner

(916) 587-9400.

Vertical	Summit	Lifts	Rating (N-I-A)*
600	7,350	3	15-80-5

Base: 6,750 feet.

Children's Ski Programs

Alpine Meadows. Snow School for children ages 4 to 6.

Boreal. Animal Crackers Children's Ski School for children 4 to 10.

Diamond Peak. Bee Ferrato's Child Ski Center. First time beginner's special for children 7 and older; second time course for experienced young skiers. The Sierra Scout Adventure Lesson for ages 7 to 12.

Heavenly. L'il Angels for children 3½ to 8. Junior Mountain Adventure for children 8 to 12.

Homewood. Ski and Play for children aged 4 to 12.

Kirkwood. Mighty Mountain for children 4 to 12.

Northstar. Ski Cubs for children 3 to 6 is an introduction to snow sports. Children 4 to 6 can enter Super Ski Cubs. Experienced young skiers from age 5 to 12 can enter StarKids.

Squaw Valley. Children's World at Papoose for children 3 to 12.

Sugar Bowl. PowderKids is for children 6 to 12. For the youngest visitor, there's the Sugar Bears Child Care program.

Lake Tahoe Region Cross-Country Ski Areas

Diamond Peak Cross-Country. Mount Rose Highway; 832-3211. 35 km marked trails, all groomed.

Eagle Mountain Nordic. (916) 389-2254. 75 km marked trails, all groomed.

Northstar-at-Tahoe Cross-Country & Telemark Center. Truckee, CA; (916) 562-2475. 38 trails, 65 km of track.

Northstar Cross-Country. (916) 562-2475. 65 km marked trails, all groomed.

Resort at Squaw Creek. Squaw Valley; (916) 583-6300.

Royal Gorge Cross-Country Ski Area. Soda Springs, CA; (916) 426-3871, (800) 634-3086. 83 trails, 323 km of track. That's not a typographical error, by the way: Royal Gorge claims it is the world's largest groomed track system with 83 trails spread across 9,000 acres with two hotels, four cafes, a day lodge, and 10 warming huts. It's located near Lake Kilborn in Soda Springs.

Spooner Lake Cross-Country. Junction of Highways 50 and 28; 749-5349. 101 km marked trails, all groomed. At the 7,000-foot level with trails from easy to difficult.

Squaw Creek Cross-Country Ski Area. Olympic Valley, CA; (916) 581-1946. 11 trails, 30 km of track.

Tahoe Donner Cross-Country. Truckee, CA; (916) 587-9484. 32 trails, 65 km of track.

Tahoe Nordic Center. Tahoe City, CA; (916) 583-0484. 12 trails, 65 km of track.

In addition to day passes, most of the above major North Tahoe cross-country ski resorts are members of a cooperative selling an interchangeable trail pass good at any of the areas for a total of 678 kilometers (420 miles) over 203 forest and lake-view trails. Call (800) 824-6348 for information.

Other cross-country centers in the Lake Tahoe region include:

Alpenglow. Tahoe City; (916) 583-6917.

Bijou Park. South Lake Tahoe Parks & Recreation Department, Glenwood Avenue, South Lake Tahoe; (916) 541-4611.

Clair Tappan Lodge. (916) 426-3632; 8 km marked trails, all groomed.

Hope Valley Cross-Country at Sorensen's Resort. (916) 694-2266, (800) 423-9949. Highway 88 in Hope Valley. 51 km marked trails, 10 km groomed.

Kirkwood. Kirkwood, CA; (209) 258-8864. 80 km marked trails, all groomed. Snow conditions: (209) 258-3000. Highway 88, 30 miles south of Lake Tahoe.

Lake Tahoe Basin. (916) 573-2600. Various trails maintained by the U.S. Forest Service.

Lake Tahoe Winter Sports. (916) 577-2940. 91 km marked trails, 8 km groomed.

Spooner Lake Cross-Country Ski Area. 749-5349. Snow conditions: 887-8844. Highway 28, 11 miles north of South Lake Tahoe, 12 miles south of Incline Village.

Sugar Pine Point State Park. Tahoma, CA; (916) 525-7982. 20 miles north of South Lake Tahoe on Highway 89.

Sunset Ranch. Tahoe Airport Highway 50, South Lake Tahoe; 541-9001.

Tahoe Paradise Sports. Highway 50 at Meyers, CA; (916) 577-2121.

U.S. Forest Service Trails. Contact Forest Service for Sno-Park and wilderness permits, snow conditions, and trail safety information at (916) 573-2600.

Ski Shuttles

Leave the driving to someone else and concentrate on your "schuss"; ski shuttle services allow you to sample more than one mountain without the need to check into a new hotel or rent a car. And they relieve you of the stress of sometimes difficult wintertime driving.

Daily shuttle bus service by Gray Line to **Squaw Valley USA** leaves from major hotels in Reno and Sparks between about 7 A.M. and 8 A.M. and arrives at Squaw Valley between 9 A.M. and 9:30 A.M. Round-trip tickets, including an all-day lift pass, were about $47 for adults; ticket/lift passes for chilren 12 and younger were $25.

You can get in a half-day afternoon at **Mount Rose** every day but Monday with a Gray Line shuttle that leaves from Sparks and Reno hotels between 10 and 10:45 A.M., arriving between 11:30 A.M. and noon. Adult round-trip tickets plus the half-day lift ticket for Mount Rose are $29.

All shuttles leave the slopes at 4:30 P.M. and arrive in the Reno area between about 5:30 and 6:30 P.M.

Gray Line also offers shuttle service from South Lake Tahoe hotels to Squaw Valley seven days a week with pickups beginning at 7 A.M.

Call Sierra Nevada Stage Lines/Gray Line Tours at 331-1147 or (800) 822-6009.

Several ski areas offer shuttle services from North Lake Tahoe locations, as well. If you're planning on skiing **Diamond Peak,** free shuttle service is available within Incline Village. Call 832-1177 for more information.

Northstar-at-Tahoe is reachable by free shuttle service between Incline Village, Kings Beach, Tahoe City, and Truckee daily. Call (916) 587-0257 for details.

In addition, the Truckee North Tahoe Transportation Management Association publishes a complete schedule of North Tahoe/Truckee public transportation and ski area shuttle services including those for **Alpine Meadows** and **Squaw Valley.** To obtain the schedule, call (916) 581-3922.

Snowmobiling

Lake Tahoe Winter Sports Center. 3071 Highway 50, Tahoe Paradise, CA; (916) 577-2940.

Mountain Lake Adventures. Kings Beach, CA; 831-4202, (916) 583-9131.

Tahoe Paradise Sports. Highway 50 at Meyers, CA (3 miles south of Lake Tahoe Airport); (916) 577-2121.

United States Forest Service. Snowmobiling is open in most National Forest lands within the Lake Tahoe Basin, provided there are at least 6 inches of snow on the ground. Recommended areas include Spooner Summit, Hell Hole, and Blue Lakes Road in Hope Valley. Contact U.S. Forest Service for maps. (916) 573-2600.

Zephyr Cove Snowmobile Center. 760 Highway 50, Zephyr Cove, NV; 588-3833. A range of tours, including two-hour guided trips running from Thanksgiving through mid-April that reach the ridge line on the Nevada side of the lake, some 9,000 feet above sea level. Prices are $69 for a single rider or $99 for double riders on one machine. Three-hour tours for experienced riders are also available. Parkas, bibs, gloves, and boots are available for rental; required helmets are free. Call 588-3833 for information.

Snow Play Areas

The California Department of Parks requires purchase and display of a permit to use Sno-Park parking areas during the season. Call (916) 653-8569 or (916) 573-2600 for information. Permits may also be obtained at many sporting goods stores, ski rental and snowmobile shops, automobile clubs, and the South Lake Tahoe Chamber of Commerce.

You don't need a lot of facilities to go sledding—a patch of snow and a saucer, sled, or cardboard box will do—but some places are nicer than others. Here are some designated sledding spots in the Lake Tahoe region.

Boreal Ski Area. 10 miles west of Truckee, off I-80 in Donner Pass; (916) 426-3666. Snow play area with two groomed slopes; plastic disk use only. $5 fee includes rental. Open weekends and holidays.

Granlibakken Ski Area. (916) 583-9896. Hill for saucers only; $3 day use fee. Saucers available for rent for $2.

Hansen's Resort. 1360 Ski Run Boulevard, South Lake Tahoe, CA; (916) 544-3361. $9 per person for three hours, including sled or tube.

Heavenly. There are several toboggan and sled hills where you can rent equipment and use the hills on the road leading to Heavenly on Ski Run Boulevard on the California side.

Mt. Rose. Undeveloped and very steep area eight miles up Mt. Rose Highway (Highway 431). Bring your own equipment.

North Tahoe Regional Park. At the end of National Avenue in Tahoe Vista, CA; (916) 546-7248. Snow hill for toboggans, saucers, and inner tubes. No charge for play area; equipment rentals available.

Old MacDonald's Enterprise. 1060 Ski Run Boulevard, South Lake Tahoe, CA; (916) 544-3663.

Sorenson's Resort. Hope Valley off Highway 88, just east of junction with Highway 89. (916) 694-2203.

Tahoe City. Off Highway 89, south of Fanny Bridge. Bring your own equipment.

If you choose to go sledding in an "unofficial" area be sure to follow commonsense rules. For example, never sled alone. Don't sled onto bodies of water or across roads or trails.

Sleigh Rides/Horseback Riding

Northstar. (916) 562-1230. Sleigh rides from the Basque restaurant through the Martis Valley. Operates when snow conditions and weather permit. Horseback trail rides open all year.

Ice Skating

Resort at Squaw Creek. (916) 583-6300. Ice Skating Pavilion and Sports Activity Center at Squaw Valley. Rental shop. Open daily Thanksgiving to spring.

Squaw Valley USA. (916) 583-6985. Olympic-size outdoor ice rink at the High Camp Bath and Tennis Club. Rental shop and lessons. Open year-round.

Chapter 28

Warm Weather and Year-Round Activities in the Lake Tahoe Region

South Lake Tahoe Attractions

Please call the numbers listed for hours of operation, ticket prices, and use fees. Phone numbers are in area code (702) unless indicated otherwise.

Heavenly Aerial Tram. Heavenly Ski Resort, South Lake Tahoe, CA; Summer: (916) 544-6263; Winter: 586-7000. Dinner reservations: 586-7000 ext. 6347. Available for sightseeing trips and for dinner at the mountainside restaurant. In the summer, hiking tours are conducted from the top of the tram.

Lake Tahoe Historical Society Museum. 3058 Lake Tahoe Boulevard, South Lake Tahoe, CA; (916) 541-5458.

U.S. Forest Service Lake Tahoe Visitor Center. Highway 89, South Lake Tahoe, CA; (916) 573-2600; (916) 573-2674. June to September, 8 A.M. to 6 P.M.; interpretive center, stream profile chamber.

Washoe Indian Cultural Foundation Exhibit. McGonagle Estate, Tallac Historic Estates, Highway 89, South Lake Tahoe, CA; (916) 573-2600.

Emerald Bay State Park. Highway 89, South Lake Tahoe, CA; (916) 525-7277. If you've got a camera, this is the place to take it for breathtaking views of Lake Tahoe; if you didn't bring a camera, buy one and bring it here.

Within the park is **Vikingsholm Castle** at the head of the bay near Eagle Falls and Creek. Tours are offered June through September, 10 A.M. to 4 P.M. Emerald Bay State Park, Highway 89, Emerald Bay, CA; (916) 525-7277, (916) 541-3030.

D. L. Bliss State Park. Highway 89, South Lake Tahoe, CA; (916) 525-7277.

Ehrman Mansion. Sugar Pine Point State Park, Highway 89, Tahoma, CA; (916) 525-7982. Tours 11 A.M. to 4 P.M. July through September.

Gatekeeper's Log Cabin Museum. 130 West Lake Boulevard, Tahoe City, CA; (916) 583-1762.

Donner State Park. Highway 40, Truckee, CA; (916) 587-3841. Memorial to the ill-fated Donner Party of 1846. Open Memorial Day to mid-October, weather permitting.

Ponderosa Ranch. Highway 28, Incline Village, NV; 831-0691. Open from

May through October, 9:30 A.M. to 5 P.M. Site of some of the scenes of television's *Bonanza* series.

Water Sports and Cruises

South Shore Boat Rentals and Marinas

Action Watersports of Tahoe. (916) 544-5387; (916) 544-0200. Boating, water-skiing.

American River Rafting. (916) 635-4479.

The Anchorage Marina at Camp Richardson. Highway 89, South Lake Tahoe, CA; (916) 541-1777.

Cave Rock. Cave Rock, NV; 831-0494.

Club Nautico. Tahoe Keys Marina, South Lake Tahoe, CA; (916) 541-8405.

The Diving Edge. 588-5262. Scuba diving.

El Dorado Recreation Area. (916) 541-4611.

Emerald Bay Kayak Tours/Tahoe Whitewater Tours. Tahoe City, CA; (916) 581-2441. Guided kayak tours of Emerald Bay, Sand Harbor, and other spots. Raft tours on American, Carson, and Truckee rivers.

Kayak Tahoe. (916) 544-2011.

Lakeside Marina. End of Park Avenue, South Lake Tahoe, CA; (916) 541-6626.

Lake Tahoe Sailboat Sales & Charters. Tahoe Keys Marina, South Lake Tahoe, CA; (916) 541-5053.

O.A.R.S. Inc. (800) 346-6277.

Ski Run Marina. 900 Ski Run Boulevard, South Lake Tahoe, CA; (916) 544-0200. You will find a discount in the coupon section of this book.

Tahoe Keys Marina. Venice Drive East, South Lake Tahoe, CA; (916) 541-2155.

Timber Cove Marina. 3411 Highway 50, South Lake Tahoe, CA; (916) 544-2942.

Tributary Whitewater Tours. (916) 346-6812.

Whitewater Connection. (916) 622-6446, (800) 336-7238.

Zephyr Cove Resort & Marina. Boating and snowmobiling. 760 Highway 50, Zephyr Cove, NV; 588-3833.

North Shore Boat Rentals and Marinas

North Tahoe Marina. (916) 546-8248.

Homewood High & Dry. Homewood, CA; (916) 525-5966.

Meeks Bay Resort & Marina. Meeks Bay, CA; (916) 525-7542.

Sand Harbor. Sand Harbor, NV; 831-0494.

Cruises

M.S. Dixie. Zephyr Cove, NV; 588-3508. Cruises Lake Tahoe daily, from April to November.

North Tahoe Cruises. Departs from Tahoe Yacht Harbor, Tahoe City, CA; (916) 583-0141. Year-round cruises on the *Sunrunner.*

Tahoe Para-Dice. Anchorage Marina, South Lake Tahoe, CA; (916) 541-7499. *You will find a discount in the coupon section of this book.*

The Tahoe Queen. Boats depart from the Ski Run Marina in South Lake Tahoe. (916) 541-3365; (800) 238-2463. Scheduled cruises to Emerald Bay, including dinner-dance cruise. Ski shuttle cruises run Tuesday through Friday. Call for reservations.

Woodwind Sailing Cruises. Departs from Zephyr Cove, NV; 588-3000. Five departures a day including a sunset champagne cruise each night on a 41-foot catamaran with glass bottom. Day trips: adults, $14; children 2 to 12, $7. Evening cruises: $20 per adult.

Fishing

All of Lake Tahoe and most of the hundreds of smaller backcountry lakes are open for fishing year-round. Certain exceptions apply to tributaries of Lake Tahoe on both the California and Nevada sides—obtain a copy of fishing regulations from sporting goods stores in the area.

Federal and state authorities regulate fishing activities in Lake Tahoe, surrounding lakes, and tributaries. For a full set of rules, contact the California Department of Fish & Game at (916) 355-7040 or the Nevada Division of Wildlife at 688-1500.

We hope you fancy trout: there are at least six variants of that fish in the rivers and lakes of the Tahoe Basin: Brook, Brown, Cutthroat, Golden, Mackinaw, and Rainbow. Golden Trout are scarce and likely to be found only in the most remote, high mountain lakes. Lake Tahoe also has Kokanee Salmon.

Fishing in Lake Tahoe is permitted from one hour before sunrise until two hours after sunset; hours for other bodies of water are similar. Most areas impose a limit of five trout, with stricter limits on scarce Mackinaw and Golden Trout.

Lake Tahoe. Locals advise getting out into the deep water on a boat; if you do fish from the shore, the best spots are where the bottom falls off sharply including Cave Rock on the east shore and Rubicon Point on the west.

Fallen Leaf Lake. Deep waters offer the most promise; fishing within 250 feet of the dam at the northwest corner of the lake is forbidden.

Echo Lakes. Shore fishing from the dam is a good bet.

Blue Lakes. High mountain lakes at more than 8,000 feet, about 12 miles south of the Tahoe Basin, off Highway 88. Locals recommend fishing from the dams.

Carson River, West Fork. A popular fishing area, south of Lake Tahoe along Highway 88 and Blue Lakes Road. **Carson River, East Fork.** Closed to fishing above Carson Falls. From Hangman's Bridge south of Markleeville to the Nevada line, there are size limits in effect.

Truckee River. Fishing is prohibited in and around the dam at Lake Tahoe, with other restrictions applied at various times of the year.

Here are some fishing services and resorts catering to anglers:

Caples Lake Resort. Highway 88, Kirkwood, CA; (209) 258-8888.

First Strike Sportfishing. (916) 577-5065.

The Outdoorsman. 2358 Lake Tahoe Boulevard, South Lake Tahoe, CA; (916) 541-1660.

Rich's Fishing Charters. (916) 541-3565, (916) 541-5550.

Sorenson's Resort. Highways 88 and 89, Hope Valley, CA; (916) 694-2203, (800) 423-9949.

Tahoe Sportfishing Company. Ski Run Marina, South Lake Tahoe, CA; (916) 541-5448, (800) 696-7797.

Tahoe Trout Farm. 1023 Blue Lake Avenue, South Lake Tahoe, CA; (916) 541-1491.

Woody's Sportfishing. Lakeside Marina at Stateline, NV; (916) 544-3086.

Wildlife in and Around Reno and Lake Tahoe

There are many, many more wild animals and birds in the wilderness and fringes of developed land in Reno and the Lake Tahoe region than there are tourists and residents to scare them away. However, it takes a patient eye to spot many of them and a lot of luck to view the big two:

Bald Eagles. Occasional visitors to Lake Tahoe in the winter, these stunning birds cannot be mistaken. An adult, with distinctive white head and tail markings, has a wingspan of as many as seven feet. The eagle, by the way, is on the way back; it is listed as one of the very few success stories of the Endangered Species Act. In 1967, only 417 nesting pairs were believed to exist in the lower 48 states; in 1994, though, conservation and environmental efforts had brought the census to about 4,000 pairs and 7,500 juveniles, and the bird was upgraded from the "endangered species" list to the "threatened" category.

Black Bear. The majestic bear, available in black, brown, and even golden hues, is no longer as common as he was when the settlers passed through. A carnivore, the black bear also shops at garbage dumps and camp sites. They're not pets, though; keep your distance.

In addition to bald eagles, other birds of note include:

California Gull. A Pacific seagull common at Lake Tahoe beaches, especially when the picnickers leave behind their daily bounty; back East we call gulls "flying rats."

Hairy Woodpecker. A hairy, uh, woodpecker, marked with a skunk-like vertical stripe down its back and a heavy black bill. The males have a small red head patch.

Mountain Chickadee. The most common bird in the Tahoe Basin, they perform circus-like acts swinging from the tips of branches in search of bugs and seeds. A mostly black body with white lines over each eye.

Red-Tailed Hawk. Readily identified by its sawtooth wingtips, this large bird—as much as two feet long—is dark brown on top and light brown below, with a red tail. You'll see them circling lazily above meadows and fields, in search of mice, rabbits, and other small prey.

Steller's Jay. The chatterbox of the forest and one of the boldest birds of the area. Deep blue wings, tail, and breast.

Western Tanager. The male has a bright yellow body with black markings on the back, wings, and tail and a red head.

Other mammals of note include:

Coyote. Rarely domesticated but often found in and around human civilizations, this dog-like animal hunts at night for small rodents.

Mule Deer. They get their name from their oversized ears, which resemble those of mules. Mule deer winter on the eastern side of the Sierras, in the Carson Valley, returning to the Tahoe Basin when the snows clear.

Porcupine. A large, nocturnal rodent that often prowls near human settlements in search of pine cones. If threatened it will turn away from an enemy, erect its barbed quills and swing its tail. Despite 50 years of cartoon action, porcupines have not mastered the art of propelling their quills—the nasty stickers become lodged when the porcupine swings its tail and touches an enemy; the loosely attached quills, which are a form of hair, become embedded in the enemy. Porcupines can grow to as much as 60 pounds in weight.

Raccoon. Crafty bottom-feeders, they will break into camp supplies and even enter some sheds or homes in search of food. The nocturnal mammal has gray, brown, and black hair with a black face mask. They dunk their food in water before eating.

Parks, Campgrounds, and Beaches

Camp Richardson. Highway 89, South Lake Tahoe, CA; (916) 541-1801.

Davis Creek Park. Highway 395 to Bowers Mansion exit. 849-0684. 20 miles south of Reno. Sites for tents and trailers up to 26 feet. Fishing. Open all year.

D. L. Bliss State Park. Highway 89, north of Emerald Bay; (916) 525-7277.

Echo Lakes. Echo Chalet, a privately leased U.S. Forest Service resort. Echo Summit Road off Highway 50; (916) 659-7207.

Emerald Bay State Park. Highway 89, Emerald Bay; (916) 525-7277.

Grover Hot Springs State Park. Highway 89 South, 3 miles west of Markleeville, CA; (916) 694-2248.

Lake Tahoe Nevada State Parks. 831-0494.

Mount Rose Campground. Route 431; 687-4384. 20 miles southwest of Reno on the slopes of Mount Rose. 24 sites for tents and trailers up to 16 feet. Elevation 8,900 feet. Open July to mid-September.

South Lake Tahoe Parks & Recreation Department. (916) 541-4611.

Sugar Pine Point State Park. Highway 89; (916) 525-7982.

U.S. Forest Service, Lake Tahoe Basin. (916) 573-2600.

Warrior Point Park. Route 445, past Sutcliffe nine miles to the end of the pavement; 476-1155. 40 miles north of Reno. Fishing, beach, waterskiing, boating.

Washoe Lake State Park. Highway 395, Washoe Lake State Park exit; 687-4319, 687-4384. 25 miles south of Reno. 25 sites for tents and trailers up to 30 feet. Equestrian area, swimming, fishing, boat launch.

Hiking Trails

The star among stars in hiking trails along Lake Tahoe is the **Tahoe Rim Trail**, a hiking and horseback riding trail through National Forest lands surrounding Lake Tahoe. Built entirely with donations and volunteer labor, 122 miles of a planned 150-mile circle have been completed, including 50 miles of the existing Pacific Crest Trail. (The current gaps lie near Tahoe City, and across Mount Rose and above Incline Village.) The trail passes high mountain lakes, streams, and meadows and offers views from as high as 10,000 feet at Freel Peak and Alpine Meadows. The trail does not exceed a 10 percent grade and is suitable for beginner through advanced hiking. For information, call (916) 577-0676. Camping is allowed along the trail; contact the U.S. Forest Service for camping information at (916) 573-2600.

Tahoe Vista Trails at Heavenly

The Heavenly Lake Tahoe ski resort offers guided tours and marked trails that lead off from the top of its tram, which operates year-round. It's a good way to take the easy way up to the 8,250 foot mark, and the three main trails offer moderate challenge with spectacular rewards.

The Tahoe Vista Trail traverses a ridge line high above the lake. The longest trail is a 2.1-mile hike to the Fremont Camp, up a series of switchbacks to the 9,000 foot level. The camp was established by Kit Carson and Colonel John C. Frémont in February 1844 when they became the first nonnatives to see Lake Tahoe.

A second trail leads to Snowshoe Ridge, named after John A. "Snowshoe" Thompson, Tahoe's earliest known skier. Thompson became a legend in the Sierra by carrying mail in the 1860s on a route that led from Placerville, California, to Genoa, Nevada, on the east side of the Sierra Nevadas.

Neumann Point is named in remembrance of Terry Neumann, a Heavenly ski instructor who was killed in a huge avalanche at this location in 1974.

Guided tours from the top of the tram leave at 11 A.M. and 1 P.M. in the summer and are free to riders on the tram. Also offered is a Sunday brunch ticket that includes the tram ride and a meal at the Monument Peak Restaurant; it was priced at $19 for adults and $12 for children in 1995.

East Shore Trails

Rim Trail South. Take the hint from the name: this is a southerly walk along the top of the Lake Tahoe world, a strenuous jaunt of about 21 miles that reaches up to 10,778 feet at its highest point.

The trail begins behind the Nevada Department of Transport building at the Spooner Summit Rest Area on Highway 50. If the views of Lake Tahoe to the west and the Carson Valley to the east from the Rim Trail aren't enough for you, branches of the trail head off to even more isolated peaks including Duane Pliss Peak, South Camp Peak, and Genoa Peak.

Rim Trail North. A slightly less challenging 18-mile hike that begins about half a mile up Route 50 from the junction with Route 28. There's a small parking area at the trailhead.

This wooded trail reaches to about 8,000 feet as it heads north. Just before Snow Peak, the trail comes to a fork. The left fork switchbacks down a steep slope to Marlette Lake, while the right fork leads to Tunnel Creek Road.

Nevada Lake Tahoe State Park. On the East Shore, off Highway 28. Trail to Sand Harbor, Marlette Lake, and the upper elevations of the Carson Range. Access from Spooner Lake at the intersection of Highways 50 and 28. Call 831-0494 or (916) 573-2600 for information.

Marlette Lake. A 5-mile uphill jaunt of moderate challenge through North Canyon to Marlette Lake. To get to the trail, park at the Spooner Lake Trailhead in Lake Tahoe Nevada State Park, northwest of the junction of Highways 50 and 28; a parking fee is charged in season.

North Shore/Mount Rose Trails

Mount Rose Wilderness. A recent addition to the protected wilderness around Lake Tahoe, it includes the land at the northeast corner of Lake Tahoe above Incline Village. For information and maps, contact the Carson Ranger District in Carson City at 882-2766.

Mount Rose Trail. A view to the north of Reno and to the southwest of the Tahoe Basin from the 10,778-foot summit. A 5-mile hike of moderate difficulty, the trail begins one mile south of the summit on Highway 431 (Mount Rose Highway). The trail crosses a high mountain meadow before making a final two-mile switchback ascent to the ridge.

South Shore/Mount Rose Trails

Mount Tallac Trail. The Big Kahuna of the southern end of the Tahoe Basin, a difficult 9-mile ascent to a view worth 10,000 words of description. The trail begins on a fairly easy level, heading for Floating Island Lake and Cathedral Lake. The trail turns steep and difficult past Cathedral Lake for the final five miles to the top of Tallac at 9,735 feet.

The trailhead can be found on Highway 89, about $3\frac{1}{2}$ miles north of South Lake Tahoe. The road to the parking area is across the road from the entrance to Baldwin Beach.

Kirkwood. Highway 88 at Carson Pass; (209) 258-6000. Along the south shore, 8,000 acres with trails for all abilities. Passes high country lakes and streams with access to Pacific Crest and Mormon Emigrant Trails.

Meiss Lake Country. (916) 573-2600. U.S. Forest Service land south of South Lake Tahoe, CA. The trails encompass 10,000 acres at intermediate and advanced levels and pass several high country lakes. Access off Highway 89, 5 miles south of Highway 50 in Meyers, CA.

Pope-Baldwin Recreation Area. (916) 573-2600. The Fallen Leaf Trail System leads to the south shore of Fallen Leaf Lake. Access from the U.S. Forest Service Lake Tahoe Visitors Center on Highway 89.

Glen Alpine Trail Head. Several hikes of moderate to strenuous challenge depart from this trailhead off Fallen Leaf Lake Road, which itself branches off of Highway 89 three miles north of South Lake Tahoe. This is a slightly less strenuous 6-mile path to the top of Mount Tallac.

Half Moon and **Alta Morris Lakes.** A moderate trail of about five miles.

Lake Aloha. A 6-mile hike that includes a high mountain meadow, three alpine lakes, and a small waterfall.

Tallac Historic Site. An easy, half-mile walk through the area of the former Tallac mansions. Accessible from the Kiva Picnic Area, or the Lake of the Sky Trail from the Lake Tahoe Visitor Center.

Echo Lakes Trail. A moderate trail that reaches deep into the wilderness to Lower and Upper Echo Lakes and several other alpine waterways including Tamarack, Lucille, Margery, and Aloha. In the summer, a water taxi offers a shortcut across Upper Echo Lake.

The trail is reached from Echo Lakes Road, off Highway 50 at Echo Summit. Bear left on Echo Lakes Road to a parking area. Upper Echo lies about 2½ miles up the trail with other lakes farther on, several miles apart.

West Shore Trails

Desolation Wilderness. Permits are required to enter the 63,475 acres of woods and lakes, and travel is by foot or horseback only. Open campfires are prohibited and overnight camping permits are strictly limited in the heart of the season, from June 15 to Labor Day.

A quota system allows reservation of half of each day's permits up to 90 days in advance, with the remainder available only on the day of entrance.

Hiking permits are available year-round at the Forest Service office in South Lake Tahoe and in summer at the Forest Service Visitor Center off Highway 89 and at some of the trailheads.

Among the most spectacular trails in all of the Lake Tahoe region is the path up Mount Tallac, which leads from near the northwestern end of Fallen Leaf Lake some six miles along and 3,400 feet up to a spectacular vista overlooking Lake Tahoe.

For information on wilderness areas, contact the Lake Tahoe Basin Management Unit in South Lake Tahoe at (916) 573-2600, or the Eldorado Information Center in Camino, California, at (916) 644-6048.

Rubicon Trail. A 7.5-mile trail of moderate difficulty along the shoreline of Lake Tahoe, passing through a number of secluded coves and beaches and reaching three miles to Emerald Point and ending at Vikingsholm Castle. The trail is reached from D. L. Bliss State Park, about 10 miles north of South Lake Tahoe on Highway 89.

Vikingsholm Trail. An easy 1-mile descent to Lower Eagle Falls and Vikingsholm Castle with views of Emerald Bay and Fannette Island. The trail leaves from the parking lot off Highway 89, about 9 miles north of South Lake Tahoe.

Cascade Creek Trail Head. Several spectacular trails lead off from this trailhead, including an easy jaunt to Cascade Falls and a difficult climb to three hidden high lakes. Located about 8 miles north of South Lake Tahoe on Highway 89 at the Bayview Campground across the road from Inspiration Point.

Cascade Creek Fall Trail. An easy nearly flat 1-mile hike to the 200-foot Cascade Falls at Cascade Lake. The falls are at their most spectacular in the spring as winter snows melt on the slopes above.

Bayview Trail. A difficult trail up Maggie's Peak one mile to Granite Lake; from there it continues on to Dicks Lake, intersecting the Eagle Falls Trail along the way.

Eagle Falls Trail. A steep and difficult 10-mile plunge deep into the Desolation Wilderness, passing Eagle Lake 1 mile along and then Velma, Middle Velma, and Upper Velma Lakes and ending at Fontanillis Lake. The trailhead is at the Eagle Falls Picnic Area off Highway 89, 8 miles north of South Lake Tahoe.

Granite Chief. A hiking area that encompasses the back sides of the Alpine Meadows and Squaw Valley ski areas, south toward Twin Peaks and Barker Pass.

Golf Courses

South Shore Golf Courses

Bijou Municipal Golf Course. 3464 Fairway Avenue, South Lake Tahoe, CA; (916) 544-5500. 9 holes. 2,685 yards. Open daily 7:30 A.M. to 7 P.M.

Edgewood Tahoe Golf Course. 588-3566. Adjacent to the Horizon Casino Resort. 18 holes. 7,491 yards. Rated as one of the top courses in the country. Open May through October. Rates $100 per player, with cart.

Glenbrook Golf Course. Highway 50, Glenbrook, NV; 749-5201. 9 holes. 2,577 yards. Mid-April to mid-October. About $30 to $35 per player. Oldest course in Nevada.

Lake Tahoe Golf Course. Highway 50, Meyers, CA; (916) 577-0788. 18 holes, 6,707 yards.

Tahoe Paradise Golf Course. Highway 50, Meyers, CA; (916) 577-2121. 18 holes. 9-hole executive course. Driving range.

North Shore Golf Courses

Carson Valley Golf Course. 18 holes. 5,700 yards. Carson Valley, NV; 265-3181.

Incline Village Championship Golf Course. Incline Village, NV; 832-1144. 18 holes. 7,138 yards. Designed by Robert Trent Jones Jr. Open May 1 to October 15. Rates $75 to $85 with cart.

Incline Village Executive Golf Course. Incline Village, NV; 832-1150. 18 holes. 3,200 yards. May 15 to September 30. $45 with cart.

Northstar-at-Tahoe Resort Golf Course. Highway 267 between Truckee and North Lake Tahoe; (916) 562-2490. 18 holes. 6,897 yards. Driving range. May through October. $48 with cart.

Tahoe Donner Golf Course. 12850 Northwoods Boulevard, Truckee; (916) 587-9440. 18 holes. 6,961 yards for championship course. Mid-May through mid-October. $65 with cart.

Bicycling

Bike trails in and around Reno and Lake Tahoe range from nearly flat tours around lakes and across valleys to steep hill climbs on the Geiger Grade, the Mount Rose Highway, and across the top of the Sierra Nevada ridge line. And there's the spectacular and sometimes challenging 72-mile coastline around Lake Tahoe, North America's largest alpine lake.

Kaspian Beach and Campground is Lake Tahoe's only bicycle campground.

Located on Highway 89 between Sunnyside and Homewood, the site is 2½ miles from scenic Blackwood Canyon and Creek. There are only ten camp sites available, though.

The **Pope-Baldwin Beach Trail** runs through several historical and educational sites along the south shore of Lake Tahoe; the 3.4-mile path passes through the Tallac Historic Site, Lake Tahoe Visitors Center, stream profile chamber, Fallen Leaf Lake, and Pope and Baldwin Beaches.

The **Tahoe City to River Ranch Path** runs approximately five miles alongside the Truckee River. Contact the U.S. Forest Service at 882-2766 or (916) 573-2600 to check on trail status.

Mountain bikers are prohibited from riding in wilderness areas, developed recreation sites, and self-guided nature trails. The U.S. Forest Service recommends several area trails for mountain bike usage: Meiss/Big Meadow, Angora Ridge Road, McKinney-Rubicon OHV Trail, Mount Watson, Brockway Summit to Martis Peak, Genoa Peak, and Marlette Lake.

Like the Lake Tahoe paths, Reno's trails also border bodies of water. Here is a selection of some of the more interesting routes:

The 6.5-mile **Truckee River Trail** begins at Broadhead Park, near Wells Avenue and Kuenzi Lane, and continues along the river ending near the Vista Boulevard exit on I-80.

The **Idlewild Route** also follows the Truckee River, beginning at Riverside and First streets and continuing 3.3 miles through Idlewild Park to Caughlin Ranch.

Bowers Mansion to Franktown is a scenic, sparsely traveled country road. This 4-mile stretch starts at Bowers Mansion about 15 miles south of Reno and makes a right turn on Franktown Road, winding its way past farmlands, meadows, towering pines, and large estates.

Bicycling to Extremes

The **Markleeville Death Ride** pits 1,500 avid cyclists against themselves as they choose to race over from 1 to 5 mountain passes pedaling from 48 to 128 miles. Markleeville is about 80 miles south of Reno. For information, call (916) 694-2475.

Bicycle Rental Agencies

Reno:
Truckee River Bike Rentals. 501 W. First Street; 786-8888.
  Bobo Sheehan's Ski Co. 1200 S. Wells Avenue; 786-5111.
  Sierra Cyclesmith. 6425 S. Virginia Street; 852-9253.
  Reno Bicycle Center. 809 W. Fourth Street; 329-2453.
South Lake Tahoe:
Adventure Sport Vehicle Rental. 2513 Lake Tahoe Boulevard, South Lake Tahoe, CA; (916) 541-7155.
  Anderson's Bicycle and Skate Rentals. 645 Emerald Bay Road, South Lake Tahoe, CA; (916) 541-0500.

Don Cheepo's Adventures. 3349 Highway 50, South Lake Tahoe, CA; (916) 544-0356.

Lakeview Sports. 3131 Highway 50, South Lake Tahoe; (916) 544-0183.

Richardson's Resort Bicycle Rentals. Highway 89, Camp Richardson, CA; (916) 541-7522.

Tahoe Sports Ltd. Crescent V Center, Stateline, NV; (916) 542-4000. South Y Center, South Lake Tahoe, CA; (916) 544-2284.

North Lake Tahoe:

Olympic Bike Shop. 620 North Lake Boulevard, Tahoe City, CA; (916) 581-2500.

Tahoe Gear. 5095 West Lake Boulevard, Homewood, CA; (916) 525-5233.

Mountain Bikes Unlimited. 10200 Donner Pass Road, Truckee, CA; (916) 587-7711.

Paco's Truckee River Bicycle. 11400 Donner Pass Road, Truckee, CA; (916) 587-5561.

Porter's Ski & Sport. Tahoe City: 501 North Lake Boulevard, CA; (916) 583-2314. Truckee: (916) 587-1500. Incline Village: 885 Tahoe Boulevard, CA; (916) 831-3500.

Sierra Cycleworks. North Shore (Kings Beach): (916) 546-7992. South Shore (South Lake Tahoe): (916) 541-7505.

Tahoe Gear. 5095 West Lake Boulevard, Homewood, CA; (916) 525-5233.

Bowling

Bowl Incline. 920 Southwood Boulevard, Incline Village, NV; 831-1900. 16 lanes.

Horseback Riding the Range

Make like a real cowboy on the wide-open ranges around Reno. Here are some stables that rent horses and conduct other Western activities in and around Reno. In wintertime, some areas offer sleigh rides.

North Shore

Alpine Meadows Stables. (916) 583-3905. Open daily June through October.

Bull Creek Ranch. 345-7600. A working ranch in Verdi, Bull Creek Ranch offers trail rides, cattle drives, roping, team penning, and cutting. They also feature hayrides, sleigh rides, and horseback riding by the hour.

Northstar Stables. (916) 562-1230. South of Truckee, California, off Highway 267, Northstar offers trail rides through beautiful, forested areas all year, weather permitting.

Squaw Valley Stables. Squaw Valley, CA; (916) 583-7433. Ride the site of the 1960 Winter Olympics. Guided rides, rentals, pony rides.

Tahoe Donner Equestrian Center. (916) 587-9400. Five miles west of Truckee, the center is open May through October for trail rides; overnight pack trips are offered in the summer.

Winters Creek Ranch. 849-1020. Located at 1201 U.S. 395 North in Washoe

Valley, offering winding mountain trails through tall pines, over creeks, and through meadows. Open year-round, weather permitting.

Wolf Creek Pack Station. 849-1105. 10 miles south of Markleeville, California, offering guided day rides or fully outfitted camping trips in the Carson Iceburg and Mokelumne Wilderness Area. Open from May 15 through the end of October.

South Shore

Borges Carriage & Sleigh Rides. Highway 50 and Lake Parkway. South Lake Tahoe, CA; (916) 541-2953.

Camp Richardson Corral. Emerald Bay at Fallen Leaf Road, South Lake Tahoe, CA; (916) 541-3113. Trail rides, wagon rides, sleigh rides in winter. Overnight and extended pack trips.

Sunset Ranch. Highway 50, South Lake Tahoe, CA; (916) 541-9001. Ride through the open meadows of the Upper Truckee River, with or without a guide. Children's pony rides and petting zoo. Hayrides and sleigh rides in season. Open year-round.

Zephyr Cove Stables. Zephyr Cove Resort, Highway 50, Zephyr Cove, NV; 588-5664.

Balloon Rides

If you've got the nerve, we can't think of very many more thrilling ways to explore the Lake Tahoe or Carson Valley than from a hot air balloon at 5,000 feet. The rides are generally offered from spring through fall.

There are several companies offering tours; most offer a one- to two-hour trip and charge between $100 and $200 per person. The trips leave early in the morning, before the air heats up and makes things even more unpredictable. The balloon pilots, by the way, have only a limited ability to steer their bags of air and they are chased by ground crews that will retrieve the equipment and passengers and bring them back to the base.

Aerovision Balloons, Inc. 265-5177, (800) 468-2476.

Alpine Adventures Aloft. Minden, NV; 782-7239, (800) 332-9997.

Mountain High Balloons. Truckee; (800) 321-6922.

Soaring

Graceful, engineless gliders soar over the mountains and meadows of the Lake Tahoe region year-round in good weather, offering a spectacular view.

Soar Minden. 782-7627, (800) 345-7627.

Soar Truckee, Inc. (916) 587-6702.

Hot Springs

Carson Hot Springs. Carson City; 882-9863.

Gerlach Hot Springs. Gerlach; 557-2292.

Grover Hot Springs State Park. Markleeville, CA; (916) 694-2228.

Steamboat Hot Springs. Steamboat; 853-6600.

Wally's Hot Springs. Genoa; 782-8155.

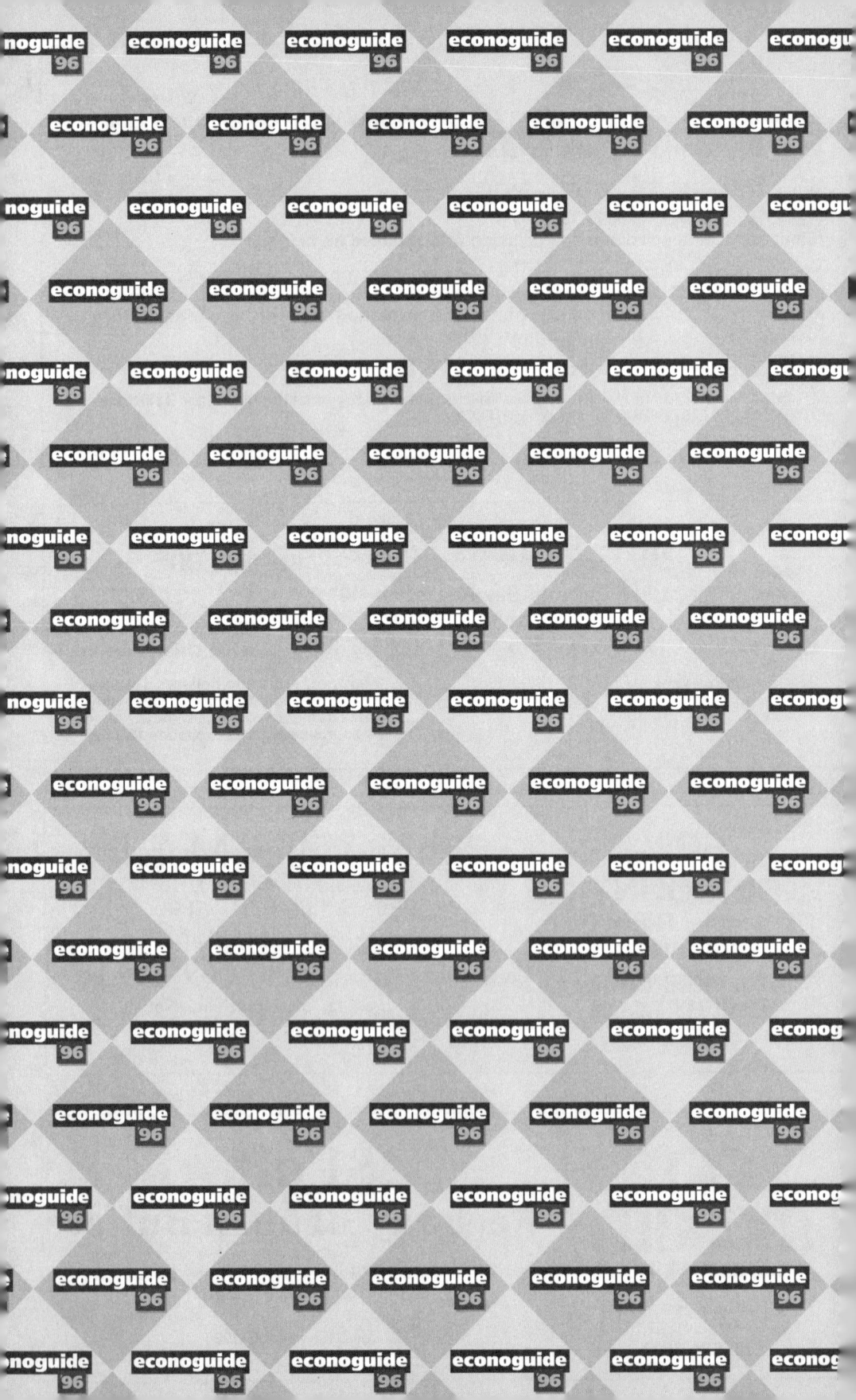

Quick-Find Index to Hotels, Attractions, and Restaurants

(See also the Contents)